CHINA, INC.

HOW THE RISE OF THE NEXT SUPERPOWER
CHALLENGES AMERICA AND THE WORLD

Ted C. Fishman

SCRIBNER
New York   London   Toronto   Sydney

SCRIBNER
1230 Avenue of the Americas
New York, NY 10020

SCRIBNER and design are trademarks of Macmillan Library Reference USA, Inc.,
used under license by Simon & Schuster, the publisher of this work.

For information about special discounts for bulk purchases,
please contact Simon & Schuster Special Sales:
1-800-456-6798 or business@simonandschuster.com

DESIGNED BY ERICH HOBBING

Text set in Granjon

Manufactured in the United States of America

1   3   5   7   9   10   8   6   4   2

Library of Congress Control Number: 2004065328

ISBN 0-7432-5752-9

Title-page photograph: Skyline of Pudong, a Special Economic Zone in Shanghai,
the financial capital of China, by Dan Bibb.

To my family

CONTENTS

CHINA, INC.

THE WORLD SHRINKS
AS CHINA GROWS

CHINA IS EVERYWHERE THESE DAYS. POWERED BY THE WORLD'S MOST rapidly changing large economy, it is influencing our lives as consumers, employees, and citizens. The words MADE IN CHINA are as universal as money: the nation sews more clothes and stitches more shoes and assembles more toys for the world's children than any other. But moving up the technological ladder, China has also become the world's largest maker of consumer electronics, pumping out more TVs, DVD players, and cell phones than any other country. And more recently, China is ascending even higher still, moving quickly and expertly into biotech and computer manufacturing. No country has ever before made a better run at climbing every step of economic development all at once. No country plays the world economic game better than China. No other country shocks the global economic hierarchy like China.

Even a casual glimpse at the news tells us that something large looms in China. The nation is making parts for Boeing 757s and exploring space with its own domestically built rockets. China has between 100 and 160 cities with populations of 1 million or more (America by contrast has 9, while Eastern and Western Europe combined have 36.). China is buying oil fields internationally and also signing exclusive oil and gas supply deals with Saudi and Russian companies. China is buying the world's scrap metal, as well as enormous amounts of steel, to fashion into products sold globally. The country is relentlessly positioning itself for ever-higher levels of industrialization. It's exporting computers with Chinese brand names. There are giant capital flows from industry to China now. It's where the world is investing. China is laying down fiberoptic at a rapid rate. China, which tried mightily and tragically to leapfrog from an agrarian economy to an advanced industrial state under Mao Zedong, now leapfrogs over many of the technologies of mature industrial states. Its phone system is more wireless than wired, and many of its big cities will soon have the most advanced rapid-transit systems in the world. Here are two metaphors, both true: China is drinking milk these days. The tallest starting center in the NBA, Yao Ming, is Chinese.

In the past, China's enormous population was hard to feed and employ. Now China's one-fifth of humanity must be seen anew: as the biggest market ever. As the customers of Citibank, Disney, Nokia, GE, Toyota, and Microsoft. As the critical mass in the coming order.

But even if you don't read the business pages, the impact of China's boom is hitting home in all sorts of ways both subtle and obvious that can be felt in our everyday reality:

- Mention an interest in China to your old friend who owns an industrial toolmaking shop and he confides that his factory, which was started by his father and has bought a comfortable suburban life for three generations of his family as well as good wages to hundreds of workers, "is getting killed by the people over there."
- Talk to your family plumber, and first he complains that he spends all day replacing broken Chinese parts, and then he takes from his bag a Chinese part he says is better, sheepishly adding, "They're actually pretty darn good now, and all we can get these days without spending a fortune."
- Run into a parent of a freshman from your daughter's high school class, a mom you've seen for years at holiday concerts in which your two girls both play viola. The mom immigrated to the United States from China in 1995 to study solid-state physics and is now a researcher at the local medical school. She says she's going back to China to join a friend's business that develops software for MRI machines and other high-tech medical devices. What about her research at the hospital? She says the opportunities in China now are too big to miss and she does not want to blame herself later.
- Mention this story to another friend, a world-famous researcher who studies the lives of cells, and he tells you that American uni-

versity biology departments now exist, in essence, to transfer knowledge from old Jewish men to young Chinese women.

- Cross the street to the all-night city convenience store run by a family of Palestinian immigrants, and notice that behind the counter where cigarettes were once sold is a wall of no-name Chinese accessories for dozens of different brand-name cell phones—batteries, car adapters, earphones, and cases—none for more than $12. They're selling great, the man at the cash register says.

- Meet a smart old high school friend who always wore thick glasses, but whose nose is now bare. He teaches English at a giant private language school in Shanghai but is home to show off the results of his $600 laser eye surgery, performed, he says, in an ultramodern Chinese clinic for a tenth the price the procedure would cost at home.

- Grab breakfast at a diner in St. Joseph, Michigan. One table over sit four men, each somewhere between the ages of thirty and sixty. They look as if they are dressed for factory work, but at 10 a.m. they sit and discuss the layoffs in the local disc-brake and machining factory of Bosch, the giant German auto-parts manufacturer that is rapidly building up its capacity in China. The company is laying off thousands of workers at its plants throughout the state, it says, to stay competitive. The men lament that there are few places to turn for new jobs. Whirlpool, Clark Equipment, and other once-solid manufacturers used to thrive in the area, but now their factories are shuttered or just shells of their former selves.

- Notice that the Armani emporium on Via Manzoni in Milan, the Italian fashion capital, revises its list of sister stores worldwide to include Shanghai.

- Head for a dim sum lunch in Chinatown and see on the corner a somewhat bewildered young Chinese man, squat, strong, and weathered, looking as though he has come to work the American railroad boom a century too late. He leans on a large bundle, wrapped in a plastic tarp and tied with cellophane ribbon, that probably contains all his worldly goods. He is one of China's untold millions of rural migrants, but has somehow—perhaps with the help of a smuggler—found his way far past China's thriving ports. He will now compete for work on the low rung of America's domestic economy.

- A contractor shows you the home of a client who has renovated her master bath. He's replaced a long, old Formica countertop with an expanse of midnight blue marble, as ornately beveled as one might find in a Venetian spa. He sees your eyes widen and recommends the same for you, saying it's Italian, it's expensive, but it's worth it. After you complain about the price, you follow the contractor in his truck to a lumberyard. Inside are giant crates of precut granite for kitchens, bathrooms, and living room mantels. Everything on them is finished and glued. If you can work with one of these tops as is, the contractor tells you, the counter will cost $450, not $8,000. The yard's owner comes over. He says buy fast, because the crates only stay in the store a day or two before he sells out. He's been carrying the counters for a year. "A guy from China came by and said he had three quarries where they cut the stone and finished it. I tried it out. Now I can't get enough."

- Wake up in Santa Barbara, California, one morning to a sky that looks as though it is painted a shiny white. The morning's newspaper reports that the sunlight is playing tricks on a dust cloud that has drifted over the Pacific from China. The cloud contains particles of loose earth from deforested land mixed with arsenic and other industrial pollutants from the country's factories.

- Buy a real pair of Levi's jeans at Wal-Mart. They are cheaper than the new pair you bought twenty years ago.

- Get invited to a "purse party" by an officemate who says she is friends with the host, a United Airlines stewardess. Her apartment, decorated with paper lanterns and silk pillows, is piled high with the latest Louis Vuitton and Prada handbags, Burberry coats, North Face parkas, leather Timberland jackets, Ralph Lauren tops, and Chanel scarves. On her table is a valise with glistening Rolex, Bulgari, and Cartier watches. "Take a Coke from the cooler," she says. "Look around. Make an offer. Think cheap, it's all knockoffs." Leave with a North Face for $20 and sharp new watch for $35. She's doubled her money. You never look at a designer label the same way again.

- Pull your Honda Civic up to the gas pump. At $2.30 a gallon it costs $30 to fill the tank.

- Drive through Houghton, Michigan, a remote town on the state's chilly Upper Peninsula. Stop by the student bookstore at Michigan Tech. On the Local Authors table is a book titled *Being a Graduate Student in the U.S.,* written by two of the university's Chinese students. The cashier reports that the book sells well in China. Stop an Asian student on campus and ask how he heard about Michigan Tech. His university in Beijing has a strong relationship with the school and his professors told him about it, he tells you. When asked how he likes studying there, he says Michigan is cold, the food is bad, and it has been hard to blend in, except with the 140 other Chinese students. The technological education, however, is excellent.

- Stop at the auto supply store for windshield-wiper fluid. Half the store is now a showroom for small Chinese motor scooters, some of which look like half-Harleys, others like Ducatis. Most cost less than $300.

- Attend dinner at the home of a discerning art collector. On the wall are four-foot-tall photographs of a ruined Chinese cityscape. Invest in contemporary Chinese art, the collector says, it's the most interesting in the world right now, and once the Chinese themselves start buying, the prices will go sky-high.

- Take a trip to Paris to see its famous attractions and to stroll the Champs-Élysées, the boulevard whose national character is usually guarded with jealous fanaticism by the French. Yet for the first time in history, "the most beautiful street in the world" is surrendered to a non-French cultural event, a Chinese parade with seven thousand costumed musicians, acrobats, and dragon dancers. That night the Eiffel Tower is lit red and fireworks fill the sky to celebrate the Chinese lunar New Year. The festivities come at a time when France is sharply critical of its Western allies, the United States and Great Britain. The show also coincides with a visit by Chinese political leaders to France to seal broad strategic and economic agreements.

- Decide at last to put your old film camera away and plunge into digital photography. Photo magazines all rave about a small new Nikon, an engineering wonder that can shoot fast, capture dimly lit scenes that would foil its best film rival, and costs half the price of similar machines a year ago. Loyal customers of Nikon trust the company for quality and innovative design. It is, after all, one of the marquee Japanese brands that helped build that country's reputation for manufacturing excellence. Holding the camera, then taking a round of test shots, confirms that this is another stellar product that only the Japanese could make. Inspect the camera more closely, however, and there in small print are the words "Made in China." A search on the Internet reveals that digital cameras from many Japanese, American, and Korean companies are made in the same Chinese factories.

- Visit an ailing elderly uncle who is home from rehab after yet another fall, but still unable to move about without help. He introduces you to Menardo, the caretaker sent by a nursing agency. Menardo is well dressed, his hair permed. On first meeting he says he is from the Philippines and has been working as a nurse for the last four months. Here in America he shares an apartment with his sister an hour away, but at home he owned a large house and had servants. He takes from his bag a brochure for his old business, a factory on Cebu Island that employed fifty workers making intricately woven straw and jute bags. He went out of business, he says, because Chinese manufacturers now sell similar bags for less than Menardo knew how to make them. It is all handwork, and his laborers made $30 a week. Chinese workers, he complains, make one-third less and work longer hours. Now he empties bedpans. With his American wage, he hopes for a new start in business, but it is hard for him to think what to make that will ever beat the Chinese on price.

China's miracle economy can come at you in a lot of ways, from all directions. And once China comes into view, it is hard not to see it everywhere.

The Supersized Workforce

Behind China's rapid economic ascendancy over the last twenty-five years is the basic fact of China's huge population. The numbers supersize nearly every facet of the country. China is home to close to 1.5 billion people, probably, which would make the official census count of 1.3 billion too low by roughly the population of Germany, France, and the United Kingdom *combined.* Put another way, China's uncounted multitude, were it a country on its own, would be the fifth largest in the world.

Surprisingly enough, China is not home to the cheapest workforce in the world. Even at twenty-five cents an hour, Chinese workers cost more than laborers in the poorer countries of Southeast Asia or Africa. In the world's most miserable corners, children carry rifles and walk minefields for less than a dollar a day. China is the world's workshop because it sits in a relatively stable part of the globe and offers the world's manufacturers a reliable, docile, and capable industrial workforce, groomed by government-enforced discipline.

The other great influence lately is the migration of hundreds of millions of peasants from the countryside now that the government allows them to leave. Indeed, the country's embrace of market capitalism over the last two decades and the end of government support for farmers are combining forces to all but evict peasants from the land. The migration is the largest in human history. It also has one of the least exact head counts: estimates of the number of people who have left for the cities to find work range from 90 to 300 million, numbers that even near the low end match the entire workforce of the United States. Move up in the range and the number tops the U.S. and European workforces combined. By 2010, nearly half of all Chinese will live in urban areas, some of them urban metropolises with populations of a million-plus that didn't even exist a few years earlier.

What these numbers mean is that the productive might of China's vast low-cost manufacturing machine, along with the swelling appetites of its billion-plus consumers, have turned China's people into what is arguably the greatest natural resource on the planet. How the Chinese and the rest of the world use that resource will shape our economy and every other economy in the world as powerfully as American industrialization and expansion have over the last hundred years.

What the American Workers
at the Harley Motorcycle Plant Knew

China's effects on the world are so great—and potentially explosive—that paradoxically it has been hard for those charged with seeing the big picture to grasp them. That, anyway, was the impression of workers and executives at the Harley-Davidson plant in Milwaukee when a trio of the most important economic officials in the Bush administration came to visit in the late summer of 2003. United States Secretary of Labor Elaine Chao, Secretary of the Treasury John Snow, and Secretary of Commerce Donald Evans arrived by bus to trumpet an upturn in the economy with one of America's iconographic companies in the backdrop. They assumed that "Hog" makers, the leather-jacketed, flag-flaunting individualists who produce America's last big motorcycle, would cheer the administration's self-described pro-business tune.

But the crowd was decidedly chilly. A cold front was blowing in from China. The United States had lost 2.9 million manufacturing jobs over the previous five years. Wisconsin had lost ninety thousand, or one in six, of its manufacturing jobs since 2000.[1] The Harley crowd had a strong opinion as to why. The companies they grew up around were fading, with orders and jobs heading overseas. Challenged on China, a puzzled Elaine Chao could only offer that U.S. National Guard soldiers serving in Iraq would be guaranteed their jobs when they returned. John Snow seemed to confuse his references to the Chinese currency, the *yuan,* with the Japanese *yen.* The astonished audience grew edgy. More than taxes, more than budget deficits or the cost of the war on terror, speakers from the floor said, China was the top issue in their economic lives. For the assembled, how the country competed with China would determine if Wisconsin could hold on to the manufacturing base it had fought to rejuvenate.

The secretaries' tour took them throughout the Midwest to dozens of stops. All along the way they met the same angry questions on China, throngs with bullhorns full of fury. Among the angry were workers and managers alike, from the left and the right. Perhaps the most vocal were the Republicans' core constituency, small and midsize manufacturers struggling under the weight of the growing productive power of the world's most populous country.

8

Those events occurred only eighteen months before the publication of this book. Today, China's economy no longer takes government leaders by surprise. What they choose to do, now that they are informed, remains to be seen, especially since the popular reactions to China keep shifting rapidly—and often on the basis of competing American political and economic agendas. China is at one moment our greatest threat, the next our friend. It is siphoning off American jobs; it is essential to our competitive edge. China is the world's factory floor and it is the world's greatest market opportunity. China's industrial might saps opportunities from the developing world, but its hungry economy pulls poorer countries upward. China exports deflation; it stokes soaring prices. China will boom; it will bust.

The truth about China is that, like all big countries, its contradictions are real. There are no easy answers in sight, just giant forces of change.

What the Numbers Tell Us—and What They Don't

By every measure, China's economy is growing rapidly. For nations, annual economic progress reports come in the form of the gross domestic product, the sum value of all goods and services traded in a nation's economy. In 2003, China's GDP was $1.4 trillion. By that measure, China was the seventh-largest economy in the world. The economy of the United States is still by far the world's biggest; with a 2003 GDP of $10.1 trillion, it is seven times the size of China's. (The world economy can also be measured by its own GDP; it totaled $36.4 trillion in 2003.)

But there are some extenuating circumstances regarding China's economic numbers. As with nearly all economic statistics from China, their reliability is suspect. The Chinese have incentives to fudge. In the past, the complaint was almost always that officials nudged their numbers up, to show they were doing a good job. Now, a chorus of doubters argue the numbers are unduly *low*. China's central planners are increasingly directing development funds more aggressively to locales officially designated as poverty zones. Thus China's east-coast jurisdictions, already the overwhelming beneficiaries of economic reform, mask their own high growth rates so that government resources don't go elsewhere. Depressed provinces have corollary motives; they work to hold on to their label even if business is starting to percolate. Perhaps for that reason, the numbers that the central government collects from the provinces do not match the figures that regional and local governments report in their own literature. China's economy is 15 percent bigger, judging by local numbers. The statistical disparities have troubled or embarrassed the central government so much that it prosecuted for fraud twenty thousand local officials who had a hand in producing them.[2]

Furthermore, the official numbers include only China's legal economy. Its underground economy, made up of businesses both unsavory and more mundane that lack a government stamp (and tax bill), is enormous but uncountable.

China's seventh-place ranking may also be too low because China pegs its currency to the dollar. The world's other major currencies go up and down against the dollar depending on market conditions. Usually a country with China's strengths would see the value of its national currency rise, but China uses the massive power of its foreign currency reserves to keep the world price of the yuan marching lockstep with the dollar no matter what its market price might otherwise be. If the dollar had not dropped against the Euro or other world currencies over the last few years, China's place would be a notch or two higher.

Some analysts already see China's place as much higher. They take into account how much a dollar actually buys in the country, which, all things considered, is a lot more than it buys in the United States, Europe, Japan, and most other places in the world where it's worth spending a dollar. Some goods—Japanese machinery, Saudi oil, French fashions, Swiss pharmaceuticals, and an hour of time from an American marketing professor—have standardized global prices. But the supply and demand that govern most of China's economy—its labor, food, rent, bricks, doctors, China-made clothes and entertainment—fall into their own local balance. In China, one dollar buys about what $4.70 does in Indianapolis. The disparity, misleadingly labeled "purchasing power parity," is reconciled in the U.S. Central Intelligence Agency's estimation of China's place among the world's economies. China's $1.4 trillion economy, in the CIA's calculations, looks more like one with a GDP of $6.6 trillion. Put another way, it makes more sense to think of China's economy as closer to two-thirds the size of the U.S. economy than it is to one-seventh.

And then there is China's rate of growth, its velocity into the economic future. For the most part, countries want to add as much as they can to their GDP. Over the last twenty-five years, China's economy has grown so fast and so large that it has taken on the mythic qualities of one of Mao's showcase farms. The United States, the country against which all others tend to measure themselves, has long had the strongest economic growth among the large industrialized democracies that make up the G7.[3] Growth in the United States is also comfortably above the average of the membership of the Organization of Economic Co-operation and Development, the world's inner clique of thirty leading democratic, market economies that together account for two-thirds of the world's economic output. From 1982 through 2002, GDP growth in the United States averaged 3.3 percent. For U.S. politicians, those years with rates above 4 percent are blockbusters, those above 2 percent are comfortable, and years showing anything less amount to political poison. In Latin America, which is often seen as China's rival in low-cost manufacturing, economic progress over the last quarter of a century has been, on average, worse than it was in the region during the Great Depression.[4] In China, however, a growth rate twice as high as that of the United States would now be seen as a calamity. Chinese officials themselves say the country must grow at *better than 7 percent a year* to create enough jobs to busy those regularly entering the job market.

China is so committed to economic growth that the Chinese often talk as though they can will it to happen. It is a necessary optimism that pervades official Chinese communication.* Orville Schell, the author of *Virtual Tibet* and the dean of the school of journalism at the University of California, Berkeley, draws a parallel between the unity of focus the Chi-

---

*Not just through the press and government communiqués, but in casual conversation. In the fall of 2003, as China was on course for yet another bell-ringing economic quarter, a Chinese diplomat new to Washington, D.C., but who had spent nine years as an economic analyst at China's embassy in Tokyo, offered his understanding of the Chinese government's prescription for Japan, still struggling against years of bad economic news, deflation, and a weak stock market. "All Japan needs to do," the diplomat said emphatically over sushi and sake at a Japanese restaurant in Georgetown, "is to follow China's model and stimulate economic growth. First they ought to get their growth up to around seven or eight percent, and then they should push their stock market up. Then they can be more like China. We know we need economic growth to keep everything together, so we make a point of it."

nese have demonstrated for anticapitalism and now for capitalism.[5] Schell argues that in both instances there is a willingness to suspend logic and see only bright tomorrows. Both cases lead to excess. In its capitalist present, China has been willing to overlook the dark side of modernization, seeing economic progress as the solution to all the country's challenges.

Not all of China's own economic experts are as blithely confident that sheer desire for growth can insure it. To the contrary. Recently, Chinese economic planners have worked hard to throw ice on their countrymen's most heated expectations. Overenthusiasm, they know, leads to economic bubbles. But controlling the power of the exuberant Chinese economy is difficult. If history were predictive of China's present, the country's economy would have burst long ago. If bubbles burst when investors chase too many projects that have no real economic value—too many factories chasing the same hot markets, too many construction projects for the local market to fill, too many bad bank loans to unsound enterprises, too many high-flying stocks in companies with no history—then China deserves to be in shambles. Instead, every time the worst is predicted for China's economy, it seems to grow faster, create stronger industries, import and export more, and attract more foreign investment money.

Since China set about reforming its economy a generation ago, it has grown at an official rate of 9.5 percent.[6] Countries in the early stages of economic reform often come up fast, but not like China. The country is closing in on a thirty-year run during which its economy has doubled nearly three times over.[7] *The surge has no equal in modern history.* Neither Japan's nor South Korea's postwar booms come anywhere close. Given the United States' recent rates of economic growth, it would take the U.S. twenty-five years to double. If the United States, which boomed in the eighties and nineties, had grown at China's rate since 1978, the U.S. economy would now be roughly its current size plus two Japanese economies added on. Nicholas Lardy, an economist at the Institute for International Economics, notes that China grew mightily even during the worldwide economic doldrums of 2001–2.

Thus does China's growth give it a place in the world economy that is far greater than its size. China still only makes one-twentieth of everything produced in the world, but on the world stage it plays the role of a new factory in an old industrial town. It can spend, it can bully, it can hire and dictate wages, it can throw old-line competitors out of work. It changes the way everyone does business.

Americans tend to focus on the huge inequality in trade between the two countries. It is a worry Americans help to create by buying ever more from China's humming factories. In 2003, the Chinese sold the United States $152 billion more in goods than they bought. Contrary to common wisdom, the trade deficit with China does not mean that Americans are spending down the national wealth at a much faster pace than ever before. So far, most of China's gains with American buyers have come at the expense of the other countries that once lured American dollars, especially other Asian economies. Americans—and the world—get more stuff in the bargain. China is winning because it can make what others did for less money. It turns once expensive items, such as DVD players, power tools, and leather jackets, into affordable impulse items that call out from store shelves. Many of us who feel our homes are running out of closet and floor space because of piles of cheap toys, consumer electronics, tools, shoes, phones, and clothes don't realize that although these items may once have come to America from other countries, the current glut is because China is now the leading manufacturer of those goods and beating everyone on price. The U.S. garment industry, for example, was fading long before China started winning orders at the expense of other Asian and Latin American factories.

The American furniture industry is another story. Its strength has been sapped almost entirely by China alone. It shows how China can come after the specialty businesses of any country and decimate them in short order. (Now it is overtaking all global manufacturers in wooden furniture, too, a convenient trend that will give the world bookshelves and armoires in which to store its other China-made purchases.) From the year 2000 until 2003, China's exports to the United States of wooden bedroom furniture alone climbed from $360 million to nearly $1.2 billion. Over the period of China's $840 million rise, the workforce at America's wooden-furniture factories dropped by thirty-five thousand, or one of every three workers in the U.S. trade. China now makes 40 percent of all furniture sold in the United States, and that number is sure to climb. And American furniture jobs will continue to fall.

Yet one irony of China's success in the U.S. furniture market is that Chinese factories have done a better job of delivering to American consumers quintessentially American and European designs than America's own workshops could. Big American furniture sellers, from department stores like JCPenney to specialty stores such as Crate & Barrel, now carry elaborately carved and painted period furniture at prices they charged a few years ago for spare "modern" styles that were easier to fabricate and required fewer man-hours.*

For other countries, China has become essential as a customer as well as a supplier. Japan and Germany currently enjoy large trade surpluses with the country because China is the now the world's biggest buyer of factory machinery, and it needs the equipment Germany and Japan make in order—yes—to produce the machinery and electronics that Germany and Japan make. Resource-rich countries do well selling China the raw materials that get reshaped in its factories, and the energy resources it needs to power them. In 2003, according to the calculations of Stephen Roach, chief economist at Morgan Stanley, the Chinese bought 7 percent of the world's oil, a quarter of all aluminum and steel, nearly a third of the world's iron ore and coal, and 40 percent of the world's cement. The trend is for bigger amounts yet to come.[8]

Future Shock

The most daunting thing about China is not that it is doing so well at the low-end manufacturing industries. Americans will be okay losing the furniture business to China. In the grand scheme of things, tables and chairs are small potatoes in the U.S. economy. The Japanese, for their part, have lost the television business. The Italians are losing the fine-silk

---

*The first floor of The Great Indoors, a national big-box interior-design chain that aims to sell luxurious living spaces to middle-class families, looks like a Sotheby's furniture auction. Tables and chests from every colonial and kingly period, highly buffed, well-weathered or hand-painted with flowers all over, make up the mock living quarters. Around it are the touches amateur Martha Stewarts love: leather hatboxes, satin tasseled pillows, jacquard ottomans, and gilded picture frames around real paintings of old-world seashores, horses and hounds, and Dutch children with cows. A large red sideboard covered with vines costs a mere $1,200. It looks enough like an heirloom costing $20,000 to make a buyer think he or she will never find something this great and this low-cost again. But he will. Costco and Sam's Club have sideboards just as fine, still in the box, for $200 less.

business. Germans cannot compete in Christmas ornaments. Everyone but the Chinese will lose their textile and clothing factories. More worrisome for America and other countries is the contour of the future, where manufacturing shifts overwhelmingly to China *from all directions,* including from the United States. Consumer goods trade on the surface of the world's economy and their movement is easy for consumers to see. The far bigger shift, just now picking up steam, is occurring among the products that manufacturers and marketers trade with each other: the infinite number and variety of components that make up everything else that is made, whether it is the hundreds of parts in a washing machine or computer or the hundreds of thousands of parts in an airplane. And then there are the big products themselves: cars, trucks, planes, ships, switching networks for national phone systems, factories, submarines, satellites, and rockets. China is taking on those industries *too.*

Follow the Money—to China

One big reason China is growing is that the world keeps feeding it capital. According to Japan's Research Institute of Economy, Trade and Industry, one-third of China's industrial production was put in place by the half a trillion dollars of foreign money that has flowed into the country since 1978.[9] In 2003, foreigners invested more in building businesses in China than they spent anywhere else in the world. In the past, the United States used to routinely attract the most foreign money, but in 2003 China took a strong lead, pulling in $53 billion to the U.S.'s $40 billion. With money comes knowledge. The catalytic role of foreigners in the country is still growing quickly; every day China receives a river of European, Asian, and American experts in manufacturing, banking, computing, advertising, and engineering. In 2003, the exports and imports by foreign companies operating in China rose by over 40 percent. Now more than half of China's trade is controlled by foreign firms, many of which import goods into the country that they then manufacture into exports.[10] Foreign companies have pumped up China's trade volume enough to make the country the third-largest trading country in the world, behind the United States and Germany, and now ahead of Japan.

Governments that try to protect their niche industries for their craftsmen must face up to a China that has an exceptionally strong hand. Do a few tens of thousands of furniture and textile makers matter when China can put a freeze on American drugs, telecommunications equipment, farm goods, or any of the other truly huge categories of products the United States hopes to export? Other countries have even weaker hands. Most of the world's countries now see China's growth as a critical engine for their own economic growth. A look at the news any day in Brazil, Australia, Canada, Mexico, Germany, Japan, and just about anywhere else tells of the world's daily balancing act to keep China happy as a customer, efficient as a supplier, and at bay as a competitor.

Orders from a Magnitude

At any given time since China started on the capitalist road, opinions about its prospects have figuratively, and literally, been all over the map. The present mood is a combustible mix of euphoria, fear, admiration, and cynicism. On those emotions ride great tides of capital, the strategic plans of businesses great and small, and the gravest political calculations in the world's capitals and city halls. The temptation is to delve into the workings of the country itself. Is its government a wise warden or power mad and corrupt? Are its people happy with their progress or intolerably oppressed as citizens and abused as workers? Will China's landscape gain more glimmer or drown in industrial muck? Will its banks collapse or successfully make themselves over into worthy world players? Will China's peasants find their way relatively peacefully into their country's urban future or will they rebel?

These are momentous questions, and the Chinese people certainly deserve concern and respect from their own government and from the world. Yet for the four-fifths of the world's population that does not inhabit the Middle Kingdom, the fact is that no matter what the Chinese machine produces for the Chinese themselves, the country's impact on the globe will inevitably and profoundly influence global life nonetheless. China does not need to boom indefinitely in order to supply the world with competitive factories. Not all, or most, or even a third or fifth, of its population needs to reach the middle class for the world to chase its markets—a mere 50 million families is enough.

Furthermore, China does not need to match America's, Europe's, or Japan's commitment to universal education or make opportunities for all its bright students to attend universities; China can produce huge numbers of world-class managers, engineers, and scientists with the far-from-universal educational system it already has now. Moreover, if China's leadership ultimately cannot reconcile itself to the free flow of information that capitalism favors, or to the growing power of its commercial class, the world's companies that now beat a path to its door will *not* turn away, will *not* abandon their factories. They have already shown that the Chinese Communist Party suits them just fine.

Barring Mao's resurrection, a push to war by a desperate North Korea or an uppity Taiwan, or an American tax on everything China ships our way, it is hard to see how China might recede back into the old world map. Tom Saler, a financial journalist for the *Milwaukee Journal Sentinel,* has pointed out that twenty-one recessions, a depression, two stock-market crashes, and two world wars were not able to stop the American economy from growing over the last century from $118 billion ($367 billion in 2000 dollars) to over $10 trillion. In constant dollars, that is a twenty-seven-fold increase. By all appearances, China is poised for similar growth in this new century. Even if China's people, on average, do not catch those of the world's wealthiest nations, and even if China's main competition continues to beat it to the best technology, China will be an ever more formidable competitor.

Certainly, if any country is going to supplant the United States in the world marketplace, China is it. Columbia University economist Jeffrey Sachs, counselor to nations, advises Americans to prepare for a world where by the year 2050, China's economy could well be 75 percent bigger than their own.[11]

But conceding China's rise does not mean conceding to China. However, it does mean acknowledging a remarkable truth confronting us all. Few working Americans have a full awareness of China's rise. How could they? It's never happened before, and it's occurring on the other side of the globe. Yet we need to know what is happening today in China—worker by worker, factory by factory—and why it will affect everyone.

That, in broad strokes, is the occasion of this book.

CHAPTER ONE

TAKING A SLOW BOAT
IN A FAST CHINA

THE BANKS OF THE HUANGPU RIVER RUNNING THROUGH SHANGHAI do not just bend. They mind-bend. For a century and a half, the currents of change coursing through modern China have been more visible from Shanghai's banks than from anywhere else. Here Western powers pushed in most aggressively in the mid-nineteenth century, and later the Japanese made their claim in 1895. The foreigners established an all-but-independent city-state to run their China trade. Western tastes mingled with China's on such a grand scale that The Bund, then Shanghai's commercial center on the west bank of the river, looked like the gleaming boulevard of a great European capital.

In the early twentieth century—until China and the world unraveled in the 1930s—Shanghai counted as one of the world's five most important commercial centers together with London, New York, Paris, and Tokyo. The city was also the world's second-busiest port. Its banks, housed in the imposing hodgepodge of broad European money palaces and slim towers on The Bund, were flush intermediaries in an irresistible trade with Western and Japanese sellers of machines, cotton cloth, medicines, and opium. Chinese factories poured out clothing, paper, and other simple manufactured goods at prices foreigners could not match at home. Commodities in vast quantities moved in both directions.

While foreigners created Shanghai as a world port, the city soon proved a magnet for Chinese looking to work in factories or, during periods of social unrest, for sanctuary. The large migration into Shanghai, and the foreigners' fears that their city would be engulfed, helped lead to the system that ultimately divided the city into separate zones, gated sections of town for the colonists, known as concessions, and the rest for Chinese. Paradoxically, the division also created China's first modern city when the Europeans imposed a formal municipal government over Shanghai. Previously, Chinese cities, though often large, did not have single municipal governments. Interestingly, the English word *modern* was transliterated into Chinese for the first time in Shanghai, and the city became synonymous with the new.[1]

This Chinese city reborn with Western management built the country's tallest buildings, was home to its most prominent banks, had streetcars and running water, beauty parlors, business suits, and French fashions.[2] The city's modernizers were not always Europeans or Americans of the standard colonial mold. Since Shanghai's modern beginning it was also the home of a small but extraordinary group of Jews, many from Iraq, Spain, Portugal, and India. Controllers of property, entertainment, and financial interests, the Hardoun, Kadoorie, and Sassoon families helped create the new world of Shanghai that was neither Occident nor Orient.

The city, however, was never new enough to wash away old prejudices. Stories are told of the notorious sign outside the British Huangpu Park that forbade entry by "Dogs or Chinese." Shanghai then, as now, collected the world's contradictions. Asia's capitalist hub was also the site in 1921 of the first meeting of the Chinese Communist Party.* The city that gave birth to the verb *shanghaied* also played host to the lost. In World War II, the city, which stood apart from the world of nations, became a refuge for as many as thirty thousand European Jews fleeing the Nazis.

In 1949, the Communists seized the country, and for the next forty years the creative power of Shanghai turned away from enterprise. Commercial life stopped dead. Shanghai's grand European architecture and the pre-1940s brick blocks that reflected the city's worldly blend withered.

Today Shanghai is again China's most proudly modern and global city. Yet the city's history of foreign domination is one of China's enduring national wounds. That collective hurt helps to fuel the insistent drive of the Chinese today, as well as China's ambivalence about what

---

*The site of the meeting is now a national museum in the middle of Shanghai's ritziest entertainment complex.

it is willing to give and take from outsiders. Historical Shanghai was corrupt but glamorous, barbaric but sophisticated, repugnant but remunerative. The Chinese government routinely trots out this darker side of Shanghai's past. The government uses the colonial history of Shanghai, once painted "The Whore of Asia," to remind its public that there's an enemy world ever ready and willing to humiliate their proud civilization.

Thus, if ever a people had chips on their shoulders, it would be the Shanghainese, chips they are urgently stacking into skyscrapers. Despite, or because of, their historical feeling of humiliation, the Shanghainese are perhaps the most assured—other Chinese would call them arrogant—among their countrymen. The Shanghainese consider themselves China's best businessmen and -women, most capable public administrators, most global in outlook, and most daring risk takers. It is no accident that a disproportionate number of the Communist Party's highest leadership came from this city, or that China has singled out Shanghai as the city that will first displace Hong Kong as the mainland's top financial center and then take its place as one of the top business and financial centers of the world.

So the middle of the Huangpu is good place to witness the rhythms of the city past and present. Traffic piles up on the water in the same way that it does on the city's overcrowded roads, and the afternoon boat tour takes travelers right into the heart of the maritime rush hour, when hundreds of barges, some shaped like oversize sampans, others like floating mountains of sand or coal, line up four or five across the width of the river under the shadows of orange-hulled oceangoing cargo ships or natty gray vessels that look like floating factories but carry gas and chemicals.

The tour boat is billed as a catamaran, but looks and rides like a slow-moving barge—with a three-story restaurant slapped on top. Except for two giant bug-eyed brass dragonheads jutting from the bow, the boat feels like a low-rent Chinese banquet hall. Filled with baroquely carved and generously marred throne chairs, banquet tables with starched but stained tablecloths, and an immobile, bored staff, the vessel is a floating ambassador from the state-run tourism sector, a nationwide empire of shabby hotels and restaurants. The boat service, one of China's first commercial tourist ventures, still peddles the Communist version of glamour even as it plies the wide gray river for three and a half hours, working its way slowly toward the intersection of the Yangtze River and the East China Sea.

Despite the river traffic, Shanghai was until recently fairly self-contained, bordered close in by a countryside of farms. When the boat tours commenced shortly after China's economic liberalization began in the early 1980s, one could still gaze across the water and see rice and vegetable fields, yards with chickens, pigs, geese, and shady trees. The Bund had grown dowdy from decades of Communist disdain, and for years few businesses saw any good in it. The grandest buildings had been taken over by regional and municipal agencies with ideological grudges to bear against the old foreign banks and hotels. Even as Shanghai bloomed throughout the 1990s, The Bund remained largely dormant, like an urban set from a 1930s Hollywood movie extravaganza that had never found another script.

Then, as Shanghai earned back its commercial bearings, it attempted to restore some international élan by leasing space in one of the big Bund buildings to a giant Kentucky Fried Chicken outlet, which at the time was a luxurious taste of the West for locals. Today, KFC is gone from The Bund, but has found new homes all over the city where it has settled into place as a popular indulgence. The Bund, meanwhile, gains the luster delivered in all world capitals by the international purveyors of lifestyle. Now one can find there Italian chocolates, Evian Spa, spruced-up boutique hotels, and world-class restaurants run by superstar chefs from Paris and New York. Three on The Bund, an entertainment complex on the waterfront, occupies an old office tower that underwent a $50 million renovation steered by one of the world's most prominent architects, Michael Graves. It includes what may be the world's most spectacular site for an art gallery, high above the river with windows out onto the water traffic and the riverfront's dancing curtain of colored light.

Making all this change possible is a city with real wealth. Average incomes in town are ten times higher than outside, with a sizable middle class that makes $10,000 or more a year, and often much more. There's an official name for the money that people make above the income they report: "additional sources." Plenty of people seem to have them. Jammed on The Bund and elevated highways are private cars that cost thousands more than they do in the United States or Europe. The Shanghai municipality requires drivers to pay a $5,000 permit just to buy one. Top models are back-ordered nonetheless. The boom in private apartments, many costing $100,000 and up, wouldn't happen in a city without lots of additional sources. A boom is fueling the boom. Shanghai property values climbed so fast that they created a whole new moneyed class in the city. Locals with enough currency and nerve to enter the housing market in the mid and late 1990s saw their property climb in value at least 20 percent year over year. Many properties doubled in price in less than three years. People bought more. Sold some, bought still more. A local scandal erupted on the news that one-third of Shanghai's new crop of luxury apartments had been bought and sold again before they were ever occupied. The result of the boom is a demographic of young Shanghainese who do not truly grasp where their wealth has come from, feeling that if they just stick their hands in the air, money will fly their way.

One of the triumphs of the Communist Party was its success in spreading the easy use of Mandarin Chinese among nearly all of China's population. The Shanghainese, of course, speak superb Mandarin these days, but immigrants to the city from other areas of China are now for the first time studying the city's local tongue, Shanghainese. Phrase books and dictionaries that help Mandarin speakers pick up the dialect are appearing in local bookstores. Shanghainese language schools have begun to pop up. All because the city's Shanghainese upper stratum of managers talk among themselves in Shanghainese, even in the presence of outside workers, executives, or public officials. The knowing nods and glances make others suspect the Shanghainese are keeping secrets. Foreigners wonder the same. Language-learning materials have begun to appear on eBay for American and European buyers.

The goal of learning the local language is to capture for oneself whatever particles of the city's energy one can absorb. Colonial Shanghai once prospered by peddling opium to locals hooked on oblivion. Now energy is Shanghai's drug, craved more powerfully by a population pouring into the city to seize its supercharged moment. Shanghai's young glow with an optimism that comes of living in a time when the local economy doubled, redoubled, and doubled again.

Behind The Bund and just visible from the boat, the city is pushing against every boundary north, south, and west. The world's construction cranes started migrating en masse to Shanghai in the late 1980s, stretching the boundaries into the sky too. More than five thousand new buildings over fifteen stories tall were built by 2004.

If the river is the best place to look up at the city, the best place to look down on it is not from one of the city's tall buildings. From those heights one must peer through a sickeningly brown smog that floats along the upper reaches of the skyline like the film at the top of a coal miner's bath. The clearest view of Shanghai's shape is found in the Shanghai Urban Planning Exhibition Hall. One of the fantasy oddball showpieces on Renmin (People's) Park, Shanghai's festive answer to Tiananmen Square, the Hall is a gleaming glassy white box of a building about the size of an urban department store. It is topped with four giant canopies shaped like inverted circus tents, making it one of the cheeriest buildings in town.

Inside one may see how thoroughly Shanghai is obliterating its low-rise past and building a high-rise future. On the third floor is a scale model of the entire city with nearly every building extant or planned, rendered as a little colorless tower. The model covers an area the size of a basketball court, and no building is more than four inches tall. What other city in the world would take a parcel of its most valuable real estate bestride its main park and devote it to a building celebrating the civic leaders' plans for the future? In another city there might be a computer image of future schemes on a Web site somewhere, a model under glass in city hall or the science museum. But not a whole building. In Shanghai, even civic propaganda falls under the spell of gigantism. And it works. Even scaled down to insect size, the burgeoning city feels like a living thing that is spreading over the earth, its horizon receding out of view.

Locals walk the elevated platform that surrounds the model looking for their homes, or the high-rises that have taken the place of their homes. The model would have looked entirely different not long ago. In Shanghai, people grew up in neighborhoods with local schools (often housed in the former mansions of the city's foreign elite), small shops, and street vendors, and closely quartered two- and three-storied homes, all of which made for intimate, self-contained communities. Kids played ball, moms hung laundry, and granddads played mah-jongg or sat with their caged birds. Today, young people who go off to school in another city or abroad, or graduates who leave the city for work, can return home after a year or two away and find that in place of their little house is a complex the size of New York's U.N. Plaza. The experience is not just physically dislocating. It gives one the sense that no matter how muscularly it is remade, the city is impermanent, that the only thing that will endure in Shanghai is ambition.

The Exhibition Hall competes for attention along Renmin Park, where the city's huge but graceful Grand Theater, designed by a Frenchman and opened in 1998, looms like a Pompidou Center reassembled as a Chinese temple. Across the street is the round Shanghai Museum, built of pink Spanish granite and designed to resemble an ancient Chinese bronze vessel, complete with rooftop arches in the shape of handles. The museum was China's first planned on the modern American model. Appeals for money and artifacts went out to philanthropists, especially overseas Chinese millionaires wanting to give something to the motherland—and perhaps get something back from the motherland too. It is the place in Shanghai where foreign tourists feel most comfortable, connecting the majesty of ancient China with the new. Through the galleries move a throng of foreigners mind-numbed by jet lag and five thousand years of Imperial display.

How Taiwan Invaded Shanghai

Not all of Shanghai's ambition is homegrown. Far from it. Though the model at the Urban Planning Exposition Hall means to give the impression that the city is in control of its destiny, the view from outside reveals how much the current Shanghai has been remade by foreign energy, money, and world-class talent pouring in. One area of Shanghai once well out of view that now rises in the skyline is the city's newest foreign enclave, the locus of Shanghai's resurgence.

In the 1990s, foreigners began rushing in again, and a whole district of the city, the Gubei New Area, was reconfigured for them. For the newcomers, the welcome mat replicated—no, topped!—the relative opulence of Taipei, Hong Kong, and other Asian cities. Huge deluxe apartment complexes the size and subtlety of giant Las Vegas hotels sprang up. Though set back several miles from The Bund, the Gubei complexes—together with those of Shanghai's other new skyscraper districts—are so enormous that they make the older buildings look like a row of town houses. And, like the international settlements of old Shanghai, which catered to the creature needs of the Europeans and Japanese, Gubei is now a city within Shanghai that replicates the prosperous Asia that lies outside China.

Interestingly, guidebooks offer virtually nothing about Gubei. *Lonely Planet Shanghai* describes it in nine sentences; *Let's Go: China* does not mention it at all. What they overlook today is likely to be exactly what tourists in the future will find so extraordinary. As with old Shanghai, Gubei is something of a foreign concession, the wholesale importation of an alien lifestyle created for and by outlanders.

The first wave of newcomers were actually returnees of a sort, the "overseas Chinese." Mostly they came from Taiwan, which made them an unusual addition to the local scene. Since their own government in Taipei has no official standing in the People's Republic, the Taiwanese arrived with little political protection, but they did bring with them money and know-how, two things Shanghai could not resist. Official Shanghai has even created a special bureau that serves as a de facto consulate for the Taiwanese, offering them the sort of resources that citizens of less murky legal status get from their governments. Accurate counts of the Taiwanese in Shanghai are hard to come by; even the city bureau cannot offer one. The official number lies somewhere between 250,000 and 500,000. Shanghai officials do have a count of the number of Taiwanese businesses in town, however; there are more than five thousand of them, representing more than $10 billion in foreign investment coming into the city. Taiwanese businesses have been moving to China so enthusiastically that there are deep fears back home that Taiwan's economy may hollow out as money and expertise migrate to the mainland.

How much is foreign investment changing the view out the riverboat window? By the end of 2003, a total of 14,400 wholly owned foreign companies were in the city, with another 13,000 businesses underwritten with foreign money.[3] In 2004, the city attracted more than $12 billion in foreign direct investment, the overwhelming share of which went for industries that export, mainly to the United States. In other words,

Shanghai *alone* attracted roughly the same level of investment as all of Indonesia, the world's fourth most populous country, and Mexico, the country that the North American Free Trade Agreement was supposed to turn into a magnet for world capital. Overseas Chinese are the most active investors, providing more than half of the foreign money spent to set up businesses. In the early 1990s, their share was 70 percent.[4]

Years into Shanghai's boom, it is still easy to feel the fever that electrified the city's early investors. Coming in close contact with China changes one's perspectives on the possible and the permissible. The river tour alone jolts the imagination, stirring up all kinds of schemes and plans to lasso one's fortunes to others' schemes that will somehow allow some small bit of the commerce of this great multitude to drift in one's direction. Matters that in other contexts might seem repulsive here glisten. There is the inescapable, peering crowd; the all-embracing political footprint of the Communist Party; the mushrooming of cities and sprawl; the common and pathological desire to exchange time for money, no matter what the social cost. From afar, these qualities in China look like demons. From up close they seize one's thoughts and look like riches. Indeed, whole countries have abandoned their worldviews as China enters the picture.

Imagine how this psychic pressure has worked on the Taiwanese, for whom China has always been in view. The island pseudonation that has lurched toward democracy and now struggles with the issue of independence feels most intensely what the rest of the world does about mainland China. Its opportunities force a rethinking of its identity. Consider the political complications of intermixing Taiwan's economic jewels with China's expanding opportunities. The Taiwanese have reason to fear for Taiwan's pesky, newly democratic soul. The Communist government insists lately that the Taiwanese who have chosen to do business in the mainland disavow the aspirations for independence of the Taiwanese leadership at home. The edict comes like the demand of a patriarch who knows his children's wealth, social connections, and identity lie within the family. In Chinese melodramas, fathers often cast out sons and daughters but find their hearts soften enough to welcome a long-overdue reconciliation. Or find tragedy when their realizations come too late. The mainlanders and the Taiwanese both wonder when the other will come around. Communist China would never change for

Taiwan's reasons. Taiwan may well change for Communist China's, but the odds are far from certain.

Up to one hundred thousand Taiwanese traveled home to vote in the island's elections in 2004, many casting ballots for the first time in their lives. The Communists banned political meetings among the Taiwanese in China, fearing open discussion of Taiwan's independence. They miscalculated. The Taiwanese working in China tend not to side with the pro-independence crowd. They already live a version of unification. The Taiwanese in Shanghai are believers. They already bet on bigger China, and not just on low-wage manufacturing industries that can pick up and move to cheaper locales on a whim. More important, Shanghai is the new home of Taiwan's cutting-edge global conglomerates. When they come into China, they don't just bring investment dollars, they bring advanced technology, business practices, and an international network tied to the world's best companies. Taiwanese banks, insurance and securities companies, and high-tech research laboratories are included in the mix.

And so too is the crowd of young internationalists who sport a style and creative energy that can mediate between the manufacturing prowess of the mainland and the less tangible, but no less essential, global technology of being cool. For the young overseas Chinese jet set—parents from China; raised in Taiwan or Hong Kong, or perhaps Cleveland, Vancouver, São Paulo, or eastern Siberia; who were schooled in the United States, Australia, or Great Britain—Shanghai is a digital, club-hopping, warp-speed update on Paris in the 1920s. Picasso is not coming, but in Shanghai, warehouse districts are being converted into galleries, while movie studios from Hollywood, Hong Kong, and elsewhere move in, creating a nexus of literati, digerati, and glitterati that China has never before seen.

No longer just for Taiwanese, Gubei also caters to Koreans, Japanese, and to other overseas Chinese, mainly those from Southeast Asia and Hong Kong. An enclave of subcontinental Indians is forming into "India Town." Now Gubei boasts fashionable department stores, five-story restaurants made up almost entirely of private rooms, and designer boutiques and upscale salons all of which set prices with a happily blind eye to the low local cost of living.

Shanghai Sex and the City

One amenity the newcomers crave in Shanghai is companionship, and Gubei grew into a district distinctly capable of keeping its growing population of mistresses and "second wives" happy. During the day, one can spot the local Chinese women who have attached themselves to men, mostly Chinese, who live in the city for business, and buy the women their name-brand clothes, high heels, and posh handbags. Sex is still one of the allures of Shanghai. The disparity of wealth between expats and the local rich on one side, and a vast population looking for a way up on the other, is a recipe for all sorts of contact. The drop in local ginseng sales is a small sign of how many men have switched to Viagra, which, with demand for it enormous, is now no longer protected in China by patent laws.

Here, the middle-aged overseas Chinese can find willing youth, burly German mechanics can find lithe girls who simply don't exist at home, and nerdy Western engineers can find girls so hot their friends at home would laugh. Outside of Shanghai's crowded clubs pass a stream of Porsche coupes and decked-out, open-top SUVs rolling to their own Chinese-rap sound tracks. Behind the wheel are the pudgy deal makers who dine out nightly with clients and party afterward, or the buff, spiky-mopped Party princelings whose connected fathers have bought them China's equivalent of a Bel Air lifestyle. One hand on the wheel, the other on the latest $800 phone, they steer their cars slowly down the street, dialing friends on the inside to assess the scene. At the clubs' doors stand gangs of bruisers who must engage in nightly brawls to keep out demanding, unwashed proletarians, who, drunk on domestic booze, insist on slugging their way into where they are not wanted.

"This is China! Who the hell are you to keep me out," they shout. "Shanghai's best hookers are in there and I want to sample one!"

Every night the police, otherwise mostly invisible in the city, come by to haul the angry away. The gate-crashers are right. The city's best hookers are inside. Expert students of the Hilton sisters, they see to it that their clothes are tight and ripped in all the right places, their high heels as long as their skirts, and their hair and makeup done up in the style of Asia's adult-comix dreamboats. They stop hearts and no doubt garner their share of foreign direct investment.

And, there are those who find that far from home they can pair up with partners of the same sex, also young, lithe, and hot. Shanghai's gay scene is lively, and Bangkok is only one time zone away. Sex does not bring as many foreigners to China as does money, but it brings them, nonetheless.

Rocket Buildings

The most stunning anachronism on the boat is not its dragon design or its moribund service; it's the sign describing the river tour to customers. The sign promises one of the most beautiful water rides in China, one where every turn reveals a lush natural vista. The endurance of the cheerful promotion speaks for the malaise of government enterprise. The sign is as out of touch with its city as a tour boat around Manhattan that still marveled at the wonders of Grant's Tomb or the magnificent spire of the Woolworth Building, neglecting entirely the appearance of the skyline and the filling out of the metropolitan region. Today, twenty years after the launch of the boat, there is no escape from Shanghai's urban landscape, nor from its surrounding factories. Up the Huangpu, city and industry stare down the dragons at every turn.

Nowhere is this contrast more dramatic than with Pudong, Shanghai's, and indeed China's, iconic glass skyline. Across the Huangpu from The Bund, and rising from land that was once fields, Pudong is a parallel twenty-first-century downtown growing in fulfillment of an implausible fifteen-year-old pronouncement that a great urban center ought to fill in for the swampy, low-lying turf. Officials call it the "Microcosm of China's Economic Miracle," and it is in fact a kind of miracle. Today, the Pudong district is home to nearly six thousand foreign-funded businesses, including the offices of nearly three hundred of the Global Fortune 500 companies (the old-Shanghai side of the river has another one hundred). Foreign businesses take advantage of Pudong's status as a Special Economic Zone, or SEZ, earning tax breaks and other incentives, including friendly relations with the Chinese leadership, which proudly pushed for the project. The development—full of needle-nosed towers, neon, and video shows playing over skyscrapers, and revolving restaurants perched high like spacecraft visiting from the pages of *Amazing Stories* magazine—projects an H. G. Wells–like vision in which a technologically advanced future delivers the Chinese from the brute realities of the present. Pudong is the propaganda of hope.

Pudong may also be one of the biggest boondoggles of all time. Where did all the money come from to build a city neighborhood that will soon match the size of Paris? The Chinese government has invested more than $12 billion in infrastructure projects just to get the land in shape for more construction. The municipal infrastructure costs aside, Pudong's building boom, like much of China's recent development, has been underwritten by a fortune of public money spent and lent with too little regard to the hard question of whether the investments make economic sense. So far optimism is keeping it up, and a whole social apparatus exists to make sure that optimism itself stays up.

So should one bet against Pudong? Maybe not. This is Shanghai after all, where buildings rocket from the earth, where the men gobble knockoff Viagra, and where the city's leaders crave projects that will drip with superlatives every time they get public mention. From their conception, buildings and public works are bulked up to be the biggest, tallest, longest, fastest, or otherwise most something.

Pudong's most recognizable landmark is the Orient Pearl Television Tower, the highest TV tower in Asia and the third highest in the world. Spiking straight into the air, the tower holds up three metallic orbs of decreasing size that are meant to look like jewels. The largest and lowest is a dance hall and karaoke bar, the next up is, de rigueur, the rotating restaurant, and the smallest orb is an observation deck. Built in 1994, the spire no longer matches Shanghai's sophistication, except that it is acquiring the sentimental affection that comes when big structures are simply present for year after year. It may even have a postmodern gloss, providing inspiration to the architects of Shanghai's newer buildings to break the conventions of joyless international style and to have fun with their buildings. City tour guides like to point out that when one's view of the tower is aligned with the two nearest bridges, it looks like two dragons playing with pearls. Yet, in front of the tower is another building that lines up in a more interesting way. It's the International Convention Center, a curved rectangular building with two large glass halls in the shape of the world on either end. As the tour boat heads up the river, people rush to the rail for a shot of the TV tower centered over the Convention Center, the tower's spike rising proudly between the two glass globes. Is it possible that the planners overlooked this possibility? Or that they were excited by it?

In 2004, Toho Pictures of Japan paid Pudong its highest compliment, making Pudong the location for the climactic fight scene in *Godzilla: Final Wars*. The big amphibian stomps through several major cities around the world in what is said to be his farewell film, but the firefight against a dragon in Shanghai is the topper. That should lend the Orient Pearl Television Tower the pop-icon status King Kong gave the Empire State Building.

But this is not all. Another one of the towers under whose shadow the tour boat passes is the shiny silver Jinmao Building, raised to a lucky eighty-eight stories in Pudong on the east side of the river. The skyscraper, which was briefly China's tallest building, houses the Grand Hyatt Hotel, the world's highest inn. The Jinmao Building, like the boat, is outwardly clad in Chinese accents. Instead of dragonheads, however, its exterior has the aggressive contours of a bronze from the Warring States epoch, or alternatively of a Chinese robot toy. It's the kind of muscular, opulent skyscraper once built in New York and Chicago to express their cities' gilded ambitions, proclaiming that Shanghai intends to takes its place among the world's top cities, but in its own sinocized version of global moneyed culture. The accents were designed by the building's American architects, the giant Chicago firm of Skidmore, Owens and Merrill, the same firm that designed the Sears Tower. Rooms in the Shanghai Grand Hyatt begin at around $240, one-quarter of the average annual income of the Chinese, who are more accustomed to paying $10 a night in the country's innumerable hotels that cater to the much bigger, less comfortable demographic.

Again, that is not all. The projects now on the boards that will finish the current decade in the Shanghai area alone include the world's tallest building, the world largest shipyard, and on The Bund, the world's tallest Ferris wheel, which at 656 feet tall will top England's London Eye by a mere 213 feet. Add to that hundreds of miles of highways in and around the city, and a major expansion of the city's ultramodern subway system out to areas of Shanghai being newly redeveloped.

Probable too is the extension of the world's fastest train, a magnetic levitation train that now runs only over a single short run between the east and west side of the river to deliver people to the new airport. The $1.2 billion "maglev" train now traverses the short route as a test for a system that may eventually provide the world's fastest intercity train, running at nearly three hundred miles per hour between Shanghai and Beijing. The test train was built by two German industrial giants, Siemens and ThyssenKrupp, in an attempt to sell the Chinese their technology, but they may not get a bigger project. The Chinese, with the confidence of the age to boost them and the easy seepage into the country of foreign technology that others have already bought and paid for, have their own ultra-high-speed trains in the works. Forty years ago when Japan was still seen as a low-cost copycat producer, its Bullet Train, the Shinkansen, helped rebrand the country as a technology leader. The train made its first run the same year as the Tokyo Olympics and was a star of the worldwide blitz of broadcast and print images that showed the country at its best and turned the Olympics into a cutting-edge coming-out party. Barring slipped deadlines, the high-speed link between Shanghai and Beijing will begin its run in 2008, the year of China's first Summer Olympics. When China's leaders weigh whether it's folly to spend $1.2 billion on a twenty-mile test run for their fast train, or $16 billion on the intercity system, they reject the logic that the money would be better spent on programs that serve the hundreds of millions of people for whom a ticket on the ultra-fast train will always be an unobtainable luxury. Investing in the nation's prestige will, it is assumed, ultimately pay dividends for everyone. Letting the world know China can top Japan also has psychic rewards that money cannot measure.

Again, this is not all! The city fathers are also planning three big bridges and four traffic tunnels, one of which will be—that's right—the world's longest. Today, the world's longest single-bridge project is outside Shanghai, but still very much driven by the city's interests. It is the planned $1.4 billion highway in the sky that will connect the road that extends south of the city to Hangzhou Bay, twenty-two miles of which the bridge will cross. The south end will connect to Cixi City, a gateway to Zhejiang Province, just to the south of Shanghai, which is filled cheek by jowl with industry.

All this local gigantism is carefully documented each day on the front pages of the *Shanghai Daily,* the English-language paper put out by the government press. It is a quick, mostly cheery read, peppered with local news, summaries of government commissions and state visits and, less prominently, wire service stories on select world events—perhaps in Denmark or Tonga—that often seem to have no conceivable local relevance. The tour boat's trash bins fill with copies even before the boat departs.

Yet, the paper is still worth reading, and rereading. Its news—like that in most of China's state-run media—is both a measure and stimulus of China's ambitions. While the rest of the world's press leads with war news, celebrity scandals, or political coverage, the Chinese press logs every effort, public or private, that is being made to push China to the top in every contest it publicly places itself. The China news, of course, also has a "lift the race" message, in which Asians, and Chinese in particular, are encouraged to try harder in all things. One day's big story might describe how Chinese mobile-phone makers are winning the contest against foreigners, painting the victory as a point of pride. The math, however, is strained, and the surveys it rests on are highly targeted. Chinese phones are not leading the market, but Chinese phone users say they hope homegrown brands will someday lead. The headlines in the paper will, it is hoped, help make the wish come true.

Great personal achievements also fill the front page. There are, for instance, top stories about the young winners of one of the nationwide English-speaking contests. Imagine an American newspaper attempting to pump up sales with the story of a hardworking, likable local boy who trounced his competitors in a conversational-French contest by giving a fine speech on the merits of international brotherhood. The Chinese press regularly carries such stories. In a country where so much rides on the achievement of the upcoming generation, and where families must bet all on the achievements of the one child that the government allows families to have, parents and grandparents apparently find the triumphs of other people's superstar children entertaining, a kind of vicarious thrill in a country where good test scores and the right academic track are as sexy as six-pack abs. Smart children, after all, hold the key to China's ascendancy. If they are diligent enough, they too may one day build the world's biggest something or other. They will certainly help build what is destined to be the world's biggest economy, and if all goes as the Chinese expect, the most influential geopolitical force in Asia and perhaps the world.

As the tour boat ride ends, the dragon bow bumping lightly against the dock, one can't help but see the destiny of China in its cities, in Taiwan's subservience, and the return of the overseas Chinese to the motherland. For now, big projects are the public prelude to dominance, parts of a national temple in the making. The vistas from the Shanghai tour boat may not be lovely to someone wanting respite from the whirring urban-industrial engine that is Shanghai, but they possess a certain beauty to those who see industrial might and architectural bravado as the path to a world where China has regained its rightful place—at the center, certainly respected and maybe even feared.

CHAPTER TWO

THE REVOLUTION AGAINST
THE COMMUNIST REVOLUTION

THE FAMILY SHOP OF LI ZHANWEI AT THE SLEEPIEST END OF SHANG-hai's Dongtai curio market sells anything and everything. The utilitarian shelves that stretch from floor to ceiling could be those of a toolshed or auto parts store, except that they are randomly filled with bits of China's material past. By the door is a small hook hung with jade bangles. Bronze flying horses, some the size of pecans, others as a big as a golden retrievers, rest throughout the shop. Glass snuff bottles painted with gauzy goddesses sit among Buddhas in dozens of incarnations.

The Lis' shop is mostly lit from the sun outside, but under a fluo-rescent lamp in a dim alcove at the back are ceramic plates embedded with hundred-year-old grime. And stashed in them are corroded coins and good-luck pendants promising one of a hundred forms of happiness. Standing on the floor are two thirteen-hundred-year-old Tang dynasty statues, which patient bargaining can free for $5 each. There are racks of bamboo calligraphy brushes said to have wolf-hair bristles and oth-ers with white rabbit hair. The Lis also have an assortment of old Chi-nese-style locks, favorites of engineers visiting from America and Germany. On the highest shelves, out of reach of casual browsers, is a line of gilded clocks from Old Europe. They are topped by porcelain gowned courtesans, trumpeting angels, or ghoulish John Bulls. Ivory mah-jongg sets, some big enough for giants and others small enough for flea circuses, stack up in neat pyramids.

The Lis also keep enough killing tools—axes, nunchakus, daggers, spears, razor-edged spades, and horse-chopping blades—to fill a Hong Kong studio's prop room. In all, thousands of things, most reproductions made in Chinese factories. To those who shop Dongtai regularly, the Lis are among the street's most honest sellers. They adhere to a candid buyer-beware ethos, and identify flimflam when asked, but only when asked.

If Shanghai and China were not changing so quickly, Mr. and Mrs. Li would not be selling anything at all in Dongtai. Their story epitomizes the enormous forces at work in China, carrying people away from their ancestral farming communities and into global commerce.

Six years ago the couple arrived with nothing from a farming village in Henan, which, with 95 million people, is one of China's many nation-size provinces.[1] Like many of the district's sellers, they still have the air of country folk about them. Mr. Li, thin and lively, carries a rough approximation of city style. His bangs look fashioned at home. His polyester pants and cuffed shirt are dressily cut but are many washes past smart. Mrs. Li, in nattier pants and a darted shirt, sports a basic ponytail. Her rosy face has high but muscled cheeks; her bright eyes scan the shop. The Lis, now at the early edge of middle age, smile easily when asked about their road to Shanghai, and their story comes out with the detail and emotion of one waiting to be told—so much so that when an Australian man wanders into the shop to trade currency and bargain for war swords, hot items in Dongtai, Mrs. Li keeps on talking. "We will never be completely accepted as Shanghainese," Mrs. Li says through a translator, "but the city has made a big difference for us." Henan, which lies two provinces inland from Shanghai, offers plenty of incentive to leave. The Asian Development Bank offers a bleak assessment of the region, describing it as beset by "high population density and limited arable land due to mountainous terrain, a harsh climate, and scarce water." When the Lis made their journey, locusts and flooding were among its more recent plagues.

The Lis arrived in Shanghai at the height of the migrants' surge into the city. The migrant count in the city alone in 2003 was 4 million. Astonishingly, 97 percent of the city's migrants soon find jobs. The Lis avoided the usual routes into construction and restaurants. When they first arrived, they spread a blanket on the street and sold what few items they could muster from a collection of bric-a-brac they'd carried with them from home. Migrant sellers are frequently arrested by the police, and for two years the Lis lived being chased from place to place. Then they won the chance to sell their wares in the top-floor flea market in the main tower on the outskirts of Old Shanghai, a bustling shopping district that has grown up around a four-hundred-year-old teahouse and garden. Today, new buildings in the style of old Chinese temples and mansions house tourist shops, hotels, restaurants, and antique and curio sellers.

The market at the top of the tower rents to sellers from all over China, all of whom are migrants trying to get their first leg up on an urban dream. The hall provides a bare-bones beginning; peddlers sit crouched over blankets, old cartons, and low tables filled with curios, some real, but mostly persuasive reproductions. The Lis proved their mettle in the market and even developed something of a regular clientele among the city's upwardly mobile looking for items to decorate the new apartments springing up all over town. But the couple could only sell so much in the cramped hall. In a shop, the Lis knew, they could stock more items, induce customers to spend more time shopping and give their family a more permanent stake in rising Shanghai.

But to expand their business, the Lis had to enter the vast but mostly illegal local lending network that finances much of China's economy and originates in the communities migrants call home. Virtually everything about the informal financing market is conducted by words, handshakes, and occasionally by written but extralegal contracts. China's large bookstores carry business books on nearly every topic of commerce but none on informal lending. It is almost never publicly reported upon except when the Chinese government occasionally cracks down on lenders. Yet this shadowy channel of capital is underwriting millions of rural entrepreneurs with city businesses. One study conducted under the auspices of the Shanghai Academy of Social Sciences, a prestigious center that doubles as a think tank and university, found that an overwhelming proportion of Shanghai entrepreneurs and independent business owners were outsiders who had moved into the city from elsewhere.

That the Lis now own a shop in one of China's great cities, where they have access to information, goods, markets, foreigners, spenders, and the arbiters of the city's evolving tastes, helps to explain Shanghai's boiling excitement. But that they upped and moved is no less important, as is the fact they were not arrested for doing so. Not long ago migrants in China were pitted against the full brunt of state power determined to keep them down home. Economic liberalization, however, made daring to move pay, and man by man the Chinese have picked up in such large numbers that the country is now in the midst of the greatest migration in human history.

One-Point-Something Billion Brains

To confront China today, you must confront her people—however many there are. The discrepancy between China's official count of 1.3 billion and Western estimates of up to 1.5 billion arises from an analysis by intelligence agencies of China's grain consumption, which far exceeds the needs of 1.3 billion people. The people presumably left off China's official number are literally hidden in the crowd. Among the excluded are children whose existence, if known to authorities, would imperil their parents' livelihoods. Also missing are China's farmers turned migrant workers who wander the country without the official permissions they need, or who have no permanent addresses. Perhaps they are construction workers who live on their job sites, shifting floors as work progresses, their only possession a bag of clothes, and moving on when work is done. Perhaps the uncounted are villagers from the hinterlands on the lam from moneylenders back home; China has a whole demimonde of wandering debtors who cannot go home again. Census officials certainly do not find them when making their door-to-door rounds.

And while China's size may be the best-known fact about the country, the human scale of those numbers is still the hardest to grasp. Recall that estimates of the number of Chinese migrating from China's countryside to its cities in recent years range from 90 million to 300 million. Either number is unknowably huge. Another 100 million to 200 million people will join the current migrants in the decade to come. These workers are themselves a formidable labor pool. To make another comparison, the European Union's workforce numbers 223 million. Japan's is 63 million. Some of China's urban centers, such as Shanghai, can add a million residents a year. Other, newly minted cities can reach the size of Chicago or Los Angeles in just a few years.

In the past, China's population, hard as it has been to fully feed, employ, and keep from descending into chaos, has often been seen as the greatest threat to its prosperity. The transient 100 or 200 or 300 million souls who now make up China's floating population are all people who legally ought to be one place but are not, who ought to have one sort of job but have another, and who are in effect a roving nation that is potentially the most disruptive group in China, and the country's least easily controlled. And yet, like Mr. and Mrs. Li, they are also the group that gives China's modernization its hunger.

Communist Plots

As China begins the twenty-first century and its populations move in search of freedom and earning power, its greatest paradox is that all of this change has happened on the watch of the Chinese Communist Party, once the most radical and fearsome enemy of private enterprise the world has ever seen. The Party's most significant reforms have been homegrown, not mandated from abroad by foreign governments or international agencies. There is planning behind them to be sure, but by and large China owes its success to a government that grudgingly acknowledged that it could not get in the way of a people determined and resourceful enough to undermine the old radical regime. Understand how China has advanced despite its impediments and one can sense how much more it will shake the world as its remaining, and considerable, barriers fall.

The most obvious example of Communist obstruction to growth has been the issue of private property. Since the early years of Communism, the Chinese government, in one form or another, has owned all the land in China. The 1949 revolution, led by Mao Zedong, ended a system of property ownership that reached back for centuries.

Mao, who had been active as a Communist since the 1920s, long believed that China's socialist revolution should originate with the peasantry rather than with urban workers, as Marxist theory holds. Through the 1930s and 1940s, during the Japanese occupation and the Chinese civil war, Mao's army of peasants endured vast hardships, including the 7,700 mile Long March. His forces were nearly eliminated but ultimately prevailed. The People's Republic was established in October 1949, at which time the Communist Party had 4.5 million members, nine out of ten of them from peasant backgrounds. Its first years were marked by a massive reconstruction of China, and the country's new prosperity and stability contrasted with the tumult and hardship of the decades before.

China's leadership soon launched a campaign against "enemies of the state," and began the process of land reform in 1950 with the Agrarian Reform Law.

In one bold stroke, the law did away with the rights of individuals to own land in China.[2] First and foremost, it stripped property from Chinese landlords, who often owned giant swaths of land, and granted the use of plots to their former tenant farmers. The reform made good on a long-held pledge by the Communists to put land in the hands of the peasants who worked it. It also did the opposite. In taking land away from the landlords they hated, the Communists also took land away from millions of peasant farmers who owned their own small plots. Before all land was forcibly transferred to the Communist state, 60 percent of China's rural population, frequently starkly poor families, held land, small as the plots might have been.[3]

The early radical Communist reform shared traits with exactly the reforms that were being made at the same time to bolster capitalism in the American sphere of influence outside China. During the U.S. occupation of Japan following World War II, General Douglas MacArthur made reform of Japan's feudal system of land tenure and the redistribution of farms to those who worked them among his top goals. Unlike the Chinese, however, MacArthur required tenant farmers to purchase their plots, albeit on extremely easy terms offered by the government. It too worked miracles: putting land that during the war had forcibly been cultivated according to the demands of the Japanese military into the hands of farmers pumped up production. And, unlike the Chinese reforms, Japan's did not lead to the violent revenge the Chinese farmers inflicted on their former masters. Whereas MacArthur's reforms stuck, and for the American occupiers and the capitalist West bought a grateful constituency of Japanese whose economic progress continued at a terrific pace, the Chinese lost momentum by enacting even more radical reforms.

Collectivization and Its Discontents

In the mid-1950s, China turned from individual land use to Stalin's Soviet model of collectivization. The USSR's collectivization program was enforced with Stalin's trademark violence, in which murder and imprisonment were made part of the Soviet Union's agriculture policy. Stalin executed thousands of kulaks, the former peasants who, like China's former tenant farmers, had been given small plots of land in a pre-Communist wave of reform. Stalin exiled millions more to Siberia. The Chinese Communists had planned to follow the Stalinist model for collectivization from the beginning of the revolution, and the Party's first wave of reform was step one toward that goal.

This more radical shift came in 1956. At first, farmers were compelled to help one another on each other's plots. All land and all property, including animals and farm tools, were collectivized. The new communes also struck at China's most basic social institution, the family. The most extreme of them moved people out of their homes into big dormitories where families could be separated. Land was worked in common by groups, typically a collection of hundreds of families.

One motivation for the change was practical. Cropland would no longer be divided into minuscule plots, each with a different mix of plants,[4] Bigger, unified tracts, the government reasoned, could be farmed more efficiently. Modern farm equipment could also be employed, insofar as such technology was available. Labor could also be freed to build dams and irrigation systems.

But, to Maoist China, it was just as important that the new system of collectivization reshaped China's vast peasant population. One of Mao's core doctrines was that the Chinese peasants and workers needed to be molded into a workforce that could easily be mobilized, not in the sense that they could be moved around geographically but for ideological campaigns and for the shifting, politically informed economic policies of the Party. China's rural labor was kept to the land where it could play the part of a "reserve army" to be called into action when needed by the Party for industrialization projects.[5] The countryside was thus deployed and redeployed in one campaign after another, each spurred on by the force of the state, communal pressures, ideological bullying, and dire consequences for those who did not go along.

The era of collectivization was thus also an era of confinement for China's rural population. When the Communists took control of all private property, they also set about eliminating the myriad small businesses that served everyday commerce in the country. Families with small stores lost them as the state assumed the role of universal shopkeeper. That forced families back onto the land full-time, even if they had already made a complete break from it. In 1956, the government issued an edict that forbade the state-owned factories, mines, construction crews, and transportation lines from hiring anyone off the farm.[6] The weight of China's internal security apparatus was also brought to bear against people trying to leave the countryside for the city.

To make matters worse, the country instituted its infamous *hukou* system, a series of laws that made the state a feudal master over its farmers. Briefly, from 1959 into 1960, while the extravagant industrialization goals adjoined to the Great Leap Forward were pushed by the Party, farmers were allowed to leave the country and join urban firms. In that short window China experienced what had been predicted: farmers stormed into the cities. (Just as they had been doing in much of the rest of the world following World War II.) Nineteen million were recruited to cities; 50 million showed up. China, however, did not prosper. It starved. Tens of millions more farmers poured into cities during the famine. Reaction came swiftly. The Party, moving to protect its urban workers, deported most rural migrants back to the countryside, where the government meant to keep them.[7]

By 1960, the Communists had all but sealed most of the country's people off, not just from the world, but from China's own cities.* Kate Xiao

---

*Following the general economic breakdown of the Great Leap Forward, the Communist Party reconceived the commune system, giving local officials more decision-making authority. The Party also moved to divest industrial planning of the ideological agendas that caused failures. One of the chief architects of the reforms, Deng Xiaoping, who later became China's paramount leader, believed strongly that China could only heal with a more practical approach to development. But the reforms did not do away with the collective system, or free farmers to move. For all his farsightedness, Deng did not see past the general fear that the country's cities would easily be overwhelmed if people moved freely. By the mid-1960s, practical reform again took a backseat to ideology.

Zhou, a native of China born in 1956, grew up during the 1960s and 1970s, the period of the Cultural Revolution and the height of the *hukou* restrictions. Zhou's early urban childhood was interrupted when her father, a college professor of English, was named a "bourgeois intellectual," and an enemy of the people. Such a label spelled ruin for whole families. Every member bore the stigma so heavily that children were shunned at school, if they could attend at all, and relatives were refused work. Life changed quickly and violently for Zhou. Her father was imprisoned in his school, and the surrounding campus was plastered with propaganda posters that accused him of sexual misdeeds. Soon afterward, Zhou's mother was attacked by the Red Guards, the radical young soldiers of the Cultural Revolution, who deemed her too beautiful and sexually active. The Guards cut her hair, then forced her to march to a meeting to be publicly disgraced. The mother's home (her parents were divorced) was searched, and jewelry and china were unearthed from under the floor. Eventually, Zhou, her sister, and her father were exiled to the countryside in Hubei Province to be "reeducated" by farmers.

In her 1996 book, *How the Farmers Changed China,* Zhou details her experience among farmers. She saw firsthand both how restrictive China's official policies were toward its rural population and how farmers found ways to force change. In describing her reaction to her new country home, Zhou captures the stark differences that existed then between rural and urban lifestyles. "For us, the village was a completely strange world. There was no electricity, no running water, no toilet. Everything we took for granted in the city did not exist in the countryside."[8] The divide that Zhou crossed separated her from her former world just as harshly as South African apartheid, American Jim Crow laws, or the ghettos of Europe exploited and anathematized whole populations.

The *hukou* system, as described by Zhou, was designed to prevent rural-to-urban migration. Family booklets served as internal passports. "Every household's booklet registered the family origin, class affiliation, personal identity, birth date, and occupation of all its members."[9] Those with rural identities who traveled to the city without proper permissions, which were hard to come by, would be detained, then deported back to their farms. A household's booklet was also required to get food from government shops. Those who showed up at shops outside the region were refused. The effect, says Zhou, was that the state destined children of farmers to remain on the farm. Only the army, a political post, or occasional temporary work in a nearby city offered any road out.[10]

Not only did farmers have to go to the state *for* food, they had to go to the state *with* food. Collectives were required to meet production goals, and their output was then delivered to the state to satisfy the needs of the cities. Farmers who grew the country's food were therefore the first to go hungry. That is why the famine of 1959 killed tens of millions of people in the countryside while city dwellers survived.[11]

The usual explanation of the low productivity of Communism blames the lack of incentives for farmers. On China's collectives, the standard complaint goes, growers, dulled by state guarantees that fed them no more and no less than their ration books allowed, had no reason to work harder than absolutely necessary. Those who thought their work could be sloughed off on others would take it easy. But this analysis neglects the enforced deprivation of farmers kept on the land. They were turned into slaves for China's cities.

China's rural population suffered then, as now, from a deep, abiding discrimination at the hand of the country's city dwellers. Before and after the Communists came to power, the cities in China were the most coveted places to live. Cities had wealth, schools, culture, and political sophistication. Cities offered a chance for social mobility. China's country folk, like country folk elsewhere, were poorer, illiterate, and tarnished with the negative stereotypes city dwellers predictably applied to them: lazy, stupid, and dishonest. And although the revolution gave China's rural population new dignity, since it had been the peasant farmers who had nurtured the Communist Party during its long fight and many of the Communist leaders were themselves country people, the Communists too found ways to subjugate the countryside.

How Eighteen Farmers Saved China

The hunger that continued to plague large swaths of the Chinese countryside throughout the 1960s and 1970s stirred the clandestine efforts of one group of farmers that have since been pushed into popular mythology by post-Mao reformers. The group came from a hardscrabble village called Xiaogang in China's poor Anhui Province. In the 1970s, families in Xiaogang lived in extreme deprivation. The farmers, with annual incomes around twenty yuan a year, were among the poorest people on earth. (At today's exchange rate, twenty yuan equals $2.50.) Many families sent out members to beg.

The official story of how they lifted themselves up is known to nearly all Chinese. It goes like this: Eighteen farmers desperate for a better way to feed their families agreed to divvy up land they farmed collectively and assign discrete plots to each family. Collectives at the time were obliged to pay a "grain tax," an allotment that went into government distribution channels. The farmers agreed that they would still pay their grain tax, but that once their obligations were met, they could sell or barter whatever surplus they could coax from the land. The proceeds would then be theirs to keep. Such a secret arrangement was illegal, and the farmers knew their pact could result in prison, or perhaps death. The eighteen men courageously signed the compact with their fingerprints in December 1978. It stated that if any one of the signatories was apprehended and punished, the others would support his family left behind.

The effects were nearly immediate, achieving in months what years of ideology and central planning could not. The yields from the land climbed dramatically. The secret agreement and its results, the official story goes, caught the eye of Beijing, where Deng Xiaoping had recently become China's paramount leader. In truth, the Xiaogang farmers were far from the first to subvert the system. Some farmers were already making small bribes to buy themselves the freedom to sell crops. Provincial officials willingly allowed the illegal experiments to proceed. Deng himself ultimately endorsed comparable agreements, citing the Xiaogang pact as a "responsible contract system with profits linked to production." With Deng's support, similar arrangements were allowed on a trial basis in the poorest provinces most desperate for relief. The scheme offered a powerful, no-cost way for a strapped government, itself struggling through a difficult transition, to lift its people.

Within a year of the compact most of the farmers in Anhui, a rural province of 50 million people, were operating under a version of what became known as the Household Responsibility System. As the stuff of myth, it helped that the heroes were peasant farmers, not city intellectuals or government planners in Beijing, who planted this new revolution. China officially instituted the Household Responsibility System in 1980. The system allowed families to grow and sell crops for profit, provided they met their quota responsibilities to the state. The market economy in China was, in fact, kick-started by farmers.

Today, the document that the original eighteen farmers signed is enshrined in the Museum of the Chinese Revolution in Beijing, and Chinese government information agencies do what they can to keep the story alive. In December 2003, the Chinese papers ran articles commemorating the twenty-fifth anniversary of the secret meetings.[12] It interviewed one of the signatories, Yan Hongchang. He is quoted as saying that the agreement was "a capitalist action challenging the socialist public ownership then." He takes issue, the report noted, with the common view that the farmers were defying Mao by going against the system of collective farming. The farmers, he said, were instead working hard to conform "to the thoughts of Mao in 'serving the people wholeheartedly.' " The Chinese news agency reports that now every family in Xiaogang has a tractor and a TV set, while some even have cars and two-story homes with living rooms. "We have built public flush toilets, reading rooms, a water tower, and a cultural square in our village," says Yan Hongchang, "and the . . . per capita income [in 2003] is estimated to be more than twenty-six hundred yuan [$313]." Instead of just trying to eke out grain, the area's farmers have also diversified into forestry and livestock.

Whether the Household Responsibility System really owes its existence to the Xiaogang experiment and whether farmers throughout the land embraced it as wholeheartedly as official Chinese histories proclaim has come under doubt among academics outside China. Some scholars point out that the end of the communal farms met considerably more resistance than the official version admits to. Perhaps as a result, China's official press apparatus continues to flog the story of the secret agreement, and the virtues of the farmers involved. No matter. From a practical point of view, the details about the origins of reform are far less important to the present than the industry and appetites the rural reforms ignited.

It was also an incredible turning of the tables when the economic reforms that effervesced out of the rot in the countryside delivered the first wave of China's new wealth to the country bumpkins themselves. What's more, the new prosperity came to the regions of China that were among the poorest, not coincidentally or out of some turn of cosmic justice, but because the people there had the least to lose and had the incentives to take the risks that utter poverty and disenfranchisement offer. Kate Xiao Zhou recalls that when China's farmers first found their way into the cities, usually illegally, to sell the produce they had harvested under the Household Responsibility System, city dwellers were dumbstruck at the money the peasants were making. First the farmers were the butt of innumerable jokes, and then the subjects of envy. The farmers' enterprise then woke the urbanites up to the possibilities of a freer marketplace.

Once farmers began to make some money on their own, they looked for ways to make money with their money. Many of the enterprises competing for survival in China today grew out of the pooled savings of backwater farmers who looked for ways to invest their newfound money in more ambitious businesses. Among them are collectives and cooperatives owned not by the central government but by members of local communities. Or they are owned as private investments by local governments. These "township and village enterprises," or TVEs, fill the gray area between public and private sectors and now make up a third of the economy. Mostly these companies—an astounding 120 million of them[13]—were originally financed by the pooled resources of farmers or set up by municipalities using their citizens' funds. They are overwhelmingly small-time companies with fewer than five employees, but some township and village enterprises have flourished and now rank among China's most competitive.

Because farmers devised ingenious structures that rarely divided the interests of the government neatly from those of investors, the landscape of Chinese businesses is dizzying. After years of reform, China is an infinite jumble of hybrid businesses that mix together the financial interests of government bodies at every level with those of officials (who may themselves be investors or otherwise reliant on corporate profits), townspeople in the role of shareholders, and other private investors. Millions of companies conflate the sectors, often in impossibly complex, opaque ways.

These murky corporate structures are often seen as an impediment to future growth, but may in fact argue the opposite case. One way to begin to understand China's impact on the world economy that is to unfold over the next few decades is to consider how far the Chinese have come *without* the property rights and laws often regarded as some of the most fundamental building blocks for economic development.*

And it all began with the sale of surplus vegetables.

Communism's Supercharged Soldiers of Capital

The long repression and then liberation of China's farmers set into play the explosion of China's market economy. But they also triggered the recent flood of migration that brought Mr. and Mrs. Li to Shanghai's Dongtai curio market. And yet, chances are that the current number of migrants is only the first wave of what is soon to follow.

Here's why. Although good population statistics in China are hard to come by, the broad trend comes through in every head count.† For

---

*Consider, for instance, how life in a mature market economy would have to be reordered if people were, in essence, suddenly allowed to own nothing of real value. Among development theorists—the economists and sociologists who study the preconditions that must exist for economic advancement—an influential strain of thought stresses the importance of property rights. The chief deficit that keeps the poor down in developing countries, the argument goes, is the absence of property rights. In *The Other Path* (1989), the Peruvian economist Hernando de Soto powerfully advances this thesis, arguing that when people do not have solid legal ownership of their homes or of whatever small businesses they manage to start on their own, they have no power to tap the value of the things in their life worth the most money. That in turn shuts down their chances to advance. They do not have assets to borrow against. Poor villagers who have stacks of paper showing that they own their homes still cannot borrow against them if there are no courts that back up their claims, nor clear rules that say which pieces of paper really matter. Such scenarios, common through the developing world, prevent the poor people who must live with flimsy rights from borrowing against their homes to start businesses. Weak property rights, according to the argument, also dissuade others from investing in the businesses of people who must build their livelihoods on legal quicksand. In test cases in Peru and El Salvador, where property rights have been firmed up, economic activities among the poor have improved and offer proof of the value of property rights.

†Unlike the strong central governments of other tightly controlled states, China's Communist government was, until recently, less than rigorous when it came to big social surveys and censuses. The difficulty is compounded by the government's frequent shifting of the definitions and categories that divide city and country.

nearly all of the last fifty years, excluding the most recent few years, the pace of China's urbanization has lagged behind that of the world as a whole. Outside China, during the last four decades of the twentieth century, the world experienced unprecedented urban growth, most of it the result of migration in from the countryside. In 1950, about 30 percent of the world's population lived in cities. That is just six percentage points under where China is *today,* while in the year 2000 the percentage of the world's population that called cities home was 47 percent. The numbers reflect high concentrations of city dwellers in developed countries, where three of four people are urbanites.

But China's urbanization is low even compared with developing countries—where 40 percent of people live in cities—that have nothing like China's industrial might. As mentioned before, China has one-fifth of the world's population, but equally momentous is that one in three of the world's farmers is Chinese. What's clear is that China's recent urbanization rush is rapidly making up for lost time. The United Nations predicts that by 2010, the vast influx of rural residents to the cities will boost China's rate of urbanization to 45 percent, and by 2030 to 60 percent.[14]

Thus, another way to view China's rapid surge in the global economy is to see it as a counterreaction to the Communists' forced removal of most of China's population from the world of commerce.* And similarly paradoxical, when seen in light of China's long-term development, the Communist collectivization campaigns in the country and in the city forged a docile and pliant workforce hundreds of millions strong.

Prasenjit Duara, professor of history and East Asian languages and civilizations at the University of Chicago, and chairman of the school's department of history, grew up in India during the heyday of Indian socialism. In his youth, in the 1970s, he was drawn to China by the country's image as a radically egalitarian state. Today, Duara's work on

---

*The Chinese themselves think of their absence from the world's mainstream as an aberration of nature. For thousands of years of human history, their country was the richest and, by the Chinese reckoning, most civilized nation on earth. The Chinese, outsiders often hear, had lively cities of over a million people when European cities were still small. When Marco Polo traveled to China (or said he did), Europe's leading cities had just tens of thousands of people. Paris, Europe's largest, had seventy thousand and London just thirty-five thousand.

China explores the manipulation of the country's historical record to serve the purposes of different generations of leaders, reformers, and conquerors. Duara sees a deep irony in how capitalism arose in China after 1978. For the Chinese, who sweated and beat themselves over Marxist and Maoist theory until they had internalized it into their bones, the irony is far more than a historical twist; it has turned their mental world topsy-turvy. Marxist theory holds that capitalism takes shape when early capitalists squeeze peasant farmers, in essence starving them enough so that the wealth of the land gets pushed into commercial, capital-intensive enterprise. In China, however, it was the peasant farmers who squeezed the Communist state to start their own businesses, and ironically it was Mao's reforms that laid the groundwork for Chinese capitalism. "The Communists made the workforce docile and organized labor to be a managed entity that could be continuously mobilized," Duara says. The social institutions the Communists created, including housing, schools, and a health care system, bled the state of resources. But in providing for the people, even at a basic level, the Communists ended up saving the nascent capitalists the price of developing a workforce.

Now, of course, this workforce is irresistible to the world's manufacturers. As American and European companies cast around looking for places to move factories or parse out production to third parties, China is seen as a place where labor and management costs can be kept to an optimal minimum.

The next historical irony may be that those same American and European companies will teach China's own companies how to utilize that same docile, compliant workforce to gain a competitive advantage against them in the global marketplace.

CHAPTER THREE

TO MAKE 16 BILLION SOCKS, FIRST BREAK THE LAW

GREEN, MOUNTAINOUS HUBEI PROVINCE STRADDLES THE MIDDLE OF China, its eastern extreme three hundred miles inland from Shanghai. Hubei's beauty is largely unknown to Westerners, except for those who saw director Ang Lee's martial-arts/special-effects masterpiece, *Crouching Tiger, Hidden Dragon,* which displayed the province's subtropical, alpine charms. Hubei is also one of the most agriculturally rich regions in China, an important national source of grains and vegetables. It is the site of China's most fabled natural wonders, the aquatic valleys on the Yangtze River known as Three Gorges. And also, of course, the site of the controversial Three Gorges Dam, the six-hundred-foothigh, 1.2-mile-long span that will create a reservoir 350 miles long, comparable to Lake Superior. Construction of what will be the world's largest concrete structure has already forced the relocation of 820,000 people with another 350,000 to go. The project will all but wipe out the contours of the gorges themselves, and several cities. The dam is designed both to generate enough electricity to power an inland economic revival and to spare the region from the violent seasonal caprices of the Yangtze.

How interesting it is, then, that despite Hubei's natural beauty and long-term potential for economic development, many of its people are leaving. Walking, biking, hanging on to the sides of trucks, and riding "hard seat" on trains, they are pouring into the tide of migrants washing over China. As much as China's reforms have lifted the lives of its rural population, the countryside is still a land of vast want. The many miracles of the new economy have refused to come and must be chased.

In Changxin, for example, a small farming village in Hubei that is representative of so many others, officials make the often-heard complaint that its best sons have all left for work elsewhere. Of the thousand villagers, three hundred are gone, and only two of the village's twenty-five Party members are under the age of forty,[1] meaning it has a broken pipeline for its future leadership. The rural exodus has taken on an inexorable dynamic that weakens the countryside with every train ticket out and gives those who remain all the more reason to leave. In Changxin, the hapless officials who are among those left behind now have trouble finding neighbors to volunteer for such essential tasks as flood control—the Yangtze River is prone to breaching—and disaster relief—Hubei sits on top of a major earthquake fault line. It is bad enough to live in a poor village, but even worse to live in one where civic life erodes with the receding emigrants.

Even midsize country towns cannot hold on to their people. Elsewhere in the province, in Chahe Township, in Honghu City, a municipality of forty thousand, one-quarter of the population has left to work elsewhere. As is typical of such towns, many of the residents still farm for a living. In Honghu that means a lean existence. The annual per capita profit for farm families is only about $12.50.[2] Extra money must come from elsewhere, odd jobs or remittances from someone who has already gotten out. To make matters worse, many fields are now left idle because the people remaining in the area are often too old to tend their family's plot. In Hubei's Jianli County, one-quarter of the arable land sits idle because two hundred thousand people have left to work in the cities. And still, the district, together with its neighbors, owes millions in taxes on its land, plus interest, money it cannot hope to pay.

But Hubei is not alone. Every rural area of China has its own bleak tale, including one county in Hunan Province that has lost 156,000 farmers to the migratory tide. Local fields, once avidly farmed, are now infested with weeds. "Why don't the higher authorities work out solutions for places like ours, a hollowed-out old-people's village?" asks a sixty-five-year-old man left behind. "Nobody [here] wants to be a village official."[3]

In some areas of Sichuan Province the emigration rates are so high that nearly every family sends someone away. In the county of Santai, which, with a population of 1.5 million, has more farmers than any other county in China, seven of every ten families have said good-bye to someone who has gone to look for a job in the cities. No wonder; Santai farmers must work plots of land only one-eighth of an acre (0.05 hectare). It is hard to make a living on a piece of land smaller than an Olympic swimming pool.* Santai's farmers are getting out of the area as fast as they can, knowing, as did Mr. and Mrs. Li, that the most meager city jobs pay better than wages in the poor agricultural areas.

Economic opportunity in China, largely driven by geography, has grown so lopsided that China now ranks among the most unequal of nations. On average, rural incomes are but a third of those in the city.[4] But statistics can't easily measure the disparity in local government services. With the advent of reform, localities now must support their own social services such as schools. In 1998, the National People's Congress cut the Ministry of Education in half, leaving rural education in a free fall. In China's poorest provinces, the odds of a child getting even basic schooling can be zero. In thirty-five poor rural areas surveyed for a recent World Bank project, four of ten children ages seven to fifteen had received no schooling whatsoever. The chances for girls are markedly dimmer than for boys. Where agriculture is hardscrabble and regional budgets prove too lean or too mismanaged to cover basic services, school becomes an ever more distant possibility. China's urban boom pulls with every propaganda broadcast from China's state good-news machine, which runs story after story about the raging success of the country's economy, which is more or less the same as running ads urging escape to the cities.

Dan Wright, the former director of the Hopkins-Nanjing Program at Johns Hopkins University School of Advanced International Studies, traveled the countryside for a year on foot talking to villagers in China's poorest regions. Wright notes the bitter irony that China's booming prosperity has deepened the deprivation for millions of China's poorest. Wright collected stories of his travels in his book *The Promise of the Revolution:* "A schoolteacher in a village complained to me that one-third of their school's expenditures . . .went toward feeding local education

---

*According to the Earth Policy Institute, population growth and the creeping loss of arable land have reduced the per capita amount of land China has under cultivation for grain by more than half since 1950. Under these circumstances, China drives up crop harvests by driving up yields, where possible.

officials visiting on 'inspection.' They traveled from one village school to the next eating and drinking," the teacher said. "And we dare not feed them poorly; they have power over us."[5]

Another strong incentive to leave the countryside is the misery inflicted by greedy, tyrannical local officials. Abuses against farmers grew to be one of the country's most explosive issues when a Chinese magazine published a report in December 2003 by Chen Guidi and Wu Chuntao, husband and wife writers in Hefei, the capital of Anhui Province. Their work, *China's Peasants: An Investigation,* caused such a sensation that it was repackaged as a 460-page book that sold two hundred thousand copies in legal editions and then, following a government ban, sold another 7 million copies printed underground.[6]*

China's Peasants sprang from the moment that Wu learned of a rural mother who bled to death following the birth of her son because she lacked the $360 her local hospital demanded for treatment. Wu, a new mother herself, decided to investigate the economic causes for the tragedy, following them as far back as she could.

The couple spent three years traveling Anhui collecting stories. At first, officials greeted their study enthusiastically. Many people read the book over the Internet, where it had been typed by volunteers into news groups. Readers were said to cry and rage at the stories in their books and on their screens. When the response proved too strong, however, the government ordered the government publisher that first produced the book to stop sales. Other journalists found themselves shamed by the book, feeling that they had overlooked the pain of their rural countrymen.

"We observed unimaginable poverty and unthinkable evil," the couple writes in their preface. "We saw unimaginable suffering and unthinkable helplessness, unimagined resistance with incomprehensible silence, and have been moved beyond imagination by unbelievable tragedy." The authors were struck that half a century of agricultural reforms had often left farmers with almost no wealth and still stuck using the most primitive farm methods while being extorted for taxes. While rural incomes have in fact climbed 90 percent since the mid-1990s, locals pay four to five times the tax they once did. To tap into the coun-

---

*A best seller by any standard. During the fifty-eight weeks that *The Da Vinci Code* spent at the top of the *New York Time*'s best-seller list, it sold roughly as many.

try's growing prosperity, local officials have in effect wiped it out for earners, levying hundreds of new taxes. Couples who want to get married must pay fourteen taxes just to register. The tax system itself is a catalyst for migration. Farmers make a fraction of what urban residents do, but the government requires them to shoulder disproportionately higher taxes than urban dwellers.[7]

The book is filled with innumerable corrupt schemes that keep farmers poor. It describes in detail how local officials in Anhui shake down farmers for payments of various kinds. Embezzlement is another all-too-common crime; funds earmarked for public improvements regularly disappear. One story that drew national attention in China tells of Ding Zuoming, a villager who was so sick of the pilfering that he demanded a public audit of the local till. The authors describe Ding as an ordinary peasant but a good student who once just missed a university education by a couple of points on the national test. If he had lived in the city, they said, he would have been able to get a better education and have led a better life. Instead, he suffered silently, stuck with his family on a farm where there was often nothing to eat. After he asked for the public accounting, he was arrested and, while in custody, beaten to death. His killers were punished, and money was promised to his family. The funds, however, never materialized. The dead man's children were forced from school and his parents, both sick, left to languish.

The government, responding both to the book and its genuine fear that the imbalance between China's prosperous zones and the countryside could threaten the country's stability and progress, spent much of 2004 declaring measures aimed at redressing the farmers' complaints. These included tax relief, subsidies, and a major effort to encourage industries to locate to China's poorer regions. Premier Wen Jiabao has personally inserted himself into efforts to get migrant workers millions of dollars in back pay from dishonest employers. At the National People's Congress in 2004 he called on members to focus on "more giving and less taking" when it came to China's peasants. The official press reports progress. Farmers' incomes are said to be climbing, up 5 percent from 2003 to 2004. There is no way to tell yet whether that is a reliable number.

But rural reforms, no matter how ambitious, can never turn China's small farms into the growth engine of China's industry. Conditions in rural China are often appalling, and the government's chief strategy to end rural poverty still focuses on getting people off the farm. Everyone knows as much. Many of China's farmers live as they did centuries ago, inhabiting houses of their own making, eating off tables and chairs made from local trees and relying on oxen and water buffalo, or their own legs, for heavy fieldwork. They live in villages where most of what they consume is grown by themselves, or a neighbor. Extra income, usually just a few dollars a year, comes to those who catch wild snakes or birds to sell. The most money comes from departed family members who send it back once they have found work elsewhere.[8]*

Borrowing Time to Buy the Future

In making the trip to larger towns and cities, migrants often face a gauntlet of exploitation, discrimination, and fear. The mass of new arrivals can be seen at the Beijing Railway Station. Often they have come hundreds or thousands of miles, sitting on hard benches or even standing. The cheapest train tickets for a journey that travels half the length of China can cost $10, but that may be all that a migrant's family made at home over the last several months. Over long journeys the air inside the trains is a putrid mix of human biology, cheap fried food, and overripe fruit. Riders, cramped, anxious, and dead tired, slip into an achy daze. As trains take migrants farther from home, they can become treacherous places. Among the dangers are roving gangs that rough migrants up and steal what little cash they have. When confided in, train police, often the thieves' confederates, take whatever migrants still have hidden. Once off the train, migrants emerge into a world they expect to exploit them, but hopefully not too badly. In the grime of the station plaza, countrymen and -women sit by their twine-tied bundles, looking around as frightened and tired as war refugees. If they are lucky, relatives or townsmen who preceded them to the city will pick them up and move them into work.

*According to the World Resources Institute, China's national poverty rate is 4.6 percent, but more than 47 percent of the population lives on less than $2 a day. China's official poverty statistics can be confusing, because some of China's very poor may subsist on their own farms but still have extremely low incomes. Rural per capita incomes are, for example, well below those of Mexico and most of Latin America.

To raise the funds for these journeys and to establish themselves in the big towns and cities, the villagers depend on their own networks of finance. In the case of the Lis, the Shanghai shopkeepers met in the last chapter, their money came from a town lender who served as a kind of bank for villagers venturing out. The Lis describe him as the richest man in their hometown but say that he does not invest only his own money. The lender collects money from other villagers who want a piece of the urban action but who cannot make the trip to the city themselves. The terms are strict. The interest rates are high by Chinese standards but well below the loan-shark rates on the streets of New York. Some pay as much as 12 percent a year, and principal is usually expected back within two or three years, which can necessitate another round of informal financing.

For most families in China, money mainly takes one form: cash. Protecting and hiding money are everyone's concern; mattresses, urns, strongboxes, and holes in the ground double as safe-deposit boxes. Shoes, socks, and homemade money belts are where money travels. Security is also a problem for moneylenders, who sometimes build their own banklike buildings to manage their cash, but then call them something else. Kellee Tsai,[9] a political scientist at Johns Hopkins University and a former analyst at Morgan Stanley, traveled the country interviewing back-alley bankers and small- and big-time entrepreneurs about their roles in the country's private credit market. She found one such lender who transacted all business through his "reading club."

Until recently it was all but illegal to lend to private businesses in China, and yet the scope of the informal finance network rivals the banking systems of other countries. This is quite an accomplishment when one considers that since the state relinquished its role as the people's universal provider in 1978, 30 million private entrepreneurial businesses have taken root in China, most of them having needed start-up capital.

How was this done? According to Tsai, one of the remarkable features of China's private lending networks is that they work without the benefit of legal enforcement. And, because land in China belongs to the state and not to its tenants, borrowers cannot put up property as collateral. Instead they risk the social capital of their families, and perhaps, if the lenders are goonish, their health and safety.

Migrants often gamble on small shops, such as the dry-cleaning shop under the shadows of the gleaming new high-rise apartments in Xujiahui, a rapidly changing neighborhood on the edge of Shanghai that is taking the form of midtown Manhattan, complete with a Times Square–like center. The cleaner's shop is a small two-room affair in a tumbledown strip that abuts the street. It shares the building with other low-rent businesses, including a food stall fronted by barrel-size, multitiered bamboo steamers that sit over boiling water all day and night, a bicycle repair shop, and a glass cutter.

The family there, whom we'll call the Chens, arrived with nothing in 2000 from a small farm village in Shandong Province. Mr. and Mrs. Chen took service jobs for their first year and then were approached by a Shanghai local businessman with a proposition. He would sell them a machine that could do both standard laundry and dry cleaning. If the couple came up with the down payment, they could finance the rest of the machine with the proceeds of the laundry service.

The Chens returned to their village and called on the local money-lender for seed capital. The village lenders there had a history with migrants. Their first wave of loans had met with unhappy results. During that time, they had relied on the traditional social pressures of Chinese society in which families and individuals work hard to preserve good relationships within a wide network of relations, neighbors, and others with whom they are connected by dint of school, work, or through friends. Preserving working relationships is essential to local life, where Chinese work hard to build, keep, and offer "face," the combination of goodwill, prestige, and social chits that help define one's place in society. When interaction is local, the shared need to preserve face serves as a highly effective enforcement mechanism against breaking promises or double-dealing. Yet when money was first lent out to migrants, all too often they disappeared into the netherworld of China's big cities and floating populations, leaving no recourse to lenders, who had few resources to track down deadbeats or to force them to pay.

To adjust to the new reality, loans are now commonly made to the family members who stay behind and who can be held responsible. Such was the arrangement for the Chens. Their family, the couple knew, would be subject to the demands of their lenders, and nonpayment would be met with severe pressure. It might manifest itself in nightly visits from collectors, who over time grow less civil. In their own village, lenders awaiting late payments simply moved into the homes of the families of those who owed, refusing to leave and demanding to be served food and drink and offered bedding until money was paid back. Such methods are highly effective. They also supply a strong incentive for migrants to take whatever jobs are necessary to deliver their families from their financial burdens. They leave town motivated and stay that way.

For rural families in China, the financial importance of migration works two ways. Villagers can invest in the fortunes of others if they enter the lending pool that fills migrants' pockets. To raise bigger money that they can perhaps use to improve their own rural homes, invest in their farms, or to build local businesses, it is best to find a way to directly tap the wealth of the urban economy. That means sending a family member off to seek his or her (three of four migrants are male) fortune. The immediate cost can be great since the person chosen to leave is usually the same person on whom those at home depend most. Families, therefore, must live without that person's earnings while he establishes himself in the city. The migrant's time away serves, in effect, as a substitute for the high price of funds on the rural credit market.

In this system, families tend not to bet on feeble members. Too much is at stake. Working one's way up at low-road manufacturing plants, mines, quarries, road jobs, or construction jobs carries high risks. In the first half of 2004, according to official counts, industrial accidents killed around 350 people a day.[10] Grueling, demanding work demands the fittest workers. China's migrant population is thus the cream of the country, people in the prime of their earning years who on average possess two and half more years of school and are ten years younger than the typical agrarian worker. Ultimately, sending someone off can pay handsomely, in many cases boosting the income of rural homes between 14 and 30 percent. That will not make most country families rich, but it can mean the difference between a subsistence lifestyle and one with a few extras. It could be extra clothing, a TV, or perhaps a new henhouse. While away, migrants also learn skills and collect contacts, which can ultimately prove more valuable than their city earnings.[11] With those they can get better jobs or start their own businesses.

It Takes a Village
to Gain Global Market Share

The network of private financing has created another urbanization trend. It turns certain rural or quasi-urban areas into hubs of industry. In the remarkable Zhejiang Province, for example, 90 percent of the businesses are private, a rate that far exceeds that of any other Chinese province. Most remarkably, Zhejiang's local businesses began almost entirely with seed capital provided by local lending networks. Brad Huang, a native of the province, a graduate of the Yale School of Management, and an alumnus of Crédit Suisse, now runs Lotus Capital, an investment fund that buys stakes of private businesses in China. By his account, Zhejiang's success stems from its having started out so poor. Among Chinese provinces, Zhejiang received among the lowest rates of government assistance, which left its largely rural population among the most destitute in China. When liberalization began, many of Zhejiang's sons migrated to China's great metropolises. Many others, however, made a go of it at home, quickly and enthusiastically seizing the chance for their own businesses.

The province's former fields are now lined end to end with factories of every description. Land at one of Zhejiang's several small airports and one sees not the usual assort of ads for travelers. No, instead of the glossy pitches for cigarettes, mobile phones, and digital cameras, the walls of Zhejiang's airports are lined with promotions for drill presses, plastic-molding machines, and industrial lathes. Today, many of China's most successful private companies and richest individuals hail from the province.

The most astonishing district in Zhejiang is Wenzhou, part city, part countryside, and all economic muscle. The district sits across the Taiwan Strait from the 22 million people of Taiwan, and for the first thirty years after the revolution, Wenzhou was the frontier land that divided the People's Republic of China from the smaller Republic of China. Even today, fighter planes and soldiers with machine guns are a constant presence in Wenzhou's airports. Yet so are streams of Taiwanese businessmen. Wenzhou's economy was starkly ignored by the government during the period when industry was developed in areas that Mao imagined would be out of reach of foreign attackers.

Wenzhou is also beset with mountains that make roads and rails difficult to build. Most of the east coast of China is liberally crisscrossed by railroads, but Wenzhou's first train line only arrived late in 1992. Between 1949 and 1981, the Chinese government's total investment in Wenzhou was a paltry $80 million, an average of $2.5 million a year. That is an especially lean number considering the government officially controlled nearly all economic activity and that given Wenzhou's population over that period, growing from 4 million to 7 million people, the area received less than $1 per year per person. Compounding its struggle as a land without, the amount of acreage allotted to Wenzhou's farmers was less than a third of the national average, and the plots more likely than not were hardscrabble.

Yet out of this marginal land emerged the patterns that shaped China's economic destiny.[12]

How? As with the famous eighteen farmers who secretly entered an agreement to run their own businesses out of sight of the rural collective, nascent Chinese entrepreneurs had to decide to break the law. Starting a private business in China was illegal. As with all illegal businesses that thrive despite the law, it took a combination of will, political skill, business acumen, and a readiness to game the system in any imaginable way, employing secrecy, bribes, and a facility with the law that could recast otherwise illegal ventures into businesses that fit some legal construct acceptable to those policing the local economy. For foreigners doing business in China, or competing against it, one of the most maddening things is the fluid view that Chinese businesses have of agreements, and their often blatant disregard for legality. But Chinese businesses grew up in an environment in which extralegality was the only option. The entirety of China's budding private sector mushroomed under the same sort of restrictions faced by American bootleggers and speakeasies during Prohibition.

In Wenzhou, private businesses, such as they were, were already taking shape before Deng Xiaoping officially began reform, yet the paramount leader saw their value and praised the region even though officially it was a hotbed of crimes against the people's state. Thus was the private economy born with a wink and a nod from the central government. And like the famous eighteen farmers, the entrepreneurs of Wenzhou were lionized for acting as if China's rules and regulations were all wrong. Deng's most quoted saying, "It does not matter if the cat is black or white, so long as it catches mice," was uttered during policy debates in the 1960s, but is invoked now to refer to the failure of the old Communist economics, which did not "catch mice," and to the new ones in which the people are given license to focus on ends and give nary a thought to means.

Once rural households were given permission to go into business, entrepreneurialism in Wenzhou caught fire. In some villages in the district, businesses were set up in nine of ten households. In just five short years, 80,000 families had set up some sort of small industrial operation, and by 1986, 110,000 had done so. The law still prohibited the businesses from growing large; employing more than five people drew immediate attention from authorities, who had the power to shut bigger enterprises down. Even so, by 1986, the villagers of Wenzhou were employing three hundred thousand workers, thus teasing off the farm the first of China's hundreds of millions of rural migrants searching for better work.

All those businesses needed money to get going and to run. Unlike much of China's boom to come, the early boom in Zhejiang, including in Wenzhou, was financed by the region itself, with virtually no foreign money to kick-start it. To get around the restrictions against lending to private firms, local businesses again resorted to their own funding networks, some of which have since grown up to become among the most powerful financial players in modern China, capable today of raising hundreds of millions of dollars for mammoth factories, private toll roads, and virtually any other project that elsewhere in China would need the capital of a state bank, a well-connected state company, or a foreign business.

And without a Wall Street lawyer or London solicitor in sight, the peasant villagers of Wenzhou devised all sorts of ingenious and novel corporate structures to gain the legal footing they needed to get money. One of these was the "hang-on household enterprise," in which a family company morphed into an offshoot of a state-owned enterprise (SOE). Through an arrangement with the older company's management, the household enterprise would cloak itself with the SOE's name, paperwork, and bank account numbers. Not only did this make the company kosher for loans from state lenders, but it also freed it from having to pay taxes. State collectives were in on the game, too, partnering with household companies in similar ways.[13] As businesses plied these new forms, they embroiled the local Communist power structure in their push to market.[14] The hybrid businesses grew to be called "red-hat" enterprises. Kellee Tsai notes that the owners of many of the fake collectives were themselves cadres, local Party officials in charge of managing farms or businesses under the auspices of the state. Local officials were actually prodded by the government to get involved as much as they were able. If that meant becoming partners with the enterprise, and getting wealthy in the deal, so be it.

The Chinese Communists, steeped in Marx, knew that the early stages of capital accumulation in a market economy taking shape were bound to be messy. Europe had its pirates and pirateers, America its robber barons, Japan and Korea had their corrupt *zaibatsus* and *chaebols,* the cozy interlocking conglomerations of banks, industry, politicians, and the military, all willing to scratch each other's back and hide each other's sins. The intertwining of interests of the private entrepreneur and the official in power has become commonplace in China. It can work in myriad ways, some highly cooperative and others highly coercive. Zirui Tian, an engineer turned economic investigator at Peking University and INSEAD, the French business school, argues that "one proof of the genius of the Chinese businessman is that he can succeed in a system that has so many restrictions."[15]

Over time, the process helped to link groups in China whose interests were not historically aligned. On one side was an aspiring middle class and business class that needed money and property rights to conduct business. On the other were the state and Party officials who were ideologically wired against business and private property. Today, there is little separation between the two. Even as regulators, the interests of officials are so complex and conflicted that reining in the private sector on any front also slashes the fortunes of those who run the state.

Whether the system can ever shake off the culture of legal noncompliance and circumvention will forever influence how the rest of the world does business in China. If the country's system of bribes, networking, and back-scratching remains the norm for decades to come, it will have a pervasive influence on the companies that enter the market, who will at the very least demand a free hand to deal with the Chinese market in the same way the Chinese businesses do.*

Cross the River by Feeling the Stones

When Deng Xiaoping emerged as China's economic steward in 1978 and the Communist Party moved to correct the radically ideological mistakes of the past, including Mao's and the Maoist Gang of Four's, these changes signaled an era of more practical leadership. Deng reenlisted China's intellectuals, the objects of ridicule and ruin during the Cultural Revolution that had just ended, to help heal the country socially and economically. Under Deng's leadership, China also deemphasized class struggle and no longer pilloried the upper class, which would soon be remade. Deng's bold reversals and reforms were carried out with a large measure of conservatism, too. Under his watch, changes in the economy were monitored closely by the Party and intellectuals drafted to support reform.

Allowing economic freedom for farmers proved one of the greatest successes. Farmers were gripped by a fever of entrepreneurialism, and millions cast around for business ideas that would supplement their meager farm incomes. Deciding which business to pursue is hard enough in a mature economy where one lives among a wide range of options. The Chinese farmers, however, had a much smaller realm to inspire them. They could conjure up memories of businesses before the Chinese Communists gained power, but even then the countryside was poor and well removed from the richer variety in China's cities. When good ideas did crop up, they were so busily copied that soon any thriving business was swarmed with competitors. Often the new industries set out to fill the enormous pent-up demand for simple everyday

---

*Steps do get taken to eliminate the abuses that most mock the state. In Zhejiang the phony business relationships came under a March 1998 directive to "remove the hat." Most of hybrids have since found their way to more purely private corporate structures. Today, banks all throughout Zhejiang must lend to private clients because that is practically all that is left to lend to, with 90 percent of all businesses now private.

necessities such as clothing, household supplies, brooms and brushes, and kitchenware.

The farmers of Wenzhou moved quickly to seize their market advantage over the inflexible state-run distribution system, sending sales representatives throughout China to hawk their wares. A whole new section of town grew up in far-off Beijing called Zhejiang Village, where migrants from the province, mostly men, clustered in a ghetto of their own making. Though the early arrivals were often richer than Beijingers, residents of the capital grouped them together with what they considered the great rural unwashed. The government tore down the village once, a tactic that met the southerners' bold willingness to skirt the law head-on. Almost immediately a new Zhejiang Village was in the works. The men who left the region to sell throughout the country developed a reputation as sexual adventurers. For those outside the province the caricature of the Zhejiang businessman is one of an arrogant rich peasant on the prowl. The entrepreneurs of Zhejiang made their countrymen jealous, which almost certainly motivated many others to seek what the swaggerers possessed.

Wenzhou and greater Zhejiang made ideal case studies for China's reformers. Deng strongly believed that economic development required measured steps and local experiments. Successful reforms could then be rolled out nationally. This contrasts to the rapid cold shower of market reform that Eastern Europe elected for itself when Communism collapsed there. Zhejiang, however, needed little encouragement to begin its own experiments, and when some government officials tried to halt its boom, they were overwhelmed by the province's dynamism. Deng's other famous saying, "Cross the river by feeling the stones," encouraged the Chinese to find their way cautiously and gradually as they moved toward a better life. The villagers of Zhejiang and the people of Wenzhou felt the stones, but they did so while running.

China's farmer-entrepreneurs were thus thrown into the reform era's soup of hypercompetition, in which hundreds or thousands of local competitors chased the same business. The Chinese often extol the cultural virtues that make them natural business owners. Foreigners, too, marvel at their frugality, capacity for hard work, and ability to manage a workforce. Culture informs the workplace all over the world, but in the case of China's resurgent capitalism, intense competition created its own culture, forcing diligence and efficiencies that were rare under collective agriculture.

A Leather Belt Factory Closes in Massachusetts
As Thousands Open in China

Merrill Weingrod, the principal of China Strategies in Providence, Rhode Island, has been doing business in Chinese Asia—first Hong Kong, then Taiwan, and now also China—since the early 1970s. Weingrod now consults to American and European companies considering moving manufacturing to China or setting up sales networks in the country. His first twenty years in the region, however, were spent on behalf of his own company, once one of America's leading marketers of leather fashion belts.

In the late 1980s, Weingrod closed his company's plant in Massachusetts and forged relationships with Chinese manufacturers instead. China has always had a leather business of sorts, and even during the most dysfunctional periods under the Communists, the state ran tanneries that were giant by any standard. China, after all, has a lot of feet to cover. Weingrod, who saw early how China's labor force would transform his industry, traveled through the country to line up manufacturers that met the standards of other Asian factories, but at lower prices.

Touring a rural region in Wenzhou while visiting leather factories and belt makers, Weingrod had a revelation. "The point at which I learned that it would be very hard, if not impossible, for me to compete against the Chinese was when I visited a Wenzhou factory preparing hides for patent leather," Weingrod says.

He recalls entering a tin-roofed Quonset hut filled with tables and two hundred workers. There barefoot men were crouched over the worst leather he had ever seen, thin layers of hide that were brittle and pocked with galaxies of holes. "This was the kind of leather that would have been thrown out in a leather workshop anywhere else in the world." But things that have no value elsewhere can have a lot of value in China, where labor costs so little. At the Chinese belt factory, the workers inspecting the hides filled in every tiny hole in the skin *one by one,* by cutting small bits of scrap leather that fit the shape of each hole. They beveled the edges of the small strips by hand with a knife, then beveled the edge of the hole in the matching direction and glued in the piece. It was as if the boss had decided that Swiss cheese ought to be smooth and hired workers to craft exact-fitting plugs for every hole. Weingrod was astonished. "You could only do that in China," he says. The belts that are produced from the reconstituted hides sell in Chinese stores for less than a dollar, a price unbeatable anywhere else.

Despite a wide network of contacts in the industry, Weingrod was previously unaware Wenzhou was so big in belts. "I remember going to a local market where the leather and belt companies sold their products," he says, "and I had never seen anything like it. It was a building about the size of a football field with eight hundred stalls manned by people all selling the exact same item."

Weingrod closed his Massachusetts factory, where two hundred workers had been employed, and reinvented his belt business to fit the inevitable shift to China. He would ultimately do better as an intermediary between American sellers and Chinese manufacturers than he could have done with his American factory. One reason: American, European, and Japanese retailers themselves were dead set on finding their ways to China and its promised savings.

In the United States in the late 1990s, Weingrod says, there were fewer than sixty medium- to large-size manufacturers of women's fashion belts—plants with twenty-five or more workers. By 1999, more than one hundred and fifty such factories operated within a ten-mile radius of Wenzhou.

The manufacture of leather goods is one of the businesses in which China has stunned competitors around the world by inserting itself forcefully into a market where it had little presence until a short time ago. Now China's leather factories provide more leather for the world's shoes and clothing than any other country. Six thousand leather goods companies turn out 460 million tanned hides, 5 billion pairs of shoes, and 70 million articles of leather clothing a year.

Belts are an offshoot of the shoe industry, and after Guangdong Province in southern China, which turns out 175 million pairs of shoes every month, including footwear for most of the better-known Western brands,[16] Wenzhou is the number two shoe-producing region in the country and has made a specialty of catering to less affluent markets. Sixty percent of its shoe exports now head to Eastern Europe and the former Soviet Union. "All this came out of nowhere," says Weingrod.

Beyond Wenzhou, Zhejiang is full of areas with similar unity of focus. An emblem of the province is Hong Dongyang, an entrepreneur whose story is now well-known in China. Hong was once a schoolteacher. She began making socks in the 1970s on a home sewing machine. At first Hong sold them along the roads near her home. She opened a stand and christened her embryonic enterprise Zhejiang Stocking Company. Hong's sock company, the first in Zhejiang Province, was predictably copied en masse by others. Today, the province is the sock capital with over eight thousand companies spinning out 8 billion pairs a year, one-third of the world's supply.

The former farmers and home industrialists are tough to compete against. Zhejiang's factories have helped make the U.S. sock market the most competitive niche in the entire U.S. apparel industry. In 2001, the Chinese makers produced 1 percent of the socks on U.S. feet. In just two years, socks imports from China to the United States jumped two-hundred-fold and now make up 20 percent of the U.S. market. That market share, however, has had a disproportionate effect on U.S. jobs.

"There is no doubt that imports have cost an awful lot of jobs in the sock industry," Sid Smith, a former president of The Hosiery Association, told the Associated Press. "Is it seventy-five percent of all the jobs? Who knows? Probably." In June 2004, four U.S. textile and trade industry groups successfully petitioned the U.S. Department of Commerce to slap quotas on socks from China. But the new quotas only slow China's growth into the market.

The Chinese makers, it turns out, have also become indispensable suppliers to big U.S. sock companies, who like what the Zhejiang entrepreneurs have done to their market. Jim Williams is the president and CEO of Gold Toe Brands Inc., a Burlington, North Carolina, company that controls half of all department store sales of men's dress socks in the United States. Gold Toe's Web site brags that "each pair of Gold Toe socks is made with pride by skilled craftsmen and carefully inspected to offer the customer the finest possible quality." The Web site makes no mention of the fact that those craftsmen are likely to be migrant farm women toiling in Zhejiang sock factories. Williams personally wrote "every U.S. congressman and every person in the government" opposing the imposition of quotas. "If you have the opportunity to source around the world," he told the AP, "you have the potential to find better quality and better prices."[17]

But in Zhejiang the leather and shoes and socks were just the beginning. Now towns all throughout the province have their own world-beating industries. One area makes billions of buttons, another has swelled the world's supply of freshwater pearls, still others crank out tools and cigarette lighters.[18] Booming Wenzhou has variously been dubbed the China Shoes City, China Electrical Appliances Capital, China Pens City, China Locks City, and Chinese Printing City; in each case it is a formidable global competitor. Landscapes that seem neither urban nor rural are nevertheless centers for their respective industries. One stretch of country road runs through a row of factories all devoted to making downspouts for home sinks, another to making industrial valves, and still another to clamps and fasteners.

To these factories come the world's volume buyers looking for voluminous discounts: big boxers such as Wal-Mart, France's Carrefour, Britain's Tesco, manufacturers of all sizes looking for parts, specialty distributors that cater to plumbers, builders, home theater installers, gift shops, neighborhood dollar and 100 yen stores, and just about anyone else in the world's wholesale yellow pages. It is against these destination factories that factories from Tokyo to Stockholm to São Paolo and Cincinnati must compete.

If You Build the Factories, They Will Come

Zhejiang, although only a tiny province by Chinese standards, is thus a magnet to migrants. Nine of every one hundred of China's wandering workers make their way here,[19] some undoubtedly from beautiful, green Hubei. In some areas of Zhejiang, a quarter or more of the population comes from outside; nearly all have come for the low-paying jobs in the local factories. The average factory wage is forty cents an hour, but is often lower. Given the numbers and the trends in migration, Zhejiang's entrepreneurs will have an ample supply of motivated, low-cost workers for years to come.

Zhejiang is an extraordinary example of a phenomenon that is repeated in varying degrees elsewhere in China. Kate Xiao Zhou recalls a rural saying commonly uttered in the early years of market reform that captures the penchant among Chinese businesses to copy other's successful formulas: "One household influences one village; one village affects one district; every village has a[n industrial] smokestack; every household emits smoke." Villages, she says, often grew up to be the national centers for production of their specialty products. But often they saturated their own markets and failed en masse, too. Areas did not rise to dominate their markets because they achieved vast scales of economies or had a few visionaries who altered their industries the way Henry Ford changed the automobile business. They achieved their market positions by playing follow the leader many times over, most on a small scale. Zhou notes that eighty thousand farm households in Zhuo County, Hebei Province, had set up small-time operations in the 1980s to produce acrylic garments. Together they sold more than 20 million articles of clothing a year and pulled in perhaps $100 million. Xiqiao Township in Guangdong was once a giant commune, but following the first glimmer of economic reform, its workers started two thousand cottage textile factories. Now it is one of the great textile manufacturing centers of the world and pulls migrant workers to its looms from all over China.

One of the most surprising facets of China's economic development is that so many pockets have sprung up all over the country. Over time it looks as though China's packs of copycat entrepreneurs can take on nearly any industry in the world and tap into the virtually bottomless labor force willing to come work in just about any kind of factory.* The

---

*China's trend is the current bright side in a global reality that has shaped local economies ever since people learned to trade. The Chinese ceramics that traversed the world's trade routes from the time of the Silk Road were the local specialties of their time, produced in ancient Chinese industrial centers that guarded their manufacturing secrets as jealously as any modern multinational corporation. The minders of the better kilns worked under a form of royal charter, and the manufacture of copycat pots was punishable under the law. Yet the enterprising Dutch literally pirated the pots, if not the technology to make them. Chinese ceramics found their way into the mainstream of Dutch commercial life after the capture of two Portuguese trading ships and the sale of their goods in Amsterdam. Tea was the primary cargo, but Ming-dynasty ceramics filled the bottom as ballast. Its sale caused a greater sensation than the tea, and a fashion was born. The Europeans had to wait over a century before continental kilns could match the delicacy and durability of

standard view of economic development is that it moves slowly from agrarian industries to low-tech commodity businesses, then moves up to more sophisticated manufacturing and service industries. China's development is so compressed it appears to take on every stage all at once. It certainly mastered the low-road manufacturing quickly. So quickly that China's new clusters of factories, by the hundreds and thousands, overwhelmed their competition.

Schumpeter in the Twenty-First Century

China's industrial competitors, including America, often misapprehend the source of China's productive strength. They fear that another centrally governed, well-planned assault on strategic industries is being plotted in Beijing. The world has already seen how effective the Japanese, Koreans, and Taiwanese can be when they focus on sectors they mean to conquer. Even Chinese government planners like to talk as though they are aping the centrally coordinated, government-financed assaults on strategic global industries that their Asian neighbors have pulled off over the last forty years. In looking at how Chinese businesses really take shape, locally and opportunistically, however, Kellee Tsai argues that nothing could be further from the truth. For a world fretting over Chinese economic competition, the entities to fear are not govern-

---

Chinese wares, but they tried mightily. Over time, the potters of seventeenth-century Delft in the Netherlands developed blue and white stoneware to mimic Ming porcelain. In effect, the Dutch then did what the Chinese do today. They took a high-priced imported product made in a high-tech setting and transplanted it to a low-tech manufacturing facility. As with the early products made by China's entrepreneurial farmers, the "china" of the Netherlands was a clunky imitation made to sell to an emerging local middle class. The Dutch pioneered markets with two tiers that created a division between true luxury products at the high end and beneath it a market for quality approximations, which though short on refinement were easily reproducible at prices a larger middle class could afford. The Dutch would become the victims of their own success, as the technology and styles they developed moved to new ceramics centers in Germany and the British Isles. Today, Made-in-China.com, an online directory of Chinese manufacturers, lists nineteen factories in Zhejiang Province that mass-produce Ming-style pottery. In the Netherlands, only one manufacturer, Royal Delft, remains in the business, and in Holland itself one can now find Chinese knockoffs made to imitate the Dutch ceramics.

ment-backed juggernauts, but enterprises that spring on the scene lean and mean, planned and financed by investors who want to make money quickly.

Moreover, the Chinese have learned that capitalism is an exercise in creative destruction, to repeat the famous expression coined by the twentieth-century economist Joseph Schumpeter. They can rarely be accused of sentimentality and, for the time being, seem to be tolerating the tremendous dislocation they are undergoing. Thus China's competitors cannot apply their own internal standards of what their own people will endure to compete. Few people working in America, for example, with the exception of illegal Mexicans working in agriculture, would willingly subject themselves to the working conditions many Chinese are eager to accept.

One of the cruelties of China's reform and the rise of private enterprise is that it is creating its own new wave of poverty, and not just among farmers. The most troubled and shrinking share of the economy is controlled by state-owned enterprises, the companies that are the legacy of China's years of central planning. Since 1978, nearly forty thousand state-owned industries have been shut down. From 1996 to 2001, 53 million people working in China's state sector lost their jobs. That is 7 million more people than the total employment rolls of 46 million at the five hundred largest corporations in the world.[20] Or, to state the numbers another way: in the four years beginning in 1998, state-owned companies fired 21 million workers.[21] *That's more than all the Americans who work in manufacturing.*

The death march of the state-owned companies began when rural villages took it on themselves to take a run at the state monopolies and started their own businesses. The Chinese leadership itself was unprepared for the dynamism of its own people. "Our rural reforms have proceeded very fast, and farmers have been very enthusiastic," Deng Xiaoping was reported telling a Yugoslavian delegation in 1987. "The development of the village and township industries took us by complete surprise. It was as if a strange army appeared in the countryside making and selling a huge variety of products. This is not the achievement of our central government. . . . This was not something I figured out. . . . This was a surprise."[22]

Just as the village and township enterprises attacked the inefficiencies of China's state-owned enterprises, purely private businesses are now displacing them. The failure of the older firms, most of which were located in rural areas, is now another factor in China's urbanization. As the county continues to coalesce around the cities, urban areas can offer an efficient environment to do business that more isolated rural areas cannot match.

Thus, while the rest of the world worries about the power of China's best factories to kill off jobs, the Chinese themselves must worry about how competition in their own country is spiking unemployment. China may have as many newly unemployed industrial workers, especially older ones, *as the rest of the world put together.* Today, state-owned companies can claim only a one-fifth share of China's industrial production. The private sector now accounts for half of what China makes and about one-quarter of its GDP.[23] That percentage will only keep rising.

All these reinforcing factors—rural poverty, huge internal migration, liberalization of financing, a self-cannibalizing frenzy of competition, intensifying urbanization—speed the high metabolism of Chinese capitalism.

CHAPTER FOUR

MEET GEORGE JETSON, IN BEIJING

CHINA'S CITIES ARE NOW THE ENGINES OF ITS ECONOMIC DYNAMISM. Metropolises the world over compete with each other for prestige, jobs, and political clout, but in China the competition among them is a blood sport.

At stake are the fates of hundreds of millions of citizens who demand that their governments deliver the benefits of China's golden age to them as fast as possible. Their general optimism notwithstanding, the Chinese know that all the money coursing through the country could become buried in backyards, mattresses, and foreign bank accounts in a trice. Tremors of economic uncertainty or political crisis could quickly end for everyone the present good thing. The Chinese often say they are culturally disposed to save and to make contingency plans for the certainty that uncertainty lies somewhere ahead—and China's citizens have the highest rate of savings in the world, socking away, on average, forty percent of their income.

China's outward optimism then, its willingness to build quickly and build big, is also a measure of its anxiety. China may be eternal, but that makes the realm of possibilities, both good and bad, all the greater. For China's vital eastern cities, long thwarted by the central government, the buzzy rush to build critical mass now, while the going is good, is the best insurance for the future. And best bought today.

Before the Communists came to power, the great urban centers along its east coast were home to 90 percent of China's industry. Shanghai and Guangzhou were particularly strong. In the 1930s, massive Japanese investment in Manchuria in the northeast of China also made the city of Shenyang, then called Mukden, a major industrial center. The

Japanese, while reviled for their cruelty as conquerors, also saw China as a place worthy of their best industry. Even by today's standards, Japan invested extremely aggressively in the country. Its businesses poured into the region for familiar reasons—the temptations of low-priced labor and large markets—but also to tap natural resources that Japan lacked.

After China's Communist government took charge, the economic advantages of China's cities and the attraction they held for global investors no longer mattered. Strategic and political considerations came first. To Mao, that meant devolving the country's industrial centers and spreading them around China. The former industrial installations in Manchuria became the early resource for the Communists' industrial development plans under Mao, as the machinery and factories brought to China by Japan's industrial cartels and other firms were crated up and shipped to newly chosen industrial centers away from the coast. So began the decades-long forced hibernation of China's urban powerhouses.

When the Chinese government under Deng Xiaoping shifted course, it turned again to its once thriving cities. Farmers may have started the commercial revolution, but China's government eventually backed reform enthusiastically, and sometimes with exceptional skill, in the urban centers it chose.

One example of the resources marshaled is the Shanghai Academy of Social Sciences. An impressive collection of intelligence, the academy is connected to the inner circle of the city's government, many of whom are its alumni. The academy is also connected to an international network of the world's foremost universities and think tanks. It is a powerful arbiter of information on China and on the country's largest city. With the academy's help, Shanghai would become the creation that showed China at its best, its space shuttle, world's fair, and Manhattan all in one.

Officials at the academy's campus, off Shanghai's bustling Huai Hai Road, greet visiting dignitaries daily, so many of them that they manage conference halls the way a busy doctor's office manages examination rooms. Foreign big shots smile and wave in surprise at the other foreign big shots passing through the corridors. In one month in 2003, more than sixty foreign journalists were newly installed in Shanghai, and most counted on the academy to give them the lay of the land. Scholars obliged out of duty to their country, city, and institution, delivering one-on-one lectures to the newcomers. They offered the academy's usual mix of informed loyalist views and bold critiques, the kind that could pass muster at the international conferences where Shanghai scholars are now in much demand. Foreigners extend invitations to their own institutions in order to leverage the academy's connections in China. Every social scientist and city official in the world, it would appear, wants to take a look deep inside China to take in the country's secret sauce, to take a bite out of its problems, to go home and say he has seen the future of the planet, good or ill. In turn, the academy sends its best scholars for extended stays at America's Ivy League and its peer networks around the world. When they return, they often instruct Shanghai on the best international thinking about how to build modern cities.

Qiyu Tu, a vibrant returnee from Harvard, is the assistant president of the Shanghai Academy and one of the institution's chief conduits to city officialdom. Tu was one of the members of a blue-ribbon commission charged with planning the future course of the city. The commission studied Shanghai's place in culture, finance, and industry. It considered how the city's layout could serve as a home to its current residents and the millions more who hope to squeeze in. As part of its investigation, the commission toured leading cities around the world. When asked what other Asian cities Shanghai can learn from, Tu says that, frankly, Asian cities are not of much interest to the Shanghainese.

"Make no mistake," he declares, "Shanghai is aiming very, very high. London, Paris, and New York are better models, not Tokyo. We plan to lead in business, finance, and culture, and the city has extremely ambitious goals for itself."

Because this is China, and Shanghai in particular, once recommendations are made, they are quickly weighed and, if accepted, acted upon. Tu's group gleaned from its travels, for example, that the world's top cities see value in their vintage buildings. To visitors, preserving Shanghai's treasure trove of old buildings is a no-brainer, limited only by the incomprehensible destruction of beautiful old European-style buildings that has gone before. Like other cities in America, Australia, or South America, where Europeans re-created their homelands in the nineteenth and early twentieth centuries, the pre–World War Two architecture of Shanghai reflects a yearning to connect with European culture, ancient and modern. Homes designed as castles, English manor houses, and French villas filled the city's elite districts. Streamlined apartment towers and town homes in the avant-garde styles of the 1920s and 1930s defined its inner urban blocks. Shanghai's large department stores were as up-to-date as any, and its better hotels boasted jazz and gilded guest rooms. The city, it is said, had one of the largest concentrations of art deco buildings in the world, now much diminished by redevelopment. Half of the city's pre-1949 buildings have already been demolished,[1] mostly over the last twenty years.

Yet not all of the city's period charms are Eurocentric. Much of the shabbiness of the old city hangs on, existing in the shadows of a metropolis seemingly redesigned only for skyward glances. There are still a few of the old wooden Chinese-style city homes, with second stories that look like the cabins of old fishing galleys, their red planks and tile roofs willfully tumbledown. Out windows low and high hangs laundry—stubbornly grimy long johns and frumpy old pants that look wider than anyone in China—strung from poles like beaten flags, a reminder that not all Chinese are as pressed and dapper as the pedestrians below. These neighborhoods hang on by a thread.

The Dongtai market, where the Lis have their curio shop, for example, was slated for demolition in 2004. Mostly likely it will be replaced with a large, modern shopping complex. The Lis will probably be relocated to a section of the new development designated for displaced sellers. Their shop, then, will become one of the many undifferentiated sources of period reproductions, devoid of the charm of the decrepit old row of shops and the ghosts of old Shanghai that visitors long to meet.

Happily, some quarters of the city retain their period charm and can be saved. For that to happen, the city must lead China in changing its tastes. Most of the country is stuck where urban America was in the 1960s, preferring nearly anything new over aging urban homes and office buildings, and still unawakened to a preservationist ethos. If Shanghai is going to best prepare itself to lure the world's greatest businesses—to get them to locate their regional or even global headquarters—to the city, the city fathers need to make sure Shanghai's older tree-lined streets with French and British homes, its vintage Jewish Quarter, and even some old warehouses and dock buildings get immediate protection. And in some places where old buildings are to be torn down, new buildings designed like those now gone—though perhaps bigger—should rise up in their place.

One of the most subtle but nonetheless stunning changes has been the decision to force owners of older houses to show them off. Historically, Shanghai's finer residences had been separated from street traffic by thick, tall walls and solid fences. The city ruled that houses and gardens need a public view, and now roads with formerly long expanses of fortresslike barriers are garden walks, and gorgeous homes never seen from the outside lend the city their magnificence and beauty.

The Chinese government has also decreed that cities dramatically expand their green space. Shanghai has done more, razing large swaths of the city to build parks and gardens. To meet the requirements, the space could have been sodded and then simply mowed. But in Shanghai, truckload after truckload of flowers in bloom are unloaded and planted on newly made rolling contours of black earth. Lakes are dug out in weeks, public restrooms built tastefully into the hills. Full, mature trees, uprooted from distant forests, are lifted from flatbeds and placed in holes and then have their trunks wrapped and their branches urged into place by wires extending to the ground. Even in its municipal gardens, Shanghai means to rival London and Paris.

To take its rightful place, the city also determined that it had to rid itself of the stench and filth of its earlier generation of industries. Paper plants, dirty smelters, chemical factories, and dozens of other categories of smokers and belchers are no longer welcome in Shanghai's environs.

Now, after Shanghai's reemergence, Tu and Shanghai's other planners must succeed at taming what has again become an inexorable drive in the Chinese economy to concentrate industry into China's eastern powerhouse cities. Shanghai, with a local GDP that is as much as 80 percent greater than that of its next two national rivals, is undoubtedly the leader, and now under the dual pressure to ascend to the greatest international heights yet still somehow not suck too much money and energy away from the rest of China.

Chen Jiahai, director of the Shanghai Academy's Development Policy Research Center, notes that from the 1950s through the 1970s, two-thirds of China's provinces relied on their own industrial networks to supply nearly everything their citizens consumed. The industries were expected to produce goods at low prices that people could afford. In practice, however, the scattered nature of Chinese industry compounded its inefficiency and, when market reforms arrived, left the regional state-owned companies weak and vulnerable. When investment returned to China's coastal cities, industry again began to concentrate there, and in forcing China's inefficient old state enterprises to give up their local markets to the better eastern producers, the market economy forced a wedge between the old and the new, the east and the west, that is making successful eastern cities ever richer and more alluring. The city of Shanghai accounts for 5 percent of China's economy and attracts nearly 10 percent of the country's foreign investment. Its growth rate comfortably exceeds the national average, as well. That makes the city a top choice for people and businesses looking for a China home. It also creates intense competition among others to catch up.

Copycat Magic

"What makes cities differ?" asked John Gunther, the journalist whose books and dispatches explained the world to Americans in the middle of the last century. "What makes one somnolent and another gay: what makes one raw and effervescent as another is sober and sophisticated? Age; geography and history; . . . relation to the hinterland; demographic variation; also factors mysterious and unanswerable."

When Gunther posed those questions in 1947, he was pondering the differences between staid St. Louis and rowdy Kansas City. Today, he would ask them of Nanjing, Beijing, and Guangdong, and hundreds of other Chinese cities on the make, trying to do nearly anything to replicate some of Shanghai's magic. City leaders everywhere want to remake towns in order to reinvent themselves as players in the market economy. The result, if things go even remotely according to plan, is a nation of cities building up so excitedly that they will be causing tremors around the world for years.

The battle to build pits the national government against the provinces, the provinces against each other, and city against city. Its weapons are the bulldozer and the wrecker's ball, the cement mixer and the crane. Posters, stamps, and magazine covers glorifying muscular machines were Communism's color and glamour during the Mao years. The difference now, of course, is that there is money to be made. When used in the efficient capitalist way, big machines make money grow. And even when used in the less efficient, inept, and corrupt capitalist way, the webs of owners and operators can still engineer fortunes.

While in China for research on how China's governments are financing the furious growth of their infrastructure, George Peterson, a senior fellow at the Urban Institute, a private U.S. research and advocacy organization, marveled aloud to a local Chinese official that his government was designing and building convention centers and water treatment plants in the time that it took him, Peterson, to write a research paper. The official smiled and told Peterson that he must be a fast writer.

"Cities build at a scale and at a speed which, until you see it, is simply incomprehensible to us," Peterson says. Cities that the Chinese consider midsize are building convention and expo centers that would do Barcelona or Orlando proud. The competition to build bigger and better convention centers has stretched even China's need for oversize everything. Cities find themselves with so much extra exposition space that they are now filling their expo centers with big-box retail stores such as France's Carrefour hypermarts and U.S. hardware giant Home Depot.

Among American cities, perhaps only Las Vegas comes close to matching Chinese cities for speed and scale. Compared with most American job sites, a big Chinese construction zone looks like an army camp urgently preparing for battle. Various construction crews, tidily outfitted according to their function—orange jumpsuits for electricians, green for steelworkers, and so on—rove the site in orderly groups as they are dispatched to jobs for the day. Work typically begins at eight thirty in morning and continues until seven o'clock at night, six or seven days a week.

The pace of construction takes on the blur of time-lapse photography. Office towers and apartment buildings frequently receive tenants well before construction finishes, and passersby monitor a building's success with busy fingers pointed skyward to count the number of lights flicked on at twilight. Early tenants share their building with the construction workers who sleep on-site, an accommodation that keeps building costs to a minimum.

The buildings go up fast, but are they any good? And what do they look like? "In the United States seventy or eighty years ago, construction costs used to be split so that twenty percent used to go for the labor to build it and eighty percent for materials," says an American architect who has several large projects in the works in China. "That is why old buildings in America's big cities often look as beautiful as they do. The architects and builders could afford to pay their crews to build elaborate stone exteriors and ornate, delicate interiors. Now the cost ratio is inverse, and most of the money goes for labor. That's why buildings now are simpler."

This dynamic is the outsize analog to what has happened in the global furniture trade. In China, where a laborer can be hired at less than $1 an hour and brings with him the skill and willingness to take on whatever tasks the job demands, elaborate and ornate buildings of every size are springing up. "It is like a dream to design for China," says the architect, groomed in the frugal discipline of American developers and city councils. "We can put detail in buildings we would never dream of at home, and the local crews build it very well."

If the skylines of Shanghai, Beijing, Shenzhen, or Guangzhou look like cityscapes from *The Jetsons,* it is because they can.

The heavy lifting that is reassembling China's cities is delivered at whatever bargain prices will still keep the tide of willing migrant workers coming in from the farms and out of shuttered government enterprises. Building cities to rival great capitals goes faster when there is a virtually inexhaustible pool of low-cost labor to assemble them, and in early 2004, more than three hundred buildings over fifteen stories tall were in the works in Shanghai.

Roller Bags of Cash

In the red-hot Shanghai housing market of 2004, the most aggressively built properties were high-end high-rise apartment buildings that were sold off as condominiums. The speculative churn on the apartments has helped the market rise between 20 and 50 percent a year for the last five years, making Shanghai among the hottest-burning real estate markets in the world. *Newsweek*'s Asian edition told the story of an Australian living in Shanghai who began hunting for a hundred-square-meter apartment in the fall of 2003. At first the apartments he visited cost $120,000.

By the time he'd spent eight months looking at forty units, prices of comparable properties reached closer to $300,000.[2]

During the boom, Shanghainese found that their city became the destination of a new breed of traveler, nicknamed the Wenzhou Mafia, not because they are criminals, but for their characteristic Zhejiang bravado and a penchant for touring Shanghai's construction sites inseparably attached to their mobile phones and roller bags full of cash.

So anxious were Shanghai's provincial neighbors to get in on the city's boom that a newspaper, the *Wenzhou Evening News,* organized real estate buying tours. Buyers swept in, snatching up properties the way other tourists buy knockoff watches and handbags. Their visible presence, another reminder that China's prosperity is often in the hands of newcomers pushing their way into old centers of power and prestige, was the signal that local officials needed to see the dangers in the heated market. Bad press and official displeasure convinced the *Wenzhou Evening News* to halt the tours, but pressure from wealthy readers back home convinced it to reconsider some months later.[3] "The central government ordered us to stop the tours, but supply and demand rather than individual behavior or administrative intervention will eventually rule the market," Dong Wenyuan of the *Wenzhou Evening News* told the *Financial Times.* The London paper reported that central government and Shanghai officials were far from the only ones worried over the arrival of the Wenzhou Mafia. Blue-chip foreign investors, including Morgan Stanley, Deutsche Bank, Singapore's Capital Land, and Australia's Macquarie Bank all had reason to wonder whether the arrival of the roller-bag capitalists would burst the bubble all over their spreadsheets.

"Shanghai property is a disaster waiting to happen," asserted Andy Xie, Morgan Stanley's economist in the region in 2004.

Was it a warning to head for the exits? Not for local builders. In the logic of China's boom, knowing a disaster is about to happen gives cause to redouble investment. In some cities, vacancy rates of new apartments run as high as 40 percent, but builders keep breaking ground on new projects all the same. When, and if, trouble comes, owners tend to wait it out until better times return.

Not every property in Shanghai needs a boom to prosper. Market lulls bring their own sorts of highs. The bust that followed Shanghai's last real estate bubble in the 1990s left hundreds of high-rises around the city unfinished. Some were the victims of too few renters, others the result of corrupt developers who cajoled the state banks or unwary investors to front the money for their projects, then siphoned much of it off for their own purposes. Some spent it on fast living, others rolled money into still more projects, many also doomed.

But in the country that resurrected itself from economic death, lifeless properties can also spring back. Shanghai's ghost buildings, recently seen as worth only what the land under them and bricks salvaged from them could bring, are now filling out. As many buyers get priced out of the city's newer premium apartments, they are moving in as renters in the once dead buildings, where the monthly costs to dwell are one-fifth, or less, than those in newest buildings. Who is moving in? Some of the newer residents are the migrants who have made it. The vast majority of them still work for poverty wages. But many make better lives, often by starting their own businesses that rely on bringing in new workers from their hometowns.

It is a familiar pattern around the world, but China is providing more upward mobility than the rest of the developing world put together. This is part of the mix that is making the country so competitive on many different levels. It can advance and build great cities while still feeding the world's demand for low-cost labor. Elsewhere, cheap work is supplied by countries climbing up the development ladder rung by rung, praying on every step that they will not falter.

How the Genie Escaped from the Bottle

Shanghai, for all its wonders, may not be China's most amazing urban transformation. Those honors almost certainly go to Shenzhen, the city near Hong Kong that until 1980 was a fishing town of seventy thousand people surrounded by rice fields. Back then the town had no bus service and visitors from outside had to work their way into town by walking or renting bicycles at the train station on its outskirts.[4]

Everything changed in 1980 when Deng Xiaoping selected the city as one of the country's first experimental centers for market capitalism and dubbed Shenzhen China's first Special Economic Zone, or SEZ. In a godlike stroke—or better yet, the keystrokes of a computer gamer playing SimCity—China's paramount leader gave rise to a city that in short order would be bigger than Paris, Montreal, or Los Angeles.

Shenzhen's location near Hong Kong, Deng reasoned, would attract the interest, and money, of Hong Kong businesses. Shenzhen would lure in foreign investors, who would bring with them technology, goods to process, and valuable foreign currency, preferably dollars. In Shenzhen, the central government could also take a lead with change. Until then, the government had played follower, fitting reforms around the businesses that China's farmers were already starting. Deng could use Shenzhen as a test case for the future of free enterprise in China.

At the time, China's leadership still did not expect private enterprise to play a pervasive role in reversing China's fortunes. Rather it hoped a few discrete capitalist zones could provide some cure for underemployment, economic morbidity, and thin state treasuries. China's reform, Deng decreed, would not abandon Marxism. Above all, it would not cede power outside the Communist Party, which was still to be seen as the guardian of the future. This decree, famously formulated as "socialism with Chinese characteristics,"* was articulated clearly by Deng in a seminal speech before the National Congress of the Communist Party in 1982:

In carrying out our modernization program we must proceed from Chinese realities. Both in revolution and in construction we should also learn from foreign countries and draw on their experience, but mechanical application of foreign experience and copying of foreign models will get us nowhere. We have had many lessons in this respect. We must integrate the universal truth of Marxism with the

---

*The phrase "with Chinese characteristics" is now often employed ironically to refer to any activities in which China has unique solutions, especially those that smack of opportunism and situational ethics. Writers make reference, for instance, to "justice with Chinese characteristics" when referring to the government's attack on Tiananmen Square demonstrators, and "democracy with Chinese characteristics" to refer to repression in Hong Kong. Frequently, the phrase is employed to refer to any cultural import that is given a Chinese spin. *Hero,* the pretty, propagandistic, and rather dull costume, martial-arts epic supported by the Chinese government, was labeled "*Crouching Tiger* with Chinese characteristics." China's space flight was in a "Russian rocket with Chinese characteristics." The trend among some Chinese yuppie men to bulk up and unbutton their shirts has been called "machismo with Chinese characteristics," and so on.

concrete realities of China, blaze a path of our own, and build a socialism with Chinese characteristics—that is the basic conclusion we have reached after reviewing our long history.

Mao had also stressed Chinese characteristics, but Deng's shift allowed "Chinese characteristics" to include free enterprise. So long as the government could keep Shenzhen's development contained, it could also contain the corrupting influence that capitalism carried with it. To make that happen, the SEZ offered unique advantages within its borders. Those who brought businesses into the zone received generous tax breaks.[5] Hong Kong had grown into one of the world's richest cities because of the role it played as an intermediary between all of China and the outside world. Shenzhen, as Chinese Communism's first indigenous capitalist city, found similar success.

As it turned out, the government found that it could not contain capitalist influences within the SEZ. The capitalist genie flew out of the bottle so fast that in the 1980s, the government tried to rein it in with a national campaign against "spiritual pollution." Pollution, it turned out, was exactly the kind of consumerism the Chinese would soon pin their hopes on.

There is no perfect historical analogue to Shenzhen's growth. Chicago's may be the closest. The Midwestern city took fifty years to record its millionth resident. Shenzhen took less than a decade, and after only a quarter of a century Shenzhen is a city of 7 million people,[6] and the fourth-largest city economy in China. Per capita, its economic output is among the highest in the country.[7]

Shenzhen's early development in the 1980s and 1990s presaged the role China would later play in the world economy. Hong Kong, a major manufacturing center in 1980, used Shenzhen as a means to keep its industries competitive by turning to lower-priced labor on the mainland, and in so doing transformed its own economy into one based more on trade and service.

Manufacturing disappeared from Hong Kong with great speed. Its once thriving electronics, toy, shoe, and textile factories have been mostly gone for more than a decade. In 1980, manufacturing comprised nearly one-quarter of Hong Kong's economy, but by 2002 had dropped to one-twentieth.[8] Whereas before, four of out ten Hong

Kongers worked in factories, by 2002 fewer than one in ten did. Wages for those workers in Hong Kong who remained in manufacturing went steadily down, giving credence to one of the big fears held by industrialized workers elsewhere in the world, that China could actually force down wages outside its own borders. Hong Kong factories were once in far more direct competition with Chinese factories than were those in the United States or Europe, but sophisticated transportation links, shipping, and telecommunications systems have in effect equalized the distance between Hong Kong and Shenzhen, and between Shenzhen and virtually anywhere else. Hong Kong's decline as a manufacturer parallels that suffered by most of the world's advanced economies, except that Hong Kong's drop started earlier and is farther along.[9] In Hong Kong, financial and business services, especially those that relate to brokering trade and to tourism, grew stronger. That trend too mirrors the drift of other economies, especially America's.

As Hong Kong's workers acquired the expertise they needed to work in a more skill-driven economy, Hong Kong's manufacturers built factories in and around Shenzhen, where millions of low-skilled mainland Chinese were moving to find work. Ultimately, the factories set up by Hong Kong's capitalists employed nearly as many people as make up the entire population of Hong Kong. By 1994, 6 million workers had found jobs in thirty thousand factories in and around Shenzhen run and financed by Hong Kongers.[10] By the end of 2002, Hong Kong investors were responsible for 60 percent of the $23 billion that had flowed into the new city since it had opened up.

It had never been the Chinese government's plan to make Shenzhen a magnet for rural migrants. The country's strict system to regulate people's movements was still in place when Shenzhen got Deng's nod to develop. Still, two out of three of Shenzhen's workers are drawn from China's floating migrants. They match the profile of that population too, making Shenzhen perhaps the most youthful city in the world, overwhelmingly populated by people under twenty-nine years old.[11] Nowhere else does youth so define a city. Cultural life, for those who can afford it, in Shenzhen exists in the form of theme parks, and at night the city rocks with the meanest techno-punk bands in China.

In fact, before Shanghai found its groove in the late nineties, it was Shenzhen that inspired a generation of young Chinese. When anthropologist Constance Clark studied the city in the mid-1990s, she found that the China's twentysomethings who had come of age as Shenzhen was growing saw the city as a symbol of all things possible. Shenzhen was where a migrant's dreams of work, adventure, and love might all come true; it was a place where one could escape the pressure of parents, family, and neighbors and get rich in one's own way. It was a place where a young person in China could remake himself, or herself, in a land where the state otherwise dictated all one's possibilities. As television spread throughout China, Shenzhen's rising played like a national drama, a civic *Truman Show* in which the lives of the city's new inhabitants and the city itself fired hearts and imaginations everywhere.

The Working Girls of Shenzhen, Part I

Unusual for China, women far outnumber men in Shenzhen. Of the city's 4.75 million factory jobs in 2002, 3.5 million were performed by women. That's according to an official tally. Independent sources say officials undercount.[12] From a certain historical point of view, the numbers are not surprising. Young women have been sought after for light industrial jobs since the beginning of the industrial revolution. In the mid-nineteenth century, American textile manufacturers pioneered the boardinghouse system. Young women, manufacturers seem to always claim, are better suited to factory jobs that require patience and small motor skills, traits men are said to lack. This enduring piece of nonsense reshapes the workforce wherever it is allowed to take hold. If it were true, watchmaking, diamond cutting, the work of locksmiths, and the painting of Persian miniatures would all be dominated by young women. In their more honest moments, manufacturers praise young female workforces for their docility. A Chinese electronics-plant manager who has worked in the United States, Taiwan, and Korea says matter-of-factly, "Men smoke and fight. They are harder to manage. They can cause trouble."

Also, despite the overall impression that Chinese workers are docile, managers particularly fear older workers, some of whom draw on the assertive radicalism learned during the Cultural Revolution to raise complaints. Protests are rising.

While the overwhelming female workforce of Shenzhen fits into a development model that works exceedingly well for China's power elite—the overlapping group of business leaders and governmental officials—the use of migrant women in China's modern industrial zones is undermining the place of older, but still working age, Chinese. As tens of millions of workers are forced out of their jobs at state-owned factories and millions more are eliminated from China's bloated government bureaucracy and military, new employment notices at the country's more thriving factories make clear that older workers—especially older male workers—are not welcome. A Shenzhen television factory's employment notice—offering jobs for $2 a day—was recently translated by a Hong Kong labor rights organization:[13]

XX TV TECHNOLOGY (SHENZHEN) LIMITED COMPANY

Recruitment

XX TV Technology Limited Company is a Hong Kong–owned enterprise, established in July 1992, in Jardine Street, Causeway Bay, Hong Kong. The company produces bilingual double-screen telephones, "bee nest" telephones, and transformers. The company achieved the ISO9002 international quality standard. We offer reasonable wages, a comfortable working environment, and transparent management. Owing to the expansion of two production workshops, we are recruiting in the following areas with the endorsement of senior management.

Production Department

Female workers, 260 vacancies

Requirements: (1) junior high school education; (2) age 18–26; (3) healthy, industrious.
Experience in electronic factories an advantage.

Pay: (1) Daily wage 17 yuan; (2) overtime pay 1:1.5; (3) full attendance bonus 45 yuan.

Male workers, 20 vacancies

Requirements: (1) two years of working experience; (2) basic knowledge of repair and maintenance. Having temporary residence permit an advantage. Pay: subject to skills.

The girls and young women who are filling China's new factories also comprise a workforce that is causing much of the rest of the world to quake. The production lines at the consumer electronics factories that now make China the world's leading manufacturer in several major categories, including televisions, are staffed overwhelmingly by women. And the factories are huge, some with tens of thousands of employees.

China's young women can, and will, fill so many jobs in the country's shoe, garment, and textile factories that they may literally undermine whole economies. Over the next ten years, for example, the textile factories of southern China are expected to take millions of mill jobs away from other workers—also mostly women—in other developing countries. Clothing and textiles alone make up 6 percent of all world exports, more than $340 billion worth. The developing world—including China—now makes more clothing and textiles than mature industrialized countries, and in some of the world's poorer places—Pakistan, Bangladesh, Sri Lanka, India, Turkey, Nepal, Laos, and Cambodia—the trade accounts for the lion's share of export earnings and is often the source of a huge proportion of manufacturing jobs.

In the past, China's clothing and textile exports to the United States have been ruled by a quota system that divvies up the U.S. market to different countries. That will all soon change, as new international trade regulations eventually eliminate the quota system and give China a clear shot at the U.S. and world market in everything made of cloth and leather. In limited areas where China has gained freer access already, it dominates now.

Neil Kearney, the general secretary of the International Textile, Garment and Leather Workers Federation, a worldwide labor group that represents 217 affiliated groups in 110 countries, voices the fears of the world outside China. In the twenty-nine categories of garments removed from quota in 2002, Kearney says, China's share of goods imported by the United States nearly tripled, while imports from the rest of the world dropped 14 percent. In some categories, China's young women workers wipe out the competition. Making bathrobes used to be a nice business in Mexico and the Philippines, but those countries lost a third of their trade while China's expanded sevenfold. Guatemala, Bangladesh, and Sri Lanka were once swell places to make gloves, but their exports to the United States were cut by as much as two-thirds when gloves made by China's women entered U.S. stores. China's success was limited so long as quotas controlled its access to the market. But, says Kearney, "This provides a snapshot of what is likely to happen when all categories are removed from quota."

The picture is similar with Chinese exports to the European Union, where China's business in many apparel and textile categories has doubled, tripled, or more. The new factories are extremely hard to beat. When China got access to markets it formerly was denied, Chinese producers undercut the existing prices in the market by 44 percent. China forced prices in Europe down 42 percent,[14] in part because the young women of Shenzhen work so hard, so long, and for so little.

Working Harder for the Money

The rapid growth of Shenzhen's industries is creating a city whose main boulevards support five-star hotels, luxury boutiques, restaurants as glittery as Versailles, Porsche dealerships, and sidewalks traversed by men with Italian clutch bags and women whose eyes are widened by makeup or plastic surgery and whose hips are hugged by Louis Vuitton leather skirts. Curiously, the accretion of money, the ostentation, and the pace are not just hedges against impermanence but the very fruits of it.

Yet until Shenzhen finds its bearings as a high tech center, or biotech corridor, its wealth will remain the top layer of a superenlarged mill town. And like all mill towns that depend on migrant women, and to a lesser degree, men, the whole point is to build a workforce that will not find its bearings, cannot organize, and will, as a whole, stay cheap for as long as possible.

During the 1980s, when student protests spread through China and ultimately culminated in the protests and government crackdown in Tiananmen Square, it was natural to look to China's young as the chief challengers to the old regime. When modern governments come unraveled, it has often been the urban young who pull them apart. The Chinese government still keeps close watch on students, and students still rear up their heads to demand dialogue and democracy.

The most volatile mass in the new money culture that inclines overwhelmingly toward urban youth, however, may not be idealists on campuses, but older Chinese, urban and rural, deprived of their worth. Large-scale protests among this group are growing more common. Marches involve as many as thirty thousand workers at a time. They take to the streets when their wages are unpaid, when the state deems them redundant and casts them off with an early, derisory pension.[15] Their fate, often overlooked in the past by a government struggling to ride the tiger of reform and growth, has recently been taken up, gingerly, by some in the government who fear for the future.

In July 2001, a public letter to Jiang Zemin, then still the president and single most powerful leader in China, hit a nerve with the central government. The letter was written around the time that the Party was seriously considering for the first time whether Chinese from the private sector might be allowed into the Communist Party. The letter was jointly written by the former general manager of a Chinese government steel company and a former high official of China's state-run labor union, the All-China Federation of Trade Unions. Neither would seem likely dissenters, but their words attacking Jiang Zemin's headlong commitment to a market economy could hardly have been stronger:

Labor has already become a commodity today. Workers enjoy extremely little of democratic rights in enterprises, and even that little they have are not guaranteed at all. . . . Workers leave their work posts, and their seniority benefits are bought out, all as they are ordered. Nowadays masses of workers have lost their jobs; they can resort to no means to halt the process. After they leave, masses of young peasants flow in. As compared with the city workers, except for the fact that the peasants are rather younger and paid less and that they have much looser relations with the enterprises, there is nothing that can result for them in improvement in terms of education, skills, and political vision and individual personality. The conditions of the workers in private businesses of either domestic or foreign investment are even worse, insufferable, and without any guarantee.[16]

Western companies that use Chinese factories are under intense scrutiny to make sure that their facilities meet standards for humane employment. Teams of inspectors rove the plants making sure they are well lit, ventilated, and that workers not toil past reasonable shifts.

Factories know the system well and have devised schemes that easily fool inspectors, using the same talents for diversion long employed to bamboozle Communist Party and Chinese government officials who inspect farms and factories to make sure productivity is high and people are happy. For factories, that often means running front and back operations, providing model facilities in one place and less ideal, but more productive, lines elsewhere. Many workers clamor to put in longer hours, which offers their best chance to get ahead in a system where steady work is often not enough to pay the bills and still send money back to those who need it at home.*

The double systems, however, can feed some extravagant wishful thinking among those whom the reality might disappoint. Michelle Mone, the Glasgow, Scotland, entrepreneur who started a bra company in 1996 while still in her twenties, may be one of those whose Chinese operations were made out to be nicer than they are. Mone's company, called MJM International, makes the Ultimo line of bras, famous for using silicon gel inserts to enhance their wearers' cleavage. She turned to Chinese manufacturing to assemble MJM's growing line of products, and the factories now keep them affordable. Ultimo bras sell for around $35.

In April 2004, Scotland's *Daily Record,* a brassy tabloid in the London mold—masses of huge headlines, red type, and photos that catch the subject in this or that act—latched on to a story about a visit Mone made to Dongguan, another larger Guangdong manufacturing center not far from Shenzhen, after relocating production there from Portugal.[17] The *Daily Record*'s coverage pulled no punches, running headlines sure to grab readers in just the way that Western brand names fear. One of the more colorful read, "£1 a day. That's what these factory girls get paid to make the world's sexiest bras and knickers. The *Record* goes to China to investigate the squalor behind the glamour." Mone made the paper's job

---

*A recent survey of workers in two thousand factories and other businesses across China, conducted by a Hong Kong newspaper, found that 72 percent of those asked reported that their jobs gave them satisfaction. Job satisfaction surveys are notoriously difficult to administer, and this one apparently did not ask the most telling question of all: "How satisfied would you say your fellow workers are?" Nevertheless, the results more or less match the impressions one gets from more informal interactions in the country. The inverse of the survey is equally interesting; the remainder of those polled, 27 percent, said they were unhappy at work, although not always for the reasons outsiders imagine.

easier by public remarks she made after her factory tour. "There is no child labor," she was quoted. "There are no ridiculous hours. The food is good and the pay is great. We pay above average." Mone, who actually stayed in a workers' dorm during her visit, then made an absurd assessment. Workers, she said, "live [in] a dormitory . . . [and] they are brilliant like a Travel Inn. . . . At MJM, directors can go home at night and put heads on pillows and not be concerned that we are using sweatshops."[18] Mone praised the plant for providing air-conditioned facilities and meals for workers' families.

Apparently Mone's view was incomplete. The paper looked closely at one of the factories that produced for MJM and reported that eight or more women shared cramped rooms, that at night room temperatures climbed to eighty-six degrees Fahrenheit, with air-conditioning available only to residents who paid for it out of their salaries of $50 to $60 a month. Young women who worked there tended to be from China's impoverished north, from where they were almost certainly recruited with promises rosier than their actual conditions. Workers are generally allowed only one short vacation a year during the Chinese New Year; much of that time is spent riding the train to get home.

Ultimo's manufacturer's plant would not pass grade anywhere in Western Europe or the United States, but in truth, it is probably better than many Chinese factories, and its jobs are much in demand. Bras from China, it is worth noting, have been one of the most contentious products in world trade. At the end of 2003, U.S. sanctions against Chinese bras caused the Chinese government to reverse a planned purchase of 3 million tons of U.S. wheat. For the world's bra marketers, however, not manufacturing in China would mean getting vanquished by others that do.

The Working Girls of Shenzhen, Part II

In 2002, government figures put the average salary of Shenzhen's women workers, many of them teens, at $72 a month. Most live in dormitories, as do the city's workingmen. China's 2000 census counted 4 million dormitory residents in the city and surrounding area. Like those in the bra factory, they usually live eight to twelve to a room. Dorm complexes can be cities within cities, housing tens of thousands of workers from a single company. Bells for work and meals send masses through corporate complexes as thick as rush hour in a big-city subway. The average workweek is seventy hours, and half of Shenzhen's workers are on seven days a week. The law mandates a workweek of half that, but overtime, whether voluntary or not, means extra money, and for many an early ticket home. Women who come to work in Shenzhen often go home to marry. If so, they do not like to wait past their midtwenties.

Many young women leave the factory jobs they came for once they realize that their pay, low as it is, is often so sucked up by expenses they cannot get ahead. And so, China's factories indirectly lead to another of the city's big industries. The young women who leave their line jobs often make their way to the city's karaoke clubs.

Put aside any pictures of karaoke you have picked up from *Lost in Translation* or *Duets*. The karaoke clubs in China are to those what the Great Wall is to a backyard fence. Shenzhen's clubs—like those in Beijing and Shanghai and nearly all the more prosperous cities—are the size of convention hotels. The focal points are hundreds of rooms inside outfitted with plasma screens and state-of-the-art sound systems. Groups reserve the rooms, and singing and drinking games begin. Jack Daniel's turned upside down into a pitcher of 7UP loosens inhibitions.

So do the women who work the places. Shanghai's biggest clubs can have over a thousand women on the premises. They look great, they sing, sit close, they flatter and jibe, and when younger and older men with money mix fluidly with younger women without money, closeness comes quickly. The karaoke girls fill a niche in Shenzhen's sex business that is less raw than that of the streetwalkers and is less secure than that of the city's mistresses. Fate, of course, can deliver the songstresses in either direction.

Victor Yuan, a Harvard-trained researcher who runs Horizon Research in Beijing, a consultancy that conducts public surveys for businesses and social agencies, led an exhaustive study of China's sex industry in 2003 as part of a multinational effort to understand the source of the country's AIDS problem. "Many girls," says Yuan, "do not see a factory job as a way to advance. The wages are low, and they have expenses to meet when they work away from home. If they work for three or four years in a factory, their life and prospects really have not improved at all."

The young women who become sex workers make at least three times what they might at a factory. And not just in karaoke bars. They sit in the windows of all-night beauty salons waiting for paid encounters, hustle movie tickets, and, like telemarketers, ring up hotel rooms on the off chance there is a willing customer. Phones left on the hook can ring all night. Big hotels are also big brothels. In October 2003, in Shenzhen's sister city of Zhuhai, Chinese police raided two upscale hotels where officials claimed to have uncovered a three-day orgy made to order by local sex impresarios. The partyers were four hundred Japanese men, which in China made the arrest welcome, convenient, and politically loaded. The widespread loathing for the Japanese has a strong sexual component, with the Japanese conquest itself often likened to rape. The sexual cruelty of Japanese soldiers toward Chinese women, most famously in the Nanjing Massacre of 1937, is still a deeply felt wound. The recent arrests were a triumph for the national psyche, but locally they caused a practical difficulty. The government clamped down on the area's nightlife and sex trade, and tourism from Hong Kong, Taiwan, and Japan dried up.

For a while, anyway.

Ultimately, the game plan for the women is to return to their hometowns, where they say they can open their own businesses, support their parents, and with money, find better husbands. "No one asks what they did while away," Yuan says. "It doesn't matter."

The region's economic-promotion offices do not include the sex trade in their local statistics, but telling numbers come from other quarters. In 2001, a count of the out-of-wedlock children produced by Shenzhen's working women and mistresses over two decades numbered 520,000.[19]

What about the rough stuff? Yuan says it hardly exists. The market will not allow it. Businesses need a steady supply of new women, and those in place are counted on to recruit their friends from home. Abused workers do not make good recruiters. It's the women themselves who decide how much they will offer clients. Some just sing. Some are touchy-feely. Some join the ride home and romp.

But the Chinese sex industry is hardly victimless. It's a big country with plenty of unpoliced brutality. And while the sex industry in China may not have the same taboos as in other countries, one taboo is highly dangerous. Men in China strongly prefer sex unsheathed. They insist on it, and pay two or three times the price of protected sex to go without. It is no surprise that sexually transmitted diseases are already a big problem. Recent estimates put the number of hepatitis B sufferers at 120 million and HIV-positive Chinese at close to 1 million. The U.N. warns of 10 million AIDS sufferers by 2010. Yet, until 2004, government authorities were nearly silent, prevention campaigns nonexistent.

There is hope. It may be no coincidence that the prevention programs come at a time when China is increasingly worried about the disparity of incomes between the prosperous eastern cities and the rest of the country. The sex industry is one of the few robust conduits of money back to China's impoverished areas. No official estimates exist, but judging from similar patterns in other countries, the amounts extend into the billions of dollars. In Thailand, Asia's other sexually lenient regime, sex workers send $300 million per year in urban income home to the countryside. In China, the numbers mean far more to the domestic economy, not just because the population is twenty-five times bigger, but because much of the money used to pay for sex is foreign money, the funds the Chinese economy is most hungry for.

In May of 2004, the government announced newly aggressive programs to monitor and treat the spread of HIV. Safe sex practices are now pushed in a public campaign, which includes free access to condoms. Interestingly enough, the announcements made rural areas the prime targets of the campaign's antiprostitution measures, not the big eastern cities.

Bright Factories, Dark City

Today, not all the dreams in Shenzhen are bright. The city fell under a cloud during a long anticorruption campaign that pinched large numbers of officials, many of them involved in million-dollar bribe schemes. The city is also a center for China's multibillion-dollar business in counterfeit merchandise. And its sex trade may be China's busiest.

The dark side of Shenzhen has been portrayed vividly, and scandalously, by young Chinese novelist Mian Mian, herself a teen migrant to the city in the mid-1990s.[20] Her stories detail the rootless, drug-addicted crowd the author fell into. "A lot of lost people came to Shenzhen from elsewhere," Mian Mian told an interviewer. "They all dreamed of using money to save their life. [Shenzhen] is such a cruel city," she says. "It has no heart. There is no such thing as friendship there. No one is your friend."

As sordid as it once was soaring, Shenzhen's sullied reputation may now steer some investment and corporate headquarters to Shanghai. The city is now one of many urban competitors. But it is still a formidable one. Even more than Shanghai, Shenzhen wields a global punch well out of proportion to its size. It is the entry point to the Pearl River Delta, the world's biggest manufacturing zone. Shenzhen is now the world's sixth-biggest port. On its docks stand dozens of monster cranes that work around the clock unloading the raw materials China desperately needs to build more cities like Shenzhen, then reloading the ships with containers filled on the loading docks at one of the world's densest concentrations of factories making electronics, footwear, watches, and jewelry.

Some valuables aren't shipped from Shenzhen's port, however. The city has also become a center for high-tech and biotech development in China, for which products travel much better by e-mail than by sea. This too is a civic competition in China, and Shenzhen has formidable rivals among older cities with longer-standing educational and research institutions. Teams from Shenzhen have recently been sent on head-hunting expeditions to the high-tech centers of Europe and America and make their pitches forcefully to overseas Chinese. The city has reclaimed seafront land for a $250 million high-tech industrial park. The new immigrants can leverage their expertise with a low-wage Shenzhen workforce of their own making and again build globally competitive industries, this time not out of thin air, but on water.

In that other once fast-growing city, Chicago, the factories of Shenzhen are doing what they first did to the industrial workers in Hong Kong. The *Los Angeles Times'* 2003 Pulitzer Prize–winning series on Wal-Mart told the tale of the Second City's Lakewood Engineering & Manufacturing Co., a maker of household fans.[21] Ten years before the fans sold in American stores for $20. Wal-Mart, an important customer, demanded that the fans sell for less. "Lakewood owner Carl Krauss cut costs at every turn," the paper reported. "He automated production at the redbrick factory built by his grandfather on the city's West Side. Where it took twenty-two people to put together a product, it now takes seven. Krauss also badgered his suppliers to knock down their prices for parts." That only took the company part of the way. To get the fans' prices low enough, Krauss opened a factory in Shenzhen and hired Chinese migrant workers for twenty-five cents an hour. Presumably, Wal-Mart was pleased. The company's role in the Chinese economy will be explored in a later chapter.

Shenzhen may have sprung up from nothing, and its workers and bosses come from everywhere else in China, but the city—like all of China's booming cities—has also pushed its way into the lives of workers and shoppers all over the world.

Where the Boys Are

Shenzhen's gender gap is one side of China's urbanization. The demands of the city's factory mix make young women more valuable there. Nearly everywhere else, however, in China the opposite is true, and this too is shaping the country's cities and their impact on the rest of the world.

One of the most unsettling news stories out of China in recent years has chronicled what is, in effect, a war on baby girls that unnaturally skews the population toward baby boys. Why? Confucianism and rural tradition are often cited as reasons Chinese families prefer boys, a bias especially prevalent outside the big cities. Family names, important links to ancestors, carry through the male line. But economic reasons also weigh heavily on families' choices. The Chinese system of tenancy contributes. Farm families get one plot of land, and since by tradition girls who marry move in with the family of the groom, a family with a boy has a better chance in the long run in the land-allotment system. Boys also give parents a far better chance of having someone around in their old age to take of them and are better able to tend a farm. Or so is the widespread perception. In the long run, the preference for boys will also cause the abandonment of many village parents. Ironically, as boys have left their villages, China's farms are increasing tended by women, and couples who get married now have a good chance of moving away from both sets of parents.

This unexpected consequence relates to China's family planning policy. The one-child policy was designed to correct what central planners regarded as one of the grossest missteps of Mao's rule, the exhortation to patriotic couples to have large families. The state, which in the middle of the twentieth century aggressively promoted large families as the keys to China's industrial might and geopolitical heft, radically shifted gears. China's rapid population growth came to be seen, probably correctly, as the greatest threat to the country's future prosperity.

Beginning in 1979, the state mandated that couples could have only one or two children. The number depends on where families live and in what order their children are born. City couples are allowed more than one child only if the husband and wife are both in their second marriages and want to have a child together.[22] In the country, families may legally have two children, provided their first child is a girl—in other words, provided their first child is not the boy most Chinese farmers really want.

In China today 118 baby boys are brought into families for every 100 baby girls.[23] (The world norm is 106 boys for every 100 girls.[24]) Doctors with ultrasound machines do an illegal but brisk business in detecting the sex of unborn children, and in the abortion of girls. One in seven girls in China is missing—either aborted, killed after birth, or abandoned. In 2001, the British Broadcasting Corporation interviewed Chen Rong, a woman who scavenged garbage in Beijing's dumps. In her wandering, Chen had found five living baby girls abandoned amid the trash and carried them home to a one-room shack, where she and her husband tended to them.

Not all of China's missing girls have parents who wish them dead. Hundreds of thousands have been put up for adoption over the last twenty years. More than fifty thousand babies, nearly all girls, have been adopted by foreign families since 1991, thirty-five thousand of them by U.S. families. Newly adoptive parents from Europe and the United States can regularly be seen pushing strollers through Beijing's Forbidden City, taking in the sights with their new Chinese babies. The United Airlines Beijing-Chicago flight is regularly filled with the coos and cries of Chinese babies swaddled in the arms of their new American moms and dads. The growing number of adoptees in the United States is creating a whole micropopulation of parents with deep interests in Chinese culture, potentially creating a strong cross-cultural bridge for the future.[25]

Some Chinese baby girls are simply never registered with authorities because families know they will count against their chances to have a boy. In the countryside, the tip toward boys was so overwhelming that the government changed its policy, allowing families whose first child was a girl to have a second.

The population policy will not reduce China's multitude for decades and will almost certainly never bring China's numbers below 1 billion people. When Mao took power in 1949 the population of China was about 550 million people.[26] By 2020, it will be at least three times that, but the one-child policy may ultimately stem the danger of a geometrically increasing population. While the rest of the developing countries see their growing populations tax the abilities of their economies to sustain them, China's population is stabilizing at a time when its national wealth is skyrocketing.*

Today in China there are over 20 million more boys and men than women,[27] and in the next decade China may have 60 million fewer girls and women than it would have had if its gender ratio were normal.[28] The first group of single children turned twenty-five in 2004, and those behind them are increasingly mismatched. The Chinese call the surplus males *bare branches*. Demographers have recently grown concerned that China's imbalance makes it prone to instability.

In their book, *Bare Branches: The Security Implications of Asia's Surplus Male Population,* Valerie M. Hudson of Brigham Young University in Utah, and Andrea M. den Boer of the University of Kent in Canterbury, England, worry that the high concentration of men looming in the near future can lead to violence. Their chief fears are that men will increasingly gang together in all-male groups, which are historically prone to

---

*Elsewhere in the world, where economies do not have China's dynamism, population growth is impoverishing. In Egypt, for example, the national economy has stagnated at a time when its population is soaring, leaving smaller cuts of its economic pie for the younger generation coming up.

aggressive behavior. They also fear that a shortage of women will lead to increasingly brutal patterns of sex discrimination. As women grow scarcer, they become more valuable as bartered brides and in the sex trade.

"We have already seen in China the resurrection of evils such as the kidnapping and selling of women to provide brides for those who can pay the fee," the scholars have written. "Scarcity of women leads to a situation in which men with advantages—money, skills, education—will marry, but men without such advantages—poor, unskilled, illiterate—will not. A permanent subclass of bare branches from the lowest socioeconomic classes is created."[29]

The arguments are compelling, but the dynamic of China's changing economy presents a less violent alternate scenario. Now, with marriageable women in short supply, and getting scarcer all the time, poor farm boys, tens of millions of them, feel they have to improve their chances by improving their station. Instead of grouping into terrorist cells or secret armies, they are leaving home to join construction crews and assembly lines.

Despite families' best hopes to have, and then keep, boys on the farm, young men are migrating to China's cities. Many do return to their hometowns and villages, but often they are those who could not cut city life. Abler men stay away in larger numbers. They send money home. In the year 2000, migrants sent home an average of $545.[30] Multiply that by 90 million workers, the low end of the estimated migrant population, and the annual sum sent back from China's cities is nearly $50 billion. The places they left behind, however, are often hellholes, homes to those too young to work and those too old to move on.

Going for the Gold

Beijing is often likened to Washington, D.C. The two government centers share a low-lying grandeur defined by their monumental public buildings. The comparison may not last. Beijing is reaching up. Struck by skyscraper fever, it is rushing to match Shanghai's jam-packed skyline. The city wants to create a sleek image and infrastructure that can attract foreign dollars as well as anywhere else. The building boom is not new to the city, but the idea that its buildings can aspire to international standards of taste is. Shanghai, which has long had its eye on attracting the world, has aggressively enlisted foreign architects to build its bigger buildings. But in the capital city the government and the developers that worked to keep government favor preferred to use Chinese architects for its high-profile projects.

The result, with a few notable exceptions, was that nearly all the large buildings on Beijing's main streets mingle Soviet-era gigantism with Chinese love for decoration. Beijing shopping centers and government office complexes often look like armories converted into Chinese restaurants. Hotels are oversize square boxes with revolving restaurants, temple roofs, or inverted concrete arches tacked on. But that is rapidly changing. The city is now a de rigueur destination for the world's celebrity architects.

Before the 2008 Olympics, Beijing will have a new crop of huge structures each pushing modern design and engineering to their limits. Budgetary realities may yet dash some plans. To create a signature stadium for the games, Beijing brought in Swiss architects Jacques Herzog and Pierre de Meuron, the winners of the 2001 Pritzker Architecture Prize, their field's equivalent of the Nobel Prize. The stadium will dwarf the pair's most famous building, the modern art galleries at the Tate Museum in London the architects fashioned out of an old power plant on the Thames. The nearly $700 million, eighty-thousand-seat stadium project has been likened both to a giant bird's nest and a block of ramen noodles. It will be enclosed in a gracefully curved, crosshatched net of steel and will be open over its center, sending a beam of white light over the city. It is a signature project meant to herald an ultramodern, worldly Beijing. It is not Beijing's grandest construction project, however. Those honors go to the $700 million National Theater Building, designed by France's controversial superstar Paul Andreu. His Beijing theater is a complex of stages nestled under an enormous glass and titanium dome. The whole thing will sit over a man-made lake to create the illusion that it is floating, while an escalator at the entrance will give theatergoers the feeling they are descending through the water.

And then there is the new headquarters of China's national television network, CCTV. It is designed by another Pritzker winner, Rem Koolhaas, possibly the world's most influential and sought-after architect. The building is a most untowerlike tower—actually two buildings coming together—rising 760 feet in the air and taking up 5.7 million square feet. Koolhaas's design does not so much point to the sky as frame it with a continuous, sharply angled loop of glass and steel. Designed to stun, it will no doubt do the job. It is also one of the first buildings to stand in what is slated to be Beijing's newest urban downtown—named the New Central Business District—with three hundred more big buildings to join it by or near the time of the 2008 Olympics.

When Robert Ivy, the editor of *Architectural Record,* America's premier architecture magazine, visited Beijing, he had to readjust his sense of the possible. "The numbers are mind-boggling. Millions of square feet of new construction render Beijing the busiest construction zone on the planet," Ivy reported. "Two thousand high-rise buildings are under way, in one form or another, in a concatenation of architecture, urban design, and construction that makes Berlin look like an opening act."[31]

As with Shanghai, and cities all over China, the architecture of the present is rising on the debris of the past, often the result of forced demolition. Beijing's traditional neighborhoods, called hutongs, made up most of the city's living space for centuries. Some of the neighborhood homes date back to the 1300s. From the outside, the hutongs look like impenetrable mazes of gangways, gates, and doors. Inside, they are clusters of houses, often built around courtyards.

While preservationists are fighting to spare the old neighborhoods, hutong residents themselves often long for nothing better than to escape their old, drafty, unheated, cramped homes, which they regard as dilapidated and unhygienic. As new buildings spring up, developers launch legions of salesmen and -women into the city's streets and bus and rail stations. Convention centers host free public fairs that show off the amenities of their new properties. Everywhere are cheerful, pushy agents flogging glossy brochures of rising projects, maps of new city neighborhoods where the subway will soon arrive, and computer-drawn pictures of the interiors: idealized modern Chinese homes complete with picture windows, cable television, heat, hot water, air-conditioning, washing machines, refrigerators, gas stoves, and tasteful corners for treasured antiques or small altars. Perhaps there is a supermarket in the building, a small tennis court, a place for grandma to practice tai chi. Less tangibly, there is the promise of some anonymity that comes with leaving an old neighborhood. Doors close tightly in high-rises, and Beijing apartments have two steel doors and three strong locks.

It is difficult for Beijingers to see past the current state of their old hutong homes to what they might be if, like the old neighborhoods of Europe, they were renovated, especially when potential buyers are under an unrelenting onslaught of messages that tell them to abandon old Beijing. Some of the old neighborhoods may be saved. Most will go. Beijing wants to outmodernize Shanghai, and that means Tokyo, New York, and London too. What place does a city block with one public toilet and seven-hundred-year-old hovels have in such plans? And it is harder still for the city to stand in the way of the moneyed developers, road builders, and government departments that push for the hutongs' removal. Unlike in the more democratic states, there are few citizens' committees, activist city councilmen, or meddling attorneys to protect the old buildings.

Far more important than preservation to displaced urbanites is the manner in which they are forced from their homes: quickly, violently, and with scant compensation. Li Yong Yan, a Beijing-based writer on Chinese business, describes the mode of Chinese urban development as "compitalist," a combination of official communist-style rule by fiat and market economy opportunism.[12]

In Li's depiction of the urban renewal process, a commercial real estate developer identifies a city block worth remaking, perhaps with a shopping mall. He takes the idea to the local municipal zoning committee, from which he obtains use of the land in exchange for rent. Remember, in China, the state owns all the land and has the power to determine how land is used and at what price.

Once the developer has pleased officials, bulldozers can follow as soon as one month later. Notices go up, crews come by and paint the walls with huge circles to denote the impending demolition, and area residents are offered compensation—nonnegotiable—set by the government. Then, according to Li, access to water mains is severed, power cut off, and bullies brought in to drag off resisters. If the conflict grows out of hand, police show up to take the government's side and help the evictors. "In the past, when China practiced socialism to the letter and the spirit, there was no such thing as commercial development," Li writes. "Now commercial real estate developments are cropping up like mushrooms all over the country. The government is raking in the land rent by the billion. To keep up all the revenue, all avenues of negotiated settlements and legal remedies are closed to 'aboriginals,' who are never in the conference room."

Not all of the land is transferred with even the minimal legal nicety of a one-month notice. In 2003, the Chinese government counted 160,000 cases of fraudulent confiscations, a number that in the heat of China's economic boil, was up twofold over the year before.[33] China may feel that it must remake its cities to compete in the global economy, and to win that competition it must take a ruthless stand against those in the way. And also make the right people rich.

The land-grab practices have recently hit strong enough resistance to give the Chinese government pause. Protest sometimes takes the form of mass demonstrations. Ten thousand protesters converged on Beijing in the summer of 2004. But in a land where protesters, and their families, are often punished, the land grabs have stirred a far more troubling form of dissent, public suicides. Many of the begrudged come to Beijing's most public places, Tiananmen Square and the Forbidden City, to make their final statements. In September 2003, a forty-five-year-old farmer named Zhu Shengliang walked quietly into the spot where the gates of the old imperial palace meet the Square and, with his wife, sat beneath the enormous picture of half-smiling Mao Zedong that still hangs on the old guard walls peering toward the great halls of the Communist government and his own mausoleum. Zhu showered himself in gasoline and set himself on fire.[34]

Self-immolation is a desperate act of protest with particular meaning in Buddhist Asia. It was made familiar to the Western world in the 1960s during the Vietnam War when monks set themselves afire, and more lately to those who witnessed the 2001 self-burning by an elderly follower of Falun Gong near where Zhu himself sat. Self-immolation is traditionally a sacrifice its victims hope will bring public change for other sufferers. It can be a powerful symbol of the failures of leadership, and therefore a dangerous one. Zhu, who survived, albeit terribly, had traveled to Beijing from the countryside of Anhui Province to protest his family's forced eviction.

The act inspired urban protesters who suffered similar fates. In another suicide attempt the following October, on China's National Day, a Beijing native jumped off a well-known bridge inside the Forbidden City. The two men achieved part of their goal, for in the months that followed, all across China protesters marched nearly every day in the biggest wave of public dissent since the Tiananmen Square protests of 1989. All sought redress against forced evictions. "In Beijing," predicts Human Rights Watch, "the clearing of new sites for Olympics venues likely will continue to be a flashpoint." So far, Human Rights Watch reports, the government has reacted with a predictable severity, cracking down on demonstrators, sending many to prison, preventing large numbers of protesters from boarding trains to Beijing, and with a tragic touch of the absurd, making suicide by protesters a crime.

In Beijing, demolitions meet the requirement of national prestige demanded by the spotlight of the 2008 Olympics. Throughout the rest of China, however, where the national leadership is working hard to establish its bona fides as the champion of the suffering common man, the interests of local officials, who want their share of the wealth and glory, clash with the national leadership's agenda, such as it is. Enforcement against corrupt local officials is so lax that local officials on the take have only one chance in a hundred of falling into the anticorruption dragnet. The rewards for local officials can be high. Those who have power to lease out government-owned land can expect kickbacks that, according to a widely accepted rule of thumb, equal 30 percent of what developers pay the government to use the land. Often houses and other luxuries are thrown in to boot.[35]

"Some regional housing projects have exceeded local economic growth and the demands of locals as well," Fu Wenjuan, vice minister of construction, told *China Daily,* who blamed local governments for half of China's urban demolitions and forced relocations.[36] "As a result, some newly built urban public facilities were never used and the land and money spent was wasted. Problems [are] triggered by local authorities who borrow money for such construction. . . . This hurts the credibility of the entire society."[37]

In the past, China has shown a willingness to endure whatever level of discontent its modernization plans stir. To build the Three Gorges Dam, the Chinese government will ultimately have to move nearly 2 million people, urban and rural alike. Individuals and groups that have protested the dam have been met squarely with police and paramilitary troops. China's development—and the fortunes of those who steer it—depends too much on unlocking the value of the land beneath its citizens' homes to allow the aggrieved to become an impediment to the future. When the world competes with the growing presence of China's cities and the might of its urbanized industrial machine, it competes against a government that can ruthlessly drive modernization.

The benefits, on balance, for the Chinese people may warrant the government's approach. Or justify its condemnation. Whatever the long-term good for China's own, China's competitors must consider the tenor of a global player whose steadfast determination to advance is enforced by an iron fist. And competitors must also consider how the messy business of deliberative democracy—where compromise slows and often halts projects that stronger-willed regimes would let advance—makes or breaks the commercial might of more open cities.

More Juice, Please

Along the east coast, and in the select inland urban centers favored by industry and developers, China's renewal is changing not just the way towns look, but how they tap the planet's power.

Strolling in Nantong, a city of 7.5 million people that has little of the shimmer of Shanghai, grandeur of Beijing, or bustle of Wenzhou, one is inevitably drawn into the downtown department stores. There the salesmen in the frenzied electronics department, where air conditioners and home heaters are sold, lead customers to a whole section of rooftop solar water heaters.

The heaters look like rows of fluorescent-tube lamps, but instead of filling with gas, they fill with water. The sun warms the water in the glass, taking much of the load off a home's electric heater. The devices on show in the store are heirs to a technology patented in 1978 by Chinese technologists at Qinghua University in Beijing and originally produced by a company the university spun off in the late 1980s for that purpose, the Tsinghua Solar Co. China has become the world's largest user of solar power for household purposes, but most uses are clever low-tech applications such as the water heaters and do not rely on photo-voltaic cells or sophisticated processes to concentrate solar energy for conversion to electricity.

But the use of solar hot water and heaters is booming. The heaters save money, but more, they replace electricity in newly overburdened cities where electricity is now rationed or is unavailable altogether during some periods. China's industrial boom, and to a lesser extent the move to modern housing and its concomitant appliances, has so outpaced the country's ability to generate electric power that the country suffers regular blackouts and brownouts, planned and otherwise. During a long crisis in 2004, Guangzhou and other cities moved hundreds of thousands of workers to night shifts to even out demand for power through the day. Shanghai businesses were instructed to send workers home when temperatures topped ninety-five degrees.

Right now, China only has 80 percent of the energy it needs to run smoothly.[38] Some areas must do without power for one or two days at a time. Some of the hardship can be softened with indigenous technology such as the solar heaters. In fact, the solar-heating section of the department store is flush with systems from many manufacturers. As is typical in the Chinese market, strong demand for a device that Chinese factories can make easily stirs intense price competition. By 2000, the Tsinghua Solar Co. was selling $370 million worth of heaters a year, but also found itself competing against at least thirty-five other companies that pirated its designs and built copies in their own factories.

Noxious Clouds on the Horizon

China's electricity shortage is, in fact, a national debacle. The country's surging use of energy resources—the direct result of China's urbanization and industrialization—is also a predicament for the world. Pollution, already a global threat before China's economic reforms, has become more troublesome with the entrance of hundreds of millions of people into new factories, cars, and homes. China's contribution to the darkening of the planet is inseparable from the ambitions of its cities, where its worst pollutants originate. As the world learned with the collapse of the Iron Curtain, inefficient Communist economies posed their own dangers to the global environment. Red governments left much of Eastern Europe a black ruin. There is a growing body of scholarship of China's own disastrous environmental policies under the influence of Mao and the first generation of Communist leaders. If left to its old ways, Red China may have had no better an environmental footprint on the world than its market-savvy economy does today. Nevertheless, the dirt kicked up by China's development adds new and growing streams of bad air and water to an already befouled world.

The average Chinese energy user still consumes far less energy than the better-off residents of the world's more industrialized, democratic nations. As usual, however, China's story rests in its big population and the velocity of its economic growth. China's cities have the world's largest appetite for steel, the fastest-growing market for cars, and a seemingly endless need for cement. Making steel and cars are among the most energy-intensive industries of all.

The manufacture of cement is one of the world's prime contributors of CO_2 into the atmosphere, which both contributes to the greenhouse-effect warming the planet and is absorbed in great quantities by the world's large bodies of water, where CO_2 threatens marine life. In an unusual move, the International Red Cross issued a caution to China regarding the pollution perils of its urbanization.[39] The warning followed troubling signs that came from the Chinese government. The first was an editorial in *People's Daily* that urged China to find ways to turn hundreds of millions of farmers into urban residents "as soon as possible." The second was a survey released by China's government environmental watchdogs that could not find one city among China's biggest 340 cities that met the standards for good air, as measured by the amount of noxious sulfur dioxide in the local atmosphere. The study did find, rather, that nearly two hundred of the cities met the standards for dangerously high pollution.[40]

Another measure of air pollution is the level of suspended particulate matter, the result of smoke, soot, dust, and droplets in the air from the burning of fuels. China's three largest cities have about three times the levels of suspended particulates than the level deemed safe by the World Health Organization. Seven of the ten most polluted cities in the world, WHO reports, are in China.

A recent and dramatic rise in pollution is a troubling example of the bind that China's development puts itself and the world in. Modernization has been called a Faustian bargain since the advent of the spinning machine, because it forces trade-offs between benefits and costs. Energy use presents the most bedeviling of choices, and China's rapidly growing energy demands have been fiendish, to say the least. Just a few years ago it seemed as though the country, which had set itself on reversing the worst of its pollution, was on the mend. Air quality improved from 1998 to 2002,[41] benefiting from government policy, advocacy from thousands of new environmental groups in China, and from the general drift of maturing industrialization, which typically grows cleaner over time as economies prosper. (Witness Shanghai's tidying up, for example.) But China's growth proved too fast for the national cleanup. In 2003, China's demand for electricity grew by 15 percent. Even if the pace abates significantly, China's hunger for energy will require enormous amounts of generating power in the future. So far, the country has answered the need for more energy by stoking its coal-fired generating plants, users of China's soft, low-grade, high-sulfur coal, among the dirtiest of fuels. These plants, the core of China's energy infrastructure, are unlikely to go away or change their ways soon.

"I Had to Bring My Wife to China"

China is on the biggest power plant building binge ever.[42] Plans extend far into the future and will soak up enormous amounts of capital along the way. In 2004, $24 billion was invested in new generators. By the calculation of Britain's *Guardian,* China adds the equivalent of Britain's entire electricity output every two years. *Eventually China will need at least the energy-making capacity of the United States.*

The Chinese government doles out the lion's share of the power plant construction business to Chinese firms, but China's goals are so huge that foreign companies are prospering from the growth of China's power sector too. The world's large industrial construction firms, such as Bechtel, are already busy building plants. International operators are running others. American giant AES runs five power plants in China, including the country's biggest. General Electric sells the Chinese giant turbines and other equipment and services; in 2003, it did nearly $1 billion in business in the country.* Japan's Mitsubishi Heavy Industries also has big contracts to supply plants with turbines, while Germany's Siemens supplies the coal plants with core technology. The price tags are enormous and represent the sort of big-ticket, high-tech trade that America, Europe, and Japan most hope the Chinese will engage in. Nothing moves trade officials in world capitals faster than the chance to place their biggest companies into the development of China's cities. Urbanizing China is where the dreams of GE shareholders and Chinese migrant workers meet.

A legion of smaller international companies—firms without huge budgets or governments behind them—are also migrating into the Chinese market. For European and American concerns, China offers a chance to sell into a market that is actually growing. At home, their governments have long restricted the building of new power plants. Environmental regulations make finding the site for a new plant nearly impossible, and communities, once chosen, usually turn strongly against the power company that proposes one. Companies that make the parts that go into power plants are often older enterprises that grew up when their local economies had their own power plant construction booms and now exist to make replacement parts, or to create innovative technology that can fit into an old system. Clyde Bergemann is a company comprising of a network of small factories and offices in Europe, the United States, and now China. It manufactures and services some of the most seemingly mundane equipment in a power plant, the boiler cleaning systems. Without the cleaners, however, power plants could not run, and with inferior cleaners, they would run far dirtier. Its China office is run by one local engineer, but on a given day it might be the rendezvous point for salesmen and engineers collecting from the company's factories in Estonia, the United States, the United Kingdom, and Germany.

Steven Winkle, an executive visiting from the company's Atlanta facility, is smitten with China, and when he talks to his colleagues, he

---

*American companies might have done billions of dollars of more business with the builders of the Three Gorges Dam if the United States had been less vocal in opposing the project. China's willingness to reward countries that do not protest its energy plans creates a powerful incentive to go along no matter what the environmental or human costs of China's projects.

cannot contain his enthusiasm for the coming giant market opportunity. "I love it here so much," he says. "It is really an exciting place. I had to bring my wife just to show her."

Winkle and the Clyde Bergemann group can only make China work for them if they keep their expenses down. They avoid the poshest Western-style hotels and use folding tables as office furniture. A year ago, the company's China office was in an unheated building. "Our venture company," he says about his corporate parent, "has a problem with growth, but China is building half of the coal-powered plants in the world." Winkle studies the Chinese economic landscape and is familiar with the Chinese government's pressing need to expand development westward. "The Chinese are going to be building whole new cities around the new power plants it develops," he says. They will also be creating industrial centers out of previously sleepy towns, provided they can bring in power. Winkle says his company has also moved some of its manufacturing to China, where he has found young, skilled workers schooled in old industrial techniques easier to find than in the company's European or Western plants.

The Chinese power market is not all opportunity, however. China's power sector has been labeled "one of China's biggest foreign investment graveyards."[43] The U.S. Commercial Service, the government arm that promotes U.S. business abroad, notes that large deals between foreign power plant operators and local power authorities have gone spectacularly bad. The service also warns that companies, whether the scale of GE or Clyde Bergemann, must expect pressure to transfer their technology to China and thus create their own competition within the country. As with other industries, the Chinese use the carrot of their vast market to extract concessions from foreign firms that will help build China's industrial might all the more. It is a policy worthy of grudging admiration with a long record of success, when viewed from the Chinese side. In the area of power generation, however, the cost of China's ambition may weigh heavily on its own people and the world. If the foreign manufacturers that lead in environmental-friendly solutions for the power industry stay out of China for fear that their technology will be aped by Chinese competitors, China will not create the cleaner power infrastructure the world needs it to have.

Meanwhile, the cost of dirty power for Chinese city dwellers is that they die younger than they ought to. An estimated four hundred thousand people die every year from illnesses such as lung and heart disease related to air pollution.[44] The cost for the Chinese countryside from urban pollution is also high; acid rain[45] pours over 30 percent of the country's land area.[46] It also spreads over other countries of East Asia. An energy specialist at the Asian Development Bank notes that China may be the source of as much as 40 percent of the air pollution in Japan and South Korea.[47] Japan, which has suffered from Chinese acid rain for a generation, pays the Chinese to clean up their power plants. From 1997 to 2002, Japan provided $3.1 billion in loans and aid to Chinese environmental projects.

Chinese pollution travels in other shapes too. A great wind-riding smog, known as the Asian Brown Cloud, travels over Nantong and other east coast cities and arrives visibly on America's West Coast via the jet stream, its Chinese pollutants measurable across the country.[48] The Brown Cloud changes world weather patterns. Scientists now see evidence that it may be reducing rain along a stretch from the forests of Washington and Oregon to the farms of the Midwest.

Unlike Shanghai and Beijing, Nantong's main streets are not yet choked with cars, but still throng with bicycles and motorbikes. The bicycle parking areas in front of the big department stores are gray and green tumbles of thousands of vintage English Standards last seen by Americans in *Goodbye, Mr. Chips*. Time and road grit have replaced whatever luster the bikes once had with egalitarian dreariness, like two-wheeled Mao suits. There is nothing ideological in them, however. In Nantong, a passable used bike costs $10, and few riders are foolhardy enough to park a colorful modern model amid the basic pile and inevitably lose it.

Soon, however, the people of Nantong may no longer need worry about losing their bicycles downtown. The city is rapidly building up the roads and highways it needs to accommodate the growing presence of cars and trucks. Nantong, which is also home to one of China's top ocean ports, recognizes that it is solidly in the orbit of Shanghai, half a day's drive to the south. Nantong intends to build itself up as a complement to the bigger city, and in some ways Shanghai would like nothing better. Nantong can absorb the smoking and belching factories that need another home. Nearby cities such as Nantong cannot help but benefit, but it too wants to put on a modern face. Bicycle and motorbike riders will be among the first to suffer.

If other cities are the models, Nantong will soon ban two-wheeled transportation from the most traveled streets. That would also put the city squarely in line with China's national policies that increasingly encourage people to own cars and thus support an industry on which much of the country's industrial aspirations now rest.

China's development far outpaces its ability to establish and administer an effective environmental regime. Because China cannot control its own polluters, the world's best hope is to reach international agreements to contain pollution everywhere else—a long shot, but necessary given China's potential to despoil the planet.

The Dragon's Horsepower

Cars have proven a mixed blessing for China's cities, and for the world. The car business in China has quickly emerged among the world's most exciting, a gamble on a global scale. It merits a closer look later in this book, yet any discussion of Chinese cities must mention the role of cars.

Most broadly, the advent of China's urban car culture has already had consequences for everywhere else cars are driven. The world's petroleum sellers do not need massive disruptions in their customer bases or their supplies to ring up huge swings in prices. Small changes in supply and demand, say a 5 percent jump in the demand for refined petroleum, have in the past sent worldwide prices soaring by 30 percent or more. China's urbanization and its car boom go hand in hand as the cities create the middle class that can now afford automobiles. That boom now helps make China a major customer on the world's petroleum markets, and its buying was one of the key factors ratcheting up world petroleum prices in 2004 to all-time highs—to $55 a barrel as recently as October 2004. In the first nine months of the year, China's 9-plus percent rate of growth was joined by a need for an additional 1 million barrels of oil every day. During that time, more than fourteen thousand new cars were also added to China's roads daily.[49]

Cars and China's electricity-hungry manufacturers live under the same sword. When the big coal plants cannot fuel industries' needs, smaller petroleum-burning plants fill the gap. Recently, factories have found that their best hedge against enforced downtime is to build their own gas- and diesel-powered generators on their own sites. Morgan Stanley's Andy Xie predicts that world oil prices will be the creature of China's demand for years to come.[50] Few analysts see the long-term effect of China's "automobilization" as anything but higher prices.

Cars in China's cities have also become the country's chief source of pollution. China's cars pollute worse than those elsewhere, because Chinese law sets far weaker pollution standards than do laws in Europe and the United States. The *Far Eastern Economic Review* reports that the U.S. State Department will not allow diplomats with asthmatic family members to work in many Chinese cities.[51]

China's central government promises to enforce stricter pollution standards in the future, but that promise will rely on the willingness of local governments to play policeman, hardly a sure thing. Even if tougher standards win acceptance, China's surging use of cars over the next two decades will make it as much of an automotive polluter as the United States. The world outside China must deal with that, no matter what China does to clean up its act. China's progress is now inextricably linked to cars, which are rightly seen as vital to China's development.

Road Warriors

The sudden appearance of China's car culture takes outsiders—and even the Chinese themselves—by surprise. Yet the car in China can also be seen as the child of the great rivalry among the country's cities. Above all, that competition is a rush to build infrastructure, not the least of which is the network of roads on which China's growing population of automobiles travels. It is arriving on the scene because China has everywhere replicated in greater numbers, and often at bigger scale, the infrastructure of the modern American metropolis, albeit again with Chinese characteristics.

Where did it all come from? China's highways look better than Germany's autobahns. Especially at night. The brightly lit roads leading out of Shanghai toward Suzhou rise high along slender overpasses and swoop through the sky and carry cars above the stalled traffic several stories below. During the city's long rush hours, the highway offers little relief, yet later it cuts travel time to a fraction and offers a view straight at the high-rise city. During the daylight crawl past the crowded edges of town, trophy buildings give way to thousands of undistinguished high-rises adapted from more or less the same plan, the one that allows such towers to get built fastest. They are in essence concrete and steel tubes, punctuated by rows of the same sliding windows and small air conditioners. In the slightly older building the windows leach—the Chinese say they "weep"—and the air conditioners relentlessly drip, leaving the exteriors covered by irregular red, black, brown, and green stripes. The oldest high-rises, vast housing projects where the old and the laid-off room in small two-bedroom apartments renting for $12 or $20 a month, exude so many minerals onto their walls that they look like geological field sites.

At night, those details disappear, so that when the electrical grid is operating full tilt, even the grimier parts of Shanghai change into a bedazzling mix of white twinkle from apartment windows and radiant color, layered through the night by neon signs everywhere. A ribbon of azure light runs along the sides of the skyway, cutting through the dark like a glowing necklace. For a highway, it is very cool. It turns the Shanghai night into one of the long-exposure shots of urban nightscapes that makes every city featured in *National Geographic* seem to move at warp speed.

Of course, in Shanghai, it's not just the cars and trains that move fast; so do local governments, developers, and highway construction crews. The highways in and out of Shanghai, built by the latest German construction equipment and with high-tech concrete formulated especially to withstand China's growing traffic, are no sooner finished than begun again. Cars have multiplied so quickly on some roads that even though they are built in midair, their lanes will soon be doubled to eight. They would grow more if engineers could figure out a way to widen them more, but for now the roads' dimensions have been stretched to the maximum.

The natural response to overcrowded roads would be to build alternate routes. China certainly has no trouble envisioning and then building new expressways. Now on the books is a national expansion to

China's network of roads that will, in effect, add the equivalent of the entire U.S. interstate highway system.

The mind can only boggle. But only for a moment, if one sobers up and considers further. Taking into account the size of China's population, the expectations that its industries will fan out throughout the country's underdeveloped regions, and the hope of the Chinese government and all the world's top automobile companies that the Chinese will eventually buy hundreds of millions of cars, a road system that is merely the size of that of the United States will not be nearly big enough.

According to the model for public works nearly everywhere in the world, overcrowded roads will stir governments to think about where news roads could be built to relieve traffic. In China it is not so simple. Nearly every inch of the new expressways in eastern China is a business, owned by the government—often a provincial or local government—that is ultimately leased out to a private-sector company as a toll road and run for profit. In between those who initially approve a highway and those who run tollbooths is a web of officials, planners, developers, financiers, engineering firms, construction companies of all kinds, and, all hope, handsome profits for everyone. Expressways fill a place not unlike a public utility, in which the government in charge provides a monopoly to a service provider, which in turn feeds money—in the United States, anyway—back to the government in the form of taxes. Where they differ is that Chinese expressways are also monopolies in the way that Standard Oil was once a monopoly. Its interest holders have strong incentives to make sure their roads have no real competition. A parallel road network would slash the tolls.

But competition does come, nonetheless. Not directly, but in the form of other roads built by other regions that want their own modern and competitive transportation infrastructure, and their own profits. Zhejiang Province pioneered the system, motivated by the same desperation that caused citizens of the province to scratch their way so successfully into the private sector. With no money from the central government to build the roads that its budding businesses needed, the provincial government struck on the idea to build roads with money raised on the Hong Kong Stock Exchange. Each road, in essence, would be its own company, and in charge of paying its own way. The companies that took control would be run as private enterprises, but the province had a large stake in them.

The plan worked, and Zhejiang's roads became hot issues for world investors—and not just among Chinese investors, but also among the world's richest investment funds and large institutions. Over the years, Zhejiang's highway-building program has proved so successful that highways in the province have never cost its citizens a cent of public money. On the contrary, Zhejiang has earned $30 billion off its roads, enough money to finance other essential social programs, such as water reclamation and schools, both of which are far above the Chinese norm. This again is the province that once received virtually no money from the government.

The model first used for the highways is now used for all sorts of public services. The central government expects China's bigger cities to build modern water-treatment facilities and mandates that they build plants that can provide drinking water to their residents. Hundreds of new water-treatment plants are planned. Only 15 percent of the Chinese have safe drinking water that comes out of a tap. To finance their projects, some governments are privatizing water supplies as well. Whether they will be as lucrative as expressways remains to be seen. Ideally the schemes bring to China efficient markets for services, in which people pay for what they use. That could lead to a society more willing to conserve. In the United States, by contrast, where the use of highways is mostly free, and water often generously subsidized, Americans tend to grossly overuse both.

The Chinese approach also feeds the rapid expansion of infrastructure. Countries that rely on tax money and popular consent to build their roads may not be able to match what the Chinese are rushing to build. In the United States, more and better highways come only at the price of higher taxes. According to the U.S. Department of Transportation's most recent report to the U.S. Congress, money currently budgeted for the U.S. interstate system now falls short of what's needed to keep current roads to top shape, let alone expand them. Politicians who push for higher gas or income taxes, even to pay for essential infrastructure, face a citizenry dead set against them.

The Chinese have recently announced that they are opening up their train system to similar private investment schemes. Nearly anything that can even remotely fit the model is being tried. When parks get built, the land around them is leased to pay for them. Municipal convention centers are built to be profitable, something that has proven nearly impossible elsewhere in the world, but may work in China (especially if centers are converted in part to big shopping malls!).

Physical infrastructure such as highways, water systems, and other civic amenities may seem less important in an age when information moves in bits and bytes and countries all over the world compete with comparable expertise even on highly technical projects. And yet, finally, it may be a country's physical infrastructure that ultimately makes or breaks its competitive strength. If the more immaterial assets in an economy can easily be replicated abroad—either by building them or moving them—then the things that cannot be moved will be what set countries apart. Old-fashioned public goods such as roads, water, energy, and municipal services will be as important as the best engineers, telecommunications, and store of patents.

Meanwhile, the urgent privatization of roads and other infrastructure utilities reveals another key to understanding why China is growing so fast. The government has unlocked the value of the land it owns beneath everyone's feet. Every newly developed block in Chinese cities takes shape in part because the land under it gains a price from the government—or a connected official.

In large measure, then, China and her cities owe their progress and pollution to the wealth spinning out of the nation's greatest common resource: the very land that the Communists sacrificed a million lives to "liberate" from private ownership.

CHAPTER FIVE

CHAIRMAN MAO SELLS SOUP

THE NARROW STREETS AND ALLEYS OF THE SMALL SHANGHAI PET Market in one of the few remaining old neighborhoods near People's Park twist around innumerable tiny shops, each with its own niche in the animal kingdom. Some sell songbirds and bamboo cages, others fighting crickets or tortoises. On the street, from bicycles rigged with half-crates, men sell bulging goldfish, ruby Siamese fighting fish, and other jewel-toned tropicals. The little fish swim in knotted, fully distended Mylar bags that catch the light and make the fish look ten times bigger and twice as iridescent.

The shoppers here look little like the swank Chinese urban professionals—American marketers call them Chuppies—riding the escalators of the city center's glitzier twelve-story malls a few blocks away. Nothing high style trades hands here, mostly objects of enduring and affordable pleasures. Pet owners everywhere show off, and these shops offer owners a variety of status symbols. Birds of fine feathers, sweet song, or rarity lend prestige to their keepers. Cages too sing a tune. The bamboo bands that ring the bottoms of a cage might be plain or etched, detailed or crudely fashioned. The minute ceramic pots that hold seeds and water come in all the grades, from stoneware to fine porcelain. More subtle are the dainty finger-length wooden finials that connect the cages to the metal hanging hooks on top. In the best cages, the finials are cut from rare hardwood blocks carved with rural scenes at postage-stamp scale. The finials can cost pennies or, as with the few locked in glass cases, hundreds of dollars. The trade in the market is unhurried and social. At the outdoor noodle shops that serve shoppers and workers, tables are shared with critters.

The pet market is also an urban hollow, where the country lives inside the city. In addition to working from the shops and the bicycles, some vendors just plant themselves where they can. With bundles the size of lawn bags by their feet, some stand by the entrances to the shops selling amphibians and fighting bugs. The market is one of the few places in central Shanghai where one can see Chinese still donned in Mao suits and ragged military outfits. Either their work is too dirty to risk nicer dress, or those in them are simply too poor to wear much else.

Pet markets in China are places where one can work, literally, from the ground up, and in the new China the ground is all some people have, as was the case with the Lis when they first moved to Shanghai. But sometimes migrants bring the ground with them. There are, for example, the two ruddy-faced women holding small bamboo trays covered with bits of peat. The women look down at the glances of citified passersby, as if they are ashamed to have walked so recently out of China's deep past. These women sell worms. They pluck them from the clods of earth on their trays one by one, taxing customers to come up with the smallest denominations of Chinese currency in their pockets.

"Can you imagine the indignity of that job?" asks a cosmopolitan woman walking through the market. "That is the lowest of the low, selling worms. Selling worms for people's pet birds and bugs." She remarks how poor the two women look, how thin, how short, how short of calories. Shanghai, she says, is *full* of them.

Distinguishing between the rural poor and the better-off urbanites is easy business on urban streets. Or so it seems to the Chinese, who can pick up the signs instantly, judging build, complexion, dialect, and fashion to make a quick assessment. There is the expected haughtiness and sneering that passes between them.

It is tempting to see the slick side of the city as the vanguard of change in China. The big city is certainly where the big money is betting. But places like Shanghai's pet markets, where the country comes into the city, show off an equally important side of the current revolution. That there is a worm market at all is just as telling as the expansion of the giant Baosteel works, the new GM Shanghai plant, or the city's building boom. The women selling worms may look to be the lowest of low, but their presence in Shanghai is a reminder that the new economy's Big Bang was set off in the country, and it is the momentum of China's rural population, once a collective but now atomized and in motion, that is changing not just China, but the world.

Before reform, selling worms for profit in a pet market would have been an utter impossibility. Communist ideology on nature, work, and class all would have conspired against it. Nature was to be conquered. Workers were to serve the state. Business that promoted a leisure class endangered the revolution.

The Communists under Mao gave themselves a mandate to radically refashion China's earth. They used the will—stoked by ideological campaigns—and the labor of the people to do it. The Party's penchant for giant public works projects is well-known.

Less well-known is how savagely the Chinese people were set against the natural world. American scholar Judith Shapiro[1] spent three years in China talking to people involved in government campaigns designed to reorder nature.[2] One campaign in the late 1950s and early 1960s, called Wipe Out the Four Pests, directed the Chinese to wipe out all rats, flies, mosquitoes, and sparrows. Mao drafted the whole country to the campaign, including a national army of young grade-schoolers. In massive coordinated attacks on birds, whole towns would conduct search-and-destroy missions for nests and bird eggs. Patrols marched through fields beating pots and pans to chase birds out. When birds flew off to more remote sanctums, antipest armies lay in wait, beating pots and drums again, allowing birds no place to land. China's population of sparrows nearly disappeared. Other birds too. And so did nature's first line of defense against locusts and other field pests.

The campaign was one of several that led in 1960 to China's great famine, and to the agricultural collapse that caused as many as 30 million deaths, perhaps the largest man-made disaster in history. To deal with the insect infestation that followed, an army of exterminators with chemical pesticides poisoned bugs and the land. The drive to rid Chinese life of birds and bugs was so ferocious that traditional Chinese artists who'd spent lifetimes painting birds and bugs in their work felt too frightened to create or show.

Pet ownership too was linked with the ruling class and their "decadent lifestyles." Chinese official ideology demonized people with servants, free time, and pets and justified violence against them.[3] Today, catering to people's free time is as good a business as any other. Official antipet sentiments are still strong, but not strong enough to block the pet trade or to close the markets,[4] which provide a living to farm families who can now ply the trade and no longer have to stake their livelihoods solely on what grains they can grow or on the government's schemes.

Thus the lowly worm sellers embody nearly every big change in the countryside, including the ability to move, to seek one's own opportunities, no matter how meager, and to satisfy China's evolving tastes for once forbidden pleasures, to enter whole spheres of life that were all but abolished a short lifetime ago.

Good Eats

Pet markets are one place where the country comes into the city. A much broader intermingling happens around the dining table. The profusion of food and choice in China contrasts starkly with the decades of deprivation following 1949. In the early years of Communist rule, land reform made significant improvements in the lot of China's rural multitudes. But food production was soon subordinated to the regime's industrial goals. During the Great Leap Forward in the late 1950s, Chinese farmers adapted to Mao's goal for China to become a top steel producer, another national project that contributed to the great famine. Farmers were encouraged to turn from the fields to steel production. They built "backyard furnaces" everywhere and gathered their families' iron tools and kitchenware to be melted in their homemade factories.

Their newly forged steel was supposed to be turned over to the state to meet Mao's goal of topping the steel production of Great Britain, still a potent symbol of colonial domination and capitalist manufacturing. The result: What little wealth rural families had went up in smoke. The steel they made in their backyard furnaces was mostly worthless globs of metal, too unsound even for simple tools. After years of mismanaged industry and farm policies, the mass of China's rural population had moved backward. The Chinese people were poorer in 1979 than they had been in 1950, and the farmers desperate.

In China's poverty diet, ingredients were meager and monotonous. During the thirty years after 1949, the traditionally elevated role of food was all but extinguished. According to the dictates of the state, Chinese farmers remained focused on grains, the crops by which the Communist Party measured its success.[5] Vegetables were often sparse; Chinese in the northern grain belt often had only cabbages, potatoes, and turnips. Food was strictly rationed. For laborers, food was little more than fuel and came by way of their workplace, doled out with chits to use at government-run depots. Even well after economic liberalization began, eating out was an exceedingly rare event. Restaurant food in China was an artless, greasy necessary evil for travelers. Restaurants were nearly all dumps run by small state-owned companies offering frugal ingredients and bare amenities.

No more. One of the great joys of China's new urbanism is city food life. Nearly all the world's important cities collect distant cuisines. (Italy's cities, which are more perfectly content with their own food, are an exception.) Big-city concierges in China can point to the flavors of France, Italy, Thailand, and Morocco, to Irish pints and Chicago pizza. America's hamburger, chicken, and coffee franchises flourish nearly everywhere and do especially well in urban Asia.

But in China, the varieties of food may be as great as the rest of the world put together. This is an extraordinary change. So is the country's renewed interest in it. Food, together with family, has returned to the center of Chinese social and cultural life. At nearly every gathering, every ritual, and every business meeting, someone arranges for a feast.

Ann Veeck of the University of Western Michigan points out that the Chinese word *renkou,* meaning "population," literally translates as "people's mouths." In the mid-1990s, Veeck lived in Nanjing, the capital of Jiangsu Province, where she studied how the lives of hundreds of food sellers and shoppers changed following economic reform. Veeck notes that the food vendors were the first wave of urban entrepreneurs.[6] At first, after years of anticapitalist propaganda, the people who ventured into the free market were those with little to lose. Most Chinese dared not start businesses, even small ones. They had felt the winds of change reverse too often over the previous thirty years of capricious rule and feared that making an attempt at private business might lead to their being branded counterrevolutionaries or criminals. Among the first people to step into the market were those who could not find an easy place in the state-run system, including people who had been released from prison and had no other work. No wonder, Veeck found, that shoppers at first distrusted private sellers.

Today, food markets of all sorts, from farm stands to big-box hypermarkets, exist within easy walking distance of nearly everyone in Nanjing, and in cities all over China. Veeck found that more than half of city residents lived within a few hundred yards of where they shopped.[7]

Noodles in the Air

At 9:30 p.m. the streets of Rudong in Jiangsu Province are markedly quieter than they are in China's bigger cities. Rudong, with about 1.5 million people, is one of China's small big cities, which is a bit surprising considering it sits at an intersection of the South Yellow Sea and the mouth of the Yangtze River. It is bound to get much less sleepy over the next few years. The city has a brand-new port that will bring in international shipping. Rudong, like nearly every Chinese city with viable industry, is also getting a surge in migration as people move off the farms.

Some of these new migrants come out at night, setting up small food stalls for people on the late shifts. There are vendors from Xinjiang, the rugged Muslim province in China's extreme northwest. They look more like their Central Asians neighbors, the Kazakhs, than they do like Han Chinese. Emigrant men from Xinjiang are a common sight in Chinese cities, where they sell popular spiced-lamb kebabs grilled over open flames on bamboo skewers. Others sell dumplings or buns.

The busiest nightspot on Rudong's main drag, however, is a simple noodle stand where a man and his teenage son work over an enormous pot of steaming beef soup. On China's streets, noodle making is a kind of performance art, and the man in Rudong is a master of the two acts that draw people in. He can take a thick flour paste and, by alternately beating it on the countertop, pulling it the length of his arms, and twisting it, somehow produce, without a blade of any kind, a thick bundle of fine noodles. Or, if the customer wants a toothier noodle, he will take the paste, hold it high overhead with one hand, and then, with a short, sharp razor in the other, make a series of lightning-fast strokes that cut broad noodles from the paste. The noodles drop through the air into the soup, where they fluff up and float to the top.

The man came to Rudong a couple of years ago from an inland farming village in the province. Most of the young men in his hometown have left, he says, estimating that seven of ten of them have gone to the city. He did not come to the city knowing how to make noodles, but he watched others and taught himself. He wonders if there are any noodle makers like him in America, if he might find a job there.

The stall is full of people from the country. A couple and their twelve-year-old daughter listen to the noodle maker's story and nod. They too came from a farm. The man was a factory worker first, but then he and his wife began making tofu at home. Theirs is a regional specialty, chewy, flat pieces the size of a tea bag that can be eaten as are or cooked in broth or a saucy stir-fry. Business is going well for them, says the sprightly and talkative woman, while her husband nods and smiles at all she says.

Their fortunes, she adds, are now beyond anything they could ever have imagined as children. All China is beyond anything they could have imagined. A new contract to supply a school with daily shipments has just come their way. The couple now have sixteen employees, all of them transplants from the hinterlands. Some sleep in a room attached to the small industrial loft they use as a factory. Their day begins at 5 a.m.

To see how they get along, the woman says, one can go to the nearby food market at 5:30 a.m. and ask for her by nickname, Xiaoping, or Little Bottle. The dimly lit building is a simple metal-roofed shell the size of a large American supermarket. Little Bottle's station is near the center and is laid out with several large plastic bins piled high with tofu pieces. She talks while she and her husband wait on three customers at once. Two yuan, twenty-five cents, buys a small handful.

She leaves her booth to offer a tour of the market. It is mid-November, but the variety and freshness of the ingredients make the market a riot of bright green, orange, and red. There are as many different ingredients under the Rudong market roof as in all the markets of New York City. Sections of the market are filled with wriggling fish and seafood, clucking chickens, and freshly slaughtered goats stretched out whole on white enamel tabletops. But no, there is no stench. (Not so in the summer, however.) The produce and stock nearly all come in daily and clear out at night. How much of it comes from within one hundred kilometers of Rudong? Little Bottle says 99 percent. How much from within fifty kilometers? Fifty percent. And from within Rudong itself? Maybe a third.

Compare that to an American or European supermarket, where goods are shipped in from all over the world, peppers from Holland, flowers from Chile, lamb from New Zealand, and fruits from Michigan, California, Spain, and Panama. The rest of the world has rationalized its production and eats out of cold storage. When the Chinese farmers took back the right to produce, they were still stuck on plots of land on fractions of acres. Yet their patches are filled with multiple crops of fine enough quality to catch the attention of their local buyers. For those whose farms are too meager—almost all are—better crops also buy a ticket off the land.

Feasts That Move

And then there is the eating, which in China is how history gets redigested. Looking up and down nearly any street in China today, one sees how the reappearance of China's culinary life alone is enough to wed people to the capitalist road. The expansion of the Chinese menu means even more in Communist China than elsewhere. In the absence of truly open expression in the press, literature, and the arts, food is one place that the mainland Chinese can find a robust expression of their culture. Unlike works on the page, a canvas, or the screen, the government need not fear that a subtly subversive message is buried in a chef's new shrimp dish or potted-duck casserole. Food is China's least imitative, most flamboyantly inventive pursuit.

Now that people move, so do China's feasts. Regional restaurateurs tote their foods from one region to another to feed the country's desires for new tastes. Food impresarios recruit chefs from all over the country. Competition has made Chinese cities among the best places on earth to eat. Food faddism thrives, creating instant and keen demand for the Chinese flavors of the month. Restaurants that capture the wave often crest with a year or two of crowds outside the door and then fade. The hearty food of Hangzhou—sweetly glazed fatty meats that fall off the bone, duck stews, and deep-fried freshwater fish with a vinegary sauce—stirred a genuine craze with restaurants popping up all over the place. The food of Chaozhou—where Cantonese food is at its most elaborate—is found in huge and expensive restaurants, some with sprawling ground floors taken up by aquariums that would make good city museums, but are instead holding tanks for hundreds of varieties of fish and seafood. The foods of southern China's Yunnan Province, a kind of

Chinese creole that blends in the tropical flavors of Southeast Asia, is a new favorite. One of the superstars of China's contemporary art scene, Fang Lijun, helped kick off the trend with a mod Yunnan restaurant in a fashionable high-rise in East Beijing. There waitresses in traditional dress tread over see-through glass floors and a rotating collection of paintings from the country's most cutting-edge artists hangs on the walls.

At a Manchurian restaurant in Shanghai, by contrast, waiters wear round silk caps with long black ponytails sewn in. Waitresses struggle along in the flowing yellow-and-gold-brocaded robes of the Empress Dowager Cixi, topped by heavy, elaborately beaded Qing dynasty head-dresses to match. The food is a hit. Young couples wait more than an hour to be seated at rough-hewn tables and on tree stumps instead of chairs. The reviled Manchu royals are rendered quaint. One of the most potent negative symbols to Communist China's peasant reformers, the empress dowager, power-mad consort and schemer, squanderer of China's fortune who sold out China to foreigners, now serves ten-course meals to teenagers with cell phones.

Colonel Mao

The restaurant scene in the cities is also where Mao Zedong is undergoing a startling transformation. He is taking on the role of Colonel Sanders. Walk into nearly any Hunan restaurant, and Mao peers from all around. Longtime capitalists are accustomed to enlisting their great political figures as pitchmen. American luxury cars are named Lincoln; so are payday loan centers. The British monarchy lends its majesty and name to the sale of umbrellas and marmalades. Then again, being a leader of a Western democracy means being in the business of protecting commerce. Mao's fame rests on fighting the capitalist running dogs, not showing them. It is in this role that his image still appears in civic venues. Mao's eminence, of course, dominates Beijing's Tiananmen Square, for example. And monumental statues of Mao, like that in Chengdu, the capital city of Sichuan, still occasionally guard public squares. No one confuses this Mao with free-market reforms or commerce. No one would really think this Mao would endorse the secret pact of the Xiaogang farmers.

In the memories of Chinese in their midforties or older, Mao remains

131

an inescapable presence. Today, younger Chinese often complain that the older generation is stilted by years under Mao's rule, during which his, and the state's, overbearing, violent, and unpredictable will made people distrustful and obsessive about self-preservation—a generalization with plenty of exceptions, but a common rule of thumb nonetheless. Don't hire people over forty, young bosses believe, because the older generation is paranoid. It's a depressing new twist on the so-called Four Olds, one of the ideas that propelled the Cultural Revolution, when people were exhorted to get rid of "old ideas," "old culture," "old customs," and "old habits."

And yet, despite the psychic costs of Mao's reign, Mao is still the country's most prevalent icon. What better personage to enlist to sell soup. Shanghai's Hunan Garden is one big jolly Mao museum. Over here there's a picture of the happy leader lighting up a cigarette. Another highlights his pre-jowly days, when he sported matinee-idol good looks. He's lying down, he's sharing a joke. Maybe he's just enjoyed a more private pleasure.

For the restaurateurs, the images suggest something else: Try Mao's favorite food. At Hunan restaurants fatty pork in gravy is a must. Mao loved it. In other Hunan restaurants, Mao statues greet diners at the entrance just like the fiberglass Colonels do at KFC. At still others he gets the Andy Warhol treatment, bigger than life in Pop Art colors.

As time goes by, the depictions of the leader get more and more daring, pushing the image as far away from the person or his historical context as those of Caesar at Caesars Palace. Do the patrons find it odd that capitalism's biggest enemy now hawks for private restaurateurs? Not at all. Mao is from Hunan, and they are proud of him.

And what of the more goofy ways he is portrayed? Well, comes the answer, they are just trying to make their restaurants stand out. Mao means nothing in the marketplace. Except where he is sold. The business of China is business.

Communist Kitsch

Capitalism's rebranding of Mao begs a question: Where is China's more radical past? In a world of truth commissions and holocaust memorials, one might expect that the hardest years of Communist rule might come under closer examination. The memoirs of Chinese writers in exile have produced one of the late twentieth century's most moving bodies of literature. Some domestic books, if told delicately, make it past censors. The 1994 novel *To Live,* by Yu Hua, told the violent, but touching story of a rich, drunk gambler who loses everything before the revolution and is then caught in the changes wrought by war and years of social engineering. The filmed version of the book, also released in 1994, is still banned in China.

With coaxing, with time, with tea and beer, older people in China do tell of their struggles through the century. More than that, they are glad to have an ear. If they get talking, and friends draw near, they nod in recognition of each other's fate, of the slogans they lived by, of the friends they loved and lost, of their own zeal. Often too they are wistful for what has been lost, when street cleaners and widget makers were as worthy as—or more worthy than—doctors and professors. When property meant so little that that there was almost no crime, and the smallest thing lost was always returned. Stories and emotions pour out, often because they have so far been unheard or are so universally shared and understood that they didn't need telling, at least among those who lived through the worst.

University students often have only the vaguest outlines of their family history. Some of this is accidental and some of it by design. The single most amazing fact about China's transformation is that it has thus far buried the grudges and blood feuds that might otherwise have consumed it. In every town and village, people come in daily contact with the same people who brutalized or humiliated them or their families, or with their brutalizers' children. But overwhelmingly the Chinese stay focused on the future. On what their country can be, on how they can be carried up by its surging fortunes. The past was good, it was bad, it was theory, it was madness, it didn't work, they move on. Hope lives.

The Communist Party may wish to relegate its failures to the dustbin of history. They are going into the sale bin instead. A whole industry exists to sell off the detritus from Chinese Communism's old days. Shops in fine hotels, antique markets, and outdoor tourist traps are packed with the stuff. Much of it is real, like the tall stacks holding hundreds of Little Red Books, the volumes that the Chinese pored over in endless hours of "self-examination," trying to recall, or divine, how to best serve Mao and the revolution.

The books are everywhere. The markets have so many Little Red Books, in fact, that one could build a palace out of them. Behind each book is someone, or some government institution, that discarded it, selling the book for a small fraction of the ten or twenty cents the books go for used. Not surprisingly, these mountains of books are often culled from the countryside, collected by the rural migrants who work networks of small-town connections to find bits of China's past they can peddle in the cities.

Just as plentiful are the thousands of pedagogical comic books, which, on account of their endless variety, are far more interesting than Mao's discarded volumes. The small books, just a few thin pages long and no bigger than recipe cards, do not match the bold drama of thick, new, Manga-inspired comics selling on newsstands. The old books stink so badly of mold and mites that few shoppers page through them. Mostly they appeal to foreigners who have learned the value of pop ephemera and are diversifying from their own baby-boom clutter.

But flip open one anywhere and there's a quaint lesson. One tells of the little French boy who made a mark in the Paris Commune fighting counterrevolutionaries. Another tells of a Chinese peasant boy with a talent for birdcalls. After his family is destroyed by evil landlords and Japanese imperialists, he joins the Communists in their fight for China, using his whistles and trills to secretly warn the troops of enemy movements. In yet another, published in 1973, the seventh year of the Cultural Revolution, children could read about the Snow Orphan, a baby girl stranded in a snowdrift and rescued by a Red Army militiaman during the war against the Nationalists. The girl, raised on a commune, grows up to be one of China's barefoot doctors. When by chance the soldier stumbles back into her life, old and blind, it is her turn to rescue him.

The most numerous comics—meaning the ones most discarded—are the Little Red Guard comics, which tell of children's battles against landlords, eggheads, and other enemies of the revolution. Kids may not have been able to play Superman in China's old days, but they could be radical revolutionaries. The comics showed the way. Now they're nearly trash.

Propaganda posters are another hot item in the markets. There is a growing international appetite for Chinese political posters, and the curio vendors have stacks of them too. For the most part, local Chinese do not buy them yet, but foreigners wade through the piles examining every smiling ironworker, whether man or manly woman, marching farmer, and noble portrait of Mao, trying to pick out the image that most incongruously combines radicalism, sentiment, artistry, and bad taste.

They are also trying to pick out the real posters from the reproductions. While the Chinese clear their historical attics, and memories, local factories are also busy making copies. Every seller knows that in May 2001, a famous auction house—Sotheby's—sold a thirty-year-old "Yankee Go Home" poster for $575. It went at Sotheby's auction of 150 Cultural Revolution collectibles.

The markets are now flooded with fake Mao memorabilia, and the more offbeat, the better. Imagine all the Mr. Peanut, Elvis, and Marilyn novelties you have ever seen and put Mao in them instead. Ceramic busts, statuettes, plates, cups, and tins appear in waves in the market, depending on whatever sellers think is catching on. Walk through the markets at monthly intervals and whole categories of Mao items appear on sellers' tables. One month three-inch ceramic medallions might be a hit. If so, next month they will come in all sizes.

Genuine Mao items do have some local appeal, and collectors can amass huge amounts of stuff. Melissa Schrift, an anthropologist at Marquette University in Milwaukee, published a study on the history of the Mao badge in 2001.[8] In the 1960s, wearing jewelry or adding other fashion touches to one's clothes violated strict political taboos. The Mao badge was an exception. Produced by the billions, in up to ten thousand variations, the minting of badges eventually burdened China's economy so heavily that the Party tried to stop the trade. When economic reform began under Deng Xiaoping, Mao badges were collected and melted down for their metal.

Now that China is richer, there is nostalgia for the badges, both among older Chinese and the young. In March 2000, *People's Daily* ran a story on a farmer with a collection of thirty thousand Mao badges. His assortment was in homage to the leader. "There's a kitsch quality that I think the younger Chinese who are collecting old badges appreciate," says Schrift. "As Westerners we think we have some kind of monopoly on ironic attitudes toward popular culture. For older collectors, there's a cathartic quality to collecting images from [Mao's rule]. It is their way of dealing with something in the past that was incredibly traumatic, but that the government would prefer to forget. It will be a long, long time before there is a Cultural Revolution Museum in China."[9]

Meanwhile, overseas Chinese have been reconceptualizing Mao for years. Shanghai Tang, the Hong Kong fashion designer, has been selling finely tailored silk versions of Mao suits, often in bold colors, and selling watches with a waving Mao on the face. And in the mid-1990s, New York designer Vivienne Tam helped establish herself with T-shirts imprinted with a picture of Mao in schoolgirl pigtails. Nothing like that would be allowed in the Chinese markets, but young collectors, glomming on to the global taste for irony and collectibility, now buy Mao badges too. Schrift notes that many older Chinese take umbrage at such collectors, who often buy Mao items as an investment. Of course, it is also the older Chinese who have unleashed the red tide of Mao items into the marketplace. Often, they can use the money.

In the commodification of Chairman Mao one can detect China's current ambition to drive away from the twentieth century. Not just to make up for lost time, but to avoid the difficult questions and recriminations that would come with a reckoning. History has instead been turned into a product, which, once sold, helps keep a reckoning at bay.* If China can make it through another twenty or thirty years without the mid-twentieth century coming back to derail it, the country will have skirted one of the most potentially explosive national legacies in recent human memory. Could any reaction be healthier? Historical grudges are the modern world's most divisive force, and China is hell-bent not to harbor one against itself. For now, the marketplace has become the answer. Chairman Mao sells soup.

---

*How long economic progress can keep history clouded over is something the Chinese leadership worries about a lot. The whole world should. In June of 2003, on the fifteenth anniversary of the 1989 Tiananmen Square Massacre, eighty thousand protesters gathered in Hong Kong's Victoria Park for a candlelight vigil to both remember the event and to push the Communist leadership in Beijing to come clean on the events and the officials behind the deadly crackdown on the student pro-democracy movement. The Hong Kong Chinese are far freer to express themselves than their mainland kin, but dissenters are under strict pressure nonetheless. The Chinese leadership sees open discussion of its past as subversive, and Hong Kong's loudmouths as a real threat. One way the government hopes to counter Hong Kong's own democratic movement is to offer the region economic incentives to keep its economy humming.

CHAPTER SIX

THROUGH THE LOOKING GLASS

CHINA USED TO BE FAR AWAY, THE ALIEN COUNTRY AT THE BOTTOM of the world. That is certainly how it would have seemed in Pekin, Illinois, during the childhood of anyone who is middle-aged today. Back in the 1960s and 1970s, Communist China was denounced on the floor of the U.S. Senate by the town's most famous son, Everett Dirksen, the fair-haired, golden-throated conservative Republican who was a forceful advocate of America's Cold War containment strategies. Yet back then, if radical China was a threat to the American dream, it was a distant one.

Local legend says that Pekin is opposite the putative hole through the earth from Beijing. The Illinois city took its name from the Chinese capital in the 1820s, using the transliterated spelling found on maps of the era. (Oddly, the founders of Canton, Illinois, twenty-five miles away, also thought their city was the antipode of its Chinese namesake, which is some 1,250 miles from Beijing.) Chinese names were popular among those platting American towns in the nineteenth century, as American traders with fast clipper ships were making fortunes in the China trade, which brought fashionable silks, delicate porcelains, and tea to the new country. There are thirty-two American municipalities dubbed Canton, thirty-six named China, China Grove, China Hill, or some such, and no fewer than fourteen named Pekin. But unlike America's new Berlins, Yorks, and Orleanses, which had real ties back to their older European namesakes, towns dubbed with Chinese names had nothing Chinese about them.

Like Shanghai, Pekin was settled on a river that was the superhighway of its day. (It's interesting to note that in the early nineteenth century, the two towns were the same size!) Pekin's waterfront is midway down the length of the Illinois River, which begins forty miles southwest of

Chicago and works its way to the Mississippi.* By American Midwestern standards, it's an old town, one where Abraham Lincoln once tried a case in a local courthouse. The town's center is a familiar main street lined mostly with two-story, solidly built brick stores. Its old bank buildings have Greek columns and poles for the American flag on top, while its newer bank buildings look like car dealerships. Its plentiful churches have handsome spires, and its schools are named for American presidents.

Pekin's population of 33,860 has changed little over the last twenty years, and housing along the city's tree-lined lanes is highly affordable by U.S. standards. In the year 2000, the average price of a Pekin home was a mere $75,000, less than half the national figure. Median household incomes in the area hover around $37,972, well below that of the United States as a whole, which comes in at $43,527. But the city provides jobs at a rate around 10 percent higher than the national average.[1]

About one in seven workers in Pekin heads to a factory in the morning. Peoria, the home of Caterpillar, the colossal construction- and mining-equipment maker, is within easy reach of Pekin, and it is a strong influence on the Pekin economy. There are thirty-five machine shops in the immediate area, and two tool and die makers. There is enough union work in town to keep manufacturing wages relatively high. Machinists make about $32 an hour, a good living by American standards.

Pekin prides itself on its large parks and small-town wholesomeness. Stories on the front page of the *Daily Pekin Times* describe the difficulties judging the annual Miss Marigold contest or, in what might make a good headline in a Chinese paper, the success of the local Unity Festival. The daily paper in Peoria carries more hard-hitting news. The big

---

*Not long ago, the Illinois River was so polluted in parts that no fish could swim its length and survive. Today it is mostly clean and a favorite for anglers, though its health is threatened by two Chinese imports, the bighead carp and the silver carp. The bottom-feeding carp were introduced into waters near the Mississippi in 1973 to clean up aquaculture ponds where baitfish and table fish were farmed. The carp escaped into the river system, where they have quickly established themselves as fierce competitors in the local ecosystem. Despite efforts to control their spread, including a large electrified barrier in the Illinois River, the number of Chinese carp is growing exponentially. Wildlife officials at the Illinois Department of Natural Resources fear the fish will advance to Lake Michigan and eventually overrun the entire Great Lakes.

papers from Chicago, 165 miles northeast, also carry the world and national news, but in their pages, aside from the listings that report the small-town sports scores, Pekin hardly exists.

For most of Pekin's history, the connection to China has been little more than a novelty, the town's ever-so-slight historical affinity with China showing up in quaint yet dubious ways. A postcard of the Pekin Theater from 1928 shows a building with a tile roof in a Chinese style and a vaguely oriental marquee advertising a Clara Bow comedy. The building is now gone. As late as 1981, Pekin's citizens still called their public high school sports teams The Chinks, finally renaming them The Dragons.

This change certainly reflected a new cultural sensitivity. Yet it took hold just in time. In Pekin, Illinois, China is no longer a novelty or far away. As with nearly every place in America, the economy of Pekin has grown inextricably linked with China's, connected not by an imaginary hole, but by the real world's shipping lanes, financial markets, telecommunications, and above all, by the globalization of appetites.

A Global Corn Maze

Pekin is surrounded by the county's rich fields, which in a state that is mostly dead flat have a gentle roll, enough to bend the light and in the summer produce an infinite spectrum of greens, including the welcome shade seen on the dollar bill. Each year, the county's nine-hundred-some farms ship more than $120 million worth of agricultural products worldwide. Feed corn and soybeans are the richest crops. Pigs are also big.

Just as China's market reforms began with farmers who tapped into the country's craving for food that was better than what the old Communist system offered them, China's growing prosperity gives the world's farmers a chance to satisfy the hungers of a Chinese population that is ever more willing to spend its newfound wealth on filling its tables. Mark Drabenstott, the vice president of the Federal Reserve Bank of Kansas City's Center for the Study of Rural America, and Nancy Novack, one of the center's economists, assessed Chinese demand in a May 2004 commentary. "A key factor in setting the bullish tone in the

[U.S. agricultural commodity markets] has been China," the two Fed officials noted. "Not only does the nation have more than a billion mouths to feed, but strong economic gains have left millions of Chinese consumers clamoring to improve their diets. In most cases, that means more protein and less rice. That shift is good news for U.S. agriculture, since two of its fortes are growing feedstuffs and meat."[2]

In other words, Chinese consumers demand exactly what the farmers around Pekin can provide. While Drabenstott and Novack acknowledge that farm prices will inevitably rise and fall, and exports go up and down, they nevertheless predict that the long-term trend driven by China is for greater demand. According to their analysis, the country is a classic growth market for food; its development mirrors the growth of other economies that over the past half century have helped turn American agriculture into an export powerhouse. The Kansas Fed's research jibes with what Ann Veeck, the scholar who looked at China's consumption patterns soon after economic reforms spread, discovered in the markets of Nanjing: when Chinese families earn more income, they spend a higher proportion of it on a better diet.

Two other trends are making the Chinese more active food buyers. Migration is one. As the Chinese move off their farms, they must buy food grown by someone else. Nothing would make the American farm sector happier than the fulfillment of China's urbanization goals, which will convert hundreds of millions of families that live off their land into grocery buyers.

The other trend is the loss of arable land in China due to the sprawl of urban centers. Nearly 17 million acres of farmland have disappeared since the mid-1990s. China's leaders express alarm about the losses. Their fears, rooted in China's history of famine and its concomitant unrest, peaked in the summer of 2004 when a fall in China's grain harvest caused the country to be a net importer of food for the first time ever.[3] The Chinese have even resorted to leasing giant swaths of land in neighboring Kazakhstan,[4] Laos, and smaller plots in faraway Cuba[5] to help insure it can control its own food supplies. The gains from those efforts will be negligible compared with the enormous losses caused by the shift in labor and land use. China's loss, however, will be the rest of the agricultural world's gain. The World Bank predicts the country's global food imports will more than double by 2020.

Much of that food will come from Illinois. In 2003, the state's seventy-three thousand farms exported more feed grain and products than those of any other state, and Illinois was the second-largest agricultural exporting state overall, with $3.3 billion in farm products sent overseas.[6]

The food trade is rarely just economic, however, and the farmers of Pekin must also navigate the geopolitical agendas of great and striving nations. With other farmers from all over America, they were among the most vocal constituencies advocating for China's 2001 entry into the World Trade Organization (WTO). They imagined a world in which the efficiencies of the U.S. farmer would make American farm products highly competitive against China's domestic production, which is largely harvested from tiny plots of land worked by too many people and too few machines. American farms average 469 acres in size, while Chinese farms average only 1.2 acres. Many of the farms around Pekin, Illinois, however, are far larger and blessed with deep, rich black topsoil and all the growing power that America's sellers of custom-blended fertilizers and bioengineered seeds provide. One American farmer working with a $200,000 combine can do the work of twenty thousand Chinese farmers working on their government-allotted plots.

While the number of American farms has dwindled to just 1.9 million, the number of jobs tied to farming is still high at 21 million, making agriculture the nation's largest employer. China's 800 million farmers are a much bigger part of China's employment picture, however, and their demands often collide with those of freer trade. After China entered the WTO, U.S. farmers encountered problems they didn't expect, and in the first year agricultural exports were down sharply.

"We worked exhaustively to get China into the WTO because it's such a potentially great market, and we expected a good-faith effort to comply with WTO rules," complained Illinois Farm Bureau president Ron R. Warfield to *Forbes,* "but we've come face-to-face with artificial trade barriers."

Chinese trade barriers come and go without warning. Ever wary of unrest in the countryside, the Chinese government is constantly rebalancing domestic farm taxes and subsidies while also trying to give Chinese farmers access to world markets when prices are good and protection from market forces when they are unfavorable. Other unexpected barriers can also pop up when the Chinese government sees the need to limit imports. Complaints over the fitness of foreign crops or their genetic makeup, likely trumped up, are common. Such measures drive exporters to distraction, preventing them from making solid business plans for their crops. Indeed, in 2002, American farmers were so uncertain about the Chinese stance on the fitness of American soybeans that they found other markets, avoiding China almost entirely.

At the same time, the Chinese themselves have been shaping up to be competitive exporters in a number of crops. In the first year following China's WTO ascension, its export of agricultural products increased; the $1.5 billion rise was four times its rise in imports. In fact, China's exports grew in some of the very goods American farmers hoped to sell more of, including corn and soy.[7]

The first year of an agreement does not tell the whole story, and American agricultural trade with China is still evolving. Farmers around Pekin hope that new trade deals between the United States and China signed in the spring of 2004 will lead China to lower its import barriers and buy half a million metric tons of American corn in the near term, and perhaps millions of tons more in years after.

Farmers who grow corn often also grow soybeans, rotating the two crops to protect against infestations of insects. Watching the soybean market now means watching the Chinese consumer, whose habits are changing as he or she becomes more affluent. Researchers at Iowa State University found that on average, the Chinese diner was consuming 440 percent more vegetable oil in the year 1999 than he was in 1979.[8] Indeed, before economic liberalization, one of the items most coveted by Chinese who were allowed to get parcels from relatives outside the country was a tin of soybean oil.

Those days are gone, but consumption continues to climb. The Chinese have been cultivating soy on their soil for at least five thousand years, and soybean cultivation in the United States boomed in the nineteenth century following the importation of Chinese and Japanese plants. It is as hard to think about a Chinese diet without soy as it is to think about it without rice. Soy finds its way into animal feed, cooking oils, tofu, additives, and sauces, among other things. And yet, the mainland Chinese still consume relatively little when compared with their wealthier ethnic kin overseas. The average Chinese diet in the PRC contains seventeen pounds of food derived from soy, while the Chinese across the

Taiwan Strait consume ten times as much. If the mainland Chinese upped their consumption to just half that of the Taiwanese, China would need to import an amount equal to six of every ten pounds of soybeans produced on American farms.[9]

Thus do the world's big soy producers see a giant market in the making. The soy products that are sent to China now come by armadas sent from the farms of the Western Hemisphere. U.S. soybean exports to China in 2003 totaled $2.9 billion, more than shipments to any other country and one-third of all U.S. soybean exports. That came after a doubling of shipments two years in a row. It was also a time when prices were high,* in part because the American crops that season came up short, due to a lack of rain and a plague of sap-sucking aphids that left plants stunted. American farmers had not had so little crop to sell since the early 1970s.

In the past, foreign sellers would gladly have picked up sales to make up for the soybeans and meal the United States didn't have in inventory. But in the 2003–4 growing season, South American crops came up short too. Compounding the lack of supply was that Latin American growers simply do not have the transportation infrastructure to get their products where they need to go in a timely fashion. Demand for grain and beans is so overwhelming that at times six thousand Brazilian trucks carrying grain for export approach port only to stall in sixty-mile-long traffic jams that take a month to move through.

The Brazilians, however, see an opportunity in China's rising demand and are determined to beat American farmers in the North America–China grain trade. For Brazil's part, strong trade and political links with China give the leftist government there a counterweight to the influence of the United States, and the two foreign governments are working hard to solidify their ties. One of President Luiz Inácio Lula

---

*So high, in fact, that some Chinese manufacturers have resorted to what some Chinese manufacturers always resort to when prices are perceived as high. They are, incredibly, counterfeiting soy products. In a rare genuine news scoop, Chinese Central Television uncovered some fuzzy—literally, it turned out—dealings in a condiment factory in China's Hubei Province in January 2004. As a result the government raided factories making fake soy sauce out of, of all things, discarded human hair, which was apparently being distilled in vats for amino acids much like those that give soy its essential qualities. Hydrochloric acid was added to make the stuff, um, digestible.

da Silva's first big trips once he was in office was to China. He brought with him four hundred businesspeople, most from the farm sector.[10] The two countries now share satellites, infrastructure projects, and technology. In the meantime, Brazil's agricultural exports tripled in 2003 to $1.2 billion and were running well of ahead of that by mid-2004.

The Brazilians see their exports quickly growing tenfold. That will give China a big economic and political foothold in Latin America. Already, Brazil has enlisted the country's support to help it gain a permanent seat on the United Nations Security Council.

"Last year, the government made the strategic decision to draw closer to China," President Lula said in 2004. He noted that China and Brazil "share similar interests regarding their social needs, imperatives of growth, and communal thinking in the United Nations and World Trade Organization."[11]

The same month that the Brazilian president arrived in China with a planeload of business and government leaders, Illinois sent its own trade mission to China. It set off with fanfare from Governor Rod Blagojevich's office. "By leading this trade mission to China, we are facilitating a match between the skills of Illinois companies and the needs of an expanding foreign market," the governor announced. "This trip should help forge relationships that will result in tremendous growth opportunities . . . today and tomorrow."

A mere five businesses from the state were represented.

China stretches into the Cornbelt in other less obvious but powerful ways. Pekin is also home to the plant of Aventine Renewable Energy, the nation's second-largest producer of ethanol, a fuel additive derived from corn. Ten percent of the American corn crop is converted to fuel. In addition to Aventine in Pekin, farmers' cooperatives are everywhere investing in small ethanol plants to fill the nation's, and the world's, fuel pumps. China recently passed Japan as the world's second-greatest consumer of petroleum, and the growing Chinese demand makes ethanol an increasingly attractive alternative. And, indeed, ethanol prices climbed forty cents a gallon in the spring of 2004, yanking up U.S. corn prices as a result, a boon to Pekin's farmers and industry.

The need of local farmers to conquer the Chinese market informs everything in the Pekin area. Just as Brazil puzzles through its infrastructure problems, Pekin civic leaders have worked with state and federal officials to fund and build highway connections that will help farmers get their goods to big ports, such as Chicago, faster and more economically. Given that recent funding for U.S. highways has been at a level too low to maintain current roads, the new road projects are a big victory. One could argue that the promise of Chinese trade with U.S. farms is buying better roads for Middle America.

American farmers will also benefit if China's appetites help lift other developing Asian economies over the long term. Those countries too will spend more on food. That's a big if. For now, China's appetite for resources has benefited the economies of its Southeast Asian neighbors, but it is still an open question whether those economies will grow at a good clip over the next decades on the strength of Chinese demand, or whether China's industrial might will cause Thailand and Malaysia to *deindustrialize* and turn back into more natural-resource-driven economies. One can also wonder if China's productive strengths will keep the likes of Vietnam and Indonesia from advancing out of the cheap-labor and natural-resource ghetto.

If the triangulation of world trade, the politics of tariffs and other barriers, and the worldwide status of pests and crop viruses weren't enough to fret about, the farmers of Pekin can even add the financial health of China's banks to their watch list. The Chinese crush 29 million tons of soybeans a year to make cooking oil, and the companies that do the crushing have long been operating at a hefty loss. In May 2004, as the Chinese government tried to engineer a way to ease the country's roaring economy, Chinese government banks stopped lending to the crushing companies. Strapped for cash, they could not pay for their imports. Ships with beans in their holds were left to idle in the northeastern port of Dalian.[12] Back in Pekin, farmers saw the price of soybean futures traded on the Chicago Board of Trade plunge 8 percent.[13]

In the long run, which is to say when historical ironies become most apparent, American farmers may actually benefit from the flight of American manufacturing to China. Not only has agricultural demand from China risen, but the powerful global effects of the Chinese economy may have made it easier for the American farmer to finance his business. That China has an overwhelming trade surplus with the United States drives down the interest rates that American banks charge borrowers (a topic covered in a later chapter). That, of course, includes the owners of America's 1.9 million farms, whose interest rates on bank loans dropped by 2.5 percent between 2001 and 2003.[14] Lower interest rates help farmers be more successful in repaying their loans[15] and have also helped push up land values, another boon for farmers, whose property grew in value considerably during the era of low interest rates. That also increased their borrowing power. No matter how one calculates it, China is sowing farmers' fortunes.

Nuts and Bolts

It's not just the farmers of Pekin who think about China, of course. There are also the workers and managers at Excel Foundry and Machine, a factory on a lonely stretch of Wagonseller Road that can only be found with a good set of directions. Excel makes parts for machinery used in heavy-construction and mining operations. There is little outwardly high-tech about Excel's shop. It is American industry in its plainest form, forging and casting metal parts that go into other companies' machines. Most of the machines that Excel parts go into— presses, industrial shovels, haul trucks, pumps, and cone crushers— reconfigure masses of earth. One of its big markets is for replacement parts of giant mining machines, the sort made by Peoria's Caterpillar.

Walking though the twenty-five-thousand-square-foot foundry makes one feel inordinately small. Eleven large furnaces can cast a part weighing up to fifteen tons. On the shop floor stand shiny new brass cylinders the size of Saturn rocket stages and cast-steel cones that look like space capsules. There are nuts and bolts that are seven feet across, and huge shafts, pinions, and rollers made for mining buckets that can lift a whole house. The company sells what it makes globally out of its own warehouses around the world.

Doug Parsons, Excel's young president, heads the family-owned business. Parsons is a fit man of medium build. He wears a suit to work, but keeps his modest office near the shop floor and greets most workers by name. Parsons has worked hard to keep Excel on the cutting edge of its niche in the casting business. He shops the world for the best machines and practices and believes the company can stay ahead only if it invests in technology.

"Any of the parts we make that can easily be duplicated by metal shops in China," Parsons says, "are handed off to an offshore supplier." Excel can make more money on these commodity parts if someone else produces them, then selling them at a bigger margin. Parsons is willing to play middleman for some parts so long as the strategy helps Excel retain its spot as manufacturer of higher-value parts. Under his stewardship Excel has already relocated 20 percent of the company's production capacity to China. Sending production of commodity parts offshore also frees up the talent and machinery in Excel's own plant. Excel can then make products that few, if any, other companies can match. That's where the fattest margins are.

In Excel's case, the biggest-ticket items include giant cast gears and big cylinders made out of highly engineered alloys. Because the parts go into the machines that extract and grind rocks and ores in the world's mines, they must be built to withstand the harshest wear and tear. In addition, since mining companies can suffer deep losses from machine failures that force long downtimes, Excel's parts must be ready when mining companies need them. Those demands add up to higher prices for Excel's parts, and they can cost more than $10,000 per piece.

Yet, Parsons knows too that today's specialty parts may be tomorrow's commodities. He realizes that to keep business that might otherwise be lost to China's cheap, uncountable, and often huge foundries, he may well have to send even more of his production offshore. Some parts will inevitably be copied by his overseas competition. "I can't predict how we might have to do business in the future, but the goal is to keep enough ahead of the competition that we can still run our factory here and do well," he says.

For now, however, Parsons's biggest problem is not how to make up for products poached by his competition; it is how to manage his company's recent growth. Excel's mining customers are running their machines all out because China has raised worldwide demand for nearly everything that is dug or drilled out of the earth. Excel needs twenty-five new employees to fill factory and technology jobs. Its human resources department has scoured the local workforce, interviewed dozens of candidates, and come up empty. It has given up looking for people without jobs to walk in and has now set its sights on recruiting from other companies.

Thus does Excel's current wish to service China's demand carry an ominous note. For all the talk in the United States and other industrialized countries about the loss of manufacturing jobs, open positions can be tough to fill. Workers with factory experience simply are not out in the market looking, and new high school and college graduates do not see manufacturing, especially basic manufacturing, as a good career bet. Meanwhile, Excel's competitors in China have the opposite problem. They must sift through a surplus of willing workers, including an oversupply of graduates from universities and technical schools who enter the workforce with superb skills.

One place that Excel's job search may lead to is Chicago. China's development as a low-cost manufacturing center is one reason Chicago is now a good place to find out-of-work industrial workers. The city and its neighbors lost one hundred thousand factory jobs over the three years ending in 2003 and, in 2003 alone, lost more jobs than any other American urban center. Nonetheless, manufacturing remains crucial in the Chicago area, employing 622,000 people in twenty-three thousand factories. Despite the job losses, the Chicago area—including counties in Indiana—remains America's leading industrial metropolitan region with $59 billion in sales of manufactured goods.[16] The fortunes of manufacturing still have immediate and powerful effects in the city. Using just one measure, the foreclosure on homes by owners who can no longer keep up their mortgage payments has recently been a near mirror for manufacturing losses. According to Foreclosures.com, an online trade publication, it is not just the immediate job losses at factories that cause hardships, but the undermining of the professional and service sectors that cater to manufacturers. The City of Big Shoulders is no longer defined by its blue-collared muscle.

When Mexican Factories Go to China, Mexicans Come to America

Interestingly, if Parsons's recruiters come looking, they may find workers who have been displaced not once, but twice: once in Chicago, and once in Mexico. Mexican migration into Chicago has grown so fast over the last fifteen years that today one in thirteen residents of the region—

around seven hundred thousand—is of Mexican descent. The surge has grown stronger in recent years as Mexico itself is losing manufacturing jobs to China.

Despite the fears of "the giant sucking sound" (to quote the quixotic 1992 American presidential candidate Ross Perot) expected by many Americans who feared U.S. manufacturing would flee to Mexico following the passage of NAFTA in 1994, in the end, both Americans and Mexicans in manufacturing proved at risk. According to the Mexican government, the country lost 218,000 manufacturing jobs when five hundred of the thirty-seven hundred export-only maquiladoras closed between 2001 and the end of 2003.[17]

Clustered along the Mexican-U.S. border, and often terribly abusive of their workers, maquiladoras tend to be the kind of low-cost assembly plants that compete most directly with Chinese manufacturers. They are often earlier, smaller versions of the big industrial barns and mega assembly lines springing up in Guangdong and around Shanghai, and compared with the bustle of the Chinese plants, one of which can *alone* employ and house 10 percent of all maquiladora workers, the Mexican versions look like dormant outposts.*

But their closings only tell part of the story. Nearly two hundred thousand more maquiladora jobs were shed from factories that are still running.[18] Frequently, pay for the jobs that remained shrank too. The Mexican Ministry of Labor says that the country's workers now earn less than they did in 1993. The *Washington Post* reports that laborers in Mexican furniture factories, which are under intense competition from their Chinese counterparts—earn half of what they did a decade ago.[19]

While Mexico's manufacturing fell into a slump, China's roared. In Guadalajara, the center of Mexico's export electronics industry, the factories of the big international companies that assemble there operate at only 60 percent of capacity now that production of high-volume goods such as mobile phones and computer-networking equipment has been relocated to China.[20] Workers at a Sony plant in Nuevo Laredo were reportedly forced to make concessions to better match Chinese labor rates. "The company began threatening to move to China when it

---

*The three factory complexes of Dongguan shoemaker Yue Yuen employ 250,000 people.

began lowering wages and benefits in 2001," recalled Nelly Benitez, a former employee at the factory. "Weekly salaries were dropped from about eight hundred pesos to six hundred pesos."[21] Or from $70 to $52. Newspapers carry charged headlines, such as the one that read "China: The Enemy to Vanquish."[22] But not much vanquishing is going on. U.S. Department of Commerce data show that from 2002 through 2003, Mexico lost market share in thirteen of its top twenty export industries, nearly always to China.

One way out for Mexico's workers, especially those in skilled trades, is to head north to the United States, where they can find work in American factories seeking to slash their own costs to compete with Chinese competition. Mexican maquiladora workers, on average, earn about four times what Chinese workers do, but they earn only about one-seventh of what American factory workers do. Employers at plants like those in Chicago found they could take on nonunionized Mexican factory workers at half the wage of the more senior workers. Part of the bargain was that employers could free themselves of having to pay added benefits, such as health care. In Chicago, one in five Mexican workers has a factory job.

A two-tiered workforce can be hard to manage, and so far Parsons has not had to scale back pay for his Pekin workers. If Excel hired an immigrant Mexican out of Chicago, it would be for his skills and availability.

Meanwhile, the riches of the Chinese workforce make Parsons shake his head. When told of a nine-year-old Shanghai company (which we will examine in a later chapter) that became the world's leader in cast aluminum wheels for cars just a few years after its founding, Parsons sinks into his chair. "How can such a company find the skilled labor it needed to grow so quickly?" he asks.

When told further that the wheel company is now in the car business turning out tens of thousands of light trucks a year, assembled largely by recent graduates of China's technical high schools using hand tools, he says, "I find that vision frightening."

Parsons has China on his mind for still other reasons. In 2003 and 2004, the prices of copper and iron, like oil, skyrocketed in response to Chinese demand, thereby driving up Excel's costs. Yet at the same time, Excel's international mining customers have been buying more

Excel products in order to feed that same Chinese appetite for commodities. Excel's business in Australia, where mines are booming, has been doing well lately. The world's largest diversified mining company is Melbourne's BHP Billiton Group. In 2003–4, it recorded the largest corporate profit in Australian history, earned in no small part because of the strength of China's demand for raw materials and the resultant spike in world commodity prices.*

Parsons himself hopes to catch some of the China boom. He has just started a new company that will build machines called Raptors, which crush rock for use in construction, including the manufacture of concrete. The new plant is being built in the Pekin Enterprise Zone, or PEZ, with the help of state tax credits. Pekin's PEZ is tiny compared with China's booming Special Economic Zones, but it nevertheless offered enough incentives to help get Parsons's new venture off the ground. He will sell and service his new machines first in the United States and hone the business to compete internationally. Until China took off, it would have been hard to see gravel-making machines as a growth business, but Parsons now has it in his mind that his new machines can fit into China's frenzied construction boom nicely.

But Excel is bucking recent trends. A 2003 survey of Illinois manufacturers found that thirteen out of every twenty firms face competition from China. Of those, 84 percent stated that Chinese competition hurt their sales by an average of 17 percent that year. Losses were expected to grow to 26 percent by 2007.[23] The vast majority of manufacturers in the survey said that they thought Chinese manufacturers could produce

---

*Australia may be the one country that is more euphoric about China's growth than China itself. The reason is that China is signing up Australia to huge multiyear resource deals that no other country can match, including tens of billions of dollars' worth of commitments to buy Australian natural gas. The Australians are so high on the prospects of growth due to Chinese demand that in October 2003 when Chinese President Hu Jintao addressed the Australian federal Parliament in Canberra, he was greeted with warm ovations. Australian leaders also lavished attention on Hu during his three-day visit, and he was praised in the local press. In contrast, U.S. president George Bush, who was in Australia just the day before, was heckled in the Australian Parliament, excoriated in the press, and merely offered a barbecue lunch with sports stars and conservative businessmen. "The United States thinks we are as ambivalent about China's rise as the United States is," a former senior official in the Australian defense department told the *New York Times,* adding that "Australia wants Washington to understand how important China is to us."

competitive products at lower cost. One reason they cited was that the Chinese can often receive financial support at far better terms than manufacturers in Illinois. That includes government subsidies and other assistance such as loans from Chinese government banks that are offered cheaply and often with little expectation that they will be paid back. For a manufacturer in Pekin or anywhere else in America to expect to get similar terms is absurd.

Lower Prices, Year after Year!

Leaving the peaceful lane that is home to Excel and driving down through the business district to the strip malls at the edge of town where people shop, one comes to Pekin's Wal-Mart Supercenter, another element of China's creeping influence on the town.

Not outwardly, however. To the contrary, the store is a bastion of brand-name America. Its colors are patriotic, its smiley-faced mascot a corporate emblem of American cheerfulness. Wal-Mart openly supported its hundreds of employees called into national service for the war in Iraq by protecting their jobs. In November 2003, at the 9th Annual American Veterans Awards, broadcast later on the History Channel, Wal-Mart was granted the Corporate Patriotism Award. Tom Coughlin, vice chairman of Wal-Mart, accepted, saying, "Wal-Mart . . . associates are proud to support our country and serve our communities. . . . Veterans are an important part of our community, representing the values that make our country great. We're honored to receive this award and our associates will continue to honor members of the military and their families."[24] What the stores today do not boast are the company's famous old banners entreating shoppers to "Buy American" and "Bring It Home to the USA."

Walking into Pekin's store, one is greeted by an elderly woman in the familiar Wal-Mart blue polo shirt emblazoned with the company name and Always Low Prices motto over the heart. She offers a tired, forced smile. Perhaps she is nearing the end of her shift. Perhaps she is someone who wishes she were happily retired, but whose pension does not add up.

Wal-Mart does not pay as well as many other retailers, but it is an embracing employer. Workers in the Pekin store range from the elderly to young people who have just entered the workforce. The company is famously forgiving of its workers' personal tastes outside work, and some of the younger clerks have rebel hairdos combed and pinned into a semblance of responsibility, their multiple piercings sparingly adorned. Some clerks are missing teeth, and some are unhealthily obese. The company is even known for taking on the mentally handicapped. In the aisles one meets workers who seem not to belong either because they are too bright or too slow, too antsy or too old, but Wal-Mart finds a fruitful place for them. Receiving an average wage of about $8 an hour (which for a year's work is below the poverty threshold for a family of four), many do not work in the store for long, however. In the United States, about half of the stores' workers leave in a given year.

At midday in the Pekin store, most of the customers filling the aisles are mothers with young children in tow, and senior citizens in pairs. The moms' carts are piled over the rims with diapers, cleaning supplies, cartons of milk, soda pop, and other groceries. The seniors do not buy a great deal and seem to visit the store as much for exercise as for merchandise.

This is Pekin's second Wal-Mart. Its predecessor opened in 1985 and is now slated to house a new Sears store. Wal-Mart is renting the old property out because the building could not accommodate the growth in products Wal-Mart sells. Pekin's newer Wal-Mart has 203,000 square feet and is one of the first wave of one thousand extralarge supercenters that Wal-Mart plans to build in the United States.

As the company's stores get larger, they take a bigger chunk out of Americans' disposable incomes and a bigger chunk of their competitors' bottom lines. Today, Wal-Mart is a big enough part of the local economy to warrant a ribbon-cutting ceremony by "Ambassadors and Directors of the Pekin Area Chamber of Commerce." Why the hoopla? Wal-Mart's three stores within a forty-minute-driving radius of Pekin make the company one of central Illinois' largest employers.

Wal-Mart's local importance in Pekin is the direct result of the company's global power. Among the things Wal-Mart shares with China is the ability to shock with its size. The retailer is now the world's largest company. Charles Fishman, who profiled Wal-Mart in the December 2003 issue of the business magazine *Fast Company,* noted that Wal-Mart is bigger than ExxonMobile, General Electric, and General Motors, and that its annual sales exceed those of rivals Target, Sears, Kmart, JCPenney, Safeway, and Kroger *combined*.[25] Wal-Mart's 2003 annual sales of $260 billion matched the gross domestic product of Switzerland, which will soon fall behind. Then again, twice as many people, 14 million in all, shop at Wal-Mart every day as live in Switzerland. And Wal-Mart's workforce of 1.4 million—the world's largest for a private company— is one-fifth the size of the Swiss population. The company plans to add the thousand new stores to its current three thousand will swell its rolls by eight hundred thousand retail workers. Between the company's high rate of employee turnover and the new store openings, Wal-Mart must find more than half a million new workers in the United States every year.

Wal-Mart's growth as an economic force is inseparable from China's rise as a manufacturing giant. No company in the world has embraced China's potential more vigorously than Wal-Mart, and no company has been a bigger catalyst in pushing American, European, and Japanese manufacturers to China. The *Los Angeles Times* series on the company in late 2003 noted that in 1995, with only 6 percent of the stores' merchandise coming from abroad, nearly everything sold at Wal-Mart was indeed "made in America." Estimates of how much of Wal-Mart's merchandise comes from abroad today range from 50 to 85 percent.

Chinese factories are, by far, the most important and fastest-growing sources for the company. In 2003, Wal-Mart purchased $15 billion worth of goods from Chinese suppliers. A whopping portion of between 10 and 13 percent of everything China has sent to the United States winds up on Wal-Mart's shelves. Writing in the *Washington Post*, Peter Goodman and Phillip Pan reported in February 2004 that "more than 80 percent of the six thousand factories in Wal-Mart's worldwide database of suppliers are in China." The company has 560 people on the ground in the country to negotiate and make purchases for the chain.[26] Goodman and Pan note that if Wal-Mart were a nation, it would be China's fifth-largest export market, ahead of Germany and Great Britain.[27] Wal-Mart's trade with and in China accounts for 1.5 percent of that country's gross domestic product.

World-Class Speed and Strength

Wal-Mart is often demonized for its part in shipping U.S. manufacturing jobs overseas. It is difficult, however, to separate the role of Wal-Mart's thousands of suppliers in the migration of manufacturing out of the United States from the larger global trends realigning how and where the world makes things. If Wal-Mart has a unique part in the trend, it is in how expertly the company has managed that trend and, in so doing, accelerated it. One way to think of Wal-Mart is not simply as a store chain, but as a delivery service devoted to bringing goods to its customers at the lowest possible price that will still yield a profit.

To that end, the company has developed what is almost certainly the world's broadest and most technologically advanced systems for finding low-cost goods and delivering them to its stores in the most efficient manner possible. Wal-Mart, for instance, has the world's largest private network of satellites, deployed to keep tabs on merchandise as it works its way around the world. It is currently implementing a system called Radio Frequency Identification, or RFID, which will track every single carton of goods sold to Wal-Mart from its creation on the shop floor until the box is carted empty out of a Wal-Mart store. The RFID system will allow Wal-Mart to manage inventories so tightly that it in effect makes Chinese factories behave as if they were down the street from the stores where their goods are sold. Smaller clothing, hardware, and toy stores, especially those owned by a community's local shopkeepers, have had trouble surviving Wal-Mart to date, but over time the company's reach across the world's supply chain makes it an ever more daunting competitor.

Wal-Mart is so strong that it alone can force companies to change the way they make things. Often that change is to move production to China. One of the ironies of global supply networks is that they often appear to take the form of exactly the kind of industrial organization they have defeated.

Merrill Weingrod, the Providence, Rhode Island, consultant affiliated with Kurt Salmon Associates, notes that international sourcing has been the norm in some large American industries for the last fifty years. "It used to be the companies grew large by vertically integrating their production, bringing the manufacture of a wide range of products and components under one roof. When Japan began to reemerge as an industrial power after World War II, the first companies that figured out they could go to Japanese factories and get things cheaper could gain a strong advantage over their competitors." Weingrod explains that while Japan did not remain a low-cost source for long, it nevertheless began the trend in which American companies made less and shopped the world more. "The shoe industry has been doing that for decades." When Wal-Mart shifted to international sourcing in the 1990s, it did so with such wide reach, and so comprehensively, that the company now looks something like the large vertically integrated manufacturers and marketers of old. While the company does not actually make anything, Weingrod says, it forges alliances with large foreign manufacturers that in essence make them captive to Wal-Mart. What's more, the company's intelligence about its own markets is so complete that it knows full well how much it costs its suppliers to manufacture for it. In some cases, Wal-Mart can even force open a supplier's books and glean costs down to the penny. That forces suppliers to produce at ever-lower prices. Its essential presence in Chinese manufacturing, where it is likely to be the dominant customer of the factories that serve it, gives the company an unmatchable power to set prices. As long as it holds its manufacturers captive, that power rises. And as Wal-Mart's pricing power gains, so does its competitive advantage over its rivals. China's low-cost manufacturing machine feeds Wal-Mart's critical mass by allowing companies to build assembly lines that are so huge that they achieve ever-greater economies of scale and drive prices downward all the more.

Wal-Mart's Chinese suppliers often make startling, market-shaking price cuts. By selling portable DVD players with seven-inch LCD screens from China for less than $200, for instance, Wal-Mart recently helped to cut the price of these trendy devices in half. Even with super-low prices, Chinese factories can sell in such giant quantities that they willingly oblige. To get ready for its big Thanksgiving sale in 2002, Wal-Mart picked Sichuan Changhong Electric, one of the world's largest makers of televisions, to supply sets under the Apex Digital brand. Changhong makes 15 million TVs a year, most of them for export. Eight of ten shipped overseas go to the United States. In 2002, its sets at Wal-Mart sold for far less than comparable models from other makers, sometimes undercutting the competition by $100 or more. The models the company delivered for the sale helped the event net $1.4 billion and led to a doubling of profits at Changhong.*

Wal-Mart's clout is felt no less by its American suppliers. When companies do business with Wal-Mart, they meet a tough negotiator that demands that products be delivered exactly on time and at the negotiated price. They must also expect Wal-Mart's push to drive prices down over time. Rather than letting manufacturers raise their prices as time goes on, Wal-Mart expects yearly reductions. The McKinsey Global Institute, a research arm of the big management consultant McKinsey, estimates that from 1995 to 1999, Wal-Mart itself drove a 4 percent improvement in U.S. productivity, the chief measure of economic efficiency. Yet, the big shift in Wal-Mart's supply base to China points to another fact. No matter how efficient Wal-Mart's American manufacturers get, most could not compete with factories in China, where wages are a small fraction of those in the United States.

Wal-Mart, says Charles Fishman, is legendary for forcing its suppliers to reshape their businesses, and just as well-known for dictating what it is willing to pay. While no companies are forced to do business with Wal-Mart, not doing business with the company means being shut out of the store where most of America, and increasingly, the world, shops. He relates the story of an American umbrella manufacturer who, facing rising costs, asked Wal-Mart for a 5 percent price hike. Wal-Mart answered that it needed a 5 percent price reduction. The manufacturer could not meet the price, and Wal-Mart found a Chinese company that could. Until recently, Wal-Mart's potential as a seller of branded clothing remained untapped. Now that quotas are scheduled to end on clothing and textiles, China will be able to export clothing freely to the United States. Wal-Mart is expected to use its links into the country to charge head-on at the world's clothing retailers. No doubt, consumers will see clothing prices drop as Wal-Mart, true to form, passes on savings to its customers.

---

*Wal-Mart's negotiating prowess was not the only factor driving low prices on the sets. The company also benefited from the vast overcapacity in Chinese factories, which can produce nine times more televisions than Chinese consumers are willing to buy. The flooding of sets into the U.S. market at such low prices also raised a red flag with U.S. regulators, who slapped $450 million in dumping penalties on some Chinese makers in 2004.

Cutthroat competition overseas forces Chinese factories to squeeze their low-paid workers by adding to their workweek or forcing over-time. In Guangdong, where Wal-Mart's suppliers are heavily concen-trated, many export-driven factories have been having trouble finding workers to meet their demanding schedules. The provincial government notes that there is, amazingly, a shortage of 2 million people on the area's assembly lines. To fill the jobs, employers must search farther and far-ther into the Chinese countryside where stories of the factory conditions are rarer and the poverty deeper.* For its part, Wal-Mart has a team of factory inspectors who tour facilities to ensure compliance with the local labor standards that require a minimum wage and restrict overtime. Its ability to police abuse is, however, limited by the ingenuity of plant man-agers, who often farm work out to subcontractors who are not subject to inspection.

So nearly every shopper in Pekin will save money by shopping at Wal-Mart—which is to say the shoppers will profit from the retailer's China connection. Of course, this very connection may also contribute to Wal-Mart's ability to drive other area stores out of business. If the town's retail landscape changes to include more secondhand shops, used-book stores, and coffee bars, it will be because Wal-Mart will have done to Pekin what it has done to so many other places—force local businesses to adjust around it. Or close.

In short, Pekin, Illinois, is not so different from many American towns. China is right around the corner.

Dreaming of a Bavarian Christmas

As the core of Pekin's shopping district has moved to the edge of town, the city's downtown shops have been vacated. Some merchants tried

---

*These strategies echo some of those in Wal-Mart stores. In October 2003, U.S. immi-gration officials raided sixty Wal-Mart stores in twenty-one states and arrested 250 immi-grants working in the stores illegally. The workers were hired by a cleaning contractor, though the officials claim that Wal-Mart had full knowledge of their presence in its stores. Several cases related to the raids were working their way through the courts in 2004. The case shows how the company's relentless demand for cost savings links the fate of low-wage Mexican workers in the United States with those in Chinese factories.

their luck in malls, while others simply faded away in the face of competition. Today, the old storefronts hold a mix of professional offices, tired antique shops, and a select few shops that are still genuine destinations. One of those is the city's one locally owned gift store, B' Ribbonned, Etc., run by Althea Geiser. Each year, when Pekin holds its Main Street Christmas festival, trees around town take on the look of an old European holiday. Some of the decorations come from Geiser's shop, which is given over to Christmas each December.

"I go to gift shows in Chicago every year to make my purchases," Geiser says. "There I mostly buy traditional pieces."

Traditional or not, nearly everything she orders is imported. Lately, the shop's top sellers come from China. Plastic ice cubes cobbled together and painted to look like snowmen fly off the shelves, and so do frilly balls made from peacock feathers. The angels, wise men, and little carolers that give the Main Street festival its old European look do well too. Geiser, however, does not buy ornaments from Europe. "They cost at least twice as much, and few of my customers would pay that if they can save a few dollars on something else."

Thus has the Christmas tree, that quintessential German symbol of holiday hopes, become a portentous indicator of the rise of Chinese workshops. On the trees' boughs, ornament by bright ornament, the companies that created the business of Christmas now hang in the balance.

Nowhere is this more true than in Rothenburg ob der Tauber, a three star destination in the *Michelin Green Guide* to Germany. The town is one of the highlights on one of the world's most celebrated tourist routes, the Romantische Strasse, or Romantic Road, the country lane that wends through Bavaria's postcard-perfect ancient towns and ends down the road from Mad King Ludwig's famous white fairy castle at Neuschwangau.

From afar, the city looks like a porcelain Christmas village, with its crowded roofline of white-stuccoed Bavarian town houses, stone cathedral spires, and ancient clock towers. Once inside the gate, the city is a maze of stone streets, shops, centuries-old homes, open churches, halls, and inns. Within these old stone walls, Rothenburg hummed with commercial activity in the late Middle Ages, when its craft guilds were so strong and wealthy that their city was governed as a free state rather than under the thumb of German kings. A hilltop location and a massive fort helped.

Rothenburg may appear virtually unchanged in the last few hundred years, but signs and portents of its future can be divined, especially if one looks across from St. Jacob's Church to the Lotus Hotel, the only inn in Rothenburg where Buddha stands guard over an arched rathskeller-style restaurant. The Lotus Restaurant is the first local restaurant to serve authentic Cantonese food, and demand these days is high.

Rothenburg is used to Asian tourists. The town of twelve thousand usually enjoys about six hundred thousand overnight stays by Japanese tourists each year. They come to Rothenburg to savor its authentic German qualities, digging into sausages and sauerkraut, smoked veal, German beer and wines. Over the last few years, however, the town's tourism board has been energetically marketing Rothenburg to Chinese travel authorities and agencies. The effort is led by the director of tourism, Johann Kempter, a man in his fifties who is as hale, elegant, and worldly as a top corporate executive.

"As a very small town with a limited budget, we are not able to get into the tremendous and great Chinese market without other partners," he says. "Germany opened a National Tourist Board in Beijing about the year 2000, and we now can cooperate with this office and another office in Shanghai as well. In the last years, we met the travel trade in different towns such as Hong Kong, Guangzhou, Xi'an." Kempter has had some success. "We're just beginning," he says, "but that's just what we did with the Japanese. There may be only a small fraction of Chinese who can afford European travel, but a small fraction of the Chinese can add up to a very big group."

One of Kempter's chief challenges has been in organizing tours that make Chinese travelers comfortable. "They really like to stay in their own groups and eat only their own food," he says, "so we make special arrangements for them." The Lotus, run by a Hong Kong family, is one place where Chinese tourists can feel comfortable. It is far from the most expensive or most luxurious hotel, but it does have silk Chinese fans over the beds.

Rothenburg will acquire more Chinese flavor in the years to come. One German marketing firm estimates that the number of tourists from the People's Republic is growing so fast—between 10 and 15 percent a year—that eventually they will overtake the Japanese. (In anticipation, Berlin has launched Chinese-language Web sites.) In 2004, 20 million tourists from China traveled abroad, around the same number as international travelers from Japan. At current rates of growth, China's globe-trotting population will rank fourth among nations by 2020.[28] Eighty-five million Chinese can now afford to travel overseas,[29] which makes the world tourism business giddy in anticipation. In 2003, twenty thousand came to Germany, though, of course, not all came to Rothenburg.

The must-see sights for tourists in Rothenburg include the Christmas shops. Such shops now proliferate in popular tourist destinations in Europe and North America, such as Colonial Williamsburg, Virginia, or Edinburgh, Scotland. In the United States, the shops have also appeared in nearly any city, town, or outlet mall that attracts high pedestrian traffic, as well as on the Internet, where one can surf Christmas shops' auction sites. Elsewhere, as in Pekin, local gift stores morph into Christmas shops when the time comes. In all these locations, one can find Italian-style glass, top-hatted caroling dolls from Dickens, and miniature piñatas, and no matter where the shops sell, a thick dose of frosty Germanic Christmases.

Rothenburg is the place where the proliferation of Christmas shops began. The first and still premier show in town is Käthe Wohlfahrt's Christmas Shop. In fact, there are several of them, and Wohlfahrt's today is almost certainly one of the small city's biggest businesses, pulling in some $22 million a year. The shops are built as scale Christmas villages, replicating year-round the holiday markets that spring up around the country. Germans are fanatical about the quality of their toys, and it shows. Inside is a riot of little lights, glitter, and frosting, with giant bows and little angels. Model trains and nutcrackers. Santas of all sizes hang everywhere, German craftsmanship on full display.

The success of the Wohlfahrt shops has not gone unchallenged, however. Nor have the high prices of its German-made ornaments. Rothenburg and other Bavarian towns now have rival Christmas shops that sell at considerably lower prices, often by bringing in imported items, including many from China. For buyers who want heirloom hardwood or ceramic ornaments painted and glazed in the traditional manner, only locally made ones will do—or at least the ones that best approximate them.

"It was evident that the Wohlfahrt company had to go to Asia to produce the items there as the clients are even looking for lower prices in the shops," says Johann Kempter, who keeps in close touch with the Christmas business so essential to Rothenburg. "I think that Rothenburg is not an island in the market, and we can't have luxury prices and luxury products only. Souvenirs and Christmas decorations as well have a great variety and diversification and follow the changes in the market. If you have a product which sells, you find copies in a very short time."

Some low-cost imported ornaments fill their expected role as slapdash, perishable merchandise. Wohlfahrt's shies away from those, but competitors do not. Most worrisome to the local German manufacturers with long histories of making finely crafted, durable ornaments is that the Chinese ornaments look better all the time.

A quick inspection of the merchandise in shops and online venues selling Chinese Christmas products shows how remarkably close Chinese manufacturers come to their premium European competition. They know their markets too, because they study them. Deutsche Welle, the German government-run news service, recently examined trade in Hamburg, Germany's largest port. It noted that China is the port's most important trading partner, accounting for one-sixth of its business, with double-digit growth expected every year in the foreseeable future. As of 2004, no fewer than 320 Chinese shipping companies had offices in Hamburg. Toys were among their highest-volume imports into Germany. German toy makers are worried enough about the competition from China that their trade association has recently pressed their members and the Chinese government into supporting anticounterfeiting measures.

At the Christmas shops in Rothenburg, the coming of the Chinese tourists is bound to be a mixed blessing. Many will drop in for mementos of their trip, but just enough will come looking around with more than casual interest, taking close stock of every rouge-cheeked piper, every fat, little-freckled, rouge-cheeked chef holding a Christmas pudding, and each smiling daisy. The tourists walking out with the largest shopping bags may be the ones least welcome. They are bringing the goods back to their own workshops.

The Elves Get Scrooged

And how are these Chinese-German Christmas ornaments made? The spirit of the holiday opens a window onto the global marketplace, when the international press is often moved to peer into the means of manufacturing toys and ornaments. Two of Washington, D.C.'s newspapers, the quirky *Washington Times,* owned by the Unification Church, and the *Washington Post,* took long looks at the holiday trade in 2003. Both wound up in Yiwu in Zhejiang Province. The *Washington Times* took a stroll through the town's own Futian Market, which, unlike that in Rothenburg, is devoted to commercial sales to merchants, nearly all selling outside China. *Seven thousand* shops sell the Christmas wares in the Futian stalls. (By comparison, the Mall of America in St. Paul, Minnesota, the largest shopping place in the United States, has a mere six hundred shops.) The market does not stick to Christmas goods. It also hawks evergreen religious knickknacks such as framed pictures of Jesus, Hindu posters, calligraphic Islamic jewelry, and, the *Times* noted, even images of the Dalai Lama, which are elsewhere banned in China. But Christmas is undoubtedly big business. Fake trees as tall as a man cost $4, and a package of six shimmering ornaments costs thirty-six cents. The bargains add up. Nationwide, China's three thousand Christmas-decoration factories exported over $900 million in Christmas decorations in the first ten months of 2003.[30]

For its part, the *Washington Post* story detailed a Yiwu factory and described how a Mr. Zhang, the owner of the Shuitou Co. in town, had little understanding of Christmas beyond knowing that it had something to do with the thousands of short fat men in red suits that pass him every day at the plant.

Zhang's facility, according to the paper, is a common Chinese gewgaw mill, with gritty working conditions. Migrant laborers earning $100 a month "squat in front of hissing machinery as they melt chips into moldable plastic, pulling levers by hand to squeeze out Christmas tree ornaments." Barefoot women shave extra bits of plastic off the molded items, and men shred and weave sharp strands of plastic into fake trees by hand.

Neither Mr. Zhang nor his workers have any comprehension of

Christmas's religious meaning, but they do know that the Christmas business is but part of the $10 billion export trade in toys and ornaments that ship out of China each year.[31] For the ornament sellers in Rothenburg, the tide of Chinese knickknacks, some of them disposable junk, but others high-quality crafts, is a backdrop to all they do.

Why Germany Must Look East to Find Itself

While German toy and craft makers deal with the onslaught of competitive Chinese merchandise, for the German economy as a whole China's economic rise has been a mixed blessing, stirred, so far, with more sweet than sour.

Unlike the trade between the United States and China, which gets more stunningly lopsided every year in favor of the Chinese, Germany's trade with China stays roughly in balance, often tipping in favor of the Germans. A key factor is that the Germans make the machines that fill the tens of thousands of Chinese factories that have sprung up in the last decade. The Chinese need machine tools, molding and forging equipment, and whole computerized electronic assembly lines. Tour nearly any of China's new megafactories making electronics, and the semitrailer-size, million-dollar automatic machines that make the guts of the devices are bound to be supplied by Siemens, Germany's premier electrical and electronics conglomerate.

The company is a major player in building up many of the big industries that China needs to be a complete manufacturing base. The company's short list of industries it supplies includes metallurgy, petrochemical, power generation, glass, cement, water processing, automotive, medical equipment, telecommunications, transportation, food and beverage production, and packaging. Siemens has some forty-five companies operating in China, employs thirty thousand people there, and sold $5 billion worth of equipment in the country in 2003. As with many companies that make up the bulk of Germany's share of the two countries' bilateral trade, Siemens sells China big-ticket items it needs to compete with all the world's manufacturing nations.

The Germans let little get in their way when doing business with the Chinese. When Chinese leaders visit Germany, they visit big factories of such companies as Siemens, DaimlerChrysler, and VW. When German leaders visit China, they ink trade deals. Politics? Human rights? Taiwan? Tibet? Those are issues for the United States and China to quarrel about, in the German view.

Even if the European market for industrial machinery stagnates, China is a market where Germany can sell enough new equipment to keep German companies growing. China is one place, in other words, where Germany has a shot at earning enough to buy itself time as it struggles to maintain the lifestyle it built for its citizens during its own fabulous boom years following World War II. The country rose from the ashes of the Nazi defeat to erect an economy that today grants its citizens one of the highest standards of living in the world. The Germans also erected one of the most generous social welfare systems in the world, a key factor that helps keep the German living standard high. And high-priced. It costs both the state and German employers, who must pay for generous benefits. In China, German companies succeed by skirting the weight of high labor costs and an expensive social service system at home.

Volkswagen, for example, is one of the crown jewels of the country's China trade. It was the first foreign carmaker to manufacture in China, and for years it was far and away the dominant carmaker in the country, with over 50 percent of the market. Now its share is closer to 30 percent, but the Chinese market for cars has grown dramatically and VW still does well. Last year, tellingly, the company's profits from China were the only robust numbers in all of the company's global markets. Without China, VW's bottom line would look like a sea of red ink. Volkswagen is doubling its bet too, announcing in 2004 that it would spend nearly $8 billion to boost production as the competition in the Chinese car market began to grow cutthroat.

The German approach has risks. As German machines are sold into the Chinese market, German engineers and corporate educators follow, teaching their Chinese customers, or the Chinese who run the plants for big multinationals, how to use the equipment to create world-class products.

In fact, one can see how the German approach distinguishes itself merely by walking after hours in any of China's cities that attract foreign workers, such as Beijing or Shanghai. Run into Americans or Brits in these cities and they look utterly immersed in the privileges of expatriate executive life—Gatsbys on the Huangpu, sporting an MBA chic worthy of a low-angle portrait in *Fortune* magazine, wearing tailored suits or preppie casual clothing that allows one to roll up the sleeves of a pinpoint Oxford shirt. There is, admittedly, a large contingent of Germans who cut similar figures, many wearing mod designer eyeglasses that give them away as surely as a plate of Bavarian *Schweinshaxe,* but there are also the many German mechanics and line managers, bulky men with wide mustaches who leave work in their coveralls and stop at the convenience stores to buy multiple six-packs of Tsingtao beer, the one first made by their countrymen in the former German-dominated port city of Qingdao.* American companies generally try to push as much management into Chinese hands as soon as possible. The Germans like to remain more hands-on.

Meanwhile, Chinese goods are making sharp quality improvements in virtually every product category. This is evident in electronics and building materials, where high-quality goods rapidly dropped in price as China's industries grew more expert and capacious. But it is also true of low-tech products such as toys, where Chinese factories have the double advantage of extremely low labor costs and, increasingly, the world's most up-to-date equipment for designing, shaping, and finishing their goods. The chief challenge to China's ascendancy in these goods is its appetite for making them, which drives up the price of raw materials. Even so, while raw material prices escalate in roughly equal measure for both countries, Chinese labor costs remain negligible by German pay standards, which, not incidentally, are the highest in the world.

Europe still does not have a dominant retailer such as America's Wal-Mart (not even Wal-Mart in Europe) that can take the lead in forcing Chinese-made goods into the retail market. What Germans face instead is a

---

*China's beer market has recently been a battleground for the world's large brewers, each struggling for a foothold in what is widely expected to be the world's thirstiest market. A report from the Access Asia research group found that beer consumption rose at the "astounding pace" of 17 percent from 1997 until 2003, even though China's per capita consumption is still far below that of other Asian nations. That means it has lots of room to grow, a fact that has attracted America's Anheuser-Busch, the maker of Budweiser, which owns both a 27 percent stake in Tsingtao and a 97 percent stake in Budweiser Wuhan, and London-based SABMiller, which owns a large part of China Resources Breweries, China's second-largest beer-maker. Dutch, Japanese, and Danish breweries are also heavily invested in China.

world everywhere forced by China to work smarter and harder, to make more efficient use of its labor and capital. Even where competition does not force German firms to move production all the way to China, the pressure to leave Germany is high. Many firms turn to the post-Communist economies of Eastern Europe, especially the Czech Republic and Hungary, to join the global fray, using those low-wage markets to get an edge on Chinese factories. That, of course, is good news for Eastern Europe, which often pits itself against Chinese manufacturers when Western European and American producers look to move offshore and when their own companies try to gain global footholds with lower-priced goods.

In Germany, the corporate smart money is way ahead of any political resolution of the forces at work. A poll disseminated by the German Chambers of Industry and Commerce (DIHK) indicated that German firms are making foreign investments at a pace unrivaled in the country's history. The big change reflects what's happening in other large economies; smaller and medium German firms that have until recently fiercely stuck close to home are joining the big German multinationals on the prowl for new markets and lower costs. To make the move, the report found, German firms are reducing their investments in their home country. Recently, Germans workers have been forced to work longer hours and take shorter vacations to help Germany's domestic industries better compete in a leaner, harder-working world, the world it helps create by bringing China up to speed. Siemens led the charge against old work rules hammered out over decades with German unions. The company threatened to move thousands of jobs out of Germany unless its workers put in longer hours at no extra cost to the company and successfully forced concessions. That hard-nosed approach emboldened Germany's smaller companies to make similar demands and to move production abroad.

For the Christmas shops in Rothenburg, the new German work rules may pose an additional problem: many of Germany's tourists now have less time and money to make the trip to the Bavarian town.

Noodle Wars

The case of Rothenburg's Christmas ornaments offers an example of how China is able to manufacture items that once appeared to embody the essence of the nation that originally produced them. Germany's artisans are not alone. The glassblowers of Italy, Belgian lace makers, the Russian artists who carve and paint enameled nesting dolls, and the batik makers of Java can all log on to the Internet and find Chinese sellers offering credible knockoffs of their national crafts. The Ningbo Topluck company makes fine cowboy hats. On www.africaimports.com one can find a variety of African-style masks and the statue of a Benin queen among the items made in China. Now that Chinese travel the world in larger numbers, they often return home with the bittersweet observation that all the foreign souvenirs are made in China.

Fifty years ago, the Japanese made similar observations. Back then their economy turned out the souvenir ashtrays, snow globes, and ceramic statuettes that were their country's calling card before the arrival of Panasonic and Toyota. It's interesting to wonder what the many Japanese tourists in Germany think as they see MADE IN CHINA labels on "German" Christmas ornaments. After all, China is encroaching on certain "Japanese" products, not just digital cameras and high-definition televisions, but also low-tech, low-cost items that are simpler emblems of Japanese identity.

One of the more curious of these items is ramen noodles, and if one wants to sample authentic Japanese ramen noodles, there's no better place than the island of Hokkaido, the island north of Japan's "mainland," Honshu, and east across the Sea of Japan from Russian Siberia. Sapporo, the island's capital of 1.9 million people, is far and away Hokkaido's largest city. It is best known internationally for its annual Snow Festival, during which a million visitors pile into the city to see huge models of castles, temples, and cartoon superheroes made out of snow and ice. To the Japanese, however, Sapporo is more prized for its hot treasures: the big, steaming bowls of ramen noodle soup that are a local obsession. This is the soup that is now mimicked in another Japanese innovation, instant ramen, the ubiquitous blocks of fried noodles that are now, with 65 billion packages sold a year, one of the world's most popular foods. A Chinese restaurateur introduced fresh ramen (ramen is the Japanese pronunciation of lo mein) to Sapporo in 1923, but it wasn't until 1946 that stalls began springing up in the city, which was still woefully short of food following the war years. Thus Sapporo became one of the progenitors of Japan's love affair with the Chinese-style dish, which has long since gone native with miso broths and other local touches.

Today, over a thousand ramen shops compete against each other in Sapporo, often within a chopstick's distance of one another. The contest is keenest in the late-night stalls in Ramen Alley and the nearby New Ramen Alley, which fill two narrow gangways right in the heart of Susukino, Sapporo's entertainment district. Nighttime traffic is not what it once was in Susukino. The decade and a half of economic doldrums in Japan have taken their toll on local nightlife, and local restaurants, bars, and private clubs have contracted along with the employment rolls and the entertainment budgets of corporate Japan. Late at night, the ramen rows suffer too now that fewer carousing salarymen are in need of the savory sobriety of a steaming bowl of fresh-cut noodles. Still, the sellers wave in the customers they can.

At other times of day, however, and elsewhere throughout Sapporo and Japan, ramen is on the rise. The food matches Japan's moment now that extreme frugality is again a virtue. If in the 1980s the Japanese chased every high-end food craze from Europe and the United States, today ramen is trendy and cheap.* The *Japan Times* reports that ramen chains "are going upscale, serving special pork and organic vegetables at eateries featuring dark-wood interiors and soft lighting."[32] Even dolled up, ramen is a supremely affordable luxury and one of the everyday products most visibly affected by more than a decade of falling prices throughout the Japanese economy. The country's shops and instant-noodle makers have engaged in a prolonged price war and race for market share. The noodle wars have become something of a national spectator sport, creating "ramen shop celebrities" out of the country's most famous vendors.[33]

The ramen war has spread to China, too, where affiliates of Japan's giant ramen producers are trying to assert their leadership. Instant noodles have caught on with the Chinese over the last decade. Indeed, sellers of noodle-making machines were among the first Japanese companies to test the Chinese market. Today, China has over three hundred companies that produce instant ramen. The noodles are popular because

---

*One of Tokyo's leading city magazines even has a weekly column devoted to the noodle dish.

they don't cost much. One yuan, about twelve cents, buys a whole pack, which is one-fifth the price in Japan. Chinese consumers also like the noodles because they are a Japanese version of a Chinese product, well-packaged and hygienically prepared.*

The Chinese government is working hard to get China's noodle industry in shape for volume exports. Japan is already one of the largest export markets for Chinese processed foods, which can arrive on Japanese shelves at one-tenth the cost of Japan's own goods. The price of food weighs heavily on the official measures of Japan's consumer prices, and the Chinese, when they provide top-quality goods, can push down grocery prices to levels the Japanese have not seen since the 1960s.

So a noodle that originated in China became popular in Japan, and then, when noodle manufacturers moved from Japan to China, the noodle became popular in China because of its Japanese appearance, and soon it may be even more popular in Japan because of its Chinese price. Thus does a simple bowl of ramen soup symbolize how tough it is to disentangle Japanese tastes, culture, and more than ever, the country's economy, from China's.

As Japanese manufacturing companies set up shop in China and sell Japanese industrial equipment to Chinese businesses, China can now make much of what Japan makes, matching Japan's vaunted quality and drastically undercutting Japanese costs. China is one of the few large countries with which Japan runs trade deficits because of this steady movement of Japanese production to China. More impressive still, China is now Japan's leading trade partner; the exchanges between the two countries topped Japan's bilateral trade with the United States in 2003. Much of what China sells Japan are goods made in new factories by Japanese companies for their home market. Big consumer electronics firms such as Sony, Panasonic, and Toshiba realized long ago that

---

*China's commercial food producers have come under close scrutiny following a wave of deaths resulting from shoddy and fraudulent products. In an April 2004 scandal, 130 people were arrested for making phony infant formula using starch and water and contributing to the deaths of twelve children. The Chinese government announced the next September that it had revoked the licenses of thirty thousand firms with unacceptable hygiene, and that it had much more work to do. Given that backdrop, and the look of many down-market eateries, a plastic-sealed, twelve-cent block of Japanese-style Chinese noodles can be most appealing.

Chinese factories could beat them on price and that they needed to move production there to survive. (The market for DVD players is an extreme example of the trend and is covered in depth in the next chapter.)

Japan's own demographic profile is another reason manufacturers are shifting production abroad. The population of the island nation is aging rapidly and its population shrinking. Japanese factories in China can take better aim at the Chinese market, which is growing as surely as Japan is losing promise. The Japanese now see their future prosperity tied tightly to China's growth. It would seem a sure thing if other countries did not pin similar hopes on China and have similar designs.

George Stalk, a director at the Boston Consulting Group, an international management consulting firm, spent years working in Japan and noticed a distinct shift in the mid-1990s, when, he says, "big Japanese companies saw that China was a big deal and that [they] had better move production there before their competitors did." Stalk notes that large Japanese sellers, like the Europeans, see China as a place where they can still grow despite the stagnation in their own home markets. "There are no firm figures on this, but one can estimate that around ninety percent of all the marginal growth at Japanese and European companies is coming from China. Japanese firms cannot get the big volume kicks they want in America and Europe, but in China, a big share of the market can give them real growth." While the Chinese market is its own plum, producing for a big Chinese market has additional global advantages. It allows Japan's big car, machine, and electronic manufacturers to gear up giant production facilities that can create the economies of scale that the Chinese have already achieved in socks, shoes, and clothes. One-third of all Japanese investment in China in recent years has gone to building factories that make electrical machinery, but an increasing amount of money is being spent on building up China's automobile industry now that nearly all the major Japanese car companies have made big commitments in the country.[34]

But all of this profitable interdependence is a sore subject in both countries. One of the most bitter paradoxes of the global economy is that the more people of different nations are linked together, the more they can feel fear, hate, arrogance, and nationalism. As Chinese and Japanese lives draw closer, the two peoples engage in an unceasing cycle of antagonism and rapprochement that betrays how strongly China's nineteenth- and twentieth-century humiliations motivate it today. And how Japan, which is today the least militaristic of the major powers and the practitioner of foreign policy that avoids conflict at all costs, remains nevertheless the captive of its formerly brutal self. Plainly put, the Chinese despise Japan.

Peter Hayes Gries, a political scientist at the University of Colorado, explores strains of Chinese chauvinism and xenophobia as it is expressed daily in the mainland press in his fascinating book *China's New Nationalism*.[35] "While it is possible," Gries notes, "to speak of the feelings of both love and hate that many Chinese have for America, it is decidedly not possible to speak about a genuine Chinese 'friendship' for Japan. The Chinese view the Japanese as the paradigmatic 'devils' *(guizi)* during World War II, and they continue to see them that way today."[36] He notes that while other foreigners can be "American devils" or "Western devils," when used alone, the Chinese noun for *devil* now means a Japanese person.[37] There may be no culture in the world that does not pollute its language and humanity with ethnic epithets. Japanese is as littered with them as any other language. But Chinese refer to the Japanese as devils so commonly that is amazing there is even enough goodwill between the countries to shake hands on anything.

The hatred comes out in ways that can astonish foreigners schooled in politically correct manners. Talk, for example, to a group of Chinese journalism students about the virtues of an open mind. Wax on about how preconceptions cloud facts and about the necessity of hearing all sides. The group will nod and smile. They will say how liberating that approach is and declare how much they like that way of thinking. Then one eager student will raise a hand and say, "Sir, I too believe we must keep our minds open. That is the only way people can really learn. I also have a very open mind," he will say gravely, "except for one thing. I hate the Japanese." The emotion comes on without any provocation, even if Japan is far from the subject at hand.

Gries notes that even when the Chinese refer politely to "Chinese-Japanese friendship," as the nation's press does nearly as a matter of routine when it covers relations between the two countries, the phrase is rife with overtones denoting Japan's place as China's subordinate. Moreover, Gries argues, public hatred for the Japanese has been an important tool for the Chinese state, which defines itself in opposition to its neighbors. Though Japan sits to the east of China, in the Chinese imagination Japan is regarded as "Western" because it was the conduit through which much of Western modernity was transmitted to China. Japan's early adaptation to Western-style business and politics allows China to define itself as the genuine Orient.

Yet, at the same time, China identifies with Japan as an economy that rapidly industrialized and succeeded in its modernization.[38] Japan's post–World War II industrial rise has been well-studied and admired in the halls of Chinese academe, and the Chinese finance ministries are well aware of the enormous investment strength of Japan's interlocking banks and multinational corporations. The Japanese, they know, must be played against Japan's most important economic competitor in China, the Germans, in a way that both countries are allowed to win just enough.* The manufacturing and export strengths of the two rivals in industrial equipment, automobiles, and chemicals square off with uncanny regularity in the Chinese market. So, for example, while a German consortium built and financed the prototype for a high-speed rail system in Shanghai in hopes of getting larger national projects, soon after the Shanghai line opened China's Railway Ministry awarded a rich $3.83 billion contract for cross-country trains to a group that included six Japanese concerns and one Chinese company. Another example involves Volkswagen, long the dominant foreign manufacturer of cars in China. When China, which until 2003 insisted that foreign car companies partner with Chinese firms (usually government-owned ones), allowed foreigners to build the first wholly owned car factory in the country, it went not to the Germans, but to Japanese Honda. Honda pledged its factory would only build cars for export back to Japan, a promise that few of Honda's competitors expect will keep the factory from eventually selling into the Chinese market.

Japan's success in winning high-profile contracts and concessions from the Chinese government speaks volumes about how willing China is to let its business interests come first, and to act in ways that seemingly contradict the country's most stubborn political grievances. If the reunification of Taiwan is one tenet of the China's political religion, hatred for the Japanese is another. Inviting in Taiwanese investors and industrialists to ignite the country's economic development, and allowing the Japan-

*In 2004, Germany's bilateral trade with China neared $42 billion, while that between China and Japan came to around $130 billion.

ese to penetrate the Chinese market with two of the most potent symbols of their postwar success, fast trains and great cars, are both outstanding examples of China's willingness to open its economy. With the exception of the United States, no other country has ever opened up more. In the case of China and Japan, it has meant checking the most strongly felt common emotion in China.

But the conflict between the two countries festers. When the Japanese consortium won its contract for the fast trains and rail lines, a group called September 18, a name taken from the date in 1931 when the Japanese began their prolonged and brutal assault on China, collected half a million signatures from people who opposed the use of Japanese technology in such an important national enterprise. And, on the other hand, radical Japanese nationalists have been known to demonstrate for their impossible dream of reenacting Japan's colonial glories, even the imagined ones. In April 2004, Japanese radicals crashed a bus emblazoned with Japanese nationalist slogans into the Chinese consulate in Osaka. Japan's officially sanctioned textbooks have glossed over Japanese atrocities, and Japanese national politicians, most notably Prime Minister Junichiro Koizumi, make regular visits to Yasukuni Shrine, a Shinto place of worship that incorporates cannons, kamikaze memorabilia, and includes among the 2.5 million war dead honored there fourteen convicted war criminals.* The Chinese regard the shrine as a memorial to Japan's murderous colonial past.

*Prime Minister Junichiro Koizumi's annual visits to Yasukuni Shrine, which began in 2001, meet strong protest from South Korea and China and stir nationalist passions on all sides. In 2003, the diplomatic tensions caused by Koizumi's visits put a halt to visits that Chinese and Japanese leaders were to make to each other's country. For their part, the Japanese set up a commission to consider a nonreligious memorial to the country's war dead, but any such proposals meet strong opposition in the country from those who note that Yasukuni Shrine provided the nation spiritual comfort while the Japanese endured the country's wars.

It is worth mentioning too that China's neighbors often find China's version of historical events well varnished, or worse, dressed up to justify Chinese aggression. Koreans are fighting a recent move by China to rewrite a long-accepted history of the Korean Koguryo Kingdom, parts of which stretched into what is now China. The new Chinese versions claim the power and scope of the kingdom was much smaller than earlier believed, a revision that strikes Korean observers as pure politics aimed at weakening any future territorial claims on behalf of ethnic Koreans in China. Never mind that the idea of the Koreans attacking China to grab territory is an absurdity today; the Chinese take the long view.

On the highest level, however, the assertive Japan that slashed, bombed, and spent its way into China in the first half of the twentieth century is not visible today, at least not from abroad. The Japanese know it is in their best interests not to trumpet their strengths too publicly. When American and European companies do well in China, they broadcast the news to their shareholders. The biggest news for Volkswagen and General Motors recently had been the success of their China operations, and it was carried on the front pages on all the world's major business publications. Search the news for profits from Japanese operations in China, however, and one can find general numbers, such as that eight in ten of Japanese companies in China make money there,[39] but little company-specific information comes up. Given China's hatred of the Japanese, no big Japanese company is likely to say it made millions or billions off the Chinese. The numbers are reserved for sharing in Japan's spotless corporate boardrooms or at private executive dinners—where, of course, noodles are likely to be served.

CHAPTER SEVEN

THE CHINA PRICE

Big news can sometimes be found in little places. In its November 2003 circular, a drily written four-page publication, the Chicago Federal Reserve Bank noted complaints from American makers of automotive parts that "automakers had been asking suppliers for the 'China price' on their purchases." The bank's analysts observed that U.S. suppliers had also been asked by their big customers to move their factories to China, or to find subcontractors there.

Over much of the business world, the term *China price* has since become interchangeable with *lowest price possible.* The China price is part of the new conventional wisdom that companies can move nearly any kind of work to China and find huge savings. It holds that any job transferred there will be done cheaper, and possibly better.

To understand this mentality it helps to remember that in the world of manufacturing the great bulk of products that roll out of the world's factories are sold to still other manufacturers as parts or software. Many common everyday objects, such as refrigerators, cameras, and cell phones, can have hundreds of parts produced by hundreds of companies. Bigger things, such as automobiles, commercial aircraft, and industrial robots, have thousands of parts and thousands of companies supplying them. By the time objects get to their end users, corporate purchasers have scoured the globe for the best parts and the best prices. Along these uncountable supply chains spread around the world, the China price rules the imaginations of corporate purchasers. For them, China has become a kind of cut-rate El Dorado, where the lowest prices mean gold. The constant push to the rock-bottom price has had a profound impact on the way the world makes things. Which means it also has a profound impact on people.

How to Manufacture Unemployment

When China's growing might is matched against the worldwide loss in manufacturing jobs, it seems that nothing can stop the China price from hollowing out the rest of the world's factories. In the United States, fears over China's economic ascendancy begin on the shop floor. A recent poll of America's manufacturing workforce revealed that one-third of workers are anxious that their jobs could be moved overseas without them. Their fears are well-placed. Although only one in eight jobs in the United States is in manufacturing, the number of manufacturing jobs lost in the United States between 2000 and 2003 exceeds the total jobs lost because a small portion of the newly unemployed were hired by the service sector. During that time, the odds of losing a manufacturing job were *fifty times* higher than losing a job in the greater economy as a whole. Manufacturing employment has been on a steady decline since the 1980s, but the most recent wave of job losses has been far out of scale to anything before. Even the great corporate downsizing of the early 1990s does not compare. Back then, four hundred thousand people lost jobs in manufacturing, just one-seventh of the number of people who suffered similar fates between 2000 and 2003.

Proof of the trend keeps mounting. The most disheartening job statistic in the United States is that for long-term unemployment, the measure of people who have been out of work for six months or more. During the three-year manufacturing slump that began in 2000, long-term unemployment doubled.[1] Long-term unemployment for those cast out of manufacturing jobs, the largest of any group, grew 260 percent.* The unemployment rate does not, of course, count the nearly 2.7 million Americans who have given up looking for work or the 4.5 million who have low-paid part-time jobs but who want better ones.[2]

Job losses hit America's families hard. When jobs disappear in America, they rarely return in the same industry or even the same place. Workers in North Carolina and South Carolina who lost jobs in the furniture industry now have to line up next to the thousands of other

*In 2000, the number of long-term unemployed in manufacturing totaled 102,311. In 2003, it reached 367,323.

workers who have lost work in the region's other big manufacturing industries for whatever job openings present themselves. A field investigation in South Carolina for the U.S.-China Security Review Commission, a Congressionally mandated watchdog panel, describes the three bleak years before 2004 when one-third of the state's computer and electronics manufacturing jobs were lost, along with nearly one-third of its textile, machinery, and appliance making jobs, and one-fifth of jobs in metal fabricating and chemicals, and one in seven of its plastics manufacturing jobs. Read another way, the state lost jobs in a wide cross section of the nation's businesses.[3] In all, 85,000 local jobs are most likely gone forever.

North Carolina, the state whose manufacturing sector has suffered more than all others, lost 160,000 factory jobs, or one in five.[4] Whole communities have been devastated. In the state's Robeson County, 10,000 out of the county's 18,000 factory workers lost their jobs over the last ten years. As unemployment has stayed stubbornly high, the income of one of every three people in the county of 123,000 has fallen below the American poverty line, a direct result of the job losses and the nearly $700 million in income that vanished with them.[5] Locals tie their fortunes directly to China. Speaking at a Robeson County political fund-raiser in 2004, Erskine Bowles, a chief of staff in the White House under Bill Clinton, met with raucous cheers and applause when, referring to the cost advantages that Chinese factories have over local ones—including loans from state banks they do not have to repay—Bowles told the crowd, "China has an unfair advantage. They don't pay anything . . . not for their equipment or buildings. We can't compete with that. They illegally ship six billion dollars in goods every year—that's three hundred textile plants closed down as a result of illegal imports."[6]

North and South Carolina have been hit hard, but nearly every state in the union has similar stories, and their departments of commerce and economic development are all but obsessed with competition from China and busily pen reports and lead seminars on how to answer the threat from China's low-cost factories. Pick up the paper in Pennsylvania, Ohio, upstate New York, nearly anywhere in the United States, and there are stories of people who, like millions of others, cannot lift themselves up after their manufacturing jobs have gone. In New Hampshire, where one-fifth of the state's manufacturing jobs have disappeared, the papers carry stories like that of George J. L. Staiti, a worker in a small metal-grinding shop shuttered in 2003. Staiti, sixty-two, sent out two hundred résumés in his search for work at another machine shop. "I've never a problem getting a job before," he told the *Nashua Telegraph*. New Hampshire ranks fourteenth among U.S. manufacturing states, and local officials complain that the job losses have eroded the local economic base. Staiti's low-tech shop was in an industry that is among the most vulnerable to Chinese competition. China is leading the world in the purchase of machines to do basic industrial tasks, whether it is fashioning metal, shaping plastic, or producing glass. It bought $6.5 billion worth of machine tools in 2003, a 25 percent jump over the year before, and its purchases continue to grow.[7]

Sometimes the last dollar made by the dead businesses is when they sell off their machinery to representatives of the same companies that killed them. At the Keeler Die Cast Co. in Grand Rapids, an auctioneer recently went through what has become a common ritual on American shop floors, selling off equipment, some of it practically new, to the highest bidders. At Keeler, the bidding was a contest between Michigan scrap dealers and manufacturers from Mexico, India, and China.[8]

"Globalization has transformed our business," Richard Kaye, an executive vice president of industrial auctioneer Hilco Corp., told the *Detroit News* in August 2004. "In fact, I don't think we've ever experienced that type of growth [in the past]. We anticipate future growth." Hilco is one of a dozen busy auctioneers that sell factories down to their cement floors. Since 2000, it had run five hundred industrial liquidations, netting $2 billion. Ominously, Kaye notes that many of his clients are *healthy* companies that are getting out of manufacturing (and into outsourcing) or that are moving their production. One of the 120 former Keeler workers told the Detroit paper that he had worked at the factory for thirty-six years but now faced a job market that could only pay him $8 an hour, half his former salary. Kendell Shangle, a Michigan scrap dealer who bid on Keeler equipment, said he attends auctions three times a week. "Every time I go, I kind of shake my head and think . . . how many jobs just got lost."

The disappearance of manufacturing jobs is a real blow to regions that rely heavily on their local factories. Factory jobs tend to pay well above the service jobs that are rising in number, especially when costly health-care and retirement benefits are added in. In the past, robust manufacturing centers have also been centers of industrial education and innovation. The service economy that is rising so quickly is in large part subsidiary to the nation's manufacturers it serves. At the 2004 world economic forum in Davos, Switzerland, Zhu Min, the general manager of the Bank of China, referred to the migration of both industrial and service jobs out of the United States and suggested that America "needs to reposition itself. Manufacturing is gone; services are going. [The United States] needs to move up the development chain."

Zhu's gloomy, quasi-apocalyptic assessment of the United States obviously overstates the problem, but he is on to something. The migration of manufacturing and service jobs are often linked. What he misses is the real possibility that if U.S. manufacturing slips away, so does the industrial expertise and infrastructure needed to create the high-value products he prescribes.

The cascade of news makes the loss of American jobs to China (and also to India, where call-center and software jobs are migrating) a political bombshell in nearly every major political contest in the country. Lou Dobbs, the popular news anchor on CNN and hundreds of American radio stations, has battled daily against companies that move American jobs elsewhere. His commentaries and guests all but liken the shift to treason. Dobbs's Web site keeps a list of nearly a thousand companies reported by his audience as job-movers, and Dobbs's passionate manifesto, *Exporting America,* may be the most direct assault on American big business by an establishment figure since President Dwight D. Eisenhower took on the military-industrial complex. To American corporations, like congregants schooled in sin by rousing sermons, the news of workers' woes serves not only as a warning but as a Darwinian playbook too. John McCarthy, an analyst at Forrester Research of Cambridge, Massachusetts, a firm whose widely cited research on the out-migration of American jobs fuels the international debate wrote, "While the press visibility [of outsourcing overseas] has spurred offshoring's emergence as a political third rail, it has also fostered an increase in overall offshore initiatives."[9]

It Doesn't Look Pretty

What's coming next for the American factory worker? A steady stream of statistics and predictions offered by America's big consultancies and financial institutions paint a bleak future. In late 2003, Forrester Research predicted that as many as 830,000 Americans would lose their jobs by the end of 2005, as American companies shipped work overseas, and that another 3.3 million would have their jobs shipped abroad by 2015. Goldman Sachs, the world's premier investment bank, predicted that 6 million jobs would leave the United States by 2014, at a cost of $150 billion in wages to Americans. A study by economists at the University of California at Berkeley predicted 14 million U.S. service jobs alone could be transferred overseas within a decade.[10] *That's 10 percent of the current American labor force.* The Berkeley researchers specifically identified China as a place that will take jobs not just from the United States, but from other developing countries that today are choice destinations for global companies in search of cut-rate facilities.

One may argue that the gloomy employment statistics do not reflect the overall health of American manufacturing. To begin with, manufacturing is still huge. Today's U.S. manufacturing sector is as large as the entire Chinese economy in dollar terms. And while manufacturing jobs have disappeared, the sheer volume of things that American manufacturers produce has skyrocketed. The key to the growth in output is the rise in manufacturing productivity, the term that describes the ratio between the value of the factors that go into making something and the value of the goods that result. Better machines, software, and advanced management techniques, for instance, now mean that U.S. companies on average produce far more per worker than they did a quarter of a century ago when manufacturing employment was high. From 1977 to 2002, productivity throughout the U.S. economy grew by half, but in manufacturing it more than doubled. Surprisingly, despite losing huge numbers of workers, U.S. manufacturers actually finished 2003 making more stuff than they did in 2001. Output was up, if only by half a percent. American manufacturers have gotten so good at making more stuff efficiently that workers in American plants now lead the world in how much they make both per hour worked and per employee.[11]

But productivity gains can have self-consuming effects. Competitive pressures, including those from American buyers who insist on ever-lower costs and from foreign industries that always threaten to undercut the cost of U.S. manufacturing, have pushed U.S. manufacturers to become productive at a pace that exceeds the growth of demand for U.S.-made goods. The result is that prices of manufactured goods have fallen while prices in the rest of the economy have raced ahead. According to the National Association of Manufacturers, over the decade ending in mid-2003, prices in the economy as a whole rose 18 percent, but prices for manufactured goods *dropped* 6 percent.[12] The researchers at Alliance Capital Management note that outside of the United States, productivity is also growing rapidly, though in many countries it begins from a drastically lower level and has not risen quite as fast as in the United States. Nevertheless, despite the global purging of factory employees from 1995 to 2002, the factories of the world turned out 30 percent more stuff at the end of the period than at the beginning.* Given that huge jump, and the constant cost pressure from China, one can only wonder where tomorrow's increases in production will take us.

The reach for greater productivity makes manufacturing the most nimble sector of the U.S. economy, yet subjects it to constant churn. Today, the American electronics business, which includes computers and telecommunications equipment, is, along with transportation equipment, a leader of manufactured goods. That market barely existed thirty years ago.

If nothing is stable in a world in which huge industries and new powerful manufacturers can emerge in a few years, and seemingly vital industries can die off or relocate even faster, then no country's industrial strengths insure it against a challenge from China. Carly Fiorina, the CEO of Hewlett-Packard who took over with a mandate to make the company into a swift global competitor, asserted in a 2003 press con-

---

*The measure of manufacturing output does not necessary mean more by volume, though the world is undoubtedly making more things. The Alliance Capital Management figures looked at total manufacturing output as measured by the value of shipments from all producers to all purchasers, including to other manufacturers.

ference, "There is no job that is America's God-given right anymore." Looking again at the great productivity gains in the U.S. economy, one sees that the biggest factor was investment in new information technology. A full 60 percent of the improvement came from better software, computers, and telecommunications links that ran and coordinated the shop floor.

Increasingly, however, the rest of the world can afford the technology to improve its own shops. Why? One big reason is that superproductive industries drive down the price of the electronics America makes best and pushes out to the world. And so do advanced-technology companies in Europe, Japan, and South Korea that all fight for the world's industrial market. Over time, the world's manufacturers, like the world's retailers, find their spheres ever more efficient, interlinked, and smaller. China can now choose its weapons, hitting on one flank with low-wage labor and on the other with improved factories bucked up with increasingly affordable technology.*

As the world shrinks, national industries begin to lose their relevance. What nation will Hewlett-Packard, the manufacturer, belong to when its goods are produced largely outside the United States? What exactly does it mean to be an American or Japanese car company when 80 percent of a car's parts come from outside suppliers overseas? And what does it mean to be a Finnish, Swedish, or American giant in the mobile phone business when your manufacturing and technology has been transferred to China to meet the needs of the foreign consumers and politicians on whom business now depends? The past, as investment advisers are obliged to say, is no guarantee of future performance. China's manufacturing might is all about the future.

---

*Following the 2000 bursting of the investment bubble that overcame North American telecommunications companies, China and other Asian countries were able to snatch up equipment to build state-of-the-art telecom networks at a fraction of their original cost. *New York Times* reporter Jennifer Schenker found that $30 billion in international telecommunications infrastructure owned by U.S. companies was sold off to foreign enterprises for $4 billion.

What Do We Talk about When We Talk about China?

In the political debate over trade and jobs, that China is the place where the world's companies choose to exploit low-cost manufacturing is well understood. But the framing of the debate implies that American consumers and businesses have strong choices in the market; in fact, China, supplying ever more goods, in ever more varieties and at ever better prices, is straitjacketing the choices of American businesses. China's size does not merely enable low-cost manufacturing; it *forces* it. Increasingly, then, it is what Chinese businesses and consumers choose for themselves that dictates how the American economy operates. Knowing this, one feels obligated to observe that the American political debate on China's economic threat overlooks this dynamic entirely.

Casting Lots to Survive

It's one thing to describe the dislocating effects of the China price, but how exactly is it forced upon corporations and workers? The answer is that each industry is prey to particular pressures and must be examined individually. Only then may one appreciate China's inexorable squeeze on industry. But this same investigation yields another insight: how China has raced so quickly up the industrial ladder.

The bellwether of American industry may well be its foundries. Casting is one of those decidedly unsexy industries that rarely come up in cocktail party conversations. But no amount of buzz could overstate its importance. Without metal-casting, the United States would boast hardly any industry at all. The U.S. Energy Information Administration of the Department of Energy notes that 90 percent of all manufactured goods and capital equipment use metal castings or are made with equipment that uses them. The American casting industry is the world's largest, with over $25 billion in annual sales. Nearly three thousand foundries are spread across the country, with a majority located in the Midwest. Most are small businesses with fewer than one hundred employees, who, on average, outearn their counterparts everywhere else in the world. The metal-casting industry once had generous trade surpluses with the rest of the world, but imported castings have doubled their American market share in the last seven years; they now have 15 percent of the market.

Imports from China are growing at between 7 and 10 percent a year, and worldwide by volume China is now the top producer of castings. The effect has been severe pressure on American foundries, 140 of which closed their doors in 2002, the last year for which the American Foundry Society has figures.

Robert Schuemann is vice president and part owner of Signicast Corporation, a privately held investment caster located at the edge of Hartford, Wisconsin.* Signicast supplies goods for more than three hundred industrial customers and makes items as basic as simple rods to complicated parts for medical devices. The table at the entrance of Signicast's office is filled with dozens of gears and brackets and other sundry-shaped metal pieces that are unrecognizable to the layman. One of the company's specialties is to design and cast single pieces where once multiple parts were used. For Harley-Davidson, Signicast took thirteen parts once used to connect the steering wheel to a motorcycle chassis and reduced it to a single rigid component that was both stronger and easier for the manufacturer to work with.

Hartford, where the company has done business since 1991, is one of Wisconsin's many midsize towns whose roads are shared by farm tractors and semitrailer trucks making their way to the loading docks of manufacturers who since the 1970s have stayed competitive by migrating out of the urban Midwest and into the more economical countryside.

Signicast, like many of them, now lives under the sword of the

---

*Investment casting, also called the lost wax process, is one of the world's oldest industrial techniques. With it, one can make intricate metal parts, from jewelry to complex turbine blades. The process requires a mold, usually fashioned from wax, that is an exact model of the object one wants to make. The mold is then used to create a second ceramic mold to surround the original. This is done by dipping the wax mold into a liquid clay slurry that dries and hardens around the original mold. The ceramic mold is than fired in a kiln at high temperature. The wax mold melts out, leaving a void in the shape of the model, and the ceramic hardens enough to withstand the pressure and heat of metal heated to three thousand degrees. After molten metal is poured into the mold, it is allowed to cool, after which the ceramic outer mold is removed and the metal part cleaned up.

China price. "Our company owns proprietary technology for producing metal machine parts with extremely high precision," Schuemann says. "As far as I know, Signicast's most valued work has no direct Chinese competition." Yet the company lives and works in a community in which companies rely on each other's vitality to stay alive. Schuemann, who has made a life in and among the cluster of Wisconsin factories that make the Dairy State one of the nation's top industrial states, sees the role American companies play in building China's critical mass of manufacturing as a threat to his business, his community, and his family.

At first glance, Hartford, a city of eleven thousand, looks as if it could be the sister city of Pekin, Illinois. Hartford too has a classic Main Street and narrow residential lanes lined with handsome hundred-year-old homes. But the town looks richer than Pekin. It sits on the edge of the lake and forest district known as the Kettle Moraine. Hartford's homes are more freshly painted than Pekin's, and its vibrant downtown is a healthy mix of mainstream stores selling furniture, shoes, and clothing, but also includes jewelry stores, galleries, and restaurants that cater to tourists and summer-home owners.

The city took shape in the early nineteenth century on land formerly belonging to the Potawatomi tribe of Native Americans. Among Hartford's first businesses were a deerskin factory and a gristmill. Over the next hundred years, immigrants from Ireland and central Europe filled out the city. Hartford earned some national fame as the home of the Kissel car company, one of more than a hundred new American automobile companies building cars in the early part of the twentieth century. Kissel made sporty, luxury roadsters from 1906 until 1931. A local museum has more Kissel models under one roof than anywhere else. After the Depression, Hartford was more notable for its lack of industry, and it still retains its farm feel. Handmade signs point down rural routes to tumbledown stands that sell from the expansive fields that edge the town. Unlike the manufacturers in Pekin, Hartford's current industries did not grow up here, but rather are corporate refugees from urban America.

Geographically, the latest wave of American industrial development is the reverse of China's. China is trying to move its rural population into industrialized cities, where its big manufacturing base resides. China is creating giant clusters of urban factories and workers—more or less the sort that once dominated the American industrial landscape.

Until the 1960s and 1970s, America's Midwestern and Northeastern cities were home to the world's most advanced factories. Detroit, which at midcentury was the epitome of a prosperous, brawny industrial American city, was during World War II famously labeled the Arsenal of Democracy. Walter Reuther, the labor leader who was instrumental in organizing Motor City for defense production, declared, "Like England's battles were won on the playing fields of Eton, America's were won on the assembly lines of Detroit." And every other big manufacturing center that offered skilled urban labor, access to rail lines, and waves of migrants—many of them rural black Americans from Southern states—willing to take nearly any factory job. The urban corridor stretching from Gary in northeast Indiana to Chicago and then up north to Milwaukee was until a generation ago the most solidly industrial concentration in the world.

In the 1960s, American cities began to lose their industrial edge. In a trend that continues today, suburbs and rural communities offered manufacturers incentives to leave their old multistory urban factories and move to flat corporate campuses. Southern states, traditionally industrial backwaters, offered manufacturers their own attractions in the form of lenient local regulations, tax breaks, freedom from industrial unions, and workers willing to sign on for far less than their Northern counterparts.

Manufacturers fled with a vengeance. Once proud industrial centers, such as Buffalo, Detroit, and Philadelphia, lost three-quarters of their manufacturing jobs.[13] Milwaukee, Signicast's first home, is no longer a compelling base.[14] The past few years have been particularly brutal on the city. Many of its biggest and stalwart private-sector employers shuttered their plants: Johnson Controls, Miller Brewing, Delco, and Masterlock. The city lost nearly half of its industrial jobs in the 1990s.

Interestingly, the new sprawling single-story factories were built to help U.S. companies compete with other foreign rivals. Signicast, a witness to the widespread plant closings and downsizings that predated the Chinese challenge, is one of the companies that now thrives.

"Beginning in the 1970s," Schuemann recalls, "it was the Japanese that made American companies afraid." Wisconsin lost fifty thousand manufacturing jobs in the 1980s.[14] Midwestern manufacturing—its new suburban and rural homes—bounced back from that challenge with a vengeance by shortening the time it took to design and deliver products and by vastly improving the quality of American goods. The Japanese did not attack American manufacturers so much on price, but on overall quality, which in the long run made their products a good value. To compete, American manufacturers learned to match, and in many cases beat, the Japanese strengths.

That paradigm still defines Schuemann's approach, which steers Signicast away from low-cost goods and toward those that perform well in the long haul. Signicast's biggest revamping came with a new plant in 1991. With it the company had a flexible facility that could be reconfigured to match whatever innovations its engineers came up with to reduce costs and speed products to customers. The plant cut labor costs by *two-thirds* and slashed product development and delivery from months to days. Robots move everything from the boxes in the warehouse to thumb-size precision parts. Workers are scarce. One feels that the whole plant is run by smart ghosts. Walking through it is a lesson in how the hardware business has become a software business. The same is true all over America, Europe, and Japan.

Signicast's migration is typical of many exurbanite companies. The company still retains its old urban plant to handle some of its work, but that plant is a far cry from the spacious home Signicast found by moving out. Hartford is now full of similar facilities. Giant, outwardly plain, low-lying factories spread almost stealthily throughout the city's fields.[15] Off the state roads that wind through the countryside, evidence of its several industrial parks appears at otherwise inconspicuous intersections in the form of large signs with a dozen or more corporate names and directional arrows. The factories themselves chug away behind grassy berms and cornfields.

For Schuemann, the biggest danger facing U.S. industry is not the difficulty that individual companies have staying competitive. Competition, he gladly admits, created Signicast and keeps it lean. His company has lately been logging in record years. What is most dangerous, he believes, is the erosion of the business environment around good companies. "American companies," Schuemann says, "need a critical mass of customers. Just as importantly, we need competitors around us to keep the manufacturing sector robust for us all."

Schuemann holds that the Chinese government keeps its country's currency roughly 40 percent lower than it would be if it traded at its fair value on the world market (an issue addressed in a coming chapter). The view is echoed by nearly every manufacturing trade group and industrial union that has weighed in on China. For Signicast's part, the wide differential has caused the company's biggest customers and potential customers to look to China, either as a place to make their goods or a place to buy parts. China now figures largely as a manufacturing and supply base for such American Midwestern giants as Caterpillar, John Deere, and Cummins Engine, and the thousands of companies clustered in the Midwest that comprise much of the American automotive industry.

Schuemann says his corporate customers also want his company to make the move to China. Customers have actually offered to underwrite the company's costs of doing so. But the company won't move. Schuemann fears that Signicast's proprietary technology would inevitably slip out the door into the industrial wilds of Guangdong or Zhejiang, and the Chinese would drastically undercut the price of Signicast's parts.

"We don't need to match the China price dollar for dollar," he says. "If we stay within twenty percent of their price, our customers will stay with us."

It's getting harder to keep them, however. The company used to have a lively business with a big local power-tool maker, but the customer moved production to China and found ways to jerry-rig substitutes for the high-quality parts that Signicast's engineers designed. "Our part was one sturdy piece and their new one is two inferior pieces," says Schuemann. "Theirs will break more easily, but it's a lot cheaper." Schuemann says the reason the company lost the business is because the big-box retailers that bought from the Wisconsin power-tool company insisted on yearly price cuts.

No matter how well Hartford's new plants are run, they must navigate a world that is fulfilling Schuemann's fears. Wisconsin's nearby industrial clusters are weakening in the face of China's growing strength in an ever-broadening assortment of industries. Schuemann's company makes parts for Harley-Davidson, and so, with the bleeding of manufacturing jobs from Wisconsin on his mind, he drove himself to the 2003 forum held in the motorcycle maker's factory by Bush administration cabinet officials Secretary of Labor Elaine Chao, Secretary of the Treasury John Snow, and Secretary of Commerce Donald Evans.

Schuemann's well-groomed executive bearing might have led the U.S. officials to expect a soft-ball question from him. Instead, he arrived at the meeting mad and lit into Snow. "What can the Treasury Department do to get the Chinese government to cut its currency's tie to the dollar?" he asked. When the secretary demurred, and his fellow cabinet members stumbled, seemingly stunned by the barrage of questions on China, Schuemann uncharacteristically lost his temper. After the meeting, he walked beside Snow and angrily asked his question again, pointing his finger aggressively at the chest of the formidable man who was once CEO of CSX Corporation, one of the largest railroad companies in the world.

"I don't know what got into me," Schuemann says, admitting he later saw that he was off-kilter. "I came that close to being arrested."

A Chinese Safety Valve

Will Signicast be forced by the China price to move some of its operations to China? It's too soon to say. But another Wisconsin metal casting company did, and its case is instructive.

The business cards of executives at Milwaukee Valve Company Ltd., located in Wuxi, a city of more than 4 million about an hour and half northwest from Shanghai, list the company's address as "End of Guangrui Road." By the outward appearance of the corrugated-tin-roofed industrial buildings that make up the small factory, "end of the road" might seem an apt description. Along the interior of a wall at the back of the factory yard is a pile of wood kindling that is used to stoke the factory's large furnace when the local electric grid is out of power. In 2003 and 2004, power dimmed often. Inside one of the barns, the furnace's orange glow heats and dimly lights a shop that looks little different from that of a sand-casting foundry early in the last century. Sandboxes are assembled manually, their negative impressions filled with molten brass, and set end to end in the black earth floor to cool.

While the method looks primitive—the Chinese have been making castings for twenty-five-hundred years—workers in Wuxi produce quality castings comparable to those made in spiffier factories in the United States, Europe, and Japan. Milwaukee Valve is a family-owned company whose manufacturing is still largely located in the United States. Its management entered China twenty years ago, soon after economic liberalization began. The company's valves are critical components in pipelines used in many industries. A faulty valve produced by one of the company's Chinese suppliers several years ago nearly ended the relationship with China. But this end of the road for Milwaukee Valve turned into the trail-head of a profitable journey. The mistake, according to the company's management, is what transformed the Chinese affiliate into a "world-class operation." Engineers from both countries redesigned the valve and changed the production process. Since then, Milwaukee Valve has stationed five Chinese quality-control engineers as roving inspectors at all of its factories in China.

Apply this learning-curve experience at the Wuxi plant to China's manufacturing economy generally, and you get a sense of how the country is moving up the manufacturing ladder so quickly. Of course, no one would be interested in seeing the Chinese improve if the cost of high quality were not still a bargain. But a bargain it remains. All other factors, such as the price of energy and raw materials, being equal, China continues to drive down the prices of goods it makes, even while learning to make them better.

Out in front of the valve factory is another telling symbol of China's competitiveness. It is a small $2,000 truck, a circus car of a truck, and one of many quaint but operable models still turned out by China's state-owned vehicle factories. In the United States, cheap trucks prone to failure and always in need of new parts would wreck production and delivery schedules by causing downtime and burden bottom lines with $50-an-hour mechanic bills. But in China, mechanics can tend such cheap trucks with the same care that pit crews tend Indy cars—and for less than a dollar an hour. In this way, Chinese factories can take advantage of all sorts of machinery that is one, two, or three generations past its usefulness in more expensive economies, because the Chinese can afford to run them and fix them.

What's more, Chinese companies work in an environment where much of what they need off of the shop floor is far cheaper than it would be in an advanced industrial economy. Roads can be built for less and factory buildings typically cost one-eighth of their price in the United States and an even smaller fraction of the price in Western Europe and Japan. Entertainment budgets to schmooze clients and government officials go much further. And nearly any industrial machinery made in China, if adequate, can shave capital expenses down to fractions of their world price. According to figures gathered by the Boston Consulting Group, Chinese-made injection-molding machines used to form plastic cost just one-third of their price in the United States; and power presses and pressure-casting machines cost just one-twentieth. Thus China wrings further cost savings from the manufacturing process, and the world's companies are forced to go there to get them.

"First there was the wholesale price, then the retail price, and now there is the China price, and it is very real," says Oded Shenkar, a professor at the Fisher College of Business at Ohio State University. Big manufacturers, Shenkar says, come into their American suppliers with the China price in hand and present ultimatums, often veiled, that the price be met.

Milwaukee Valve and Signicast do not compete for the same customers, but they operate in the same industrial environment. By making valves in Wuxi, Milwaukee Valve is assured the China price. Signicast is only assured of having to compete against it.

Play It Again, a Billion Times

One reason the China price can be hard for manufacturers elsewhere in the world to beat is that the price is produced in the unique stew of China's evolving business culture. Competing against manufacturers from most other places in the world requires understanding the particular dynamics of the culture and political environment that competition grows out of. Nevertheless, for most of the world, the forms that companies take are familiar and the bags of tricks governments can pull out to promote their native industries are filled with standard-issue tax breaks and local improvements but offer few surprises.

In China, however, the game is far more complicated. First and foremost, the country's huge population changes fundamental rules. It makes companies operating on superslim margins look like huge successes.

China's irreproducible ability to drive prices down can be seen in one of the world's favorite machines, the humble DVD player, a device now so commonplace it is nearly disposable. Chinese-made DVD players now sell for as little as $30 at electronics chains that once stocked players at thirty times the price. They are also a staple at discount stores. During the Christmas season of 2003, the deep discounts on players caused a post-Thanksgiving rush so frenzied that reports of an in-store stampede made the national news. Giant shipments of no-name but competent DVD players are stacked on the floors of unlikely sellers, such as grocers, pharmacies, and automobile supply stores. DVDs are displayed by cash registers, where, like candy bars and tabloids, shoppers are expected to snatch them up without forethought. If the average car dropped at that rate DVD players have, a Porsche 911 would now cost $1,500. Personal computers have also plummeted in price, though a 97 percent price drop in a top-of-the-line PC would deliver a machine at about $75. Chinese manufacturers make 60 percent[16] of the DVD players sold worldwide. In 2000, today's Chinese volume champs made almost none.

When the machine was first launched in the United States in 1997, it cost $1,000 and was as soberly designed as a black limousine, long and strong enough to hold the weight of a heavy TV. The machines were made in Europe and Japan and sold by the world's top brands. Ten companies, most notably Philips, Sony, and Toshiba, controlled the technology through the DVD Consortium. New entrants into the market paid a licensing fee to the Consortium.

Sign up they did. DVD players became the most rapidly and widely accepted consumer electronics appliance of all time, and eventually DVDs emerged as the world's first choice for recorded video entertainment. In the beginning, success looked like a long shot. To home movie buffs the format seemed evolutionary, a way to see movies at home more clearly and in a form that was easier to navigate than videotape. Initially, in 1998 and 1999, it seemed that the evolutionary changes were not all that compelling to consumers, who were so slow to take it up that the electronics trade press described the DVD market as in crisis.* The

---

*In February 1998, *EETimes,* a trade magazine for electrical engineers, wrote of "a handful of component makers . . . betting on the wild card of the vast but unproven Chinese market to jump-start DVD sales, which have been slow to take off in the West."

players were, however, revolutionary in ways invisible to most consumers. Like CD players before them, DVD players moved entertainment content from the analog world of over-the-air broadcast TV, movies on film, and videotape to a digital format. For the first time, movies could be copied perfectly by anyone with the digital equipment to set up shop. The switch to digital formats and the relative ease of copying content made DVD players a huge hit with the Chinese. And ultimately, it was Chinese companies that pushed DVDs into the forefront of consumer electronics worldwide.

Another angle on the story of the DVD player can be seen far from the Dutch and Japanese laboratories and boardrooms where the technology was born and launched.[17] According to Chinese economists Lu Feng and Mu Ling, who are documenting a history of the Chinese VCD and DVD industries, the Chinese dominance in DVDs has its immediate roots in the early 1990s. Then, prerecorded movies were available almost exclusively on VHS videotapes. The Chinese, however, were looking for a way to watch movies at home that did not rely on videotape or the videocassette recorders that played them. Per capita income in China in 1992 hovered around $400, and the mechanical construction of VCR machines and the license fees required by foreign patent owners put them out of reach in the poor country, even for middle-class families.

An alternative technology was beginning to take shape in the labs of the world's electronics giants. It was VCD, or video CD. The format is built around one of the first mass-market standards for digital video, MPEG 1, a precursor to the higher-resolution MPEG 2 format that eventually because the basis of DVD technology. The MPEG 1 format never scored big in the United States or in the home markets of its pioneers, Philips, Sony, Matsushita, and Japan Victor.

While attending a convention for the broadcast industry in Las Vegas, a Chinese researcher and entrepreneur named Jiang Wanmeng had a brainstorm.[18] Jiang saw a demonstration of an early-stage consumer technology that could digitize movies and show them on a computer. Digital machines already existed for broadcast professionals, but they were editing machines that cost hundreds of thousands of dollars. Jiang saw the potential for the new chip, being shown by an American company named C-Cube, to provide the guts of an inexpensive movie player for the still-unformed Chinese market.

In addition to digitizing motion pictures, the technology Jiang saw also compressed the resultant video files so that they could fit on a disk in the same way songs from analog audiotape could be transferred to a CD.[19] Jiang formed a company to support the development of the new chip and spent several million dollars, facilitated in part by the government of his province, to get the work done. Using the same Motorola computer chip that once ran the benighted Apple Lisa computer, Jiang rigged up a movie-playing, disk-based machine that could attach to a television and mimic nearly all the functions of a VCR. VCD players could not record, however, and they relied on disks that could not hold a whole movie. But anyone with the right equipment could make good, inexpensive digital copies of movies on CDs. Jiang and company quickly assembled an operation to do just that.

Suddenly, China had the hardware and software it needed for a new industry. The Chinese government moved quickly to back the standard. It saw a national VCD industry as a chance to leapfrog with digital home video over the rest of the world, which was still wed to analog videotape.[20]

The VCD player was born in an effort to escape license fees necessary to import VCR technology, but where the easily copied VCD disks were concerned, there was no pause. In shops and on the streets, premium films from all over the world were available at less than $1 apiece. A cycle soon began in which the market was flooded with titles, and as the market grew, new companies would come along to make still more machines. The American company, C-Cube, that developed the chip for Jiang developed better chips that made the machines extremely easy to manufacture.[21] In just three years, more than three hundred companies were making VCD players. The few big foreign electronics manufacturers that briefly dominated the market soon found they could no longer compete and exited the VCD player business. Hundreds of Chinese companies eventually failed too, but with so many of them vying for buyers, vicious price-cutting became the norm. By 1998, two years after their introduction, the price of VCD players had dropped from $400 to $110, according to Lu Feng and Mu Ling, and annual sales had soared to nearly 19 million units.

Wilf Corrigan, a digital media pioneer who now heads LSI Logic, the company that ultimately took over C-Cube, notes that player sales soared when prices dropped toward $200, still an enormous amount of money in a country where hundreds of millions of people don't earn that much in a year. Yet often the players were used communally, offering a village's only reprieve from the hours of mind-numbingly bad programming served up on government television stations. In 2001, another 29 million machines were sold. In three furiously paced years, China rose from having no domestic industry for recorded movies to the world's largest market for players and almost certainly for content.

Lu and Mu argue that the major difference between the failed Chinese VHS market and the VCD market was that Chinese companies designed the indigenous machines so that they could be made using China's abundant low-cost labor. That drove prices for machines and disks lower still. The combination of Chinese technology and Chinese labor, the economists argue, was a classic case of creative destruction, in which a killer product finely honed to a local market pushed out less desirable competitors. Today, China and Southeast Asia, where VCDs also became popular, have an installed base of one-quarter of a billion players.[22]

The VCD market has given way in China to the superior DVD technology, which was the big foreign brands' answer to the VCD. Chinese manufacturers rushed into DVD players even more heartily than they did into VCDs, and although they did not start out strong in the DVD market, they have ultimately taken the lion's share in the newer format too. Amazingly, DVD players, superior to VCD machines in every way, are now the cheaper of the two.

None of the machines would have met with nearly the same success had not the Chinese market supplied the public with a steady supply of cheap, pirated films on disk. Nearly everywhere in China, new releases can be bought for around ninety-five cents. Chinese consumers are also helped because few of China's hundreds of DVD-player manufacturers pay the proper fees to license the foreign technology that goes into their wares. And yet, in a strange twist, the rogue ways in which the Chinese disk and player makers have flooded their own markets and driven down prices have also been strong forces behind the popularity of DVD players *worldwide*. The DVD, it can be said, owes its success to the China price.

The VCD and DVD boom points to another competitive strength of

China's huge population beyond its capacity to send legions of low-wage workers into new factories. China's huge domestic market allows manufacturers to gear up to sell vast numbers of goods quickly and to profit on the size of the market even where their profits per sale are low. Indeed, only low prices make the high-volume strategies succeed. With many things, such as consumer electronics, the world's going price for equipment is far too high for the mass of Chinese consumers, so Chinese companies find ways to drive prices drastically downward.

In such a brutally competitive environment, only the strongest and smartest survive. Most of the three hundred companies that made VCD players vanished, and hundreds of companies in the DVD business have also closed. In the tumult, China's manufacturers short-circuited one of the most predictable trends in consumer electronics manufacturing. For most of the last twenty years, Corrigan of LSI notes, technology originated in Japan at high prices. "Typically," he says, "a new technology would be released at a thousand dollars in Japan, and it would take two years to drop below a thousand and make it to the U.S. and Europe, and it would take a total of five to seven years for it to make it into the mass market." In the past, consumer electronics were built by vertically integrated companies that controlled most of the manufacturing required to make their devices. That meant they could set the schedule for how long it took for their products to reach the mass market.

What the VCD and DVD markets taught the Chinese was they could build devices from components provided by outside companies, often American and European ones. Companies such as LSI could provide computer chip sets that were nearly complete solutions, called reference designs. With the chip sets, Chinese manufacturers could focus on what they do best, assembling the machines with their armies of affordable labor and assessing the local market for what Chinese consumers need. Whereas before it took three to four years for new features to get worked into consumer electronics, at a higher price, the competitive Chinese market forces manufacturers to shove more features into their machines more quickly. And to lower their prices while they are at it. New and better features for players are engineered and installed in players in a single season instead of over years.

Ironically, the low quality of pirated movie disks egged manufacturers on to make better players. Pirated disks, economists Lu and Mu point out, need not adhere to quality standards and often they do not play well. Sometimes they don't work at all. When players that could correct for the flaws in less than perfect disks proved popular, the chip-set makers provided manufacturers with ever better technology to minimize the grief caused by sloppily made copies.

More capable players made the market for disks even better. The recent appearance in China and Southeast Asia of "super error correcting" DVD players means that even botched copies of movies that would not play on any previous machine run smoothly. Antipiracy advocates regard the new players as diabolical. In addition, the Chinese players began to incorporate technology that allowed them to read multiple digital formats. Not just VCD or DVD for instance, but also files for digital photographs, MP3 music files, and karaoke disks. Chinese players are now so chock-full of features that Japanese and European machines costing several times more cannot compare.

How did the Chinese no-name DVD players arrive in America? A year before they began stacking up on the floors of American drugstores, a back channel of distributors had already forged a market on eBay. Brands such as Sampo, Malata, Conia, and RJ Tech, hardly household names in North America or Europe, were being advertised to buyers who wanted machines that were low cost, capable, and perhaps most importantly, could play disks from all over the world.* China's excess capacity in DVD players was also showing up in sundry shops in American Chinese, Southeast Asian, and Indian neighborhoods that catered both to ethnic locals who wanted to watch foreign films and to others who wanted to copy rented DVDs to videotape.

Then the floodgates to American stores opened. European regulators, frustrated over the failure of many of China's DVD manufacturers to pay license fees to the DVD Consortium, drastically restricted the sale of Chinese-made DVD players on the Continent. China's manufacturers, already building up large surplus inventories, shipped players out of

---

*Normally, DVD disks are coded so that they cannot be copied and can only play on machines sold into the geographic region where the DVD disks were purchased. The U.S. is coded Region 1, so that a European player, coded Region 2, cannot play U.S. disks. This prevents sellers from arbitraging disks from the cheaper U.S. market to the more expensive European market.

their warehouses into the hands of American buyers. Players that hit American stores for $30 left China for $20. With chip sets costing between $7 and $10, and license fees, when they were paid, costing roughly the same, not much room was left for profit. How aggressive have the Chinese been at slashing prices? On average, the profit on a DVD player exported out of Guangdong, where seventeen of twenty Chinese machines are made, has sunk to a single dollar.[23]

A rescue was soon in the works. In December 2003, the Chinese government announced that it would back a new standard for digital movies that would improve on DVDs. Called EVD, for "enhanced versatile disk," the technology was developed by a new consortium of Chinese corporate, academic, and government groups. While EVD delivers six times the resolution of a DVD, it is no more revolutionary than the evolution of VCD to DVD. In its first year out, EVD looked like a flop. Players were far too expensive for the Chinese market. To shine they also require a high-definition television, something that is still a rarity in China. In the future, prices will make all the difference.

Thus the global consumer electronics market has reached what may be a huge tipping point; if Chinese makers back the new standard and begin to produce EVD players in quantity, China—not Sony, Philips, or Microsoft—will have set the standard for the next big thing in home video. Behind EVDs' still uncertain success stands the lure of the great mass of China's frugal but hungry consumer class, whose few pennies are enough to drive Chinese manufacturers toward an unbeatable China price. After its first year, EVD seemed to face an even more uncertain future than DVD did in its early outing. The backers of the EVD format must battle rival standards for high-definition content on disk developed by the usual suspects from Japan and Holland, and a new player, American giant Microsoft. Even with the Chinese government behind it, the EVD group may not have the marketing power to beat their more seasoned rivals. But should the likes of Microsoft and Sony insist on high prices for their technology, EVD may well find a critical mass of consumers in China at a lower price, and then it will conquer the world's wallets and eyeballs.

But no matter what happens to EVD, the Chinese are here to stay in global consumer electronics. At the 2004 Consumer Electronics Show, an entire pavilion was dedicated to dozens of Chinese manufacturers, large and small alike. On the main exhibition floors at the Las Vegas Convention Center, Chinese companies commanded imposing booths alongside the likes of Japanese and Korean giants Panasonic, Toshiba, Pioneer, and Samsung. The daily press lunch was hosted by RCA Thomson, the large French consumer electronics company that in 2003 sold 70 percent of its television market to one of China's largest TV manufacturers, TCL. Simple VCD players and even DVD players were a rarity at the 2004 show, their low prices making them uninteresting commodities. DVD recorders and flat-panel televisions, however, were everywhere, shown by a seemingly countless number of big brands, up-and-comers, and unknowns. Most would be delivered to consumers out of Chinese factories. Three years earlier, the Chinese were barely a presence at the electronics show. Now the rest of the world fights to keep up.

CHAPTER EIGHT

HOW THE RACE TO THE BOTTOM IS A RACE TO THE TOP

THE STREETS AND HIGHWAYS OF CHINA ARE FILLED WITH ROLLING museums of everything that has ever moved on wheels. Head four hours north of Shanghai on the bus to Rudong, where one of China's newest and still lightly trafficked toll roads gives way to land still off the highway grid. There one ends up on the rough two-lane highways that have crisscrossed China forever, running past tiny one-counter private shops that have sprung up by the millions since economic liberalization. Most sell hot food, crackers, and soda, and many also sell cement bags, porcelain plumbing fixtures, and other weighty necessities of the world's greatest building boom. Moving materials in and out of the shops and along the roads are big old military trucks and trucks that are not so old but come out of factories that still make them according to Soviet-inspired designs. Their big flat beds get stacked so high with materials that they look like moving mountains. These lumber down the roads taking every bump carefully. Newer trucks, which look more like up-to-date European models from Mercedes or Volvo, hot-rod past them. Smaller trucks take up most of the road, often pickups with beds customized with oil tanks, chicken coops, or benches for paying customers. And there are buses of every size, from double-deckers topped with giant canvas mounds for luggage down to minibuses for small outings. Motorcycles, virtually all of them Chinese brands copied from old Japanese bikes, also carry imprudent loads, the rear of their vinyl seats taken up with bundles of sticks, paper, steaming baskets of food, and mothers with babies on their laps and packages around their wrists. Farther down-market still are the motorized bicycles, often rigged against the elements with plastic cabs around the seats. In the slowest lanes, bicycle rickshaws and microtrucks ride with front ends that stick out like anteater noses on wheels, their small, exposed put-put engines perched right over the front wheels, kicking out so much heat, smoke, and noise that the driver's cab is several feet back. China is in a hurry these days, and these wheelbarrows married to go-carts clog up the roads and elicit fury from drivers of anything that can go more than ten miles an hour.

And then there are the cars. Over 120 companies make passenger cars in China, a number that far exceeds the roster of any other country and that signifies both China's nascent industry and long history as a nation of automotive tinkerers. At the turn of the last century, before the advent of real mass production, the United States had roughly the same number of carmakers as China today. Kissel in Hartford, Wisconsin, was one. Dozens of these Chinese manufacturers are just small firms cobbling together cars any way they can. Some make models based on old Soviet cars and European compacts several generations past. Others paste together the parts and designs of multiple manufacturers depending on which parts can be had—often dubiously—in the market.

"Many Chinese consumers are so hungry for cars that they don't care what they look like if the price is right," says Michael J. Dunne, whose Bangkok firm, Automotive Resources Asia, helps Western car companies navigate their Chinese businesses. "Right now, there is a large volume of demand on the low side of the market, and upstart Chinese companies are building knockoffs that buyers who just want transportation can settle on."

Among these many car manufacturers are a small number of larger, thriving ones that in many cases were started with the pooled resources of local governments. These wholly domestic firms play a role in how much a Chinese economy car built for export will eventually cost and what it will look like.

The Wanfeng automotive factory is a good place to see these gathering forces of China's automotive might. Morning there begins with a neat line of employees doing calisthenics to martial music over a PA system. The blue-uniformed workers, nearly all of them young men, make for a clean-cut, well-pressed company line. The Japanese introduced courtyard exercises and company songs to the world back in the 1970s when that nation seemed to have the world's best industrial jobs.

Today, Japan is stumbling out of malaise, and its dwindling pool of young laborers lack the compulsion to work like hell. That striving Japan of old still sets a good example for would-be world-beaters, as Wanfeng's management knows, but the Chinese manufacturer goes one better. Its employees regularly have their spirits revved at company boot camps run by People's Liberation Army drillmasters, who inculcate the twin virtues of patriotism and hard work.

The results are impressive. Nine years ago Wanfeng started hammering out motorcycle wheels by hand in a Chinese garage; a few years later it was the number one seller of aluminum-alloy motorcycle wheels, first in China and then the world. The company soon became a top national and global seller in alloy automobile wheels too.

Wanfeng may well have received some help on the way up: the company's video that describes its rapid ascent does not identify the early contracts that enabled it to grow so fast, nor whether Wanfeng had insider connections to government companies in the motorcycle and car businesses. Nor is there anything in Wanfeng's literature about how the private company secured its financing, despite the fact that national banking laws have all but prohibited state banks—every bank, in effect—from lending to the private sector. Wanfeng today is nonetheless scrappy, aggressive, and capable. In year eight, it set up its automotive works in a large new factory in an industrial stretch outside Shanghai; now it annually turns out sixty thousand vehicles that look great, come with every modern luxury, including leather seats and full Chinese-made DVD video systems, and purr when driven. And if you squint just a little, these new cars look remarkably like Jeep Cherokees.

In contrast, Wanfeng's factory itself is a bare-bones machine. Most tellingly, not a single robot is in sight. Instead, hundreds of young, low-paid men newly turned out from China's burgeoning technical schools man the assembly lines with little more than large electric drills, wrenches, and rubber mallets. Engines and body panels that would, in a Western, Korean, or Japanese factory, move from station to station on automatic conveyers, are hauled by hand and hand truck. This is why Wanfeng can sell its handmade luxury Jeep tributes in the Middle East for $8,000 to $10,000. The company isn't spending money on multimillion-dollar machines to build cars; instead, it's using highly capable workers who cost at most a few hundred dollars a month, which means that the yearly pay of seasoned Chinese workers is less than the monthly pay of new hires in Detroit.

Driving a Bargain

Wanfeng is growing quickly, but its survival is in no way guaranteed, for the car business in China today is arguably one of the most competitive in the world, as manufacturing capacity explodes along with demand. Chinese and foreign automakers have invested $12 billion over the last decade in building automobile factories, with half of that amount spent just since 2002. One-third of the global growth in vehicle sales is coming from China, and within the next fifteen years, perhaps sooner, China is destined to emerge as the largest auto market in the world. China bought just over 2 million new cars in 2003, while the mature U.S. market has long been stable at roughly 17 million cars a year. Even with periodic sputters, China's long-term growth will be huge. China is on track to surpass Germany as the number three auto producer before 2010, to pass Japan by 2015, and then be just 4 million sales a year shy of the U.S. market, which it will pass in due course too.[1] The country's domestic market potential, like everything else in China, is mind-boggling. The Chinese middle class, a group expected to spend heavily on cars, will soon top 100 million.

The most visible brand around Shanghai is Volkswagen. The company sells three of every ten new cars in China and is so strong in this region, where it also makes most of its cars, that traffic jams can look like VW sales lots. The company's Shanghai works has two main lines. One makes the virtually indestructible Santana, which was the first Western car mass-produced in post-Mao China. Like old friends, they are so extraordinarily dependable that their owners don't easily give them up. Nearly all of Shanghai's battalions of taxis are red Santanas, a testament not only to the car's durability but also to the clout of the Shanghai government, which is a partner in the autoworks. VW's Santana assembly line still builds cars the way cars were built in Germany in the 1970s, relying heavily on manual labor. VW also has an ultramodern assembly line in China, perhaps the company's best. It turns out VW's premium Passat, which in China's market is considered a luxury car and is pitted against the world's other luxury makes, Mercedes and BMW among them. VW will more than double the number of cars it builds in China by 2008, when it expects annual sales there of 1.6 million vehicles, a number that will continue to mark China as VW's top profit center worldwide.

Yet for all VW's strength, it is losing market share in China as more companies move in from abroad and as the domestic manufacturers learn to compete. General Motors, the number one automaker in the world, is now number two in China. It sells one of every ten cars in China and is also working to double its manufacturing and sales with a target of 770,000 cars by 2006. Ford was a latecomer and until recently was only willing to inch into the Chinese market, waiting until it could be confident it could make money there. But if money speaks, Ford's doubts must be over. It now has two large plants in the works and is spending over $1 billion to get them online as soon as possible. Industry insiders wonder whether the company has moved in too cautiously to make up for its late entry. VW and GM will add more manufacturing capacity to their current production than all of Ford's new ventures.

Honda, Toyota, and Nissan all have plans to grab big shares of the Chinese market too. VW and the American carmakers are finding themselves in a familiar bind. Despite the loathing the Chinese have toward the Japanese, they hold Japanese cars in the highest regard and are willing to pay high premiums and bide their time on long waiting lists to get them. In the meantime, the competitors of the Japanese are building so much capacity they may end up flooding the market. Deflation is already a fact in China's car market, with prices dropping as the world's automakers collect an infrastructure around them that gives them access to lower-priced parts made locally.

Parts in the Puzzle

For national economies outside of China, it is the gathering of manufacturing inside China to serve the big auto companies that may yet prove the most worrisome. These are the first-, second-, and third-tier manufacturers that make and supply the thousands of parts that go into a car but are not made by the automakers themselves. These companies are the heart and soul of the industrial sectors of the world. Even countries that are minor players when it comes to whole cars are big players in the parts business. Mexico and Canada don't make a lot of cars compared with the United States, Japan, or Germany, but they make a lot of car parts. In the United States the parts business is one of the big engines of our national economy. Domestic U.S. auto-parts makers sell $750 billion worth of their products around the globe every year. Overall, the automobile business accounts for more than a trillion dollars, or about one-tenth of America's gross domestic product.

As with other industrial sectors, the automobile industry, from the makers of small commodity parts to the big carmakers, works like an unstable planetary system. As bits and pieces of it move around, they acquire gravity and attract other pieces of the business. As big carmakers establish production in China, they drag along the companies that supply them. And as suppliers move to China—even if they moved in order to make parts less expensively for the American market—the big companies more willingly move too, more confident that the industrial infrastructure they need to produce efficiently is taking shape in the new market.

Few businesses feel this pull to China more intensely than auto parts. "Suppliers feel increasingly pressured to move manufacturing abroad," said Antonio Benecchi to *Automotive News* following a study that his firm, Roland Berger Strategy Consultants, conducted for the Original Equipment Suppliers Association, the biggest trade group for parts makers. Benecchi studied seventy companies that together do $72 billion in business a year. He found that the North American car business is moving abroad in waves. The two largest American parts companies, Visteon (an independent company spun off from Ford) and Delphi (spun off from GM), both have multiple plants in China and aggressive expansion plans. For each, China means added billions in sales. As in other sectors, few industry watchers expect the two parts giants to keep their China-made parts for the China market alone.

Not all of the movement is going to China. Much is heading to Mexico, Eastern Europe, and to various cut-rate Asian locales. But there's no doubt that the pull of China is the most inexorable, since unlike other markets, China offers both low-cost manufacturing for export out of the country—back to the United States, for example—and the promise of an incredible local market. General Motors bought $200 million worth of auto parts in China in 2003, a mix that includes parts made by both local firms and global suppliers working in the country. And that is not including the parts GM bought from its own China operations. The company says that its Chinese purchases for export will rise 2000 percent to $4 billion over the next five years.

For the big U.S. automakers and their European peers, whatever moves they make into China pay global dividends. Once in the country, they can assess the local manufacturing environment, learn who the best Chinese manufacturers are, and bargain locally based on the knowledge they glean about their suppliers' costs. As in the case of Wal-Mart, insider knowledge in China then becomes a power hammer to swing over the heads of suppliers everywhere else in the world. GM and Ford have already told their network of suppliers that they ought to be prepared to shave their costs significantly *every year.* It is plainly understood that asking suppliers to lower prices is merely another way of telling them they ought to be prepared to meet the best price out of China, even if they are making their products in Japan or Germany. GM, which buys more than $80 billion worth of parts a year, now has in force a clause in its supply contracts that gives its supplier thirty days to meet the best price the company can find worldwide or else risk immediate termination thereafter.

Delphi, the world's largest auto-parts maker, certainly feels the push into China. Its China business crossed the billion-dollar threshold in 2004—at the same time it laid off workers in its U.S plants.

The global market for Chinese parts is also helping create global players out of China's local parts companies. The largest of them, the Wanxiang Group, has thirty-one thousand employees and does nearly $2 billion in business a year, much of it with giants such as Delphi and Visteon. Chinese companies are also finding willing customers in the huge aftermarket for parts that go into car repairs.

In all, China exported $6.5 billion worth of parts in 2003, *more than double what it did the year before.** Tellingly, if one keeps in mind what's happened in DVDs and other exported products, Wanxiang also plans to expand abroad.[2] It already owns bits of American makers Universal

*Of China's car part sales to foreign manufacturers, $2.8 billion went to GM alone.

Automotive Industries and Rockford Powertrain and has new operations in Germany and Australia too.

But creating a Chinese industrial base with its own center of gravity is not all win-win for the world's automakers. Once the automakers have a world-class supply chain in place, populated with strong Chinese companies tutored by their foreign partners in management and technology, they also have strong competitors on their hands. The same holds true for the giant auto-parts companies, which have their own networks of suppliers beneath them. Inevitably their technology and expertise leach out to the local economy in ways they cannot control. Delphi, for one, is fed by a host of local second- and third-tier suppliers that provide it with parts, but only if they can bring their plants up to Delphi's high standards. "Our second-tier suppliers must conform to the management and quality controls that meet Delphi's culture," says Jinya Chen, president of Delphi China. "It is fair to say that Delphi is bringing a culture of quality to China."

The market in China gets particularly knotty when one considers that big global automakers must partner with local, usually state-owned, firms to do business in the country. The auto sector is one of the few in which the Chinese government still twists arms to get foreigners to enter joint-venture relationships with the state. And yet, the state companies are not all hindered in their relationships. They can, for instance, enter into multiple joint ventures with multiple foreign firms. On top of that, the Chinese government has decreed that in joint-venture arrangements, all intellectual property brought to the arrangement by one of the partners is owned equally by the other partners. For Western and Japanese companies with vast stores of proprietary technology, the law is a bad deal. It gives their Chinese partners the right to distribute that technology outside the firm to whomever they please. That puts the Chinese companies in the unique position of having the ability to combine top technology from several partners into their own vehicles.

China's unmistakable long-term goal is to rank among the world's leading car-producing economies, and free access to technology is one quick ticket there. "It can cost an American or Japanese automaker between one billion and two billion dollars to develop a new car," notes Professor Oded Shenkar, who has made a career out of observing Asian automakers, beginning with the global ascent of the big Japanese companies in the 1970s.

The loose passing of intellectual property in the automotive sector, Shenkar argues, equates to an enormous state subsidy. Detroit might have to sell hundreds of thousands of cars to earn back its development costs on a particular model, but Chinese manufacturers that simply expropriate the models can earn back their money almost immediately. "Also if you knock off another company's model, there is no way the original manufacturer can beat you on price." The Chinese knock-offs also do not have to pay for advertising, since the models they ape are usually heavily promoted. "There's one more savings," Shenkar adds. "If you're an imitator, you only have to imitate the successful models. The Chinese tend to borrow only from the tried-and-true cars."

The realities of technology transfer in China also help the domestic car companies as know-how passes from advanced foreign companies to needy domestic ones through back channels. VW found its own proprietary parts *built into* a domestic rival's new cars. At Shanghai's big auto show in 2003, GM was shocked to find that a $9,000 small family van it was just unveiling had *an exact double,* priced at $6,000, at a Chinese manufacturer's booth down the same row. The cheaper vehicle was produced by a company called Chery, which was owned in part by GM's big Chinese joint-venture partner, Shanghai Auto. Perhaps to Shanghai Auto's credit, it reportedly quickly divested itself of its interest in Chery. For its part, the Chinese government ruled as it usually does in cases where Chinese companies are liberally influenced by their foreign competitors. It decided GM had no evidence for its case.

Shenkar fears that much of the activity dangerous to the long-term health of global car companies is transpiring under the radar of American industry, regulators, and the public. In June 2002, *China Daily,* one of the government newspapers, ran a short, tantalizing item announcing that 252 Chinese-made economy cars had been shipped by Tianjin Automotive Xiali Co. to Port Everglades in Florida, the first Chinese cars exported to the United States. A Boca Raton company, the paper said, planned on receiving 25,000 Xiali cars over the next five years. The small cars were the same models that swarm Beijing as bumpy red taxis, get fifty-six miles to the gallon, and cost under $6,000 in China. The cars never made it to American showrooms. Presumably they were shipped off to down-market climes where warranty service comes cheap. Nevertheless, the news item pointed toward a trade network gearing up to sell Chinese auto brands in the United States.

"No one is paying attention to Chinese exports. Most people think they aren't exporting at all yet," says Shenkar, "but they already are."

He means not just Chinese brands, but global-brand cars that are made in China. Last year VW exported between sixty thousand and seventy thousand cars made in China to Australia. Others are heading toward the Middle East. Honda, the company that makes the most coveted cars in China right now, has convinced the Chinese government to let it build a wholly owned factory—the first of its kind for a foreign company—in China by promising the government that every car made in the plant will be exported. Toyota recently revealed that engines made in its China plant will end up in cars destined for the U.S. market.

Shenkar says that our blind eye to Chinese exports reminds him of how America acted when the Japanese car companies first made their presence known offshore. "No one took them seriously. American carmakers said that the foreign models were a fad." Shenkar describes China's limited exports so far as the tip of the iceberg. The country already makes more cars than it needs, and in a few years it may be making several million more cars a year than it can sell at home. "The whole world has overcapacity right now. The Chinese, like everyone else, will be looking to export to sell all those extra cars."

So, ironically, high demand in China is pushing prices down globally. Even in a country where demand is growing geometrically, and where the world's carmakers are investing billions, there's a price war. This decade, prices for cars in China have been dropping between 10 and 20 percent a year, a trend that is expected to continue. When sales growth slowed in 2004, the big foreign car companies quickly slashed thousands of dollars off the prices of their cars. Buick, which is enjoying something of a second coming in China, where it is commonly regarded as the car that offers the best value for the money, cut $5,000 from the price of its Regal sedan. VW cut all its prices by 11 percent, and Hyundai by 10 percent.[3] The worldwide trend of car prices is already deflationary—over the last twenty years they've risen more slowly than broader price indexes—and China's exports will exert greater downward pressure still.

The Chinese market's ability to drastically push down the prices of automobiles is a prospect that is both frightening and tantalizing. Frightening because steep deflation in cars has the potential to deflate entire economies, throwing millions out of work. Exciting because, well, who wouldn't want a good car for a third of the cost?

A few supercheap cars already exist. Wanfeng, the company that exports Jeep Cherokee clones to the Middle East, has already shown that it can make an impressive export car for $10,000 in China, provided it doesn't have to brave too tough a regulatory market abroad. Koreans currently make the lowest-priced sedan in the United States, the KIA Rio, which lists with no extras at $9,665. That buys basic transportation: 103 horsepower and the road feel of a kangaroo. One reviewer, struggling to say something nice, wrote that if you "keep engine rpm up . . . the Rio can stay with the flow of traffic on the highway." The earliest Chinese export car might not be much better. "A first automotive product here," speculates Kevin Smith, editor of *Motor Trend,* "would represent the bottom of the market in features, refinement, and quality, but it won't be too far behind its competition." Smith points out that it took the Koreans ten years to get their cars up to a quality acceptable to American buyers. He thinks the Chinese may get there in half the time.

What will the first Chinese cars made for the American market look like? Auto insiders can only speculate. Michael Dunne of Automotive Resources Asia believes it will be a plain vanilla knockoff of some other country's economy car. Paul Lienert, a veteran Detroit automotive columnist, expects it to have licensed or "borrowed" technology on the inside, to come equipped with a decent four-cycle engine, radio, and air-conditioning, but have some Chinese design spin on the outside. If that means it will conform to current consumer tastes in China, the car will come with a touch of glitzy gold trim.

So where might one buy a Chinese car when it gets here? To keep cars cheap, a new entrant would have to find an alternative to a dealer network, which both adds costs and takes time to develop. When Subaru broke into the U.S. market, it sold cars through gasoline service stations. Pep Boys' Auto Parts stores in the United States are already selling Chinese-made motorcycles and off-road sport bikes. Some are dead ringers in miniature for American-made motorcycles, while others look as if they just drove out of the pages of a Japanese comic book. Retail stores would be an easy alternative channel. Costco and other big-box retailers are a solid possibility. Costco already parks SUVs at store doors and has negotiated no-haggle prices with car dealers around the country. And the stores are already warehouses for the industrial output of China, a sign that their distribution channels are ready for the first wave of Chinese cars coming to America.

China Calling

The experience of Motorola, the U.S. telecommunications giant, offers another lesson in how China's size changes the rules of competition and consumption there and everywhere else. Every month, 5 million new subscribers sign up for mobile-phone service in China. The country's 300 million mobile-phone users make China by far the largest such market in the world (and hundreds of millions more accounts are coming).

Hence the world's makers of handsets need to be in China. It gives them a chance to grow at a time when the big European and U.S. markets are saturated. Not that it's a seller's market: for equipment makers, China is also the most competitive, changeable environment in the world. New manufacturers appear out of nowhere; new phones materialize daily at big-city stores. Currently there are eight hundred handset models to choose from. Young urban consumers change phones on average after only eight months; they sell them to someone else or pass them to family members. Mobile phones in the hands of migrant construction workers, whose annual wages might not even cover the cost of a phone, are a common sight in Shanghai and Beijing.

This mobile-phone market in China was invented by Motorola. The story goes back twenty-some years. For Robert Galvin, the company's former and longtime chief executive, China in the early- to mideighties promised a market that could more than make up for Motorola's having been foiled in Japan for years. But first the company had to develop a top-drawer telecommunications infrastructure. In an unscripted bold stroke at a dreary state ceremony during a tour of the country, Galvin turned to the minister of railroads and asked him whether he wanted to do a good job as minister and be done with it, or whether he wanted to create a world-class society. In doing so, Galvin tapped a thick vein of economic patriotism.

Motorola's company archives on its move into China are deep and open. They show that Galvin and his team knew that eventually the transfer of technology to China would sow formidable Chinese competitors. Nevertheless, Motorola decided its best strategy was to get into China early. Before long, Motorola's reports to China's political leaders—infused with the same missionary vocabulary on industrial quality that had made the company a model for American manufacturers—were soon parroted by China's leadership. Galvin also brought Motorola's best technology to China. The proof today is in the size and efficacy of the country's mobile communications network: calls get through to phones in high-rises, subway cars, and distant hamlets—connections that would stymie mobile phones in the United States.

What no one at Motorola anticipated was how crowded the Chinese market would become. Nokia and Motorola now battle for market share in the Chinese handset business. German, Korean, and Taiwanese makers figure strongly. And all these foreign brands are now facing intense competition from indigenous Chinese phone makers.

"Competition goes through a cycle in China," says Zirui Tian, a researcher at INSEAD, the French business school, "At first the foreigners can make things at much lower cost than the Chinese. But as local companies come along to supply the multinational companies, the supply network expands very fast. Then local Chinese manufacturers can start to source their parts in China and drive the prices of their products far lower than the multinationals."

One of Motorola's most important suppliers is the battery maker BYD Company Ltd., based in Shenzhen, near Hong Kong. In only a decade, the private company has gone from virtual invisibility to owning more than 50 percent of the global market in mobile-phone batteries. Before BYD, phone batteries were made in highly automated plants, like those run by Sanyo and Sony in Japan. But BYD, like Wanfeng, stripped robots and other machines out of the manufacturing process and replaced them with an army of workers. By paying for Chinese salaries, and not for million-dollar American, German, or Japanese machines, BYD slashed the price of batteries. Initially the company could not meet Motorola's quality demands, but the American company sent a team of engineers to work with the upstarts, and six months later BYD earned a Six Sigma certification, a universally recognized badge of quality (which Motorola itself invented). That in China machines can be replaced by people for huge cost savings and *without sacrifice in quality* changes the competitive landscape of the global marketplace. When Motorola and Nokia were pressed to lower their prices by Chinese competitors, they turned to BYD.

One of the biggest challenges facing Motorola and other global manufacturers is that Chinese suppliers are getting too good. Their quality, low-priced parts have helped create new, homegrown, and extremely aggressive competitors. More than 40 percent of the Chinese domestic handset market now belongs to local companies such as Ningbo Bird, Nanjing Panda Electronics, Haier, and TCL Mobile. Ningbo Bird will produce 20 million handsets in 2004 and is likely soon to nudge its way into the ranks of the top ten mobile-phone makers in the world. The domestic makers have become so strong that when Siemens found its mobile handset business in China wanting, it joined with Ningbo Bird to gain both low-cost manufacturing and a developed distribution channel. Yet Motorola can't exactly exit the Chinese market. If it did, says Jim Gradoville, Motorola's vice president of Asia Pacific government relations, the Chinese companies that emerged from the crucible of their market would be the leanest and most aggressive in the world, and a company like his would have no idea what hit it. So Motorola stays. Already the largest foreign investor in China's electronics industry, Motorola plans to triple its stake there to more than $10 billion by 2006.

325,000 New Engineers Each Year

How does any company cut costs and raise quality simultaneously? It hires the smartest, most energetic people it can find in China.

"Look, China is the most exciting place in the world right now to be a manufacturer," says Mark Wall, president of the greater China region for GE Plastics. His operation sells the plastic pellets used to make everything from DVDs to building materials. Within two years GE will sell $1 billion in advanced materials, including plastics, in China. Wall, who came to China from GE Plastics, Brazil, describes a country in love with manufacturing like no other, where engineers come in excited and readily work long days. Where university students clamor to get into engineering and applied sciences. Like many American manufacturing executives in China, Wall talks about working in China with the delight that young computer whizzes felt when they found cool in Silicon Valley. Wall says he feels at home. He loves it.

GE, meanwhile, has every plan to capitalize on the local zeal for manufacturing. It recently opened a giant industrial research center in Shanghai, and by next year it will employ twelve hundred people in its Chinese labs. The company has also set up scholarship programs at leading Chinese technical universities.

GE will have no shortage of good candidates. The government is pouring resources into creating the world's largest army of industrialists. China has 17 million university and advanced vocational students (up more than threefold in five years), the majority of whom are in science and engineering. China will produce 325,000 engineers this year. That's five times as many as in the United States, where the number of engineering graduates has been declining since the early 1980s. It is hard to imagine Americans' enthusiasm for engineering sinking lower. Forty percent of all students who enter universities on the engineering track change their mind.

The ability of American industry to stay ahead of its international competition rests on the national gifts and resources that the United States devotes to innovation. Certainly, the confidence of big American companies like Motorola, General Motors, and Intel, all of which have billion-dollar-plus stakes in China, is based on the brainpower they have at home. The research gap between the United States and China remains vast. In December, Washington authorized $3.7 billion to finance nanotechnology research, a sum the Chinese government cannot easily match within a scientific infrastructure that would itself take many more billions (and years) to build.

Yet when it comes to more mainstream, applied industrial development and innovation, the separation among Chinese, American, and other multinational firms is beginning to narrow. Last year, China spent $60 billion on research and development. The only countries that spent more were the United States and Japan, which spent $282 billion and $104 billion, respectively. But again, China forces you to do the math: China's engineers and scientists usually make between one-sixth and one-tenth what Americans do, which means that the wide gaps in financing do not necessarily result in equally wide gaps in manpower or results. The United States spent nearly five times what China did, but had less than two times as many researchers (1.3 million to 743,000).

For now, the emphasis in Chinese labs is weighted overwhelmingly toward the "D" side—meaning training for technical employees and managers. Nevertheless, foreign companies are quickly moving to integrate their China-based labs into their global research operations. Motorola has nineteen research labs in China that develop technology for both the local and global markets. Several of the company's most innovative recent phones were developed there for the Chinese market.

Motorola's newest research center is located forty minutes from Chengdu, the capital of Sichuan, a province in southwestern China. Sichuan is slightly larger than California, but three times as populous. There are about 107 million people in the province, forty-three universities, and 1.2 million scientists and engineers. Sichuan's fragmented transportation system prevents Chengdu from rivaling the eastern powerhouses as a manufacturing center, but the city is promoting the advantage of its plentiful, relatively low-cost brain pool with its new research corridor, the West High-Tech Zone. And Motorola regards its building—subsidized generously by the development zone—as a world center for software engineering. The company now employs more than 150 developers there and has plans to add hundreds more. That will pit it against a growing number of the world's top research-driven enterprises taking advantage of Chengdu's largess: Intel, Ericsson, D-Link, Siemens, Alcatel, Mitsui & Company and Fuji Heavy Industries of Japan, and more than two hundred other firms in one of the area's special tech districts.

In all, foreign companies have established between two hundred and four hundred of their own research centers in China since 1990. China's *People's Daily* has reported that most of the world's largest transnational corporations have set up research and development projects in China. In part, tax incentives attract such financing. But the biggest incentive of all, of course, is access to China's consumers.

What is the likely outcome of all this R&D investment in China?

Even more overcapacity. Just as China's abundant unskilled workers feed the world more shoes and more gadgets than it needs—or at least more than it can absorb without forcing prices down—China's abundance of newly skilled industrialists threatens to swamp the world's most highly prized high-tech markets. In the past three years, foreign investors have invested or pledged $15 billion to build nineteen new semiconductor factories. China imports 80 percent of the semiconductor chips it needs, $19 billion worth, and the government has made it a point of national pride to end the country's dependence on foreigners. Industry observers seem to agree that China will be able to compete with the world's leading semiconductor makers in a decade, but even before that it may exert strong downward pressure on chip prices. Is there a coming recession in the chip market? Morris Chang, the influential founder of Taiwan Semiconductor Manufacturing, the world's largest dedicated independent semiconductor foundry, asked an industry gathering. "Yes, I think there will be," he said. And who will cause it? China, thanks to all the capacity it's building.

Plunging into Soft Tissue

Given how quickly China means to climb the industrial ladder, perhaps the next question is whether any commercial technology is beyond an imminent challenge from China. Gal Dymant, an American-Israeli venture capitalist in Beijing, believes the answer is that few will be. One of the companies Dymant works with, a database publisher named Asia Direct, produces an annual *China Hi-Tech Directory*. Tracking the directory's updates year to year gives Dymant an informal measure of the shifts in Chinese industry.

The first thing one notices about the directories, he says, is how much thicker they grow every year, particularly in industries where there have been mammoth foreign investments. In 2003, Asia Direct's directory grew considerably fatter in the sections devoted to China's domestic mobile-phone manufacturers and suppliers, broadband communications, and in companies establishing themselves in cities outside of China's eastern powerhouses. The manufacture and sale of integrated chips is also soaring, along with healthy gains in China's software and information-services markets. Then again, every section in the directory has grown, including biotechnology, semiconductors, and Internet development, areas in which Chinese firms have newly established themselves, many now in partnership with the world's leading technology-driven companies.

Casting a seasoned eye across the investment landscape, Dymant finds medical equipment to be one of the most promising areas for the future. He is putting together an investor group to build a Chinese version of one of the world's most advanced and costly medical devices, the magnetic resonance imaging (MRI) machine, a $2-million, room-size miracle of technology that captures detailed images of soft tissue in the human body. Patients are placed within a magnetic coil and bombarded with radio waves. Because different atoms in the body respond differently to waves, physicians can see abnormalities in the areas that the MRI captures. Although they are expensive, MRI machines can spare patients exploratory surgery in some cases and in others make available diagnostic findings that were once impossible.

"The talent is here to build anything," Dymant says. "We think we can develop MRIs for about sixty percent of the price they are built for in the United States."

That's a big claim. Although the $4-billion-a-year MRI market is destined to keep growing, especially as the machine itself evolves for a greater number of uses, actually making a marketable MRI machine is a considerable undertaking. The process requires the best of the world's expertise in several highly technical fields. A Chinese industry would involve physicists with up-to-date knowledge of nuclear resonance and superconductivity. It would need programmers and technicians who can handle precise 3-D-magnetic-field design. It would require experts in materials science who understand magnetic materials, and others who design and steer the manufacture of the latest in integrated circuits.

Yet Dymant does not want to just build *a* machine, but one worthy of challenging the ones produced by the likes of Philips, General Electric, Siemens, and other companies that bring the best technology into their MRI devices. Making an MRI device that is even slightly out-of-date would pit China's industry against the large market in used machines that already supplies hospitals outside of advanced industrial countries with cut-rate, but still highly useful, equipment. No, a new industry would have to build machines that are as flexible and usable as the best, but much cheaper. "In China, it can be done," says Dymant, "because the expertise is here and available at much lower cost."

Would a Chinese-made MRI have Chinese-made computer chips in it? If not immediately, then soon. In a special October 2004 issue devoted to China, *Fortune* magazine focused on the success that Intel has had in seizing market share and racking up profits in the country, won with daring investments and marketing strategies.[4] The company's success would seem assured except that China's market for computers and microprocessors, though big, is still growing so fast that Intel's future in China faces serious challenges from latecomers, including Chinese companies that are finding ways to challenge Intel's seemingly unbeatable technological lead.

Researchers at the Chinese Academy of Sciences, working with BLX, a chip-design firm that was started by academy scientists, claim to have come up with a chip, called Godson 3, that equals Intel's best chips from four years ago. To bring Chinese chips up to Intel's current level of technology, BLX has joined with Intel's American archrival Advanced Micro Devices, which has its own designs on Intel's place in the Chinese market.

Speaking to the press, Dr. Li Guojie, chairman of BLX, and the director of the Institute of Computing Technology, Chinese Academy of Sciences, said, "The partnership between AMD and BLX is a win-win solution. We are pleased to collaborate at a deep level with a world-class company like AMD who is committed to explore this market with BLX not only for China, but also for increasing visibility of Chinese design and technology globally."

The arrangement also shows the tight links between China's government research arms and its efforts to acquire advanced technology. By playing foreign firms against one another in the marketplace, China will soon push to the top ranks of chip manufacturers.

A similar process may well make China into a strong competitor in advanced medical devices. The world is full of technology firms that compete to provide parts and software for MRI machines. They will be working hard to crack the China market and will inevitably be offering their best technology to firms such as Dymant's that are looking to create a Chinese MRI industry.

Taking a Pill for the Pain

The potential market for cutting-edge Chinese-made MRI machines suggests the changes coming to Chinese health-care practices, even in a society where private health-care insurance policies are rare and most medical care is provided pay-as-you-go. Although traditional Chinese medicine will remain entrenched in the culture well into the foreseeable future, the demand for Western medicine is soaring. China's drug industry is big, with sales of $7.5 billion in 2004. China also exports $3.5 billion worth of Western medicines, which are particularly welcome in countries with few regulatory screens and a need for low-cost medicines.

The great American and European drug companies—among the most profitable enterprises in the world—know this, of course. Not that they tread into the Chinese market easily. Rather, they enter knowing full well they face a China often unwilling to honor the precious patent and trademark protections upon which the profits of drug companies depend.

Unlike most businesses, the pharmaceutical industry is an open book to new entrants because the components and chemical mechanisms of all drugs sold in advanced economies are available in documents on file with government regulators. Foreign drug companies beyond the power of effective regulatory regimes can easily comb government records for the formulas of products they can reproduce themselves. The value of this information is enormous. For example, Pfizer, the maker of Viagra, had $45 billion in revenue in 2003 and spent $7.1 billion on research and development.[5]

Until recently, nearly every drug sold in China was a copy of a foreign drug, a fact reflected in China's meager pharmaceutical research and development. Allan Zhang, senior economist at Pricewaterhouse-Coopers, notes that in 1999 total R&D in China's drug industry did not match the budget of any single large global drug company. "Up until now," Zhang writes, "this strategy has made economic sense for a developing country like China: while it takes Western companies about ten to fifteen years—at an average of $250 million—to develop a new medicine, copying new medicines takes only three to five years, at a cost between . . . $60,000 and $120,000."[6]

China's willingness to protect foreign drug companies from poaching is improving, but is still far from predictable. Pfizer lost its patent protection for Viagra in China when the government ruled the company's patent application did not adequately describe the use of the drug's key ingredient. In addition, the drug, according to the ruling, failed to meet the "novelty requirement," which for Pfizer turns out to be a kind of catch-22, since the requirement means, in essence, that drugs that have successfully been copied in China before they are marketed by their foreign originators have no chance for patent protection. The ruling left open the door for the makers of Viagra's low-cost equivalents, which in China are—as they would be anywhere—big sellers. Local press coverage of the Viagra ruling made a point of mentioning that one Viagra pill costs one yuan to manufacture but sells for ninety-eight yuan, something sure to pique the attention of margin-squeezing Chinese manufacturers and perhaps encourage more copycats to rush to market.*

Although Pfizer fought the ruling, not every company sees value in mixing it up publicly with the Chinese government. In the wake of the fight over Viagra, British drug giant GlaxoSmithKline simply gave up its patent rights to a key component of its highly successful diabetes drug Avandia when its initial efforts to enforce its rights met a court challenge from three Chinese competitors. The company did not comment on the motives for its capitulation, but one can wonder whether some behind-the-scenes deliberations convinced the company that its success in the Chinese market over the long haul requires it to sharpen its political standing before it sharpens its legal briefs. The key in China is to stay in

---

*The vast majority of Chinese pharmacies, the kind that dispense Western-style medicines, are still government-run and look it. Druggists in long white lab coats that look as though they were salvaged from a World War II hospital ship dispense medicines after prescriptions pass through three or four layers of the microbureaucracies of the shop. The stores themselves look like vintage hospital dispensaries, devoid of the advertising and special offers that scream from the floors, walls, and ceiling of a Western chain store. Viagra exists somewhere on the guarded shelves of the government shops, but it is available only by prescription. Chinese customers need not brave the scrutiny of the pharmacy to buy the drug or knockoff versions of it. Sex stores are booming in China, which despite China's ostensible prudery, is not so surprising. China is the source of much of the erotic knick-knacks that are sold around the world, especially the latex and plastic varieties. China's sex stores display those unabashedly; the boxes even sit in their windows looking out onto busy streets. They also sells chemical aids, and lots of Viagra-like stuff.

the market, and many companies are willing to make extraordinary bargains to preserve a place. The Chinese government is far from enamored with the Western tendency to push disputes into court and, to its credit, forces negotiation on a wide range of issues that in other countries would be attacked with lawyers. And to its further credit, the results of negotiation tend to weigh heavily toward the interests of the Chinese players. Or in the case of Pfizer, to side with the country's Davids against the Big Pharma Goliath.

Another factor is most certainly at work too. The Chinese government is by far the largest purchaser of drugs in the country, and it's in its budgetary interest to keep prices down.[7] Its strategy often works; many important drugs cost less in China than they do nearly everywhere else in the world.

The Chinese are tough with foreign drug makers for yet another reason: the world's largest pharmaceutical companies are by nearly any measure among the most successful businesses in history, and China has little desire to remain a nation of copycat drug firms. Medical and related biotechnology research is among its top scientific priorities. In fact, China is developing a large population of researchers working in the life sciences. In biotech alone, the country boasts fifty thousand research scientists, with another forty-five hundred graduating from universities every year. China also works hard to attract Chinese scientists who have been trained and have worked abroad. The Shenzhen biotech corridor is one example of a local government luring scientists to private enterprise, but across the country there are similar efforts to attract foreign-trained scientists into Chinese academia. China offers returning scholars high positions and salaries commensurate with what they were making abroad.

The country is still far behind the well-resourced labs of America, Europe, and Japan. The advanced R&D processes used by multinational drug companies, for instance, are still rare in China.[8] Remedy, however, will likely come quickly from foreign companies setting up research in China. According to the British pharmaceutical trade magazine *Scrip,* China's allure goes beyond its affordable scientists to what the magazine delicately calls China's "freedom of research." That is the country's willingness to forge ahead in areas that other countries, the United States in particular, have found ethically sticky.

At the top of the list is research on human embryonic stem cells, which faces none of the religious objections that conservatives in America have raised to stymie research in U.S. labs. *Scrip* points out that China's willingness to charge ahead has led to several potent research partnerships between medical centers, universities, and multinational companies. To name two among many, Swiss giant Roche has joined with the Chinese National Human Genome Center in Shanghai to investigate diabetes and schizophrenia, and GlaxoSmithKline is working with another Shanghai research center to develop an advanced lab for recombinatorial chemistry.*

Beyond such high-profile collaborations, China has hundreds of biotech laboratories (some focused on agriculture) and a growing number of start-ups each year. The country is pouring no less than $600 million a year directly into biotech research,[9] much of it aimed at a rapidly growing market. Frost and Sullivan, a New York research and consulting firm with offices worldwide, estimates that the Chinese biotechnology market will grow at 13.5 percent a year and soon reach $8.8 billion in sales. The growth will come as China's own firms mature, and as global companies move to tap China's brains at bargain prices.[10]

Greg Lucier, the president and CEO of Invitrogen, a company that yearly sells a billion dollars' worth of tools and technologies to biotech research labs, describes China as having "one of the most developed sets of scientific communities that we see outside the United States and is really quite strong in terms of agricultural biotech and gene therapy."

Lucier notes that from 1998 until 2004, China made a mark as one of six countries involved in the Human Genome Project, and that its scientists continue to decode genomes and make them available to the research community worldwide. He also points out that it was China that introduced the world to a complete genome for rice, "a very important development." The country's growing population and shrinking stock of arable land lend urgency to this agricultural biotech research, and China already has one of the highest concentrations in the world of

---

*One of China's politically awkward advantages for drug companies is that the country has an extremely large population of untreated sick people who can be enlisted into drug trials at low cost. China's millions of AIDS sufferers are one such group, and its 300 million smokers are another.

genetically modified crops growing in its fields. In human medicine, China has been an early adopter of gene-therapy drugs; it was one of the first countries where Gendicine, a drug for use with certain cancers, was commercially sold. "They really are on the cutting edge of gene therapy as we see it," says Lucier.

The commercial potential of China's biotech, Lucier allows, is just beginning to show, yet he warns that China has a way of creating big businesses fast. Lucier measures China's future in the millions' worth of annual sales his company already makes, and the $100 million of cumulative sales it expects to make by 2006. As a veteran executive at General Electric, Lucier saw how it took China only five years to develop into a billion-dollar market for MRI machines and other advanced medical products. "There's a very fast-growing, affluent health-care population coming in China that will want the type of very expensive drugs that come out of biotech," he says.

Flights of Fancy

All those American and European drug company executives arriving each day by jumbo jet in Shanghai and Beijing to scout the challenging Chinese market enter the country's spotless new airports knowing that the cost of doing business may be the forfeiture of the wide profit margins that popular drugs and medical devices earn worldwide. But they may not realize that the very airplane they've arrived on is, like their proprietary pharmaceuticals, a product highly prized by the Chinese.

Few industries pit nations as fiercely against one another as aerospace. The intense competition between U.S. aircraft maker Boeing and European Airbus is particularly visible, but competition among a worldwide assortment of smaller aircraft companies and components manufacturers is just as heated and far more geographically diverse. Brazilian, Russian, Canadian, and German companies vie for the growing market in smaller passenger jets, for example. The civilian aircraft industry may also be the most demanding of governments for financial and political support. Boeing, which is seen as a vital strategic manufacturer in the United States, receives billions in government defense money. (The once seemingly indomitable company now struggles to compete in both its defense and civilian aircraft businesses. Between 1998 and 2003, Boeing's workforce dropped from 238,600 to 157,054.)[11] The ownership of Airbus is divided up among companies with strong links to the national governments of Britain, France, Germany, and Spain, and the company became the world's leading aircraft maker on the strength of massive government subsidies and favorable treatment from government-owned European airlines.

The benefits of much of that largess now find their way to China, the world's largely untapped market for aircraft. Although China has long manufactured warplanes, including a new light fighter designed to fulfill the needs of the military export market, as well as missiles, the country has not yet built a wide-body commercial passenger jet to a global standard. Projections for growth of Chinese air travel are enormous. Airbus estimates that the Chinese market will grow fivefold by 2022, and that the country will need at least thirteen hundred planes that seat one hundred or more people to meet the demand. That makes China's skies a $140 billion market,[12] and the world's aircraft makers will do whatever is necessary to reach for it. Only the U.S. market would be bigger.

By the standards of the new Chinese economy, Boeing has a long history in the country. As with telecommunications, air travel is a networked business whose growth depends on increasing connections between points. Boeing saw early on that its involvement would give it a place in a market destined to explode. Its efforts paid off in aircraft sales. Today, Boeing planes have a 65 percent share of the Chinese market. Boeing has also played an important role in the development of China's aircraft industry, helping Chinese companies grow into suppliers of key parts of its aircraft. The company reports more than three thousand Boeing aircraft worldwide incorporate major parts and assemblies from Chinese suppliers. By 2010, Boeing will be buying $1.3 billion worth of parts in China each year.

"Boeing's industrial partnership with China is real and current," David Wang, president of Boeing China told the Chinese press in 2004. "Our emphasis is that these programs should be able to add value to our Chinese partners as much as possible as soon as they can." Wang's remarks are a public show of how willing Boeing is to move technology to China as quickly as possible.

The willingness to prep local suppliers and bring in foreign technology is an important part of the bargains that aircraft companies make to gain access to the Chinese market. Airbus and all other major sellers in China's aircraft market play the roles as best they can too. China prudently alternates which aircraft makers it buys planes from, giving it leverage to forge the best terms on price and technical transfers from each of them. A 1999 report issued by the Bureau of Industry and Security arm of the U.S. Department of Commerce observed that "despite the obviously enormous opportunities present in China's aviation sector . . . U.S. aerospace companies, represented primarily by Boeing . . . and several parts suppliers, appear to be willing to make significant concessions to Chinese state planners in coproduction agreements in return for increased market access." The report goes on to give credence to complaints that U.S.-based aerospace firms "have already agreed to onerous conditions in order to win access to the market in the PRC by acceding to coproduction deals and technology transfers." It also cites remarks by an executive at supplier Allied Signal (now part of Honeywell) who expresses hope that the company's technology transfers will buy it a place in the Chinese market, calling the move "recognition by senior management that there's just a tremendous future market potential for aerospace in China, and we need to be there."[13] As in all industries, China's entry into the WTO disallows forced technology transfers, but it is unlikely to hamper aerospace firms locked in an intense global battle from bartering their jewels for advantage.

As a result of its toughness, the Chinese government can now proclaim the country as a major center for aircraft parts and whole planes. The manufacture of a newly designed regional jet by China Aviation Industry Corp I, a state-owned aviation company, is being undertaken with technical support from Boeing.[14] The company expects to make China's first large aircraft by 2018. "China's aviation sector will be incomplete without developing its own civil aviation industry," Liu Gaozhuo, the company's president, said in *China Daily*. "Neither could China elevate itself as an aviation power if it does not develop large aircraft by itself."[15] Liu also recounted how past efforts to create a homegrown aircraft failed, in part because China did not have the intellectual property rights to make many of the components needed to get a plane off the ground. The country's new large plane, he claimed, will be built with intellectual property owned by the Chinese. He did not elaborate how much of that will have been cajoled out of foreign companies as a condition for their role in the Chinese market.

It is natural for countries to use their market power to gain whatever commercial advantage they can. Faulting the Chinese for extracting concessions from companies that want to play in its yard would be faulting it for demanding what its corporate suitors have willingly agreed to. And if the Chinese usurp technology that is not rightfully theirs, it is hard to argue that the corporate victims, at least in aerospace, could have expected otherwise. Companies such as Boeing and Airbus have made their choice. They participate in China's great aviation market because China's growth gives them a chance to sell hundreds of planes outside their mature markets. Without China, perhaps neither would prosper.

But while they make their bargain with the Chinese, global aerospace companies create an aircraft industry that will eventually meet them head-on. China's regional jet, its government-owned maker claims, is a success because it costs millions less than the competition. If China's large aircraft undercuts the competition and finds a captive market among China's airlines, as Airbus once found in Europe, then the world's aircraft makers will need a new survival strategy. If so, most likely they will appeal to their own governments for subsidy, no matter which Chinese gambits have come back to haunt them.

CHAPTER NINE

PIRATE NATION

- A brewery near the coastal city of Tianjin counterfeits Heineken and Budweiser beers. Its fake brews are sold in restaurants and "other entertainment establishments." Beer counterfeiters in China tend to use shoddy glass bottles, and consumers have repeatedly been hurt by exploding bottles.
- Food counterfeiters in China have targeted Coca-Cola, Starbucks, Häagen-Dazs, and several foreign cheese brands.
- Procter & Gamble shampoos Head & Shoulders and Rejoice are faked in Lanzhou in Gansu Province, south of Inner Mongolia.
- A Shenzhen company makes fake Cisco and 3Com network cards.
- In Sichuan Province, counterfeiters set up a fake prison to manufacture forty types of phony brand-name cigarettes. Police said it was unclear whether the workers had been hired or kidnapped by the counterfeiters. China is said to produce 100 billion counterfeit brand-name cigarettes a year. Fakes found on the market in London contained a third more nicotine and carbon monoxide, and three-quarters more tar, than legal brands. They also frequently contained strange ingredients such as plastic or sand.
- Officials in Kenya seize huge shipments of counterfeit tires and batteries made in China.
- Thousands of Chinese-made items of counterfeit Tommy Bahama, Polo, Ralph Lauren, Tommy Hilfiger, Hermès, Lacoste, Hugo Boss, and Emporio Armani clothing and other designer-brand merchandise valued close to $1 million were seized from a trading group in Apex, North Carolina. "We are constantly on the

231

lookout for suspicious sellers on eBay, at flea markets, and, as in this case, operating under the guise of being a legitimate business," stated a spokesman for Oxford Industries, the parent company of Tommy Hilfiger.

- When Nintendo's own team of antipiracy investigators joined Chinese law enforcement officials in a 2004 raid of an electronics factory in South China, they found ten thousand counterfeit Game Boy cartridges. The haul was minuscule compared with the amount of piracy the Japanese game company faces in China, where cartridges for its Game Boy machines, which were designed to discourage copying, are cloned relentlessly. Nintendo claims to have lost $720 million in sales in 2003 as a result of piracy, though its dedicated teams seized 4 million fake cartridges. The company, whose share of the legitimate game market is under pressure, can ill afford to cede too many of its immensely popular Game Boy games to pirates.

- Despite public announcements of a national crackdown on makers of counterfeit eyewear in China, half of the eyewear and lenses sold on Renmin Road in Guangzhou, one of China's busiest eyewear marketplaces, are fake. Frames that mimic Gucci and Versace cost between $.80 and $2.50. There are even frames labeled Louis Vuitton, though the fashion house does not make any such products. When Guangzhou officials in charge of quality supervision tested lenses in the wholesale markets, they found that 80 percent of them were substandard and put users' eyes at risk.

- Ford Motor blames counterfeiters of auto parts for $2 billion a year in lost sales. The company took part in a raid of a Chinese factory making brake pads and turned up seven thousand sets of counterfeit pads. In 2004, GM investigated four hundred counterfeiting schemes, including the one mentioned in chapter eight involving the alleged theft of the specifications of an entire car, which a Chinese rival then allegedly built. The U.S. Department of Commerce estimates that automotive companies could hire 210,000 more employees if the counterfeit auto trade disappeared.

- Syngenta, a world-leading Swiss agrochemicals company, successfully sued Chinese competitors for pirating its patented advanced insecticide Thiamethoxam. The Swiss press lamented that the action was likely to have little effect.

- In July 2004, two Americans arrested in Shanghai were caught with 210,000 counterfeit movie DVDs.
- When Creative Technologies, a Singapore maker of consumer electronics and computer parts, introduced a small, innovative, and patented MP3 player called the MuVo, company executives patrolling the markets in Shanghai soon found knockoffs made by forty different companies. Sim Wong Hoo, Creative's chairman, told a trade association meeting in Singapore that when one counterfeit operation is closed in China, another making Creative clones springs up. "You can't sue them all. How can we fight them?" he asked. Creative has resorted to using Chinese manufacturers to make bargain versions of its products for the Chinese market, to be sold below the price of the more polished versions the company sells elsewhere.
- In a case with broad implications for China's multibillion-dollar investments aimed at making the country a world leader in the manufacture of computer chips, one of the world's contract chip makers, Taiwan Semiconductor Manufacturing Co., Ltd., or TSMC, filed suit in a U.S. federal court against an upstart mainland rival, Semiconductor Manufacturing International Corp, or SMIC. The mainland company has caught up with foreign rivals in such a short time that an analyst at Goldman Sachs argues the company will soon be the world's third largest provider of chips. SMIC received some help from its German and Japanese technology partners. But SMIC's Taiwanese rival contends that the mainland company waged a long campaign of industrial espionage and corporate raiding. Memos produced for the lawsuit allegedly sent by SMIC executives to spies in TSMC detail the many proprietary processes the newer company hoped to steal. "Sorry for the long list," the memo's conclusion is said to have read, "but we need a lot of material to set up the new operation." SMIC is also said to have raided TSMC for 140 key personnel, including its head of R&D and a manager of its technology-transfer division.
- Hundreds of thousands of pirated copies of J. K. Rowling's Harry Potter books have been sold throughout China. Their success is so pronounced that Chinese counterfeiters have produced their own

original volumes of Potter stories and sold them under Rowling's name.

- Officials in four of China's eastern provinces broke up a ring of medical inspectors and phony pharmaceutical sellers and seized forty thousand boxes of fake rabies vaccines made only of saline solution. The fake vaccines were sold to rural clinics in areas of China where rabies is still a serious threat.

- When Yamaha sued in China to stop Chinese manufacturers from selling unauthorized copies of its motorbikes (which outnumber genuine Yamahas many times over), the Japanese company's representative helped prove its case by driving three real Yamaha motorcycles into the court to compare with the fakes. Yamaha was awarded a mere $109,000 in damages. Japan's Ministry of Economy, Trade, and Industry contends that of the 11 million motorcycles produced in China in 2002, 9 million were imitations of Japanese products and attributed the significant decline in the sale of Japanese bikes in China to the fakes.

- A Beijing court ruled against Toyota when the company brought suit against Geely, one of China's largest private automobile manufacturers. Toyota complained that Geely used Toyota's logo on one of its cars and the Toyota name to sell it. The court ruled that China did not recognize Toyota's logo, one of the best-known corporate marks in the world.

- Officials in Shenzhen raided an electronics manufacturing group that ran four factories making fake brand-name DVD players labeled Toshiba, Panasonic, Sony, Philips, Sanyo, and others. Prior to the raid, the group won a government award for being "an honest private company."

- China's central government announced a plan to crack down on the sale of fake bird-flu vaccines.

- Ninety percent of Microsoft products in China are pirated.[1]

China, the world's factory floor, is also the center of the world's $250-billion-a-year business in counterfeit merchandise. Estimates of China's share of the counterfeit trade range between $19 billion[2] and $80 billion.[3] One trend that looks certain is that as China's share of world trade climbs, so will the world's supply of counterfeit goods. According to Carratu International, a leading British corporate investigations firm whose practice focuses on abuses of intellectual property, 9 percent of world trade today is counterfeit, but as China's presence in global markets grows, the counterfeit trade will more than double before the end of the decade.[4]

Stolen in Plain Sight

Does China officially care about what it is doing? You can't tell by checking the label; if China's commitment to wipe out commercial counterfeiting were judged by the laws that the country has on its books, the Chinese government would look as strict about poaching as any in the world. In the past few years, the country has made a great show of cracking down on the illegal counterfeiting of DVDs, CDs, and clothing. Newspapers and nightly television news programs regularly feature stories about government raids on massive counterfeiting operations. Hundreds of thousands of DVDs and duplicating machines seized here, a warehouse of CDs there, and trucks full of sham designer handbags somewhere else. Considering that a generation ago China had virtually no laws protecting intellectual property, and a long cultural history that values copying and borrowing,* the raids against counterfeiters might be deemed impressive signals of the government's desire to enforce its own statutes.

Yet the supply of fake goods on the street and in the markets never seems to drop. The latest fashions from the Milan runways still arrive in season in China's alleyways, and Hollywood films are still sold off the backs of bicycles the same week they premiere in America. What's more, the raids that do occur are puzzling. Why are some intellectual-

---

*The argument that Chinese culture, which values conformity and honoring masterworks, has been more disposed than others to copy literature, art, and commercial products is common. A cold glance around the world ought to make the Chinese look less exceptional in this regard. Strong intellectual property regimes are a relatively recent invention, and they exist not because some cultures are less willing to pirate and counterfeit than others, but because some are more willing to police the widespread urge of their own constituents to infringe in the interest of providing an environment that creates more choices for consumers, and ultimately economic growth.

property pirates nabbed in one place on one day, but still operating freely and openly nearby? The purposes behind the publicized raids are always obscure, and the Chinese who read about them are skeptical about taking the raids at face value. Are they the result of turf wars among the government fiefdoms that are themselves knee-deep in counterfeiting? Did the raided factories push the Party's tolerance of violent and eroticized Western entertainment too far? Did they pirate a movie backed by the Chinese government?* Or was that day's demonstration of will just a show for a foreign trade group coming to China to—yet again—express its grave concerns over intellectual-property theft?

In the end, no matter who is led off in handcuffs on the evening news, everyone in China who has something to buy or sell knows little changes the national addiction to fake goods. And in the end, no one really expects the Chinese government to successfully crack down. The most common punishment against counterfeiters is to confiscate the stock of products they have on hand. Nothing more.

The larger truth is that the Chinese economy has staked a great deal on its counterfeiters. They provide the people with affordable goods. Often, as in the case of medicines and medical devices, some foods, school textbooks, and clothing, counterfeit goods are essential goods, meaning that any government crackdown, in effect, taxes China's needy consumers. Counterfeiters also serve their country by usurping foreign technology China desperately needs to meet its industrial goals. The counterfeiters give China's growing number of globally competitive companies the means to compete with powerful foreign rivals who are forced to pay full fare for proprietary technologies. And in a broader geopolitical context, China's counterfeiters deny the world's advanced economies, America's and Japan's in particular, the wherewithal to sell to China the valuable designs, trademarked goods, advanced technology, and the world-beating entertainment products that the Chinese urgently desire but cannot yet produce on their own.

---

*Movies that received significant support from the Chinese government are hard to find in bootleg bins. In 2003, *Hero* was one of the titles that apparently no one dared to copy, but was widely sold in an officially licensed version in the DVD sections of major department stores and bookshops.

When challenged, Chinese officials complain that piracy poses too large a problem for them to police. The country must first focus on feeding its people and encouraging economic development, they say. And they are right. Nothing about counterfeiting really upsets the government enough to act forcefully. If the sellers of DVDs suddenly found a brisk market for disks that promoted Tibetan independence, the virtues of the banned religious sect Falun Gong, or Taiwan's admission to the United Nations, these DVDs would certainly disappear overnight, and all those anticounterfeiting laws on the books would find ready application.

Chinese officialdom also has more at stake in the survival of counterfeiting than in its demise because China has innumerable local jurisdictions, each with its own enforcement regime. Daniel C. K. Chow, professor at the Moritz College of Law at Ohio State University and one of America's leading legal experts in Chinese intellectual-property enforcement, testified before the U.S. Senate's Committee on Governmental Affairs in April 2004, "No problem of this size and scope could exist without the direct or indirect involvement of the state. In China, the national government in Beijing appears to be sincere in its recognition of the importance of protecting intellectual-property rights, but national-level authorities are policy and lawmaking bodies, whereas enforcement occurs on the ground at the local level. At this level, local governments are either directly or indirectly involved in supporting the trade in counterfeit goods."

Counterfeiting, Chow explains, creates jobs and supports entire local economies. The large markets throughout the country, some with a thousand or more sellers in one place, are managed by local authorities, who often play the dual roles of regulators and investors, collecting license fees in one role and rents in the other.

Brand Awareness

For years, Beijing's premier venue for designer knockoffs was the long row of 147 rudimentarily enclosed shops called Silk Alley. The market opened in 1984 and has grown into one of the top tourist destinations in the city, attracting ten thousand visitors a day.[5] Here, East European men dressed in worn work pants and beat-up leather jackets hurry through the shops with fifty-gallon trash bags, filling them with stacks of phony Esprit socks, Calvin Klein briefs, and Lacoste shirts for resale elsewhere. Here, the flight attendants for the world's premier airlines, dressed in uniform for their afternoon departures, stroll through with multiple rolling suitcases, filling them with watches, handbags, sunglasses, fountain pens, cigarette lighters, cashmere sweaters, silk ties, and leather jackets, all dead ringers for genuine merchandise sold in shops worldwide. For them, Silk Alley acts as wholesaler for "purse parties" in their home ports.*

Despite this brisk business in fakes, the diverse economy of Beijing is not nearly as dependent on counterfeit industries as are other cities. Chow notes that Yiwu, the city in Zhejiang Province that is also a center for the holiday-decoration trade, is well-known as a center for commercial piracy. Every day, says Chow, two hundred thousand customers visit thirty-three thousand wholesalers in Yiwu selling one hundred thousand different types of products. Over 90 percent of the consumer products sold in Yiwu are bogus. "Most of the businesses that sell counterfeit and infringing goods in Yiwu negotiate a fixed amount of taxes to be paid to the local government. . . . The trade in counterfeit and pirated goods has transformed Yiwu from a poor farming town into an economic model that other towns are seeking to emulate." Clamping down on the infringers would shut down the area's economy. "Because the costs of a crackdown at the local level can be so severe, counterfeiting is heavily defended at local levels."

In Guangdong, where a high concentration of factories have been financed and built with foreign money, and where Chinese-owned

---

*One gauge of the irresistibility of the Silk Alley counterfeiters is the occasional visits by officials who ought to be anywhere else. While returning from a trip to China in July 1998, Charlene Barshefsky, the Clinton administration's tough-as-nails trade negotiator, was caught entering the United States with forty fake Beanie Baby stuffed animals purchased at a Silk Alley stall for her daughters. The toys were most likely black-market versions given their Silk Alley origin and the prolific trade in fake Beanie Babies at the time. The problem of fakes in China was so prevalent that Ty Inc., the toy's maker, had successfully lobbied U.S. Customs to restrict Americans from reentering the country with more than one Beanie Baby. Barshefsky clearly did not know the rule. In August 2004, Italy's Foreign Minister Franco Frattini caused a flap when he bought a fake Rolex in Beijing.

factories tool up with the world's best industrial machines to produce goods for export, the quality of counterfeit merchandise has also benefited. Manufacturers make copies of Rolex watches that can fool Swiss watchmakers and phony electrical components that can sneak undetected into the parts bins of the world's stereo and automotive-control makers. In some big categories of products, such as clothing, *nearly all* of the goods that appear on the Chinese market looking like branded, patented, trademarked, or copyrighted material are faked.

Walking down Huai Hai Road in Shanghai, one can find many of these international brand names, the ones that fill the world's fashion magazines. But as one gets within a couple of blocks of the large outdoor collection of stalls called Xiangyang Gift and Fashion Market, the soldiers of the counterfeit economy go to work. They call out to passersby asking if they want designer watches, purses, DVDs, and, whispering, porn DVDs. Shoo them away and more swarm near asking the same questions. Outside the market, newsstands sell European magazines devoted to fine watches. Inside the market, watch sellers try to find the ones that shoppers point to in the magazines. Usually the sellers have it in the case out front, but for the better watches, they usher buyers through back alleys past touts and guards on watch, up back stairs to rooms that look like shabby apartments, but are in fact showrooms for whole lines of fake watches.

Take a seat, and the apartment dwellers go to work, pulling out valises from under the beds and lifting up the false bottoms in their chests of drawers to pull out even more cases, each filled with dozens of knock-off models. The fakes come in three grades, from clunky steel approximations to fine, exquisite copies. One complex chronograph is copied so well, for example, that one needs the original instruction manual to learn all of its dozen or so functions, which include dual alarms, a split-time stopwatch, and phases of the moon.

One can't quite help but be impressed. The thought occurs that somewhere in China all these thousands of different and ever-changing models of watches are made in factories that have the fine tools and human know-how needed to reverse engineer the crystals, faces, and inner workings of the watches—minute springs, gears, and self-winding mechanisms. Add up all the Longines, Rolexes, Ebels, Swatches, Patek Philippes, and many other brands, and the task to run a watch company so that it stays current seems to take the skills not unlike those needed to build artificial hearts, corneal implants, and precision parts for satellites.

What China's Smartest Students Know about Counterfeiting

No country has a monopoly on smart people. What differs around the world are the constraints that people live under and the incentives they have to channel their energies. If one is willing to accept that there is a like range of intelligence in most places, then it comes as no surprise that China has lots and lots of smart people. When high school students across the country are given university entrance exams for what are, relative to China's population, a small number of university slots, the students who gain admission to China's best schools are an extraordinary group of bright, inexhaustible, and ambitious students.

Once in school, they live in tight quarters, not so unlike those given the migrant women who work in Shenzhen. Crammed six to a room, with no private space to speak of and perhaps just a single large table for all to sit at and a flickering fluorescent lamp overhead, China's university students rarely fail to display the diligence that delivered to them the treasure of higher education.

Beijing's Tsinghua University is China's leading university for science and engineering.* The struggle to get in and stay in forges tight bonds, and students stick together long after graduation. The Tsinghua Entrepreneurs' Forum is one way that former students stay in touch. The Forum holds monthly meetings in a Beijing hotel, and there the Tsinghua graduates who are brave enough to start their own tech businesses come to swap stories and strategies and to network. Some are recent graduates, others are refugees from government work or large Chinese or foreign companies, and still others have returned from advanced study abroad.

*But rivals abound. Just as the Massachusetts Institute of Technology must compete with Cal Tech and the University of Michigan, Tsinghua contends with Nanjing University and Shanghai's Fudan University. But for the Herculean intellects that top China's science exams, Tsinghua is the place.

China today is the land of the start-up, and the Tsinghua alums are as anxious to seize their golden moment as Silicon Valley entrepreneurs were to seize theirs in the 1990s. The Tsinghua group speak excellent English. They read the world press on fast Internet connections and are denizens of China's growing number of department-store-size bookstores, with row after row of shelves lined with business books by Dale Carnegie and Zig Ziglar, Western finance professors, quality gurus, and biographers of model capitalists. The Tsinghua alums know important dates and deals from the lives of Henry Ford and Michael Dell, whom they read about as eagerly as the American managers at the Beijing Jeep factory pore over *The Art of War*.

With the endless variety of opportunities springing up all around them, one would expect the best and the brightest from China's top science and technology university to be brimming with ideas for innovative businesses. Silicon Valley was, after all, where the choice killer applications were far outnumbered by thousands of big, dubiously practicable, but exuberantly creative dreams. Yet if one goes around the room and quizzes the entrepreneurs on their businesses or plans, there's a surprise. A few are venturing into creative fields, such as bottling modern, chemically consistent versions of traditional Chinese medicines, while others with army connections are working on military and security technologies.

But of the group of eighty or so in the Forum, a surprising number, perhaps half, are working on developing services that run on mobile phones. Some work on games for the phone. In 2004, companies that sold message and entertainment services to cell phone users rang up $460 million in sales. In China, mobile phone users use their handsets less to make voice calls than to take advantage of a variety of other services. Short Message Service, or SMS, is one. The Chinese send hundreds of billions of abbreviated text messages to each other each year. For consumers under the age of twenty-five, phone messaging is often preferred over calling, mostly because it costs much less to send a message. There are also social reasons. It is easier, for one thing, to gossip in public exchanging silent phone messages. It is also easier to break awkward news. As anyone with a busy appointment schedule in China soon learns, few people now call to say they will be late or a no-show; they send a text message.

But messaging to friends is just the start. Some of the services send out daily bulletins to people's phones that contain jokes, celebrity news, poems, touching stories, or English lessons. The market is big, but the concentration of interest at the Tsinghua gathering is at first glance puzzling. Compared with China's big industries of manufacturing, construction, real estate, or retail, phone entertainment is not all that huge.

Why then does the phone messaging and entertainment business attract so much talent? The chief reason is that these smart entrepreneurs know that it is one business where their good ideas and designs cannot be stolen. That separates phone messaging and entertainment from virtually every other realm of creative development in China, where designs and content that offer a whiff of a chance that they will grow popular are aped and sold in a flash.

Phone message and entertainment services, however, must be sold through the companies that are the primary sellers of mobile phone service. A company that has a great game for a mobile phone sells it over the phone, sharing revenue with the phone company. A game might cost just seventy or eighty cents, but it can be sold a million times or more in China's big market. And since people can only play and update their games by going through their phone service, money is guaranteed to go to the developers and rightful owners of the software. Smart people like the Tsinghua entrepreneurs have all kinds of great ideas for all sorts of businesses, but they also know where their talents can be rewarded and protected rather than stolen.

Contrast that with other thriving markets in China: fashion, software, movies, music, spare parts for machines, automobiles, and branded food. In each, standard legal protections such as copyrights, patents, and trademarks exist mostly in law books but not in actual practice. In China's market, anything worth protecting is the first target of pirates and counterfeiters. Remember, the country pulled itself into the market economy when its people screwed up their courage and circumvented nearly every rule in the Chinese government's playbook. Nearly the whole of China's twentieth century was spent overturning one set of rules or another. The Communist rise to power was a reaction against the rules of the old China and of foreign powers. Mao's belief in continuous revolution punished Chinese whose understanding of governmental and societal expectations was static. Confucians, democrats, fascists, Soviet-style Marxists, schoolteachers who stuck to their lessons, landlords, peasants, business owners, and factory workers, anyone and everyone lived through one period after another where following the rule book of the day before brought tragedy the day after. China is a country where the public has repeatedly learned that rules spell disaster and that finding ways around them offers hope and dignity.

How normal it is, then, that the central markets in China's cities, where people shop for clothes, music, movies, machines, and software, look to outsiders like thieves' dens where all the world's recognizable products are bootlegged on a nearly unthinkable scale.

Windows Opening Everywhere

Travel nearly anywhere in China where people work with computers and the difficulties faced by the Tsinghua entrepreneurs are obvious. In China's big cities, computers and software are often sold in modern, multistoried, indoor malls. Beijing's Bai Nao Hui mall, transliterated as Buy-Now, is one of the biggest. Two buildings, each one on its own city block but connected by a pedestrian bridge, hold hundreds of shops and stalls, most catering to some segment of the personal computer market. Walking into the mall is itself like walking through a souped-up computer. Whole booths sell nothing but circuit boards or storage drives or monitors, their products stacked up tightly in the glass cases that protrude out into the mall corridors. Up a level are the sellers of whole machines. Dozens of brands of laptop computers sit on the counters, many wrapped tightly in cellophane, others open and playing DVDs. Some sport famous names such as Sony, IBM, and Dell, but many are tagged by brands unknown outside China or Taiwan. And therein stands an important difference.

Buy a new computer at a shop in Tokyo, London, or New York and it comes with an operating system, usually Microsoft Windows, and usually a suite of software to get you started typing documents and crunching numbers. Computer makers in those markets pay license fees for that software and pass the prices on to their buyers. Buy a domestically made computer in Beijing's Buy-Now, and it will likely come without a licensed operating system and almost certainly without official versions of other software. Those additions, Chinese buyers and sellers believe, simply cost too much. It goes back to the consumer mantra in China that anything that can be reproduced costs too much if it is sold at a price that is more than a little above the cost of the media it is copied onto. The official version of Windows, for example, comes on fancy hard-to-pirate holographic disks and requires online registration to activate, features that add $40 to $60 to the price of a computer elsewhere. But in China, where it only costs a few moments of a seller's time to install a pirated version of Windows onto a new machine, paying the official price now seems absurd to nearly every buyer.

The upper floors at Buy-Now are the most amazing of all. They comprise one store after another, each with shelves stacked floor to ceiling with boxed software. Most of it comes in the long, thin boxes that DVDs are usually sold in, with printed covers that resemble the printed covers of the official licensed versions. Then again, some popular titles have several different packages, some of which show their designers tried to make an authentic-looking case, and others clearly meant to broadcast the illegitimate provenance of the precious treasure within.

One of the mall's biggest hits is the Adobe Creative Suite, a package of graphics programs that includes nearly everything businesses need to design, illustrate, and edit their publications and presentations. It lists in the United States for about $750. Though Adobe Creative Suite is one of the world's favorite software products for making documents and photographs look beautiful, in China it is often sold in cases with covers that look as though they were cut and pasted by careless grade-schoolers.

Chances are, however, that the software will work splendidly. Often the packages sold in China's bootleg stalls perform *better* than legitimate versions, because the sellers have gone to the trouble of updating their wares with all the original manufacturers' updates, a somewhat tedious process that buyers who pay full price have to go through on their own. Bootleg Windows XP, for instance, gets higher marks for stability and security among the Tsinghua crowd than the XP that Microsoft sells directly.

In the mall, nearly any popular package is for sale, including virtually every PC game ever sold, many of which have long disappeared from retail shelves outside China. For those Chinese gamers who like American football, there are copies of Electronics Arts' popular John Madden football game from most of the last five seasons. There are ways to race nearly every kind of virtual vehicle on the digital roads, skies, or in innumerable alternative universes.

One reality that the shops drive home is that the world of software is amazingly fecund, and for every smash hit there are dozens or hundreds of failed products. And yet, when prices drop down to between one and two dollars a disk—the range for virtually every package sold at Buy-Now—even the dead products stir interest. Imagine how the world's taste for experimentation might be whetted if the biggest online sellers of software in America, Europe, and Japan were turned into dollar stores. The software market in China, as with its market for recorded music on CDs and movies on DVDs, is one big dollar store.

Consider further how well one's own office or factory could shop in such a place where a shopping cart could be filled cheaply with most of the applications needed to run a world-class business. Every computer would have full versions of Microsoft Office, computer-aided design programs, and packages for computer programming that otherwise cost thousands of dollars. Each would also have great software for creating and launching Web sites, for preparing spreadsheets, for running eBay sales, doctoring photographs, editing videos the way Hollywood does, for remixing music, or, if one's business depended on it, for designing industrial machines, running assembly lines, or simulating drug tests.

Yes, imagine that. Then see it when one walks into Chinese offices, where one finds off-brand computers with hard drives full of thousands of dollars' worth of software for which no one has paid more than a pittance. Perhaps most remarkable of all, the computers are bookmarked to Web sites where any software that the user has overlooked is stored, fully hacked and cracked, so it need not be registered before using, and is ready for download, for free. That means that the Chinese software market hardly needs the Buy-Now sellers at all, except that they burn and package the software that is available for free.

How big is the Chinese market in pirated software? The Chinese use more than nine bootleg software packages for every legitimate one.[6] The Business Software Alliance, a trade group of U.S. software manufacturers, puts the annual loss in sales to the world's software industry due to Chinese piracy at $3.82 billion.* When compared to the $8.16 billion that Microsoft earned in its 2004 fiscal year, the sum may not seem all that heinous. Yet the number may also reflect a gross undercounting. The Chinese bought nearly 10 million personal computers in 2004.[7] Assuming that nine of ten of them have some combination of pirated versions of Windows, an office suite, two or three of the most popular bootleg applications, including Adobe Photoshop for editing pictures and Acrobat for making documents, or perhaps Macromedia Flash for Web-based graphics, and throwing in some games and a program to copy and play DVDs, the lost sales easily shoot over $10 billion a year. Given future sales over the coming decade—lately PC sales have been growing better than 10 percent a year—and the cumulative losses will grow to $150 billion or plausibly even twice that.[8]

There is, however, an inherent absurdity in this kind of theoretical accounting. If piracy were by some miracle eliminated from the Chinese marketplace, Chinese consumers could hardly be expected to rush into legitimate stores by the millions and buy software packages worth hundreds or thousands of dollars. The vast majority do not have the money to spend $1,000 on software. The Chinese recognize this fallacy, the illogic of which lies at the heart of their argument that software is so expensive that overlooking piracy is okay.

The issue comes back to purchasing-power parity. Looking at the $500 retail price for a current copy of Microsoft Office Professional, Chinese businesses must weigh what $500 would buy in other goods and services in China. Given that high cost, the Chinese argument goes, foreign software is out of their league and would rarely be purchased at the legitimate price. "Because there is no competition, the price of Microsoft products is much too high," Li Wuqiang of China's Ministry of Science and Technology complained to *Newsweek*.[9] Who, the Chinese ask, is harmed when software is pirated by those who would never otherwise buy it? If there is no profit to be made, there is no loss to count, right?

---

*The worldwide rate of software piracy is 39 percent, meaning that nearly four in ten installed copies of software programs come through shady channels that offer legitimate software companies nothing. Even in the United States, where the software piracy rate is 23 percent, bootlegs run a lot of computers. The Business Software Alliance says piracy in the United States, when measured by how much money it would take to buy the software that is pirated, costs the software industry $6.5 billion a year.

This argument has some persuasive power and has forced global software companies to consider whether they ought to lower their prices in the Chinese market. Microsoft has long claimed it is unwilling to do so, but it made big deals to supply licensed copies of Windows to China's largest PC manufacturers, who together control about 60 percent of the local market.

But Microsoft will not profit from all the manufacturers' sales. The companies are engaged in a bitter price war that has pushed the cost of respectably equipped personal computers down to around $350. The catch is the machines are sold *without* Windows operating systems. Instead, customers must arrange for their own software. Recently, a localized version of Linux, the low-cost open-source system, has been catching on in China. If it gets too popular in China, Microsoft knows, the open-source movement will have a giant base from which to challenge the dominance of Windows worldwide.

Microsoft thus finds its hand forced. When the Chinese government insisted that Microsoft open up the secret source code to its operating system or risk losing government business to open-source software, the company agreed. And under pressure from China and other countries to reveal more trade secrets, Microsoft has offered a free license to sixty governments and international organizations under which the company hands over its once-secret blueprints for its flagship Office suite.

If Microsoft's answer to piracy and open-source software in other countries is any indication, the company has almost certainly considered slashing the price of Windows in China. Privately, Microsoft executives admit that even pirated versions of its software in China have proven something of a blessing. And the company has recently opened up channels in which it can distribute Microsoft software for free itself while still maintaining some high ground. The company pledged to spend $750 million in China to train software and hardware developers. Part of that sum will be counted against software the company gives away as part of the program. These efforts give the company a defense against the open-source movement.[10]

Meanwhile, Chinese software users like to point out their take of Microsoft's own reputation, which to them puts the company in the same ethical league as Chinese users. When one preppy shopper browsing at an especially well-stocked booth at Buy-Now examines a copy of OneNote, a new Microsoft Office application for organizing and sharing notes and intelligent doodles, he turns the box over and studies the English information. When asked through a translator why he does not simply buy it at the low price and test it at home, he answers back in accented but idiomatic American English that he wants to see how the program works with his other Office applications. (It turns out he spent time as a student in Southern California.) He says he has them all and will buy this one too since it doesn't cost so much in China as in America.

Does it bother him that he's loading up on pirated software? He shrugs. "Microsoft takes software too," he says, rattling off a list that many of China's computer savvy seem to know by heart. "It took Windows from Apple, Internet Explorer from Netscape, PocketPC from Palm."

Try to argue Microsoft's case and the buyer interjects, also on cue, that real Office software is expensive.

When the software-shop conversation is related to a U.S. trade official speaking on background, the official shakes his head grimly. "Nothing has a higher priority in our trade policy than the fight to protect American intellectual property," the official says. "It is every bit as important an effort for us as the war against weapons for mass destruction. We focus on it very intensely."

The level of commitment reflects the level of the challenge. While negotiating with the United States, the Chinese side is quick to point out that while it tries to move ahead with intellectual-property protection, the United States and most of the rest of the world are moving backward. Music file sharing over the Internet began with Napster and continues unabated. Now CD and DVD burning and swapping are also commonplace with American teens and college students. The coverage of Microsoft's court battles in the Chinese press made it easy to liken the company's practices to those of China's software users. At the very least, the multiyear battle waged against Microsoft left the question open whether the U.S. government, states' attorneys general, and powerful corporations had a case that Microsoft was an inveterate rule stretcher and agreement bender.

The Chinese have a point. Microsoft, one of the great prizes of

American capitalism, rarely hesitates to use its market power to gain advantage, even engaging in daring brinksmanship with the law. Of course, the United States and other advanced economies do have courts, and lawbreakers can be, and often are, brought to justice. Supporters of Napster, perhaps the most audacious piracy scheme in U.S. history, also had their grandiose justifications for the service, but it was eventually forced to end its life as a conduit for free music, only to come back as a paid service.

When tackling the issue of intellectual-copyright protection, officials from the United States, and from other countries with property worth protecting, must see their task not as a legal issue but as an exercise in global political power. For now, it appears that China gains far more from the free flow of pirated goods than it loses, and believes that the economic violence it wreaks in other economies matters little.

The open-source challenge in China and in other developing countries also presents a new wrinkle to the issue of how low-wage countries, especially China, can get a competitive advantage over advanced-technology companies from high-wage countries. In richer markets, Microsoft has a strong argument that its software ultimately costs users less than open source. While open-source software is initially cheaper, because of the diffuse way in which it is developed and serviced, its implementation, tweaking, and service in the long run can exceed that of the Windows system, which in Microsoft has a strong developer behind it and huge community of companies and IT professionals that know it well.

In China, however, where the cost of programmers and code-tweakers is far lower, the cost of taking on a Linux-based system and maintaining it does *not* make it more expensive than Windows in the long run. The disruptive potential of China's low labor costs to the dominant software monopolies is real. If Chinese companies can assert an advantage by migrating away from American and European software, American and European companies will have to find a way to assert similar savings. Just as Chinese competitors taught Motorola that it needed to rely on Chinese suppliers for parts to its mobile phones in order to compete in China and around the world, Chinese companies may introduce the world's corporations to new sources of operating systems and business software.

Robbing Competitors
of Their Competitiveness

Piracy has a still more pervasive effect on the world economy. Yes, it robs some sales that might otherwise have been completed legitimately. But, more ominously for a world that is struggling to find ways to compete against China, piracy helps create and strengthen Chinese competitors who may never have shown up in the first place unless they had great business tools to steal. Consider again the argument that software is too expensive for the Chinese to buy so it is okay to pirate it. Are not trucks and lathes and injection-mold machines also expensive? No one in China suggests that Chinese companies raid German, Japanese, and American parking lots and warehouses for trucks, lathes, and injection-mold machines, though any one of those machines could mean far less to a company's success than the software it runs.

SAP AG is a giant German software developer that provides software systems to companies big and small that need ways to coordinate manufacturing, sales, accounting, and other corporate tasks. It is one of the most successful software sellers in China. The big-ticket systems it creates are often highly customized and do not travel well from one company to the next. SAP has had its share of poachers nonetheless.

Klaus Zimmer, the head of the company's China unit, told Reuters how one large Chinese company had paid SAP for 250 software licenses but was later discovered to be running 3,000 copies.[11] Assuming the company paid a license fee based on how many iterations of the software it planned to use, its software costs—before it was busted—were only one-twelfth of what they would have been had it paid in full. Custom software for such large organizations can cost millions. Not paying for it can save millions. Which is to say nothing of the Windows software that SAP software usually runs on top of, which in this case was probably also pirated. Of course SAP was robbed of profits on the deal.

But one must also calculate the cost of the competitive advantage that the usurper exerted over the companies whose products it was trying to beat in the marketplace. "A lot of intellectual-property professionals see the problems with China as a legal issue," says Andrew Mertha, a political scientist at Washington University in St. Louis, "and only pay lip service to the economics of it." Mertha spent the late 1990s in China working with officials in the Chinese government agencies charged with protecting patents, copyrights, and trademarks. "In information technology, for instance, people fail to take into account the irresistible demand for cheap software precisely because it is that price that people need to stay competitive. By calculating the loss as just the loss of sales by software makers, people miss seeing how American industry really gets nailed."

Mertha says while Western software companies spend some resources monitoring how their products are sold, no one is out looking at all the ways in which Chinese industries using nearly free software gain advantage. He adds there is social capital involved, as well. The importance of connections within a social network—*guanxi*—in modern China ties closely to the country's sad experience with rules. Mertha points out that *guanxi* weakened during Mao's reign when the ideological excesses of continual revolution pushed the Chinese to sever traditional relationships. "It is no accident," he argues, "that *guanxi* came roaring back after the Cultural Revolution. When the state failed to keep order, people turned back to the network system that could create some social control and in which people could trust one another."

Within that system, people are expected to promote the interests of their network. "If you have two people who are charged with buying software for a business, one of whom decides he is going to play by the legal rules and pay hundreds of dollars for a copy of Windows or Office, and another one who goes out and buys essentially the same thing for a couple of bucks, the first guy is going to be seen by the others in his network as a schmuck, and the second guy will gain credit for making the right decision. No one is going to trust the first guy to be smart about anything after that."

Study the computers of most of the Tsinghua entrepreneurs, and chances are they are stacked with cutting-edge programs developed by the world's leading tech firms. Tour one of the start-ups that is working around the clock to come up with a product that cannot easily be stolen and ask whether the software being used to create the new package is itself licensed, and one gets knowing smiles and an oblique answer: "You know, the people who work here are very smart."

Reverse Colonialism: How Sweet It Is

China's failure to police intellectual property, in effect, creates a massive global subsidy worth hundreds of billions of dollars to its businesses and people. Seen another way, China's vast counterfeiting schemes act on the rest of the world the way colonial armies once did, invading deep into the economies of their victims, expropriating their most valued assets, and in so doing, undermining their victims' ability to counter. As China grows into a great power, the wealth transferred into the country by stealing intellectual property will propel it forward.

But should China be blamed for behavior that robs the rest of the world of wealth it has spent generations accumulating? Perhaps. Yet perhaps the rest of the world also needs to examine itself. China is merely acting as other nations do when presented with the chance to increase their wealth and power. So far, pilfering intellectual property has cost China little and benefited it tremendously.

Moreover, hundreds of billions of dollars in foreign investment into the country has made the world's best technology easily available to China's infringers. By investing in the country's manufacturing infrastructure, by providing the expertise, machines, and software China needs to produce world-class products, the world is also helping assemble the biggest, most sophisticated, and most successful illegal manufacturing complex in the world.

So, as foreign investors stake their own prosperity on China's, they push China into the position where it can play rule maker. In the not so distant future, when China matches the world's largest markets and is among the world's most advanced and prolific manufacturers, it may well have the brand names, entertainment industry, and technology that set the world's standards. In a country that still bitterly remembers the humiliation of colonization, turning the tables by pilfering the property of foreigners will not cause much remorse.

CHAPTER TEN

THE CHINESE-AMERICAN
ECONOMY

Perceiving the effects of China's global reach is easy if one flaunts a brilliantly phonied Swiss watch on one's wrist or enjoys a cheap new Chinese DVD player at home. And certainly those who have lost or who might lose their jobs to Chinese factories feel China's presence acutely. But China touches Americans, and by extension the rest of the world, in other realms every day. Taken as a whole, these forces show that beyond the fate of one industry or another, beyond issues of labor or piracy or even the recent high price of oil, caused in part by rising Chinese demand, America's economy and the world's are now inextricably bound up with China's. Although describing these bigger, omnipresent effects begins with some abstraction, once grasped, they are as tangible as the change in one's pocket.

First, the Good News

Walk into nearly any retail store, examine price tags and labels, and it is clear that China saves consumers enormous amounts of money. How much? Gary Clyde Hufbauer, one of the first-rate economists at the Institute for International Economics in Washington, has done some rough math using China's 2003 trade numbers with the United States that shows just how much China saves American consumers.

"From time immemorial," says Hufbauer, "most American and Japanese businesses have been reluctant to move their manufacturing to new locales unless they can save at least ten to twenty percent with the move."

When one considers that the nearly $150 billion worth of manufactured goods coming from China to America are, by and large, goods that once came from somewhere else, the magnitude of the savings begins to come into view. But the savings that come directly from China's factories are just the beginning. China's prices have a downward pricing effect on the rest of the world's manufacturers that dwarfs the savings offered by Chinese goods alone. Hufbauer figures some $500 billion in goods come from countries that are China's low-wage competitors. Another $450 billion in goods come from the high-wage American and Japanese companies that compete with China's producers. That adds up, he says, to nearly a trillion dollars' worth of additional goods whose prices are pushed down by Chinese competition. Even a conservative estimate of the effect is impressive. If the savings to the United States on that near trillion dollars of non-Chinese trade are just 3 to 5 percent, instead of the 20 percent the Chinese can deliver, the average American household enjoys further savings that start at about $500, Hufbauer calculates. People who spend more get an even bigger China bonus.

One way to put the numbers in perspective is to consider how $500 per household matches up against the much ballyhooed 2003 tax cut pushed by the Bush administration and passed by the American Congress, a cut that was justified in large part as a way to pump consumer spending into the U.S. economy and help lift the country out of its economic rut. The Jobs and Growth Tax Relief Reconciliation Act of 2003 was designed, President Bush said when it was signed, "to deliver substantial tax relief to 136 million American taxpayers . . . adding fuel to an economic recovery."[1] For an American family of four earning $75,000 a year, the savings from China could easily have equaled at least half of the $1,100 in savings that the tax cuts delivered.*

---

*Savings from tax cuts or in the form of discounts on merchandise each give money to consumers to spend or save as they please. Yet in relation to the larger economy, discounts and tax cuts are very different events. The 2003 tax cuts, which U.S. politicians claimed "returned" $130 billion to Americans, actually distributed cash out of more federal debt being heaped on the citizenry, which, for its part, turned around and spent some $150 billion on Chinese goods.

The Price Is Right

The downward pressure from Chinese manufacturers even shows up now when the prices of raw materials rise. In the past when raw materials climbed in price, their costs were hurriedly passed on to consumers buying finished goods. Thanks to competitive pressures both on and from Chinese manufacturing, that dynamic has changed. While China's economic boom helped run up the cost of steel, copper, aluminum, nickel, plastics, and nearly every other important industrial commodity in 2003 and 2004, the prices of cars in major markets dropped. Chinese factories churning out cheap car parts were one cause. When in December 2003 cotton climbed to its highest price in seven years, the price of clothing in American stores was down for the year.

In fact, in the United States between 1998 and 2004, prices fell in nearly every product category in which China was the top exporter. "The manufactured goods that have dropped in price the most are those made by China," says W. Michael Cox, chief economist for the Federal Reserve Bank of Dallas, citing figures assembled by the bank for its 2003 annual report, published in 2004. Personal computers, the most outstanding example, dropped by 28 percent, televisions by nearly 12 percent, cameras and toys by around 8 percent, while other electronics, clothing of all sorts, shoes, and tableware also dropped in price.[2]

The declines are impressive in themselves, but considering that the U.S. cost of living rose 16 percent[3] over the same period, the price drops forced by goods shipped out of China provided especially welcome relief.

China will continue to offer Americans more bargains as time goes forward because the vast majority of imports into the United States still come from countries that pay relatively high wages. Meanwhile the portion of U.S. imports from low-wage countries continues to rise, especially from very poor countries. Over the past quarter of a century, there has been a surge of imports into the United States from the fifty-eight countries where people earn one-twentieth, or even less, of what Americans do. (The list of countries includes such trouble spots as Haiti, the Congo, and Nepal, and also more promising locales such as India and

Indonesia.) But where trade with the United States, and indeed most of the rest of the world, is concerned, China plays a bigger role than all of the other low-wage countries combined. Led by China, the increases in goods from low-wage countries show up both in the sheer volume of trade coming into the United States and as a proportion of what Americans buy overall. In 1981, the United States imported $319 billion (using constant Year 2000 dollars) worth of goods and services from abroad, an amount equal to just 6 percent of the country's gross domestic product. By 2001, however, Americans bought $1.44 trillion in imports, making up more than 14 percent of the GDP. Over that same time, goods from low-income countries went from just 4 percent of imports ($12.8 billion) to more than 10 percent ($144 billion). By 2011, low-income countries, primarily China, should account for 24 percent of everything Americans buy from outside the country's borders.[4]

The Price Is Not Always Right

So are the prices that Americans pay on Chinese goods the lowest possible? Usually, but not necessarily. It depends on what's being sold and whether that industry can successfully lobby the government for protection.

"One of the big problems of economic specialization is that it creates special interest groups," observes Cox, who believes that economic policy ought to be aimed primarily at providing a better deal for consumers. "In the political process, politicians usually end up representing suppliers who can donate large amounts to their campaigns." Cox argues that this imbalance can leave consumers woefully underrepresented. Manufacturers' groups lobby policymakers because their industries have huge stakes in trade policy, but in any given industry, an individual consumer's interests might add up to just a few dollars a year.

For example, when the Bush administration slapped quotas on Chinese brassieres in November 2003 to protect American manufacturers, it may have saved the American bra industry from millions in losses, while the cost of the quotas to the typical bra buyer might have been only ten or twenty dollars per year. The manufacturers, Cox says, can send all sorts of people to Washington to make their case, but no consumers are going to make the trip just to save a few dollars on whatever product is up for discussion. And so, the biggest group with the most billions at stake has the smallest voice.

It is a bitter kink of fate that among those who need the China savings most are those who have lost their jobs because their employers needed to cut costs and raise productivity to meet the China price, or because they worked for businesses that could no longer compete on any terms. "Wal-Mart is the best thing that ever happened to poor people," says Cox. In his view, where the consumer is king, even the practices that U.S. businesses commonly call "dumping"* by Chinese manufacturers ought to be seen as a boon. "Don't call it dumped," he says, "call it treasure."

Cox's view of the primacy of consumer interests, though widely shared by American economists, is hardly an accepted truth around the world. Countries whose industries face competition from China must make harsh choices that weigh the competing interests of businesses and consumers. Choosing for the consumer requires putting faith in the very economic churn that is now making China a supercompetitor. And it truly is an act of faith. Economists teach that by embracing the tumult of the free market, nations give themselves the best chance at prosperity. But most of the world remains unsold on consumer-centric capitalism. Europe, Japan, and the developing world largely focus their economic policies on protecting their industries, their workers, or both, ahead of the interests of consumers.

Bonds That Tie

China's competitive challenge not only pits Americans against themselves as shoppers and workers but as investors too. Lou Dobbs, the influential CNN financial commentator whose vociferous stand against companies that outsource jobs overseas was mentioned in chapter 7, serves as an example of this entanglement. As a commentator, Dobbs

---

*What American manufacturers call "dumping" in common parlance rarely matches economists' definition of the practice, which is the selling of goods below what it costs producers to make them, though for various reasons already noted, Chinese producers can often make goods for below even the raw-materials costs of manufacturers elsewhere.

finds deep fault with companies that abandon American workers, but as an investment adviser he recommends the shares of companies that have eliminated American jobs while taking big stakes in China and India.

This dilemma is played out throughout the economy, where nearly everyone has varied interests that incline against one another. Even union workers who lose their jobs often have a stake in companies whose success is increasingly determined by their ability to make it in China. The China bets are made through investments held by pensions and retirement accounts. Many state governments in the United States have considered laws that would ban sending state contracts to overseas companies, and yet the states' employees, as beneficiaries of giant pension plans, are stakeholders in the largest investment pools in the world. These pools are obliged to maximize returns for their participants and, within acceptable levels of risk, give them the best future possible. They typically subscribe to the dominant theories of portfolio management that dictate that large investors should diversify their investments globally, and they would be foolhardy not to invest in China, which is often described in financial literature as a "once-in-a-lifetime growth opportunity."

Thus, America's largest pension funds invest in Wal-Mart, Motorola, GE, Philips, and the thousands of other companies investing billions in China. What's more, these giant institutional investors are now scouring China for Chinese companies to invest in directly. The pension plans of universities, hospitals, and in some cases, entire countries also chase the same investments.

On the Money

Investors trying to avoid an economic stake in China will find it no easier than avoiding contact with the American economy, Japan's, or OPEC's. It cannot be done.

The reason, of course, is that China's currency is pegged to the American dollar.

What does that mean exactly? Since 1997, China has maintained the value of its currency at about 8.3 yuan to the dollar, where it still stood

258

in late 2004, as this book went to press. It is an old-fashioned but effective way to manage a currency. Before Richard Nixon freed the dollar in the early 1970s, the world's major currencies all had fixed rates of exchange against each other. At the center of the system were gold and the U.S. dollar. Countries could take the dollars they had acquired in trade and present them to the United States in exchange for gold, which was sold at a fixed rate. It was then illegal for Americans to own gold bullion in quantity, and the large stores of American gold were maintained solely by the U.S. government, which bought and sold it at an official rate set by the old international currency system.

Today, when the dollar rises or falls against other world currencies, China's yuan moves in tandem with it. China is the only large trading nation that pegs its currency to the dollar. It does so by mandating that whenever the yuan is converted to foreign currency, the transaction must be made at the official rate and through a state-controlled bank.

Other countries, especially other countries in Asia such as South Korea and Japan, which similarly rely largely on exports for their economic growth, also intervene aggressively in the world's currency markets. They act when their own currencies appreciate enough against the dollar so as to damage their ability to export. They too influence the currency markets using the power of their enormous reserves of foreign currency, wading in to buy and sell currencies in hope of bullying and cajoling the world's currency traders. But they can only bully and cajole the rates, not control them.

Why is China the only big player that maintains a fixed exchange rate? Hufbauer explains that the Chinese regard foreign exchange, especially dollars, as "supervaluable." Dollars in China, he explains, fill the role formerly played by gold in the United States and other countries once on a gold standard. The Chinese central bank is keeper of nearly all the dollars in the country. Dollars accumulate in the government's account as Chinese businesses that have earned money from foreign sales exchange their dollars for yuan, and when foreign investors bring money into the country to buy businesses or property. In the first half of 2004, China's total foreign exchange reserves topped $460 billion, a staggering amount. In size, that puts China's cumulative dollar account at roughly equal to a third of its gross domestic product. (Seen another way, it nearly equals the value of everything that was bought and sold in 2004 in Brazil, the world's fifteenth-largest economy. In theory, China could show up one day and use its cash to buy up everything Brazilians purchase in a year.)

To help keep control of its currency, Hufbauer says, and to thwart the possible emergence of a large black market, China offers its businesses and citizens an incentive to turn in their dollars to government bankers: the government overpays for dollars, giving back more Chinese currency for greenbacks than a free-market buyer might if the yuan were not controlled.

For a long time, few companies and countries complained about China's policies. At first its economy was not prosperous enough or big enough to warrant concern. And when an Asian financial crisis struck in the late 1990s and the currencies of Korea, Indonesia, and Thailand collapsed, China, which could have devalued its currency, stuck by its dollar peg and was lauded for bringing stability to a most volatile situation. While it took several years for the troubled economies to begin a rebound, China's kept chugging right along, the pegged yuan making its exports irresistible bargains to the world outside and attracting the foreign investment that is pushing the country.

But now, in the eyes of most of the rest of the world, China fixes its exchange rate too far below what it would be if the yuan were allowed to be traded freely on world currency markets. Among the most forceful critics of China's currency policies are American domestic manufacturers such as steel mills, casters, plastics molders, and machine-tool makers. Through their trade associations, they argue that China artificially depresses the value of its currency against the dollar by as much as 40 percent, a figure that is decidedly on the high side of estimates.*

But American manufacturers who do move production to China often realize savings that would seem to support the claim. Of course, the currency rate affects more than the items China makes; it affects the means of production too. (If the currency is so lopsided, factories that cost a million dollars to set up in China ought to cost $1.4 million elsewhere.) Held up only by the Chinese government's currency manipu-

---

*Estimating where the value of China's currency would sit if the yuan were freely traded is as much art as science. Economists at the Institute for International Economics estimate the yuan is undervalued by between 15 and 25 percent against the dollar.

lation, China's global bargain bin, claim American manufacturers, is artificial and thus unfair.

American lawmakers, picking up the complaint, cite the charter of the International Monetary Fund to claim that China's currency controls and manipulation are illegal. The charges are mostly a bluff, and few actually expect that an international court would ever adjudicate issues of China's currency policies. Whether China acts illegally or not is subject to how one reads the minutiae of IMF rules.

In practice, notes Jeffrey A. Frankel, an economist who served as a member of the Council of Economic Advisers under Bill Clinton and is now at Harvard's Kennedy School of Government, the legality of China's currency policies matters little since there is virtually nothing one government, even that of the United States, can do to change the way another big country decides to run its currency. Frankel also points out that "when U.S. lawmakers accuse China or other countries of illegally manipulating their currencies, they often allege a violation of vaguely worded U.S. laws, rather than any multilateral agreement."

When China was invited for an informal sit-down with the representatives of the G-7 countries in October 2004, the price for its meal ticket was to hear out the urgings of foreign finance officials fed up with China's currency peg. At the G-7, China, as is its habit, agreed to change eventually, but made no promises as to how or when.* Instead, the Chinese made clear they would be resolute in promoting the course they regarded as in their own interest, and everyone else's. "What we are trying to do is create the conditions for a market-based exchange rate," Li Ruogu, deputy governor of China's central bank told a gathering of Washington bankers at the time of the G-7 meeting. "If you force China to change, it will hurt the U.S. You destroy a goose that will give you a golden egg."[5]

---

*Letting the world know when a country plans to make a major move on its currency is a recipe for disaster. It is hard to know what the G-7 officials really expect when they make demands on China to set dates and prices for its currency, since anything the Chinese announced in advance of real measures would cause the rest of the world to adjust as if the change had happened at once. Much of the investment made in China in 2003 and 2004 had a speculative component, anticipating a change upward in the value of the yuan against the dollar. Foreign investors rushed to buy property and to set up factories while Chinese prices were, in effect, suppressed by the currency peg, hoping for a quick bump up after readjustment, when their Chinese investments would be worth more in dollars.

Currency regimes and markets are fleeting, and news about them changes quickly. Yet some features of China's long-term currency strategy will remain important to the well-being of the rest of the world no matter what comes in the short term of prodding the Chinese government. These longer-lasting verities are tied to bedrock goals the country is unlikely to repudiate anytime soon: China must develop to lift its people out of poverty and that depends on a currency that offers the country's whole economy at bargain prices. Moreover, China can be counted on not to act too radically or too swiftly. Chinese leaders know that doing so would threaten not only China's economic growth, but would rattle the economies of the rest of the world as well.

Dollar Daze

China, however, is not the only country that depends on a low yuan. In an ironic twist of geopolitical and economic fortune, the United States has developed a peculiar addiction to China's currency regime. That, in turn, has made much of the world dependent on the pegged yuan as well. This knotty codependence grows out of the size and manner of China's efforts to keep its currency where it wants it.

In the international financial markets, nations' currencies, much like any other commodity, are subject to ups and downs based on the underlying fundamentals of the economies they represent, and to booms and busts resulting from the speculative emotions of the world's money traders. Usually, when demand for a country's products rise worldwide, so does the value of its currency. A nation's currency, like other commodities, comes in limited supply, and when the world's buyers want some of it—to buy products the country sells—they must bid against other countries to buy it. When demand is keen, the purchasers must trade more of their currency for less of the one they want. If, for example, the world suddenly craved only Norwegian sweaters, it would rush the currency market to buy Norwegian kroner.

That, anyway, is the way things are supposed to go. From the American viewpoint, it might seem that world demand for Chinese goods far outstrips Chinese demand for the world's products. As mentioned before, this is not the case. China's exports more or less equal the value of its imports. In fact, 2004 imports into China actually were worth more than the country's exports. As a matter of demand, then, China's currency would seem to face little upward pressure, except that private citizens have been bringing foreign money into China to acquire local assets, a trend reflected in China's enormous reserves of American dollars.

If China simply spent its dollars, it could flood the world market with American currency and quickly drive the dollar down. But China, no fool, is not interested in pushing the dollar down. So instead of selling its dollars, it *lends* them to the United States by purchasing U.S. bonds.

The logic here is complex; because China buys so much on the U.S. bond market, China actually pushes up the price not only of U.S. currency, but also of American debt overall. And because any change in the yield on a debt instrument usually moves in the opposite direction of any change to its value, China's heavy buying of U.S. Treasury bills and other forms of public and private debt serves to push *down* U.S. interest rates.

For example, China almost certainly has a large stake in the market for bonds issued by Fannie Mae and Freddie Mac, the companies that buy home mortgages from banks and thrift institutions and resell them as bundled securities. This means that billions of dollars' worth of investments belonging to the Chinese are plowed, indirectly, into the American real estate market, and that an ever increasing share of Americans' mortgage payments pour into the coffers of the government of China.

China keeps tight wraps on the value, composition, and trading of its portfolio, but Wall Street commonly assumes that the country also owns a large amount of high-grade U.S. corporate bonds, intertwining its national fortunes all the more with America's blue chips—many of them the same corporations reaping fortunes in China itself. Thus does China indirectly profit from American corporations profiting in China.

As long as China is an aggressive lender, Americans—whether borrowing for their own private purchases or acting in the roles of taxpayers—can borrow money at low rates. Much of the recent boom in real estate prices in America, especially in the East and West Coast markets, is attributable to these low interest rates. And low American interest rates help keep interest rates low worldwide, a boon for borrowers everywhere.

That includes China. Low interest rates in the United States inform how Chinese banks lend, and their resulting low domestic rates have propelled China's dangerously fast and loose industrial development—leading to overcapacity in nearly everything its industries manufacture and to a highly speculative real estate market.

Thus do the effects of China's currency peg ripple around the world and back again. Because of the peg, America does not experience price changes forced by a changing yuan, but other nations do. As the euro climbs against the dollar, for example, Chinese goods become cheaper for Europeans to buy, and investment in China from Europe all the more affordable. As high Chinese demand pushes up the price of raw materials, Americans buying these raw materials feel the pain just as the Chinese do, but if the euro drops against the dollar-yuan combination, Europeans are more pinched.

China's currency peg touches everything.

Golden Eggs in a Cuckoo Nest

The talk about golden eggs from China's bankers makes a strong point. Americans and Chinese have become reliant on each other's most controversial habits. The Chinese need a low-priced currency to keep their export machine going and create jobs. But maintaining the yuan's low price also means that Chinese consumers are stuck with a currency that would otherwise buy more for them on the world market. China's diligent savers suffer too since their bank deposits are tied up in accounts that earn low government-mandated rates of return, as the government, in effect, siphons off money from savers to maintain its currency peg.

Relatedly, China's vast export earnings earn less than they ought to when they are invested in U.S. debt securities that offer modest yields, when investments in the Chinese economy can return ten times as much (albeit on riskier terms).[6] Seen from that view, the people of China, who earn on average just one-fortieth what Americans do, are indirectly subsidizing the insatiable shopping of Americans, who acquire ever more goods at the same time that Chinese consumers are hampered from buying goods from abroad.

The obverse of this peculiar relationship is that China lends America all the money it needs to spend itself silly. Not that China plays this role alone. Japan is also a huge creditor to the United States. Much of the rest of the world plays a role too. Foreigners now own 40 percent of all U.S. treasury securities, while total U.S. debt to foreigners tops $2.2 trillion. China's share, however, is growing most impressively. In 2004, its $480 billion stake in the U.S. securities markets, a little less than a fourth of the total, was double what it had been only two years before.[7]

These vast sums help fill deep holes. The U.S. financial landscape is littered with record debts of all sorts, much of it financed by lending from China and Japan. America's government debt grew by $1.7 billion a day in 2004, reaching $7.5 trillion. Moreover, in 2004, Americans collectively owed $9.5 trillion in mortgages, automobile loans, credit cards, and other personal debts, a staggering $84,454 per household.[8]* Americans' household debt, in fact, has never been higher. Instead of taking advantage of the lower interest rates to refinance and reduce their debt burdens, many Americans have regarded cheap money as an opportunity to go out and spend *more*. That's just the way exporters like it. The U.S. government has seen fit to do the same. Rather than use the period of low interest rates to pay off national debt and keep annual budgets in balance, as the Clinton administration did, the Bush administration set record budgets, slashed taxes, and ran up record budget deficits so big that paying off the national debt may never be possible. The people of China are financing that profligacy.

The spendthrift habits of the United States are reflected in its growing trade deficit too. U.S. consumers buy one fifth of the world's GDP, an increasing amount of which is purchased on credit. (In 2003, Asia financed over half of America's trade deficit *and* government budget deficit.[9]) Jeffrey Frankel notes that the U.S. trade deficit roughly corresponds numerically to the total of the surpluses of all the world's trading countries that are in surplus.

Other countries get drawn into the relationship, often powerless to resist. China and other surplus-generating countries do eventually reach the limit on the amount of U.S. securities they can buy. The European Union is one place they turn to buy more. Because the euro does not trade at a fixed rate against the dollar, and thus not against the

---

*On top of that, when future obligations that the U.S. government has already committed to pay out get added in, each household's share of government debt is a staggering $473,456.

yuan, the purchase of euro securities pushes the euro up against the currencies of both the U.S. and China. For European consumers, that makes Chinese goods less expensive. And for Europe's businesses, it makes competition with Chinese businesses intense. In the near term, Germany may have the most to fear. China, Hufbauer says, is coming on strong against three core German industries—chemicals, machine tools, and automobiles.

Having Your Currency and Eating It Too

Nimble companies can play the circle of American debt, Chinese lending, and low-priced yuan from all sides. Patrick Lo is the CEO and cofounder of Netgear, a maker of networking equipment headquartered in Silicon Valley that in 2003 had sales of $300 million. Lo has tailored his company's manufacturing and marketing to take maximum advantage of the countries' countervailing roles within the codependency.

"The mission of Netgear is to connect everyone on earth to a broadband connection," Lo says. "And from day one we knew we needed to be a global business. You cannot have a product that is designed in the United States, manufactured in the U.S., and marketed out of the U.S. and expect it to be a global product. It is impossible." Instead, Netgear takes advantage of the unique advantages offered by different corners of the technology manufacturing universe.

How? The answer begins with a description of Netgear's most visible products: elegant, small silver boxes, most the size of a slim paperback book, that sit next to millions of personal computers around the world. They come in all the varieties—adapters, gateways, routers, access points—needed to set up wired and wireless networks in homes and small offices. Netgear has carved a place in the crowded networking equipment market by offering products that are nice to look at and easy to set up, an important factor, since change in the networking industry moves at warp speed. New standards, products, previously unknown competitors, and waves of new, mostly Chinese-made, equipment find their way into stores, catalogs, and eBay all the time. Netgear itself introduces, on average, one new product every week, either in response to a competitor's newest model or as the innovation that will be copied within weeks.

In his constant battle to move new products into the market at aggressive prices, Lo has organized Netgear to leverage the peculiar financial codependency of the United States and China.

"Americans are more willing to spend than anyone else in the world right now," says Lo, whose products get their design and marketing in California, where the company can stay close to American tastes and needs. Netgear, founded in 1996, began life by working with a Taiwanese manufacturer that made Netgear's boxes and helped design the technology inside them.

Yet manufacturing in Taiwan ultimately became too expensive, so Netgear asked its Taiwanese manufacturer to change its function. Instead of making the products, it would engineer them and manage the manufacturing at a third site run by yet another company in China's booming technology corridor near Suzhou in Jiangsu Province outside Shanghai. A new factory there was designed from scratch to allow for highly flexible manufacturing that could change with every newly designed tech product that companies such as Netgear want to bring to market. China is full of such late-generation manufacturing facilities, which exist to be hired out by others who need floor space, advanced equipment, and a workforce on call. Netgear's factory of choice was outfitted with the latest robotic equipment for assembling circuit boards and laid out so workers coping with manual assemblies could integrate seamlessly and flexibly in the production lines. Netgear would help manage the quality control and purchasing out of an office in Hong Kong.

The company's current strategy involves a state-of-the-art distribution of talents and functions to meet the realities of the global marketplace. The U.S. operations figure out what the world's hungriest consumers will buy. Yet it keeps its company's own employee count to the bare minimum. Only 210 people work for Netgear worldwide, meaning it has $1.5 million in sales per employee, a high ratio for the electronics industry.* Their Taiwan affiliate is tapped for the tech prowess it acquired when that island was a low-cost hub, and China, now the lowest-cost place to make things, is where final assembly is done.

---

*In 2001, Sony had 180,000 employees worldwide, with sales of $58 billion, or around $322,000 per employee. In 2003, Intel had 78,000 employees worldwide with $30 billion in sales, or around $385,000 per employee.

"China gives us a way to move to the next level," Lo says, referring both to the world economy and the fortunes of his company. "Because of low-cost manufacturing, a lot of leading technology can now come out of China." In Netgear's case, it *must* come out of China. With such keen competition the company needs the boost offered by China's ongoing efforts to keep its currency depressed. "China helps us because they need to keep a lot of people employed," says Lo.

The incentives offered by China's currency policies to agile companies like Netgear do not sit well in those businesses more firmly bound to their U.S. manufacturing base. The IPC,* a U.S. trade association representing twenty-two hundred firms that design, manufacture, and assemble electronic components, are among the most enraged among the political coalition pressing American lawmakers to break China's policies.

"China's manipulation of the yuan has had a devastating effect on U.S. manufacturers," said Dan Feinberg, chairman of the IPC Government Relations Steering Committee, when the group gathered en masse on Capitol Hill in April 2004 to lobby for change. The group called China's currency actions "direct violations of their commitments under the World Trade Organization and the International Monetary Fund."

From the standpoint of consumers, however, the price cuts China facilitates make a world of difference. In Netgear's experience, products that move to the high-production, low-cost factory lines in China explode in the marketplace. Over the last three years, the basic equipment for home networks has dropped from $500 a unit to below $100, while moving data around the house much faster in the bargain. The term *network effect* describes how technologies gain critical masses of users and applications the more that they connect users with each other. It is not surprising that computer networking equipment has an enormous network effect when its price drops. In 2002, 9.2 million American homes had networked computers; by 2007, that number will top 28 million as low-price equipment from Netgear and others moves data files, music, and movies around the home, between computers and digital home entertainment centers.

---

*Despite its initials, the IPC's longer name is the Association Connecting Electronics Industries.

Will the Yuan Ever Rise?

Is this cycle of codependency sustainable? Almost certainly not. An eventual reversal is necessary. The United States cannot take on ever-bigger debt and amass huge trade deficits indefinitely. Frankel, who notes that Americans now pay out greater dividends to foreigners than they take in, now live in the world as *renter*s rather than as landlords. Renter nations live precariously.

"When Asians pull out of our markets, Americans may discover abruptly that interest rates climb and the value of the assets—stocks, homes, businesses, almost everything—declines," Frankel says. "When other countries have gone through similar crises, people panicked. Whether such a crisis might lead the U.S. to also lose much of its political power, it is hard to say. It is certainly possible."

In the worst scenario, the United States' willingness to fritter away its national wealth to finance private consumption and unproductive government spending would extract a permanent price on the economy, sending the United States in a downward spiral that would be hard to escape. Indebtedness would lead to the kind of crises that have saddled such big spenders as Argentina and Brazil and doom the United States to a future without the fiscal tools to lift the economy from the doldrums. "We would not be able to get out of recessions by cutting interest rates," says Frankel, describing the impotence of an America too deeply in debt. "There would be no way to provide the kinds of fiscal boosts, such as tax cuts, that inject spending money into the economy. Our problems would no longer be as short-lived as we're used to, but last for generations."

Thus do the routes to prosperity chosen by China and the United States put both countries at grave risk. Without the United States to buy Chinese goods, China cannot sustain its growth; without China to lend money to the United States, Americans cannot spend. Without the twin engines of the United States and China stoking the fortunes of other nations, the rest of the world might also sputter.

But the worst scenario need not be inevitable. China's currency adjustment could come gradually. A cheaper dollar may teach Americans to save again and forge disciplined government budgets.

CHAPTER ELEVEN

THE CHINESE CENTURY

CAN AMERICANS AND THE REST OF THE WORLD SEE WHAT IS HAP-pening in China? On the face of things, it seems so. After all, the global media now covers developments in China with both an earnest desire to document its rise and a bemused awareness at its unabashed con-sumerism. The daily press reports on the stream of Chinese fads and marvels. The financial papers follow the world's money to China's door, and one after another, trade magazines such as *Automotive News* and *Modern Plastics* have begun to look like China newsletters. At times it appears that everything that can happen is happening in China. In the space of one month in the fall of 2004, China held its first Euro-pean-style Formula 1 car race on a new $320-million track, hosted an NBA exhibition game with its new global basketball star Yao Ming, and staged its first Spanish bullfight in a stadium converted into a full-fledged bullring, all in Shanghai, all to enthusiastic crowds. So too comes the news that Hooters, the restaurant-and-bar chain, will offer its curvy American fantasy to Chinese diners in eight locales; that Star-bucks will add hundreds of new outlets in the land of tea; and that an adult-products expo attracted four thousand manufacturers of sex aids and huge crowds. There are the daily announcements of new ways that the world's big and small investors can take a piece of the China action with a simple phone call to a stockbroker. There is the story that Bill Clinton's 2004 memoir,* like Hillary's in 2003, was pirated and liberally

---

*Writer Alex Beels took the trouble to translate pirated Chinese editions of Bill Clinton's *My Life* back into English for *Harper's Magazine*. One Chinese version of the text turned Clinton into an avid Sinophile, putting words in the former president's mouth describing how Chinese technology left America's "in the dust." In another version Clinton says his hometown of Hope, Arkansas, has "very good feng shui."

rewritten with Chinese characteristics; that China consumes half of the world's pork; that FedEx will now service many Chinese cities directly; and so on.

The news bites, however, reflect an illusory China as much as a real one. To see how China is really changing, and to react wisely to how China is changing the world, one must see beyond the amazing stories. This sounds simple, but strong forces fight against it. On the one hand, the news stories that come out of China are far from complete. News in times of momentous change is bound to miss much of the big picture. In China's case, where the news is tightly controlled, such gaps are inevitable. On the other hand, the rest of the world has worthy distractions: war, for one; domestic politics too. One can complain, in vain, about unworthy distractions, as well. The very demographic group—the eighteen-to-thirty-four-year-old population—that ought to be most focused on the coming Chinese century is also the one most brilliantly diverted by entertainment and news-lite that detail the trials of celebrities and reality-TV neurotics. What a shock it would be if a roommate on *The Real World* were wrestling with his or her future by studying Chinese, or perhaps luring the roomie next door into some lucrative industrial piracy. (How prosaic it would be to find their Chinese counterparts studying English or poring over American drug patents.) More troubling still is how the public, in developed countries especially, willfully avoids the difficult questions about preparing for and managing the inevitable, earthshaking changes stirred by China.

Where Have All the Factories Gone?

There is no bigger question than what will happen to the future of work. If it seems lately that the local news regularly offers obituaries for nearby factories and the middle-class jobs they provided, and gives the impression of an industrial exodus, that sense may better reflect the economic trends than any of the regularly announced government statistics that track job losses.

Despite widespread concern about the transfer of jobs to low-wage countries, the U.S. government still keeps no official statistics tracking jobs that move, other than those voluntarily reported by companies making a change. (Most companies, of course, have disincentives to report their decisions, given the caustic response to such shifts.) Better numbers would be useful to quantify the trend or to debunk it. From what is known, and as has been argued here already, productivity improvement is responsible for the vast number of manufacturing jobs lost in the United States and around the world, a trend closely tied to competition from low-wage manufacturing in China.

Nevertheless, the daily news offers regular evidence that many jobs are in fact being exported to other assembly lines in faraway places. Actually adding up these reports, one by one, news outlet by news outlet, confirms that job shifts are happening frequently and all over. The monumental task of counting these stories has been conducted as part of a periodic attempt by the U.S.-China Economic and Security Review Commission to address the statistical gap.[1] One recent count, covering the brief period from January 2004 to March 2004, is far from comprehensive but telling.*

The study looked not only at the United States but to Europe, Latin America, and other Asian countries, as well. In the three months covered, 58 U.S. companies, 55 European companies, and 33 companies from other Asian countries all announced plans to move jobs to China. The numbers were up dramatically from just three years before. Over a comparable period in 2001, only 25 U.S. companies announced shifts to China.† Another big change: many of the companies moving jobs from the United States to China in 2004 simultaneously moved jobs to other low-wage countries.

By extrapolating the number of lost jobs from the first three months to the entire year, the study concludes that U.S. work sites moved four hundred thousand jobs to other countries over the course of the year, twice the number that had moved three years before. Yet the numbers

---

*The study, completed in October 2004, was devised and conducted by Dr. Kate Bronfenbrenner at Cornell University and Dr. Stephanie Luce from the University of Massachusetts at Amherst. The two scholars tracked media reports that appeared online and in corporate research during the three months under investigation.

†During the first three months of 2004, there were also announcements of 69 U.S. shifts to Mexico, 31 to India, 39 to other Asian countries, 35 to Latin American and Caribbean countries, and 23 to other countries including Eastern and Western Europe and Canada. In all there were 255 shifts out of the United States.

collected by U.S. government agencies, which are at least as thorough and obsessive in gathering economic data as any other government in the world, vastly underestimated the jobs being moved overseas. The U.S. Bureau of Labor Statistics, for example, captured less than one-fifth of the jobs that left.

Of the jobs moving in 2004, one-quarter went to China. Yet the role of China in the migration is far disproportional to its numbers. The pressure that China puts on other low-wage countries to drop their labor rates makes these countries then become more attractive to American enterprises looking for cut-rate homes. Such is the case in the Mexican maquiladoras where workers are forced to accept wage concessions under threat of losing their jobs to lower-wage workers in China. Auto-parts maker Delphi is one of Mexico's largest private-sector employers with 70,000 workers on its rolls. In 2003, the company had 5,000 workers in China, a number Delphi made clear would rise. The company also made clear that it expected Mexico to work on its incentives, including tax breaks, if it expected to keep Delphi fully committed to Mexico.[2]

China's role in the shift is also evident in the mix of jobs that are now exported. In 2001, American jobs that went to China were concentrated in industries such as electronics and toys, for which low-wage countries are always attractive. By 2004, the shifts were well-divided among a much larger cross-section of industries that more closely mirrors the full American industrial landscape. The study found that the companies most actively moving jobs to China in 2004 were large, publicly held, highly profitable, and well-established. Nearly three out of four of the workplaces that shipped jobs out were branches of U.S. multinationals.

Perhaps predictably, jobs performed by members of labor unions are among the most vulnerable to the lure of China. Not only are unionized industries at great risk of having their American workplace liquidated by bosses who find very cheap, nonunionized shops in China, but the shift of unionized shops in one industry can cause a bandwagon effect among nonunionized companies in the same industry that also move jobs abroad.

The effect on the American economy is far-reaching. Eviscerating organized labor also weakens the one constituency that can best organize to protect the interests of workers in the halls of government and in the boardroom. Without that voice, the global ambitions of big companies can more easily cut their current employees out. When William Burga, president of the Ohio AFL-CIO, testified in September 2004 at congressional hearings regarding China's impact on manufacturing, he noted that had he come before the panel two years earlier, he would have been speaking for one hundred thousand more union members, but the subsequent shrinkage of manufacturing had cut the union rolls in the state from 850,000 members to 750,000.[3]

Even more disquieting than the rash of news about jobs already lost is the prospect of what the future may bring to Americans and other countries. What are the chances that a country's workforce will assert itself when the corporate drift to China and other low-wage destinations undercuts labor's power to press itself onto the national agenda? Or when American, European, and Japanese factories are driven by software ghosts running machines with skills no human can match? As factories grow ever more productive while shaving their payrolls to the bone, whither the middle class that since the end of World War II has pulled up the world's advanced economies? Is the developed world destined for a falling tide that will strand all boats?

"The only way to maintain our security and prosperity is through relentless innovation," says Deborah Wince-Smith, president of the Council on Competitiveness, a coalition of American corporations, labor groups, and educational institutions. Wince-Smith argues that the economy's capacity for innovation is the key to raising productivity, which itself is the most important component of competitiveness and economic growth.

Michael Cox of the Dallas Federal Reserve argues that the chief problem for the United States is that it does not have enough global entrepreneurs. He notes that the country can stand to export far more manufacturing and service jobs than it does already, provided that Americans have the skills and creativity to offer the world new products and services. "There's no reason we can't have one of every four Americans working at home leveraging the work of ninety-five people elsewhere in the world," he says. "If we did that, we would completely employ our whole labor force."

There is, however, an important catch. Innovation happens best not when smart people work in small groups or geographic isolation but when they have the benefit of an environment that gives them deep knowledge of their industry. Chip designers who are removed from assembly lines do not get the feedback from the factory pros that help them optimize their designs. Software firms that work far from the world's tech corridors do not benefit from the crosscurrent of workers who come and go among firms, or from the ideas shared with industry pals over lunch.

For America to stay the most innovative economy, it must also be *the most complete economy.*

One of China's most potent economic weapons is its ability to attract entire industry clusters, acquiring the critical masses of companies that catalyze the creative ferment that leads to rapid innovation. Global telecommunications and regular air links may go a long way to closing the distances for Cox's American army of global entrepreneurs, but Americans stringing together opportunities in distant lands will have to spend a lot of time re-creating the network of relationships that has been lost as America's industrial clusters depopulate, devolve, or both.

Cheap Talk

To go global, Americans will also need to take some basic steps first. A recent count of Chinese-language students in American high schools came up with just fifty thousand, while in China there are nearly as many people learning English as a second language as there are people who speak English as a first language in the United States, Canada, and Great Britain *combined.* English-language instruction still has a long way to go in China, however. Native speakers would find the spoken English of many Chinese English teachers hard to decipher. But the country has made a start, and for now, reading English, not speaking it, is China's strength. That may change, as it did in Europe, as more and more English-language entertainment finds its way into people's homes and as multinational businesses, where English classes are common, offer incentives to workers to improve their skills.

That Americans have few non-Chinese people learning Chinese is a measure perhaps of how slowly schools adapt to important change. Certainly, the United States would have little trouble attracting native-speaking teachers of Chinese if the national will to do so were there. One might argue that it is better to devote students to learning other subjects while kids in China put in the time to learn English, which, after all, is spoken in workplaces everywhere. China's willingness to push English is a boon to the rest of the world that wants to set up shop there; English competence is akin to good infrastructure. And for China itself, English speakers provide the key to scientific and technical advancement. That works two ways. Foreign firms with Chinese R&D labs can take better advantage of their talents if they require no translation.

One must also ask who will be the better global managers, native speakers of English working in China who rely on their bilingual local managers to interpret and order the workplace or Chinese managers who can deal with their workers directly in their first language and communicate with their international counterparts in English? Of course, the presence of tens or hundreds of millions of English speakers in China also expands the kinds of work that Chinese companies can take on. India has grown into a software and service center for global companies on the strength of its English-language-speaking workers. China is poised for a similar move and Indian companies already fear the competition.

Can We Really Stay in the Game?

Competitiveness requires a highly educated workforce. On that score, the news in America is not promising, especially when one looks at grade schools and high schools where the vast majority of American students are not getting the skills they will need to be sharp enough to flourish in a future informed by China.

In 2004, ACT, the independent organization that administers academic assessment tests to millions of American schoolchildren every year, took stock of American schools overall. Of the 1.2 million graduating high school students in 2004 who took ACT's college admission test, only one in five had scores showing they were ready for college courses in English, math, and science. Only a quarter had scores that predicted they would get a C or higher in their first college biology course. The numbers were slightly better in math, but still dismal, showing that only two in five American high school graduates could earn at least a *C* in a first-year college algebra course.[4]

The plain fact is that a lot of American public schools are pretty lousy, despite decades of earnest effort to improve them. Americans never tire of schemes to correct their schools, focusing in one place on an open curriculum, in another on test scores, and in still another on self-esteem. These may all be worthy ideas, but are rarely effective enough by themselves. Local, ideological, cultural-religious, and special interest politics also cloud reform. The freedom of Americans to overspend on unproductive consumption at the expense of education leaves schools underfunded. (In many places around the country, property owners militantly oppose efforts to raise property taxes to improve the local schools. California's Bay Area, land of the tech millionaires and knowledge workers, cannot afford routine maintenance for its schools and has had to ask teachers to take pay cuts.) To make matters worse, the higher-wage attractions of the private workforce for people with even modest science and math skills, or those possessing marketable creativity who might otherwise be teachers, keep essential talent out of the classroom. American high school teachers of science and math too rarely have university degrees in science or math.

One can only despair about the education system until there is a fundamental shift in the public will so that schools become the top national priority of a people firm in the knowledge that every lesson not learned will equal a job not earned.

If American primary and secondary schools fall short, is not American higher education still far superior to that of any other country? Yes—for now. But the comparative strengths of American universities to turn out the world's highest skilled workers are fading. The challenge to America's engineering programs to produce American engineers has already been covered. Equally threatening, however, is the decreasing ability of American universities to attract the best and the brightest foreign students. Part of the problem may be short-lived, as foreign students who were denied visas because of security concerns following 9/11 begin to gain entry once the United States has a faster screening system in place. In the short time since 9/11, however, other countries have learned how to attract the world's best students, and the United States is just one of several destinations the bright can choose.

Ignorance Isn't Bliss

As old-line manufacturing jobs disappear, it's axiomatic that citizens of advanced countries prepare for the knowledge economy, a global workplace that favors intellect over brawn. Students seeking careers and workers looking for new ones are often directed to pursue a job in the brainy post-industrial workplace. Yet, often, the job of the knowledge worker is misunderstood. Silicon Valley computer programmers were once seen as the epitome of knowledge workers, but many still found their jobs easily transferred to low-wage programmers overseas. Most vulnerable were those once high-paid coders who did the grunt programming on pieces of other people's projects.

Knowledge workers, the thinking now goes, must possess more than rule-based skills used to perform complex but discrete tasks that are easily transferred to someone else who has mastered the same rules. So despite years of expensive schooling in a field that once promised a secure lifetime of employment, many programmers now find that they are defenseless against outsourcing. In contrast, their colleagues who conjure up new applications for software, new uses for computer chips, and new ways to manufacture them have seen their incomes go up.

Another misunderstanding of the knowledge economy is that it applies mainly to high tech industries and communications. Countries can only compete against China's low wages and high skills if they have a population that is ready to make nearly any job a high-tech job. "There are no low-tech industries," says Deborah Wince-Smith, "only low-tech firms."

Even a farmer is a knowledge worker in the modern American economy. Visit a corn and soybean farmer in Pekin, Illinois, and the intellectual component of his work is soon apparent. The day may begin with a visit to a computer, where he checks and analyzes the day's crop prices at the Chicago Board of Trade, uses the latest regression models to adjust his futures and options hedges in the commodities market, and then hits a key to send in his order over his online brokerage account. He may also check the satellite reading of that day's weather. In the field, he runs a marvelous farm machine, the John Deere 9650STS fast-loading combine, which is very possibly the most productive farm machine ever made and features an automatic steering system, a GPS satellite navigation link to lead it around the field, and computer controls that monitor harvesting. Deere designed the machine to be so automated that even after a long day in the field, a farmer will feel little fatigue. That can leave him fresh enough to shop for the hybrid seeds he will plant next season, choosing from among a wide variety of crops genetically engineered in the nation's advanced public and private agriscience labs. Today, American bean and corn farmers can offer products on the Chinese market at lower cost than Chinese farmers, most of whom are among the lowest paid workers on the planet.

Similarly, if American farm-equipment makers find ways to automate fruit picking, then Washington apples and Florida oranges will give Chinese fruit growers a run for their money. (Though this will cause more joblessness among the Latino migrant workers who pick oranges and apples.) As American labs pioneer ways to embed pharmaceuticals in food and engineer disease-resistant crops and fruits and vegetables with novel and irresistible flavors and textures, the food-loving Chinese will long to import them.*

As American factories of all kinds morph into high-tech shops, the workers who are left to manage them must be skilled enough to operate and service complex machines, handle inventory and work-flow databases, and they must have the core knowledge necessary to adapt to new technology that enters their workplace. In the service sector, jobs that once required little education at all will increasingly demand high skills, especially those jobs that can justify better-than-minimum wage.

Remaking every laborer into an advanced knowledge worker is an impossible dream. Yet creating an American education system that produces the most knowledge workers possible is not a dream, but, again, a matter of national will.

Right now, no such national will exists.

Such a consensus will probably take a crisis to achieve. When threatened in the past, Americans supported large-scale educational change,

---

*Even farmers who reject engineered crops as "Frankenfood" can be sophisticated knowledge workers, using computer models to schedule plantings and crop rotation and thus increase the yields of organically grown crops and better preserve the health of the soil.

most notably when the Soviet Union woke up the United States with the launch of the Sputnik satellites in 1957.* Ironically, it will not be Communist militarists that most threaten the U.S. standard of living, but a Communist-capitalist rival that is a much more formidable economic competitor.

How close is the United States to a competitive crisis? After all, China has yet to introduce the kind of world-changing technology or consumer products that are the hallmark of advanced economies. But it will. The genius that has so far poured into creating great factories will soon be evident in great products and great brands that will offer the world unsurpassed quality and refinement: Japan will have to share the shelves in high-end electronics and photo shops, France and Italy will vie with China in the luxury apparel and accessory market; and South Korea will have trouble staying ahead of Chinese shipbuilders.

Nations can find that their competitive edge against China can suddenly disappear with the movement of a single person. In May 2004, Steve Chen, one of the most admired designers of supercomputers in the United States, joined Galactic Computing Shenzhen Co., Ltd., a company backed by Hong Kong investors and several Chinese universities. The enterprise, set up to create world-class supercomputers in China, has already showcased a computer fast enough to place it among the top 250 fastest computers in the world. "In terms of momentum [in supercomputing, China is] the most rapidly ascending country in the world," David Keyes, a professor of applied mathematics at Columbia University, told the *New York Times*. In an October 2004 story headlined "China to Lead Supercomputing Sector," the *China Daily* declared that the country may well be home to the world's fastest supercomputer in 2005, and that "the nation will hold all intellectual property rights to the bionic processor and its relevant applications." Chen, who immigrated to the United States from Taiwan in 1975, did graduate work at

---

*Back then the United States saw itself as technologically weak compared with the Soviets, and educators, scientists, and mathematicians rallied to address America's gaps. Local governments and federal lawmakers increased their support for science and math education, and established new programs and standards for schools. The Sputnik-inspired reforms were far from perfect and inspired a generation of critics, many of whom believed the educational methods of the day discouraged creativity. Nevertheless, the era's zeal and focus are models for the challenges that face the American workforce today.

the University of Illinois and later worked for supercomputing pioneer Cray Research. Chen told the *Times* he joined the Chinese company because venture capital for supercomputing had dried up in the United States.

But there are other ways that time is short. China could emerge overnight as the world's largest maker and consumer of movies, computer games, television programming, and music. All it would take are a dash of expressive freedom and the joining of Chinese talents with global media companies. Beginning in November 2004, the country allowed Chinese companies to enter into joint television-production ventures with foreign entertainment companies, such as Viacom, Sony, and News Corp., for the first time. Remember the country's rising facility in English. Millennia of Chinese storytelling and performing traditions will find their way into modern media as the fabulous creativity and obsessive dedication of China's performers will transform world entertainment. Byte by byte, China will enter the world's homes, workplaces, and mindshare in ever-growing degrees. There will be nothing material, intellectual, or cultural beyond the reach of the world's most populous country. For America to stay productively employed, its skills, sophistication, and imaginative power must remain world-class, every day better than ever before. *America itself must become a new place.*

A Forced Smile

How can the United States adjust to a competitive challenger that has strengths unlike any other that America has ever faced? Are the transfers of talent, technology, and capital part of an inevitable dynamic? Or does the United States, or any other country, have the power to shape a future in which everyone prospers?

Americans looking for answers and action must also find a way to move America's leadership to see China's rise as every bit as worthy of national attention as the rumblings in more obvious political hot spots. While all eyes turn to the so-called clash of civilizations between Islam and the West, in the long run China will have the most profound impact on the world. Instead, despite occasional misgivings offered in factory towns and tariffs slapped on imports at the height of campaign season, American leaders tend to view China's rise as the fulfillment of a free marketer's dream, where global investors will shepherd the country into wealth, democracy, and peaceful interdependence with the rest of the free world.

It is a lovely theory, and it may ultimately be true. There is, however, no evidence upon which to base such a prediction. Which exactly of the world's large, highly nationalistic, dictatorial, Communist-capitalist countries offer a historical analogue? Answer: There is no other such country. Alas, where China is concerned, optimism itself is not always cause for optimism.

Chinese officialdom works hard to reassure the world that the country is no threat. Perhaps the most impressive accomplishment of the Chinese Communist Party is that after years of fomenting despair and uncertainty, it has discovered how to instill China with optimism. In a land where the vast majority of people still live in a present of bleak shelter and almost no money, optimism is an essential resource, and it gushes where one would expect, in the government-controlled media, where editors and reporters must whistle happy tunes.

For example, Hong Kong's *Sing Pao Daily News*[5] reported that before the big 16th Party's Congress in September 2004, the Ministry of Propaganda issued thirty internal instructions to China's media outlets reminding them to correctly guide the public and to beef up positive reporting with "happy stories about good people."* News organizations were instructed to not run stories about petitioners coming to Beijing to seek remedy for the loss of their homes. State-mandated optimism also pours forth in the country's provincial and municipal offices, where the

---

*Particularly galling to the Ministry of Propaganda were reports in *China Youth Daily* about a concert by female pop singer Song Zuying. The singer, the report said, was paid $50,000 to sing four songs in the poor city of Wanyuan in Sichuan Province, and local officials were directed to buy $165,000 in tickets. The article touched nerves because of the impression that Ms. Song is a special friend of Jiang Zemin, at the time, China's premier, and the implication that the concert was also a special favor to her. The Ministry's directive for positive coverage was, in part, a response to "factual errors" such as those in the story of the concert. The *China Youth Daily,* one of China's largest papers, is affiliated with the Communist Youth League, which at the time was widely regarded as an ally of Hu Jintao, then in a leadership struggle with Jiang Zemin, but now China's undisputed head.

scale models of grand projects—many of them still in search of financing from private investors—sit proudly on officials' desks.

Not all the cheerleaders in China speak Mandarin. Many speak only English, German, or Finnish, and work at Western companies plying the Chinese market or at large consulting firms that see in China a place where they can lead their large corporate clients through complete makeovers. Back home, corporate officers whine about onerous government regulations, employment laws, legal liabilities, and the weight of their pension and health care obligations, complaining as if their own governments were their worst adversaries. In China, meanwhile, executives and their corporate communications staffs turn into another breed. Anxious to please the Chinese government, they serve as informal agents for the Ministry of Propaganda, tying their corporate message points to China's official line.

One gauge of the how influential the good news machinery is in China is the nearly automatic responses that Western residents in the country give to the questions that outsiders are disposed to ask. Inquire, for example, about the country's human rights record, which by any Western norm is abysmal. Mention any horror—the Tiananmen crackdown, the brutal repression of farmers' protest movements, the occupation and cultural domination of Tibet, China's more-than-friendly relations with foreign regimes so bad (including Burma, North Korea, the Sudan, and Iran) that most other big countries shun them, or the ongoing, often violent subjugation of religionists, including followers of Falun Gong, Tibetan Buddhism, and Roman Catholicism. Offer concerns about how China censors the press, watches and blocks how its citizens use the Internet and telephone text messages.* State the plain fact that the Chinese do not allow big families. Ask about China's one-party system, reminding the listener that the Communist Party is fixedly antidemocratic and self-perpetuating. This is just a short list of the most common grievances against China, but the issues have not changed much over time. Naturally, there is a Chinese side to each issue.

---

*Chinese users of the World Wide Web report that the words and phrases Chinese censors look for when screening Internet communications have included, along with obviously politically charged references, such words as *freedom, hypermart, naïve, paper, making, peacehall, playboy, simple, bignews, tibettalk,* and *VOA* (Voice of America). The government says it watches over electronic communications to "block false political rumors."

And, since papers are the organs of power, the Chinese government fills them with answers to Western doubts. Many of the government's reasons deserve some consideration. What's more, China's system does seem to be providing much of the country's population with a better life, a fact that is routinely cited to explain China's slow-going political reforms. China remains, however, a land of ironfisted political repression and, on the local level especially, pervasive government gangsterism. To a visitor engaging expatriates on the big issues, however, it is striking how thoroughly the transplants parrot the views of China's state propaganda. They say that they feel safe in China, that the country needs stability not democracy. Chaos, goes the argument, is China's gravest enemy and rapid reform would risk it. The Chinese state takes the poor seriously, they say, and America has its own problems, such as a national willingness to go to war.

"It's amazing how it works on you," says a member of the German-language foreign press corps. "Even as a reporter I find myself getting sucked into the message. The thing is that as soon as I step out of the country, I can better see things for what they are. You have to give the Chinese credit. They are really good at the mindshare game."

This pressure to toe the party line has a strong effect on how the world deals with China's rise. Because American and other foreign executives are expected to toady to the official Chinese version of reality, important economic security and trade issues are never discussed as thoroughly as they ought to be in the world's other capitals. The very group of foreigners that has the most at stake in China is expected by the Chinese government to always be on its best behavior. Companies with interests in China that raise the key issues of trade barriers, currency values, Chinese government attempts to rig business in favor of Chinese companies, or whether the Chinese are paying full fare for technology can expect certain grief from Chinese officials. Heaven forbid that American or European companies raise flags over China's environmental degradation, labor rights, or religious freedoms. American executives repeatedly describe, in confidence, sotto voce, the many governmental roadblocks they face in China, but then plead that their stories not be told because they are still in negotiation with the Chinese government and fear anything negative they say would torpedo their hopes of gaining whatever sliver of the Chinese market they hope to secure. When complaints must be raised, they often come through the collective anonymity of foreign trade associations or informally through diplomatic channels.

Playing the Triangle Offense

If Americans are to fully appraise China's significance, they must also recognize how the fact of America makes China strong. The world leaders who now make frequent visits to Beijing accompanied by entourages of industrial ministers, trade secretaries, and business leaders certainly come to ink billion-dollar deals. But that is not all. They also come to talk power, and power not just for themselves but *against* the United States. For all of the world's serious grievances against China, it is the only country that can counterbalance the economic and political weight of the United States.

When, for example, French president Jacques Chirac made a return trip to China in October 2004 with four ministers and fifty-two French executives, their high-level meetings included, as expected, discussion of the sale of the cream of French industry: superfast trains, Airbus planes, nuclear power plants,* and military hardware. (In all, the French president netted some $4 billion in orders.)[6] But the talks also included a chorus of signals that France regarded its relationship with China as a bulwark against world dominance by America. Chirac made clear that he would not publicly criticize China's human rights record. Chirac also made thinly veiled, but much appreciated, comments against Taiwan, which during Chirac's visit had approached the Communist government seeking to reduce the six hundred missiles China points at the island.

Moreover, the very nature of the trade itself had an anti-American cast. Chirac and Chinese president Hu Jintao presided over a ceremony in which the French Atomic Energy Commission officially signed on to lend its considerable expertise to the Chinese Ministry of Sci-

---

*China plans to build thirty-two nuclear power plants over the next twenty years, and France, the United States, and other governments of countries with nuclear power industries have moved into high gear to capture parts of the business. The Chinese, no doubt, will pit all against each other and end up with the best technology mix possible and a strong Chinese nuclear power plant industry as well.

ence and Technology to develop Linux open-source software for PCs, servers, and handheld computers, thus allowing the French to help the Chinese defeat the American company Microsoft while providing a gift to the Chinese people that may bode well when it comes time to hand out contracts for nuclear power plants.

Speaking of Chirac's 2004 trip to the *International Herald Tribune,* Jean-Pierre Cabestan, a China hand at the French National Center for Scientific Research in Paris, observed that "France likes to play the China card against the United States. Chirac has a multipolar vision of the world, and economics is a crucial part of it."[7]

But France is hardly the only European country to play its China card. David Shambaugh, director of the China Policy Program at George Washington University, says "the breadth and depth of Europe-China relations are impressive, and the global importance of the relationship ranks it as an emerging axis in world affairs."[8] Shambaugh notes that Europe's trade with China is accelerating rapidly, having grown 25 percent in 2003 and up nearly 40 percent again in 2004. The European Union and China are each other's largest trading partners and will soon exchange more than $200 billion in goods. As of 2004, Europeans have invested more than $40 billion with promises to pour in $30 billion more. China is now home to more than eighteen thousand firms established with European Union money and talent.[9]

On the geopolitical front, France and Great Britain hold joint military exercises with the Chinese armed forces (as does the United States) and the European Union has more cooperative military operations in the works. Chirac is only one of sixteen European leaders who have lobbied hard for an end to the international embargo that bans arms sales to China, disregarding United States concerns that any advanced weapons China buys may well be used against the United States, should China move aggressively on Taiwan. Also noteworthy, says Shambaugh, are the Communist Party's hundreds of exchanges with political parties throughout Europe made on the premise that the continent's social democrats have much to teach the Chinese about political evolution and reform.*

---

*Shambaugh also notes the irony of China's regard for the European social welfare state in light of the efforts in Europe to roll back the states' welfare models (partly as a response to the low-wage competition from China).

Do China and Europe make easier partners than China and the United States? The answer is probably yes. Europe has no historical or political affinity toward Taiwan and adheres strictly and unambiguously to a one-China policy. In addition, the European Union nations have little strategic interest in Asia, while the United States, in contrast, maintains a powerful military presence in Asia and the Pacific and has important territorial concerns and nonnegotiable claims.[10]

Most important, China and many of the European Union countries are increasingly distrustful of the United States. While once it was the United States that urged China to give up its revolutionary fervor and join the mainstream of nations committed to a stable world, now China flourishes under the status quo, and its desire to lift itself up depends on a world with as little turmoil as possible. From the view of France, Germany, and a majority of the European Union nations, China is a more committed partner to world stability than the United States, which is now seen as willing to push violently against international norms. France and China, Shambaugh observes, lead efforts to constrain the United States through such multilateral institutions as the United Nations, and by creating a multipolar world. Germany, Spain, and the Scandinavians follow.

Whether or not one thinks America was right to go to war in Iraq, one may see why many European countries are now wary of the United States. After the end of World War II, the United States stuck largely to an agenda of containment, in which it joined with Western Europe in a unified front against Soviet Communism. To the world, it was reasonable to assume that U.S. foreign policy would remain more or less constant across different American administrations and legislative majorities. That changed when the United States commenced the policies that led to the preemptive war against Iraq. The fear over the U.S. stance is that the American route to liberty is cleared with the rapid deployment of tanks, missiles, and troop convoys, not by the gradualism that unwound Communism over forty years.[11] Right or wrong, American foreign policy no longer seems so constant, and to China and its new close allies in the European Union, the Europe-China axis provides a contingency plan against American volatility.*

*Just one day before the 2004 U.S. presidential election, the Chinese press was host to a confusing round of analysis focused on American foreign policy. Qian Qichen, China's former foreign minister, wrote in *China Daily* that foreign policy under George Bush was

Yet as Europeans leverage China's economic growth into a multipolar world and find in their new partnerships a counterweight to U.S. dominance, they risk trading one set of perceived dangers posed by Americans for new dangers posed by a richer China.

Although China's long-term military and geopolitical ambitions are beyond the scope of this book, the perils of the European approach are suggested by the writings of John Mearsheimer, the influential political theorist from the University of Chicago and a proponent of the "realist" school of international relations, which aims to recognize the lengths that states, big and small, go to maximize their power and thus ensure their survival. Taking a long historical view of power politics in his 2001 book, *The Tragedy of Great Power Politics,*[12] Mearsheimer argues that great powers reliably seek military dominance over their spheres of influence and perpetually look for ways to demonstrate strength over their rivals. China's ability to offer a convincing military challenge to the United States is still a long way off. (A recent U.S. Department of Defense report concluded that China's military power would not even equal tiny Taiwan's until 2006.) Nevertheless, the country's rapid economic ascendancy is transforming its military into a richer, better equipped, technologically improved fighting force and is also giving the country ever greater clout in shaping its strategic relations with other nations. The pacifying influence of America's overwhelming military power in Northeast Asia has long kept armed conflict in check. As China rises and Europe triangulates, that peace could grow dangerously strained.

China Kicks at America's Asian Footprint

China's relationship to Europe is naturally a compelling topic to both Americans and Europeans. But both groups must also pay attention to China's role in Asia too. In recent years, the Chinese government has

marked by its "cocksureness and arrogance" in its attempt to "rule over the whole world," and that Americans have ruined global cooperation in the war on terrorism by taking unilateral action. American diplomacy, he said, was backed by arms and the threat of preemptive attack. Backpedaling, the Chinese government quickly declared that the comments were not sponsored by the government. Days afterward, the paper's offending column was excised from the *China Daily* Web site.

declared that it is interested only in a "peaceful rise," not in regional dominance. In November 2003, at an international meeting on the Chinese resort island of Hainan, one of the Communist Party's senior foreign policy officials presented other Asian nations with a vision of the region "rising together" in peace and prosperity. The language struck some other countries as plainly offensive, reverberant of the similar but hypocritical claims once made by Japanese imperialists in Asia and later by the first generation of Chinese Communist ideologues.

The Chinese government, cognizant of the jitters of its neighbors, repeats its peaceful intensions publicly and often.[13] In 2003, China joined the ten members of ASEAN (the Association of Southeast Asian Nations) in what was billed as a treaty of friendship and cooperation, and China agreed to procedures aimed at avoiding military brinksmanship over several long-standing territorial disputes with Southeast Asian countries. China also agreed to conduct joint military maneuvers with the ASEAN countries.

The agreements, however, can do as much to fan suspicions about China's ultimate goals as dampen them. Regional agreements within Asia, like the diplomatic proximity to Europe, help China insert itself into a process that can ultimately weaken the regional footprint of the United States. China is most willing to push sensitive buttons in regard to Japan. In late 2004, Beijing granted Chinese exploration companies permission to explore for natural gas in an area of the East China Sea that pushes against, and perhaps into, a marine economic zone that Tokyo regards as Japan's. After laying claim to the area, Beijing quickly called for negotiations, thus entangling Japan in a dispute that will test the smaller country's military and political resolve and give China's leadership yet another propaganda point with which to stoke anti-Japanese sentiments.

Meanwhile, hungry China is now the largest market for goods from other Asian countries. Take away the growing Chinese demand from resource-rich Southeast Asia and for high technology products from East Asia's production lines, and the rest of Asia would have little export growth at all. In 2006, China's trade with Southeast Asia should match the region's $120 billion trade with the United States.[14]

Consider China's relationship to Indonesia, the world's fourth most populous country with 200 million people and a long enmity toward the

Chinese. It shows how thoroughly China has been recast in the region. In the 1960s, Indonesians endured violent political upheavals, much of which they blamed on the Communist Chinese for meddling in the domestic politics of the largely Muslim country over the last three decades of the twentieth century. Indonesia was also the scene of sporadic but intense anti-Chinese riots, directed at the 1 percent of the nation's population that is ethnic Chinese but whose families have resided in the country for hundreds of years. With the emergence of China as a potent economic engine for Southeast Asia, and as a model for economic development, attacks against Indonesia's ethnic Chinese have all but disappeared in the past few years.

But China's rise has not been the boon to Indonesia that it has been to its neighbors. Instead, the country has lost much of the low-wage shoe, garment, and electronics assembly businesses that have since moved to Chinese factories. In addition, despite their own ambitious market reforms, Indonesia has been unable to attract anything near the amount of foreign investment that streams into China. Rather than anathematizing China, Indonesia and its ASEAN partners now allow China to join regional discussions.

One of China's goals in all of this politicking is to diminish U.S. influence in Asia. But China has a long way to go. The United States, and its military, has strong ties in the region, with uniformed personnel stationed in the Philippines, Japan, and South Korea;[15] alliances with India and Pakistan; and plans for reestablishing links to the Indonesian military, one of the world's largest armed forces. The China-U.S. match in Asia is a slow power game, but it is afoot.

Aggressive Tendencies

Chinese nationalism, as mentioned earlier, is rising in parallel with China's globalization. State propaganda often seems directed at laying the groundwork for future territorial claims and is a constant source of diplomatic tension.

On the Taiwan issue, China's rhetoric on the use of force is unambiguous. China's capacity to drive its desired goal of unification has been buttressed by its economic growth and integration into the world economy. On one hand, an economically strong China has had an easier time diplomatically drawing the rest of the world closer to the Chinese position. On the other, China's technological advancements have pulled the shores of Taiwan closer to the reach of the mainland's military. China firmly declares that it is free to use force against Taiwan should it see the need. Indeed, China has spelled out a broad range of circumstances in which it would launch an attack, each vague enough to justify an invasion at any time. Among them are a formal declaration of independence by Taiwan, an intervention in Taiwan's internal affairs by a foreign power, and the advent of civil unrest on the island. When in the spring of 2004 the streets of Taipei were filled with angry protesters following the disputed national election, the mainland press was filled with grave concern from the Communist leadership, who publicly reserved the right to invade Taiwan to restore order.

Usually the most bellicose declarations appear in the Chinese-language press, but more recently the country has been saber rattling in the English-language editions of *China Daily*. "America has the industrial capacity and Japan the technological edge plus money to perfect their nuclear-missile defense system within the next decade. As soon as that is completed they will find a ton of reasons to attack China. No matter how we plead to them to maintain peace in our world they will never listen," ran a "Readers Voice" opinion column in the paper, written in response to overtures from Taiwan in October 2004. "China's promise of a 'peaceful rise' means that when she is strong enough to take all the marbles she will not act like a hegemon and will be fair in her dealings with the rest of humanity. Even then, China will go on acting as a responsible member of the international community, treating nations rich and poor, big and small, black and white equally."

Striking a tone reminiscent of the most colorful propagandistic prose of the Maoist era, the writer further declaimed that "one must not confuse such a goodwill promise of 'peaceful rise' with the unprincipled, cowardly position of failing to resist aggression from a technologically superior foe and letting the aggressor choose the time and place of a preemptive military confrontation. Therefore, it is pure gobbledygook muddleheaded thinking to put an 'ultranationalist' label on such self-evident righteousness."[16]

The United States Department of Defense, in its 2004 assessment of

China's military strength, interprets this stepped-up pressure on Taiwan as evidence of China's increased confidence that it can succeed in taking over the island if it makes the move.[17]

There are also more pragmatic reasons to expect a richer China to grow increasingly assertive. The country is building a global network of mining and petroleum firms and will eventually see the need to patrol the world's sea-lanes, over which its precious cargoes travel. New oil pipelines to China will soon reach up from Thailand and down from Russia and will require the resolve to make sure they do not get shut off for political reasons.

China's growing international clout need not inevitably expand the country's military ambitions or lead to a confrontation with the United States. Skillful diplomacy can do a lot to head off a conflagration. The interdependency of the Chinese and American economies certainly creates strong constituencies for sanity. Yet even a peaceful rise has important consequences. As China's new economic might helps it acquire geopolitical clout, its growing political power and strategic presence also hinder the rest of the world's ability to force China to compete on a level economic playing field.

This year the French may see their interests aligned more deeply with China than with the United States, and the United States may choose to slight France in favor of its own ties with China. Yet is it really in France's economic interest to play the Chinese against the United States? And is it in Germany's interest to compete at all costs to win Chinese business that might otherwise go to Japan? The worldwide competition for the good graces of the Chinese government means that there can be no unified front for the rule of law, compliance with the World Trade Organization, or sanctions against a government that muscles companies to transfer their patents. There will be no workable effort to pressure China on the environment, on labor rights, or perhaps even on its geopolitical ambitions.

With the world's billions bet in the mainland and the world's governments and businesses co-opted to the Chinese message, can the Taiwanese, for example, expect that any country would fire a gun on its behalf should the Communist government decide to invade? It is doubtful. How much would the Chinese have to nip at the territorial edges of the Philippines, Indonesia, South Korea, or Japan to get U.S. or

European warships to engage? As other countries compete for the economic and political advantage that will win them Chinese deals and friends, China is accumulating an impressive hand, filled with foreign investment dollars, the world's best technology, and new strategic powers. China has little problem setting the rules of the game and no problem breaking them.

Cooking with Gas

China is also deploying its national wealth in ways that may catch competitors off guard. A September 2004 story in *China Daily* headlined "Cash-Rich, Commodity-Starved Mainland Shopping Spree" announced the beginning of an "overseas acquisition march fueled by swollen foreign exchange reserves and a need to secure natural resources."[18] The article in the government-run paper describes how China's nearly $500 billion in U.S. dollar reserves would serve as a war chest for the acquisition of foreign companies, especially resource and commodity firms. Chinese state-owned firms have spent at least $5 billion on overseas oil and gas fields in the past ten years, the paper reported, but it cited a recent $550-million takeover of a South Korean oil refiner as evidence of China's new willingness to buy entire companies abroad.

The article went on to describe just how much money China's government firms could have at their disposal once they make up their shopping lists. "Mainland firms have enough cash to win over rivals worth $10 billion, enough to buy a company such as Woodside Petroleum, Australia's largest listed oil-and-gas firm, and Unocal and Devon Energy of the United States," it confidently predicted. "Meanwhile, PetroChina is looking at the oil assets owned by top Canadian oil and gas exploration firm EnCana in Ecuador. The assets, by some estimate, are worth more than US$1.5 billion. Money is not a problem for PetroChina, which earned US$8.5 billion last year." Following the strategy of experimentation that rolled out economic reform over time, China is entering some international corporate waters studiously before its makes bigger moves. A Chinese company bought two power plants in Australia, purchases meant to serve as training grounds for learning about the competitive power-supply market.

China's economy will remain a hybrid of private companies and large government-owned firms in key industries such as power generation, resource mining and exploration, transportation, truck and car manufacturing, as well as large private-sector firms with inextricable links to government agencies and officials. Chinese companies with government links will continue to be able to draw on government resources that even the world's largest private sector firms cannot match.

In the past, for example, the open spigot of money out of China's banks has helped bankroll goliath domestic firms. Now those companies are turning their sights on foreign acquisitions. A consortium of Chinese government-backed firms made a spectacular $5-billion bid for Noranda, Inc., Canada's largest mining company, in late 2004. The consortium includes several Chinese state-owned enterprises whose structure allows them to double as big, publicly traded firms while the state remains the dominant shareholder. The group includes Baosteel, the $10-billion giant that is now the world's fourth largest steel company, and Jiangxi Copper, China's top copper refiner. The consortium has access to foreign capital on the world's security markets while keeping its links to China's government banks. The world's other mining companies, such as American copper giant Phelps Dodge, can only raise money the old-fashioned way, by justifying its investments to private-sector lenders and shareholders.

The Chinese strategy is not risk free. The Chinese people may find themselves saddled with assets for which their public companies have overpaid. Then again, government-sponsored buying sprees of mineral companies can help give the Chinese the power to set prices in the world market and to ensure their own supplies. One sign that China is heading for both a boondoggle and a buying spree is the 2004 rush on the Canadian stock markets, where half of the world's equity finance for mining firms is raised. Not only did share prices soar, but mining companies from all over the world rushed to list their shares in anticipation of a speculative boom caused by Chinese buying.

An economically big China that is still the sum of impoverished parts may also find reasons—some economic and some political—to follow the paths of other superpowers and assert its armies. If the rush to spend some of its massive dollar reserves on foreign companies and resources does not deliver China into the economic company it means to keep, or even if it does, China may see the need to spend more of its money on the world's weapons market.

China's rise means the world will need to get used to a different kind of economic superpower, one that has huge numbers of people poorer than those living in countries that China has surpassed. In such a country even a small rise in the national standard of living results in an enormous change in the total size of the national economy.

As usual, the story may be told in the numbers. Today, the United States can claim both the world's highest income among large countries and the world's biggest economy. But if per capita income in China (measured by purchasing-power parity) were to double overnight, the size of China's economy would instantly top the U.S. economy. China would still be a very poor country; its per capita income would still only match the level in Botswana, and one-quarter of America's. If, however, the incomes of the Chinese come up to a mere half of those in the United States, a standard of living that the Chinese someday aspire to, China's economy would be *two and half times as large* as America's.

How China's scale and relative wealth play out in the future truly beggars today's understanding.

CHAPTER TWELVE

ONE LAST STORY

Back in Shanghai's busy Dongtai Market, the Li family awaits news about whether their atmospheric stretch of shops will be bulldozed for another mall or, in keeping with the city's new resolve to preserve some of its period charm, spared and spruced up. Whatever the fate of the market, the old world of the antique and curio sellers is butting up against nearly every trend reshaping China and the world. The small shops offer a reminder that the sweep of history creating giant Chinese corporations and forcing the world's largest companies to rethink their global strategies is also remaking the lives of Chinese shopkeepers and Americans far removed from the most prominent manifestations of China's rise.

A few stores down from the Lis' jam-packed shop is an even smaller space with its own mix of genuine collectibles and reproduction whatnot. It is the shop of the Zhai family* from Henan Province. An average of ten or twelve foreigners browse the Zhais' shop every day. Aaron Shershow, an American resident of Shanghai, is a regular visitor. By all appearances, there is little to distinguish Shershow from other *waiguoren* (the Chinese version of "gringo") strolling Shanghai. He looks around as if everything were new to him, yet also as if it might be gone tomorrow. A man of moderate height in his midthirties, Shershow wears a baseball cap over his black curly hair. As he walks, his shoulders slump and his hands tuck halfway into his pockets as if he were killing time in a suburban American mall.

His meandering, however, is far from purposeless. The Dongtai shopkeepers know that Shershow looks over their wares carefully and that on any day he is a potential customer. Shershow is also a friend to

*All the names in the shopkeeper's family have been changed.

297

many of the sellers. They take to him readily. The American learned Mandarin Chinese in his high school in Massachusetts, and later in college and during a year in Taiwan. He speaks the language with little accent and a warm smile, finding ways to make every word reassuring. His conversation is sweetened with frequent nods and interjections of "I see," "I understand," and "This is fascinating." He has also learned Shanghainese, a feat that astonishes locals and opens communications all the more.

Shershow loves the Chinese people, and it shows in his rapport with them. The big economic and geopolitical issues all seem like distant nonsense in his life in Shanghai. His concerns involve his social life and everyday business. Will he meet friends for dinner at a favorite dive or splurge at a popular new French restaurant? Will his landlord sell to developers the old Shanghai house Shershow rents? How can he make more money without driving himself mad in the city's supersonic rat race?

Before settling in Shanghai, Shershow worked in Hollywood. He moved to China to join the production teams of Western film projects that came to China to shoot. Shershow has a knack for getting Chinese and American crews to work together and on schedule, and he has worked on several big television series and films in Shanghai. For instance, he has his own team of carpenters, all from a single rural village in China, whom he can set loose to build any prop or set. He swears they are as good as any in Hollywood, and of course, cost nothing near the price of tradesmen in California. Film work, however, is far from steady. After the SARS outbreak in 2003, it dried up altogether. But in China, where new businesses are just an idea and few dollars away, Shershow came up with an alternate plan to tide him over. He started his own small Internet sales business.

Joining a friend in Los Angeles, Shershow picked out several items from the Shanghai markets and offered them on eBay.* Those that tested well included traditional baskets, army uniforms, and Chinese versions of Tin Tin comic books (unauthorized versions from the 1970s and 1980s, completely rewritten by the Communists to remake Tin Tin, the

---

*The name of Shershow's firm on eBay is Yellow Mountain Imports, and its eBay screen name is ymimports.

bourgeois Belgian boy detective, into an agent for class struggle). Chinese editions of *The Art of War,* unsurprisingly, do very well, too.

The export business grew into a microenterprise that mirrors the Chinese economy. Shershow now employs a local manager, a Chinese friend who coordinates bulk buys and shipping prices, and he even has hired a migrant worker who comes in every day and packs up goods for bulk shipment to Los Angeles, where another friend ships them out to customers who buy the goods on eBay. The migrant worker, a twenty-year-old farm boy, is so thrilled with the opportunity to learn how to use a PC that he will gladly perform any task.

Shershow's manager convinced him to list for sale tea thermoses made in the manager's hometown. The thermoses, common in China, are handsome, painted acrylic jars that have screens in their lids so they can be filled with tea leaves and replenished with hot water all day. The leaves stay put and the tea flows through the top. American stores carry nothing like them. On eBay they caught fire, and Shershow's operation now fills whole shipping containers with tea thermoses and other items for American buyers.

Lately, however, Shershow has noticed that the shopkeepers in the Dongtai Market are also trying their luck on eBay. "They're all over the eBay site now," Shershow says.[1] "If you walk down the street you can see the shop owners packing goods into Styrofoam boxes all labeled for mailing to eBay buyers." In an ad hoc inventory of eBay sellers, and possible competitors, Shershow found 56,000 items offered by sellers in China, with 31,000 of them in the category loosely defined as antiques. Thousands of Chinese sellers also offer computers, electronic components, musical instruments, cars, cheap DVDs, look-alike watches, and even real estate.

The new sellers are something of a problem for Shershow's business. Like the world's makers of auto parts and microchips that face constant poaching, Shershow finds enterprising competitors passing themselves off as his operation. On eBay, it is difficult to keep success a secret from other sellers. If his venture finds a product that sells well, the Chinese sellers post the same items in their listing and lift wholesale the language Shershow has carefully crafted to pique interest in his items. Often too, Chinese sellers hawk inferior versions, but do not flag them as such.

Nevertheless, Shershow believes his crew can easily stay ahead of the imitators by choosing better items that are more in keeping with Americans' tastes, especially their quirky demand for offbeat collectibles. No Chinese sellers have yet caught on to the Tin Tin market. For that reason, when Shershow is asked by a Dongtai seller about how to conduct business on eBay, he often obliges, both to keep his friendships on the street strong and to get a look at what the sellers are up to.

It was just such a request that led him to the cramped upstairs room where Zhai Ming, the twenty-four-year-old son of the Zhai family, runs the family's international operations. The slight Zhai Ming greets Shershow in a sweater and tie, his hair pomaded and neatly combed back. He talks in a faint, nervous tone as if the American were a doctor making a bedside call.

Shershow eyes the setup, which to an uninitiated American would look something like a Mississippi mud shack stuffed full with scavenged office equipment. Shershow, however, sees more. The Zhai apartment is not a humble beginning, but a huge step up from a much humbler beginning in the provinces. The family's commitment to buy computers required grave sacrifice, and they see their future riding on what Zhai Ming can do with them.

A few moments after Shershow arrives, Zhai Ming's father, Zhai Young, comes in to say hello. The father arrived in Shanghai in 1992 after a long military career. His fortunes might be higher had he not been caught in the political crossfire following the 1989 Tiananmen Square protests. As it happened, the older man had been a soldier assigned to serve in the detail of bodyguards for China's former premier Zhao Ziyang, who was also from Henan Province. The former premier had a distinguished career in the early years of Mao's rule but was persecuted during the Cultural Revolution. He went on to become a popular reform figure and held many government posts from which he advocated economic and political change. Policies laid out by Zhao Ziyang greatly influenced China's turn toward a market economy, and the country's new wealth owes much to his vision. In a fateful decision, he advocated that the Chinese leadership enter a dialogue with the students who occupied Tiananmen Square. He lost all his posts, was placed under house arrest, and has stayed under supervision ever since.

In China, where military and political connections can offer a path to wealth and power, the former premier's fall from official grace was almost certainly a blow to the Zhai family. On hearing the outline of the former soldier's story, Shershow nods his understanding, signaling a deeper knowledge of what has been left unsaid. Though the humble Zhais do not talk about the impact of the political change in their lives, preferring to focus on their success in building up their small business, the family's will to succeed in the system that both set them back and now allows them room to prosper is strong. In China, there is also an optimism that defies the state, one in which people see their success as their own triumph despite the disappointments that official China has dealt them. China's private sector is full of people driven to prove they can overcome the reach of the state.

Now Shershow asks about the setup. The whole operation is handled on two locally built computers that are linked by Chinese-made networking gear to a broadband Internet connection. The office, which must be reached by climbing a rickety outdoor staircase and ducking past low, dripping water pipes, also doubles as the bedroom and kitchen of Zhai Ming, his wife, and their baby. Its crumbling walls use old advertising calendars as wallpaper, and the family's clothing hangs all over on lines and nails planted in the walls. As Shershow sits down on the jumble of covers on top of the bed that acts as a bench, Zhai Ming's wife, buried unseen in a quilt, wakes and gives him a start.

"What do you think of the Internet?" Shershow asks Zhai Ming.

The young man takes a deep breath and puts his hands in the air to signal that he is about to explain something big.

"It is a new world for me," the young man says with humble amazement. "Before my world was restricted to our family shop and our circle of friends and relatives. I did not have the opportunity to explore or to meet people from far away. Now I am communicating with people over the world." He pauses to think of how exactly to describe the impact on him.

"It is as if the whole strange world is shrinking into this house." Zhai Ming says he spends far too many hours on the computer because he finds it too fascinating to turn off. Some of the shop's Internet customers, he says, want to become friends. A woman from Australia writes to ask him about his feelings about China and his life. He says he is reluctant to say too much and that he is embarrassed by his limited used of English, which relies on dictionaries and a Web site that translates both Chinese and English. He does answer her though, out of a heartfelt fear that he will hurt the woman's feelings if he is too shy.

Zhai Ming and his wife struggled with the English-Chinese dictionary and figured out how to set up an eBay seller's account and how to get paid with credit cards, which are new in China but indispensable for international online sales.

On their first night, they put ten items up for sale and sold four. Suddenly they realized that the Internet allowed them to keep their store open through the night and have access to the 60 million buyers who visit eBay every day. Only a fraction actually buy Chinese collectibles, but that small contingent is perhaps the biggest, most motivated pool of buyers in the world.

The Zhais' stumbling block is their presentation. Out of the two hundred items they now offer for sale on eBay, only one in five sell, and of buyers who commit to purchase, only two in five pay. The Zhais distrust their own descriptions, and they have asked Shershow to help.

Shershow sits at one of the Zhais' computers and pokes around. They have all the software they need to make beautiful Web pages for their wares. That includes all the late edition software that lives on nearly every computer, plus auction management software that keeps track of inventory and activity on eBay. Shershow shows the young man a better way to organize his sales using the software—a small but valuable technology transfer. Shershow then pulls up the description of a seemingly old Chinese oil lamp. The English is only intermittently intelligible and even then the description is so extravagant that it would raise suspicions from nearly any buyer. The Zhais' biography also needs work. Shershow sets out to make the necessary changes.

While Shershow works, he asks Zhai Ming if he has any complaints about his computers. Zhai Ming says no, adding proudly that nearly all his technology is made in China, and most of it nearby. The price of equipment is dropping, he says. Of course, much of the equipment that Zhai Ming's customers use is also made in China, and the price for it is also dropping rapidly.

The prevalence of affordable Chinese technology is opening up the world to amazed people in China such as Zhai Ming, shifting the way the country spends its money and time. By conducting the family business at night while his shop is closed and by communicating with his new friends on the other side of the earth, Zhai Ming reaches beyond the China where minds are controlled and where one's family fortunes depend on its local social standing. Shershow embodies the other side.

In China these days all kinds of connections pay off. In the decrepit Dongtai slum, not so far from the gleaming skyscrapers filling with Western and Chinese companies, the Zhais see a good life in the making.

It is not only China's big companies and its government's grand designs that are changing the world. Change also comes from hundreds of millions of modest enterprises that reach deep into China to make what the world wants. We might remember that America grew strong on the enterprise of its own immigrants who arrived with little and whose American dreams often began by selling goods from wagons and suitcases. Most of China's dreams also begin with modest means.

Those dreams are now the most powerful force in the world.

NOTES

INTRODUCTION:
THE WORLD SHRINKS AS CHINA GROWS

1. See stats in "Another 500 Manufacturing Jobs Are Lost," by Joel Dresang, *Milwaukee Journal Sentinel* January 22, 2004, http://www.jsonline.com/bym/career/jan04/201935.asp.
2. Chi Lo, *The Misunderstood China: Uncovering the Truth Behind the Bamboo Curtain* (Singapore: Pearson Education, 2004), 22.
3. United States, Britain, France, Italy, Canada, Japan, and Germany.
4. Mark Weisbrot, "Latin America's Stunted Growth," *BusinessWeek,* June 15, 2004.
5. Schell spoke of the comparison on Boston's WBUR's radio interview show *On Point,* July 14, 2004.
6. China's GDP statistics are a constant source of controversy. Some argue that the numbers are systematically overstated, while others claim that the country's latest numbers are too low, understated perhaps to keep a lid on worries about the economy getting overextended.
7. No other country has doubled more than twice during the same period.
8. Art Pine, Bloomberg News, "China Steals the Spotlight on the Global Stage," *International Herald Tribune,* July 7, 2004, http://iht.com/bin/print.php?file=528123.html.
9. These figures come from "China in Transition, China Surpasses Japan to Become the World's Third-Largest Trader—but the 'Workshop of the World' Is Still Fragile," Japan's Research Institute of Economy, Trade and Industry, March 23, 2004.
10. According to Japan's Research Institute of Economy, Trade and Industry, 80 percent of the exports and 60 percent of the imports of foreign companies are categorized as "processing trade," meaning that the goods pass through China just to get finished—at low cost—and shipped back out.
11. Ian Garrick Mason, "Next Challenge: Capitalist Competition," *Philadelphia Enquirer,* July 18, 2004, http://www.philly.com/mld/inquirer/news/special_packages/sunday_review/9185839.htm?1c.

CHAPTER ONE:
TAKING A SLOW BOAT IN A FAST CHINA

1. Leo Ou-fan Lee, "Shanghai Modern: Reflections on Urban Culture in China in the 1930s," *Public Culture* (Society for Transnational Cultural Studies, Duke University

Press) 11, no. 1 (1999), http://www.uchicago.edu/research/jnl-pub-cult/backissues/pc27/04-Lee.html.

2. Leo Ou-fan Lee, in "Shanghai Modern," assembled a longer list of modern emblems culled from 1930s literature of the city. It included cars ("three 1930-model Citroëns"), electric lights and fans, radios, "foreign-style" mansions *(yang-fang),* sofas, guns (a Browning), cigars, perfume, high-heeled shoes, beauty parlors (in English), jai alai courts, "Grafton gauze," flannel suits, 1930 Parisian summer dresses, Japanese and Swedish matches, silver ashtrays, beer and soda bottles, as well as all forms of entertainment—dancing (fox-trot and tango), roulette, bordellos, greyhound racing, romantic Turkish baths, dancing girls, and film stars.

3. "Shanghai Forsees 10% Growth in FDI in 2004," Xinhua News Agency, March 26, 2004, online.

4. Yasheng Huang, "Why Overseas Chinese Dominate China's Exports," Project Syndicate, June 2001, http://www.project-syndicate.org/commentaries/commentary_text.php4?id=596&lang=1&m=contributor.

CHAPTER TWO:
THE REVOLUTION AGAINST THE COMMUNIST REVOLUTION

1. For some stats on Henan, see http://www.unescap.org/pop/database/chinadata/henan.htm and http://fpeng.peopledaily.com.cn/200104/02/eng20010402_66597.html and http://www.adb.org/Documents/News/2000/nr2000157.asp.

2. This summary of the history of land reform draws on the paper "Land Reform in Rural China Since the Mid-1980s" by Fu Chen, John Davis, and Liming Wang in *Land Reform 1998/2,* published by the Sustainable Development Department of the Food and Agriculture Organization of the United Nations. It also draws on *Women and Land Tenure in China: A Study of Women's Land Rights in Dongfang County, Hainan Province* by Jennifer Duncan and Li Ping, published by the Rural Development Institute, Seattle, 2001.

3. The 60 percent number appears in Chen Jianyuan, *Zhongguo shehui: yuanxing yu yanhua* (Chinese Society: Original Pattern and Transformation) (Shenyang: Liaoning Renmin Chubanshe, 1988), p. 142, and is cited in English in Kate Xiao Zhou, *How the Farmers Changed China: Power of the People* (Boulder, CO: Westview Press, 1996).

4. David Zeng, "Evolution of Agriculture and Agricultural Practices in China" (paper presented at the 2003 International Fertilizer Association Regional Conference for Asia and the Pacific, Cheju Island, Republic of Korea, October 6–8, 2003).

5. Dorothy Solinger, *Contesting Citizenship in Urban China: Peasant Migrants, the State, and the Logic of the Market* (Berkeley: University of California Press, 1999), 27.

6. Zhou, *How the Farmers Changed China,* 34.

7. Peter W. Mackenzie, "Strangers in the City: The *Hukou* and Urban Citizenship in China," *Journal of International Affairs* (Columbia University, New York City) (Fall 2002), 305–22.

8. Zhou, *How the Farmers Changed China,* xx.

9. Ibid., 34.

10. Ibid.

11. Ibid., 35.

12. "Shaking Chairman Mao's Collective Economy 25 Years On," carried on Xinhua Online, December 12, 2003.
13. *Asia Week,* March 7, 1997.
14. Figures cited in Shenghe Liu, Xiubin Li, and Ming Zhang, *Scenario Analysis on Urbanization and Rural-Urban Migration in China, Interim Report* (Laxenburg, Austria: International Institute for Applied System Analysis).

CHAPTER THREE:
TO MAKE 16 BILLION SOCKS, FIRST BREAK THE LAW

1. Goh Sui Noi, "China's Rural Rot," *Straits Times* (Singapore), January 24, 2004.
2. China.org.cn, "Hollow Villages in Rural Areas," http://china.org.cn/english/2003/Jul/70357.htm.
3. Ibid.
4. Xinhua, "Survey Shows Increasingly Large Urban-Rural Income Gap in China," Chinagate.com.cn, February 25, 2004, http://www.chinadaily.com.cn/chinagate/doc/2004-02/25/content_309540.htm.
5. Daniel B. Wright, *The Promise of the Revolution: Stories of Fulfillment and Struggle in China's Hinterland* (Lanham, MD: Rowman & Littlefield Publishers, 2003), 63.
6. A year after the book appeared in China there was still no published English translation, but an Internet-based group of Chinese speakers called the China Study Group took turns at translating the stories.
7. Some of the summary of *China's Peasants: An Investigation* comes from an excellent treatment on the book prepared for The Great Britain–China Centre by Wenran Jiang.
8. Wright, *Promise of the Revolution,* 71–73.
9. Kellee S. Tsai, *Back-Alley Banking: Private Entrepreneurs in China* (Ithaca, NY: Cornell University Press, 2002). Also interviews with Ms. Tsai in October 2003 and February 2004.
10. "Accidents Kill 350 People in China Every Day," Reuters, July 20, 2004.
11. "A New Economics of Migration: Perspective from China," Center on Rural Economies of the Americas and Pacific Rim Working Papers, October 30, 2001.
12. Wenbo Wu, "Entrepreneurs from Wenzhou: A Case Study of Economic Freedom in China" (paper presented at the 2004 Annual Meeting of the Public Choice Society, Baltimore, March 11–14, 2004).
13. Tsai, *Back-Alley Banking.* Also interviews with Ms. Tsai.
14. Throughout China it is also common for this process to work in reverse, producing a garden-variety political corruption in which privileged party and government officials use their positions to forge lucrative business and kickback deals. This is the kind of corruption the central government publicly works against and launches anticorruption campaigns to root out. It is also one of the most explosive issues in China today. The government itself has noted that bribes, extortion, racketeering, and smuggling are problems throughout its ranks.
15. Zurui Tian is also the founder of the Beijing Entrepreneurs Forum, a group that develops support networks for business start-ups, mostly in high tech.
16. Yue Yuen, a shoe manufacturer based in Taiwan, runs the world's biggest shoe factory in Zhongshan, Guangdong. A May 17, 2000, article in the *San Francisco Chron-*

icle described the plant as being as big as a city with thirty-five thousand employees, most of whom live in high-rise dormitories owned by the company. As of 1999, the paper reported, Yue Yuen produced 14 percent of all branded athletic footwear sold worldwide, as well as 14 percent of nonathletic casual shoes, a total of 87 million pairs.

17. "Sock Makers Seek U.S. Protection from Chinese Imports," Associated Press, June 29, 1994.

18. Anthony Kuhn, "Land of the Big Tycoon," *Newsweek International*, "Issues 2004" issue, http://msnbc.msn.com/id/4402795/site/newsweek/.

19. Evelyn Iritani and Marla Dickerson, "People's Republic of Products," *Los Angeles Times,* October 20, 2002.

20. "World's Largest Corporations," *Fortune,* July 26, 2004.

21. "Reforming China's Economy: A Rough Guide," Royal Institute of International Economics, http://www.riia.org/pdf/research/asia/ReformingChinaEcon.PDF.

22. This is a version of Deng's remarks quoted in *People's Daily,* July 13, 1987, and referenced by Zhou.

23. "China Private Sector Needs Help to Flourish Further," *Asia Finance,* December 2003, http://www.financeasia.com/articles/B29F64E2-8A29-45C7-8BFF51D86A37F237.cfm; and http://www1.chinadaily.com.cn/en/doc/2003-12/03/content_286741.htm.

CHAPTER FOUR:
MEET GEORGE JETSON, IN BEIJING

1. Cathleen McGuigan, "Building Up, China's Biggest Cities Are Struggling to Balance Modern Design with the Historical Structures," MSNBC News/Newsweek, October 12, 2003, http://msnbc.msn.com/id/3158255/.

2. Karen Lowry Miller, "Bursting Bubbles," *Newsweek International Edition* (online), July 12, 2004, http://msnbc.msn.com/id/5359494/site/newsweek/.

3. Richard McGregor, "Wenzhou Gang Stirs Fears for Property Prices," *Financial Times,* July 10, 2004.

4. Constance Clark, "The Politics of Place Making in Shenzhen, China," *Berkeley Planning Journal* 12 (1998): 103–25.

5. Ibid.

6. Dexter Roberts, Bruce Einhorn, and Frederik Balfour, "Can Shenzhen Keep Its Cachet?" *BusinessWeek Online,* February 17, 2003, http://www.businessweek.com/print/magazine/content/03_07/b3820130_mz033.htm?mz.

7. Alex Frew McMillan, "Shenzhen Props Open the China Door," CNN.com, November 26, 2002, http://www.cnn.com/2002/BUSINESS/asia/11/26/china.shenzhen/index.html.

8. Stephen W. K. Chiu, "Country Report, Hong Kong (China), Recent Trends in Migration Movements and Policies in Asia, Hong Kong Region Report." Chiu, a professor of sociology at the Chinese University of Hong Kong, prepared the report for the Workshop on International Migration and Labor Markets in Asia, Japan Institute of Labor, Tokyo, February 5–6, 2004.

9. Robert Rowthorn and Ramana Ramaswamy, "Deindustrialization—Its Causes and Implications," International Monetary Fund, September 1997, http://www.imf.org/external/pubs/ft/issues10/.

10. Clark, "Politics of Place Making," 103–25.

11. Ibid.
12. Michael Dorgan, "Shenzhen, China's Economic Engine, Powered by Migrant Women," Knight Ridder Newspapers, July 23, 2002, http://www.realcities.com/mld/krwashington/3720235.htm.
13. "Chinese Labour and the WTO," Hong Kong Confederation of Trade Unions, June 2004 (cover).
14. Neil Kearney, "Disaster Looms for Textiles and Clothing Trade after 2005," International Textile, Garment and Leather Workers Federation, February 9, 2003, http://www.itglwf.org/displaydocument.asp?DocType=Press&Language=&Index=5 95.
15. Charles Wold Jr., K. C. Yeh, Benjamin Zycher, Nicholas Eberstadt, and Sung-Ho Lee, *Fault Lines in China's Economic Terrain* (Santa Monica, CA: Rand National Defense Research Institute, 2003), 19.
16. Ma Bin and Han Yaxi, "A Letter to Comrade Jiang Zemin and the Party's Central Committee," July 15, 2001, translated into English in the *Monthly Review,* May 2002, http://www.monthlyreview.org/0502cpc3a.htm.
17. Simon Parker, "The *Record* Goes to China to Investigate the Squalor behind the Glamour," *Daily Record,* April 27, 2004, http://www.dailyrecord.co.uk/news/tm_objectid=14184308&method=full&siteid=89488&headline=-pound-1-a-day-name_page.html=.
18. Ibid.
19. Alex Perry, "Crossing the Line," *Time Asia* (online), August 8, 2004, http://www.time.com/time/asia/biz/magazine/0,9754,108014,00.html.
20. Jonathan Napack, "Banned in Beijing: A Rebel Writer's Message," *International Herald Tribune,* February 8, 2001, http://www.iht.com/ihtsearch.php?id=9977&owner=(IHT)&date=20010208000000.
21. Abigail Goldman and Nancy Cleeland, "An Empire Built on Bargains Remakes the Working World," *Los Angeles Times,* November 23, 2003, http://www.latimes.com/business/la-fi-walmart23nov23a,1,7637894.story.
22. Married couples who are themselves only children may also have two children.
23. "China's Unwanted Girls," BBC News Online, August, 23, 2001.
24. "China's population growth 'slowing,' " BBC World Service News, March 28, 2001, 6.
25. Whether the Chinese will have any affection later for the abandoned girls is an open question. One hopeful story is that of the Chinese adoptee Kailee Wells, who was found abandoned on the steps of a teachers' college in Hunan Province. In 1998, after a year in an orphanage, she was adopted into the family of New Mexico couple Owen and Linda Wells. Kailee was later diagnosed with aplastic anemia, a severe condition that blocks bone marrow from producing new blood cells. The child did not respond to conventional treatment, so her mother made several trips to China to search for Kailee's natural parents, to see if she might find a genetic match in a person who would offer Kailee transplanted stem cells for an advanced genetic treatment. Failing in that, she then appealed to Red Cross societies throughout China with links to scientists at China's bone-marrow registries and umbilical-cord blood banks. The goal was to see if they might discover a match from their databases. Umbilical cords are especially well suited to the harvesting of stem cells, and after screens of tens of thousands of records a match was found.

26. The first modern census in China was in 1953, when the population was counted at 583 million.

27. "China's population growth 'slowing,' " BBC World Service News.

28. Ma Guihua, "Checking Imbalance in Gender Ratio," *China Daily,* May 26, 2004.

29. Valerie M. Hudson and Andrea M. den Boer, " 'Bare Branches' and Danger in Asia," *Washington Post,* July 4, 2004.

30. Melinda Liu, "Rural Riches: China's Migrants Are Starting to Return Home as Savvy Entrepreneurs with the Cash to Prove It," *Newsweek* special issue, May 2004.

31. Tim Johnson, "Chinese Cities Building Skyward," *Detroit Free Press,* October 28, 2003.

32. Li Yong Yan, "China's Compitalists: Worst of Both Worlds," November 12, 2003, http://www.atimes.com/atimes/China/EK12Ad03.html.

33. Jehangir Pocha, "Demolitions Straining Families in China," *Boston Globe,* July 9, 2004, http://www.boston.com/news/world/asia/articles/2004/07/09/demolitions_strain ing_families_in_china/.

34. Sara Meg Davis, "Demolished: Forced Evictions and the Tenants' Rights Movement in China," *Human Rights Watch Reports* 16, no. 4 (C) (March 2004).

35. He Qinglian, "Where's the Boom of the Chinese Property Industry Coming From?" five-part series in *Epoch Times,* beginning May 5, 2004, English.epochtimes.com/news/4-5-5/21264.html.

36. "Eviction Protests in China Soar, Thousands Converge on Beijing," Radio Free Asia, August 3, 2004, http://origin.rfaweb.org/front/article.html?service=eng&encod ing=10&id=142746.

37. "Complaints on Home Demolitions Soar," Chinaview.cn, Xinhuanet, http://news.xinhuanet.com/english/2004-07/06/content_1576039.htm.

38. Peter Cochran, "Uncommon Sense: Energy Worries," Silicon.com, July 29, 2004, zdnet.com./2100 1107 5288374.html.

39. Ed Lanfranco, "Red Cross to Caution China on Urbanization," United Press International, May 6, 2004, http://www.washingtontimes.com/upi-breaking/ 20040506-125126-8127r.htm.

40. Ibid.

41. Andrew Batson, "China's Choke Hold over Asia," *Far Eastern Economic Review,* July 8, 2004, http://www.feer.com/articles/2004/0407_08/p028china.html.

42. Jonathan Watts, "China's Growth Flickers to a Halt," *Guardian Unlimited,* July 4, 2004, http://www.guardian.co.uk/china/story/0,7369,1253545,00.html.

43. Kimberly Song, "Succeeding in China: Meiya Power, Rules Can Be Negotiable," *Far Eastern Economic Review,* August 5, 2004, http://www.feer.com/cgi-bin/prog/print easy?id=11322.7718350576.

44. The estimate comes from the World Bank and was cited by an AFP dispatch of July 29, 2004, "China's Dependence on Coal for Energy Causing Pollution at Home and Abroad," www.channelnewsasia.com/stories/afp_asiapacific_business/view/98147/1/.html.

45. Sulfer dioxide is the dominant acid precursor of acid rain in China, followed by nitrogen oxides.

46. "China: Environmental Issues, Country Analysis Briefs," Environmental Information Agency, Department of Energy, July 2003, http://www.eia.doe.gov/emeu/cabs/chinaenv.pdf.

47. "China's Dependence on Coal for Energy Causing Pollution at Home and Abroad," APF, July 29, 2004.
48. James P. Miller, "Asian Pollution Ill Wind for U.S.," *Chicago Tribune,* May 3, 2004.
49. "Trafficking in Traffic," *Kansas City Star* (*Wall Street Journal* wire story), July 27, 2004, http://www.kansascity.com/mld/kansascity/business/9249382.htm?1c.
50. "China Factor Driving Oil Prices," CNN.com, May 24, 2004, http://www.cnn.com/2004/BUSINESS/05/24/china.oil.demand/.
51. Ben Dolven, "The Great Car Crush," *Far Eastern Economic Review,* November 27, 2003.

CHAPTER FIVE:
CHAIRMAN MAO SELLS SOUP

1. Judith Shapiro first gained fame when, as one of the first Americans to work in China after the country began to reopen, she fell in love with a Chinese national and after much struggle with local authorities obtained Deng Xiaoping's permission to go ahead with the wedding. She told the story in her memoir, *Son of the Revolution,* written with her then husband, Heng Liang. Shapiro now teaches environmental politics at American University in Washington, D.C.
2. Judith Shapiro, *Mao's War against Nature: Politics and the Environment in Revolutionary China* (Cambridge: Cambridge University Press, 2001).
3. Peter J. Li, "Politics and China's Wildlife Crisis," for the Hong Kong Anti-Cruelty Society, 2003.
4. Permit fees for dog owners can cost hundreds of dollars, a fortune for most Chinese. And still there are occasional campaigns to eliminate pets, such as periodic sweeps through cities during which dog owners must watch as a local warden clubs their dog to death in front of them.
5. Ann Veeck, "The Revitalization of the Marketplace: Food Markets of Nanjing," in *The Consumer Revolution in Urban China,* ed. Deborah S. Davis (Berkeley: University of California Press, 2000).
6. Ibid.
7. The numbers of overweight and obese Chinese are growing along with the country's food choices. AFP, the French news agency, reports that there are now 70 million Chinese with severe weight problems, a number that reflects a rising trend that, should it stay on pace, will mean that China's obesity rates will match those of the United States in twenty years.
8. Melissa Schrift, *Biography of a Chairman Mao Badge: The Creation and Mass Consumption of a Personality Cult* (Piscataway, NJ: Rutgers University Press, 2001).
9. Melissa Schrift, interviewed in "Mao's New Collectivism," *Chronicle of Higher Education,* January 17, 2003.

CHAPTER SIX:
THROUGH THE LOOKING GLASS

1. As of July 2004, U.S. unemployment registered around 5.5 percent, while that in the Peoria-Pekin area was 4.9 percent.
2. Mark Drabenstott and Nancy Novack, "Roar of the Dragon: The Asian Upside for

U.S. Agriculture," *Main Street Economist,* Center for the Study of Rural America, Federal Reserve Bank of Kansas City, May 2004, 1.

3. Jonathan Watts, "China's Farmers Cannot Feed Hungry Cities," *Guardian,* August 26, 2004, http://www.guardian.co.uk/china/story/0,7369,1290852,00.html.

4. "3,000 Chinese farmers to farm abroad," *China Daily,* December 17, 2003, http://www2.chinadaily.com.cn/en/doc/2003-12/17/content_291308.html.

5. "China to Lease Overseas Farmland to Solve Food Problem," *People's Daily,* May 24, 2004, http://english.people.com.cn/200405/24/eng20040524_144221.html.

6. Jim Paul, Associated Press, "ADM, Food-Makers Reap What Agriculture Sows; State Relies on Farms, But Not All Pastures Are Green," *Peoria Journal Star,* December 1, 2003.

7. Fred Gale and James Hansen, "China's Exports Outpaced Imports During WTO Year One," Electronic Outlook Report from the Economic Research Service, United States Department of Agriculture, FAU-79-02, August 2003, 2.

8. Cheng Fang and John C. Beghin, "Urban Demand for Edible Oils and Fats in China: Evidence from Household Survey Data," Working Paper 00-WP 245, Center for Agricultural and Rural Development, Iowa State University, August 2000.

9. Dwain Ford, First Vice President, American Soybean Association, testimony before the U.S.-China Security Review Commission, August 2, 2001.

10. "Brazil's Lula on Offensive to Boost Brazil-China Alliance," AFP, Channel News-Asia, May 22, 2004.

11. Ibid.

12. "Soybeans Stranded in Chinese Harbors," UPI, *Washington Times,* May 18, 2004, online edition.

13. "Soybeans Have Biggest Drop in Week as China Demand Seen Slowing," Bloomberg Online, April 28, 2004.

14. Nancy Novack, "Rising Farmland Values: Some Implications for Rural America," AgDM newsletter, Center for the Study of Rural America, Federal Reserve Bank of Kansas City, July 2003, http://www.extension.iastate.edu/agdm/articles/others/NovJuly03.htm.

15. Jason Henderson, "Will the Farm Rebound Lead a Rural Recovery?" *Economic Review,* First Quarter 2004, http://www.kc.frb.org/PUBLICAT/ECONREV/PDF/1Q04hend.pdf Federal Reserve Bank of Kansas City.

16. Dave Carpenter, Associated Press, "Windy City Diversity: Chicago Battles Loss of 100,000 Manufacturing Jobs with Increasing Services, *Peoria Journal Star,* November 30, 2003, http://www.pjstar.com/services/news/manufacturing/b1curgnn011.html.

17. Juan Forero, "As China Gallops, Mexico Sees Factory Jobs Slip Away," *New York Times,* September 3, 2003.

18. David Bacon, "NAFTA's Legacy—Profits and Poverty," *San Francisco Chronicle,* January 14, 2004. Bacon puts the total job loss at four hundred thousand.

19. Mary Jordan, "Workers Falling Behind in Mexico: For Many, Wages Still Lower Than before '90s Crisis," *Washington Post,* July 15, 2003.

20. Geri Smith, "Wasting Away in Mexico: Despite SARS, Mexico Is Still Losing Export Ground to China," *BusinessWeek,* June 2, 2003.

21. David Bacon, "Anti-China Campaign Hides Maquiladora Wage Cuts," *ZNet* (the online arm of Z magazine), February 3, 2003, http://www.zmag.org/content/showarticle.cfm?SectionID=19&ItemID=2949.

22. Forero, "As China Gallops."
23. "Impacts of International Trade with China on Illinois Manufacturers," survey of 161 small and medium-size firms by the Illinois Manufacturing Extension Center and The Center for Governmental Studies, North Illinois University, August 27, 2003.
24. News release from The American Veterans Awards, "Wal-Mart to Receive Corporate Patriotism Award," PNN Online, November 23, 2003, http://www.pnnon line.org/print.php?sid=4847. The awards were broadcast on the History Channel in February 2004.
25. Charles Fishman, "The Wal-Mart You Don't Know," *Fast Company* 77 (December 2003): 68.
26. John Schmid, "American Drive to Buy for Less Has a Price," *Milwaukee Journal Sentinal,* December 30, 2003.
27. Peter S. Goodman and Phillip P. Pan, "Chinese Workers Pay for Wal-Mart's Low Prices," *Washington Post,* February 8, 2004.
28. "Chinese Tourists Bring Vitality to German Market," *People's Daily,* May 3, 2003.
29. Deutsche Welle, November 16, 2003.
30. "Yiwu, China—Increasingly around the World, Christmas Is 'Made in China,' " *Washington Times,* March 29, 2003.
31. Peter S. Goodman, "America's Christmas Is 'Made in China,' " *Deccan Herald,* November 17, 1999.
32. Natalie Obiko Pearson, "Ramen Makers Go Upmarket in Search of Fresh Clientele," *Japan Times Online,* April 30, 2004.
33. Setsuko Kamiya, "Food Makers Find an Escape Route: Cobranded Instant Noodles Point to a Way out of Deflation," *Japan Times Online,* August 14, 2002.
34. Gordon Feller, "Japanese FDI and China Challenge," *Japan, Inc.,* December 2003.
35. Peter Hays Gries, *China's New Nationalism: Pride, Politics, and Diplomacy* (Berkeley: University of California Press, 2004)
36. Ibid., 10.
37. Ibid., 153.
38. Ibid., 36.
39. Feller, "Japanese FDI and China Challenge."

CHAPTER SEVEN:
THE CHINA PRICE

1. Economic Policy Institute, EPI Brief Number 198, "Educated, Experienced, and Out of Work," March 4, 2004, http://www.epinet.org/content.cfm/issuebriefs_ib198.
2. Brian Deese, "That Rosy Unemployment Rate," Center for American Progress, September 13, 2004, http://www.americanprogress.org/site/pp.asp?c=biJRJ8OVF&b=186379.
3. Charles W. McMillion, briefing paper for the U.S.-China Economic and Security Review Commission, "Field Investigation on China's Impact on the U.S. Manufacturing Base, Columbia, South Carolina," January 30, 2004.
4. "Kerry Works to Bring North Carolina into Play," CNN.com, August 20, 2004, http://www.cnn.com/2004/ALLPOLITICS/08/20/kerry.jobs/.
5. American Sociological Association, press release, "Hill Briefing on Social and Economic Consequences of Job Loss Draws a Crowd," March 30, 2004. The press

release details the testimony of research sociologist Leslie Hossfeld from the University of North Carolina, Pembroke, along with other community leaders from Robeson County, North Carolina, on the rate and impact of job loss in that rural county at a congressional briefing on March 30 on Capitol Hill.

6. Tim Wilkins, "Bowles Finds Support in Robeson Fund-Raiser," *Lumberton (NC) Robesonian,* July 1, 2004.

7. Joe Jablonowski, "Metalworking Plants in Asia Boost Investment," Metalworkers Inside Report, April 5, 2004.

8. Louis Aguilar, "Michigan Factories on Auction Block," *Detroit News,* August 16, 2004.

9. Ed Frauenheim, "Study Supports Controversial Offshore Numbers," CNET News.com, May 17, 2004, http://news.com.com/Study+supports+controversial+offshore+numbers/2100-1022_3-5213391.html.

10. University of California Haas School of Business, press release, "UC Berkeley Study Assesses Potential Impacts of 'Second Wave' of Outsourcing Jobs from U.S.," October 29, 2003, http://www.haas.berkeley.edu/news/20031029_outsourcing.html.

11. U.S. Department of Commerce, "Manufacturing in America: A Comprehensive Strategy to Address the Challenges to U.S. Manufacturers," January 2004.

12. Franklin J. Vargo, "Impact of Chinese Imports on U.S. Companies," testimony before the Committee on House Appropriations Subcommittee on Commerce, Justice, State, and Judiciary, May 22, 2003.

13. Robert Fishman, "The American Metropolis at Century's End: Past and Future Influences," *Housing Policy Debate* 11, no. 1 (Washington, DC: Fannie Mae Foundation, 2000) 204.

14. See Mark V. Levine, "Stealth Depression: Joblessness in Milwaukee since 1990," http://www.uwm.edu/Dept/CED/publications/stealth_depression803.pdf.

15. See interview with Terry Ludeman, chief labor economist, Wisconsin Department of Workforce Development, *JS Online,* January 20, 2004, www.jsonline.com/news/state/jan04/201241.asp. For information about Hartford, see http://ci.hartford.wi.us/.

16. Evan Ramstad and Phred Dvorak, "Asia's Upstarts Shake Up Consumer Electronics," *Wall Street Journal.* In the *Miami Herald,* December 29, 2003.

17. Chinese economists Lu Feng and Mu Ling interviewed participants in the Chinese DVD market for their study, "Indigenous Innovation, Capability Development and Competitive Advantage: The Origins and Development of the Competitiveness of Chinese VCD/DVD Industry," presented at the BHC/EBHA meeting in Lowell, Massachusetts, 2003. The authors stress China's technological advantages as primary reasons for the ascent of the Chinese DVD industry, not low-cost labor.

18. Ibid.

19. Video files were produced in the MPEG 1 format.

20. Interview with Wilf Corrigan, LSI Logic, January 9, 2004.

21. Lu Feng and Mu Ling's research argues that Jiang could have bargained for a better deal with C-Cube.

22. Corrigan interview.

23. Michael Kanellos, "DVD Player Profits Down to $1," CNET News.com, August 9, 2004.

CHAPTER EIGHT:
HOW THE RACE TO THE BOTTOM IS A RACE TO THE TOP

1. John McElroy, "Be Careful in China," *Ward's Auto World,* September 1, 2003.
2. Alysha Webb, "Chinese Suppliers Make a Mark Overseas," *Automotive News,* June 28, 2004.
3. Frederik Balfour and Chen Wu, "China: Letting Up the Gas," *BusinessWeek,* September 20, 2004.
4. Fred Vogelstein, "How Intel Got Inside," *Fortune,* October 4, 2004, 127–36.
5. Malorye A. Branca, "The Fabric of Discovery: Pharma's Genomic Harvest," *Bio-IT World,* March 17, 2004, http://www.bioitworld.com/archive/031704/horizons_horizons_pharm.html.
6. Allan Zhang, "The Future of China's Pharmaceutical Industry," *Pricewaterhouse-Coopers Executive Perspectives,* 2001, http://www.pwc.com/extweb/newcolth.nsf/docid/ 4CE903FAD5FB1DF985256A31007820CB.
7. Branca, "Fabric of Discovery."
8. Manuel Torreblanca, "The China Syndrome," *Scrip,* April 2004.
9. Greg Lucier, testimony before the U.S.-China Economic and Security Review Commission, February 12–13, 2004, 118.
10. Ibid., 123.
11. "Boeing Takes on Additional Staff," *BBC News World Edition,* July 18, 2004, http://news.bbc.co.uk/2/hi/business/3904285.stm. The article describes Boeing's plan to add three thousand workers in 2004.
12. "Air Travel Expected Strong Growth," *China Daily,* July 14, 2004.
13. *China Technology Transfer Report—Part 2,* Bureau of Industry and Security, U.S. Department of Commerce, 1999, http://www.bis.doc.gov/DefenseIndustrialBase Programs/OSIES/defmarketresearchrpts/ChinaGuides/China2.pdf.
14. "China's Plane Parts Industry Takes Off," *People's Daily,* January 1, 2004.
15. "China's First Large Aircraft to Fly by 2018," *China Daily,* March 17, 2004.

CHAPTER NINE:
PIRATE NATION

1. Selected sources for the anecdotes:
    Beer: "Anti-Counterfeiting Headlines," *QBPC Newsletter,* Quality Brands Protection Committee, February 2004, http://www.qbpc.org.cn/en/about/newsletters/02-2004/file; "Manufacturers Must Target Chinese Mass Market," *Food Production Daily,* September 9, 2004, http://www.foodproductiondaily.com/news/news-ng.asp?n=54731-manufacturers-must-target.
    Coke, Häagen-Dazs, Starbucks, and cheese: "Manufacturers Must Target Chinese."
    Shampoo: "Anti-Counterfeiting Headlines," *QBPC Newsletter,* Quality Brands Protection Committee, June 2003, http://www.qbpc.org.cn/en/about/newsletters/06-2003/file.
    Network cards, fake cigarettes, and counterfeits in Kenya: "Anti-Counterfeiting Headlines," February 2004.
    Tommy Bahama, etc.: "Tommy Bahama Helps Crack Counterfeit Ring," press release, PR Newswire—First Call, September 21, 2004.

Nintendo: Bloomberg, "Games Pirates Winning Streak," *The Standard, Greater China's Business Newspaper* (Hong Kong), June 4, 2004, http://www.thestan dard.com.hk/txtarticle_v.cfm?articleid=48192.

Eyewear: Olivia Chung, "Eye Piracy Damages Partnership Prospects," *The Standard, Greater China's Business Newspaper* (Hong Kong), November 27, 2004, http://www.thestandard.com.hk/txtarticle_v.cfm?articleid=43639.

Car parts: Joann Muller, "Stolen Cars," *Forbes.com,* February 9, 2004, http://www.forbes.com/global/2004/0209/020_print.html; "Anti-Counterfeiting Headlines," February 2004.

Syngenta: "Anti-Counterfeiting Headlines," *QBPC Newsletter,* Quality Brands Protection Committee, June 2004, http://www.qbpc.org.cn/en/about/newslet ters/junenl/file.

Pirated DVDs: "ICE and Chinese Authorities Dismantle Major Counterfeiting Network," press release, Department of Homeland Security's U.S. Immigration and Customs Enforcement, July 30, 2004, http://www.ice.gov/graph ics/news/newsreleases/articles/073004seizure.htm.

Creative Technologies: John Lui, "Creative to Make 'Clones' of Own Products," CNET Asia, November 11, 2003, http://asia.cnet.com/news/industry/0,,39158663,00.htm.

TSMC and SMIC: Sumner Lemon, IDG News Service, "TSMC Lawsuit Alleges SMIC Stole Chip-Making Secrets," *InfoWorld,* December 22, 2003, http://www.infoworld.com/article/03/12/22/HNtsmclawsuit_1.html?; Sumner Lemon, IDG News Service, "SMIC: U.S. Courts Have No Jurisdiction over TSMC Claims," *InfoWorld,* March 8, 2003, http://www.infoworld.com/article/04/03/08/HNuscourts_1.html?platforms.

Harry Potter: "The World's Greatest Fakes," *60 Minutes,* August 8, 2004, transcript at http://www.cbsnews.com/stories/2004/01/26/60minutes/main595875.shtml; John Pomfret (*Washington Post*), "It's Harry Potter versus the Pirates," *International Herald Tribune,* November 2, 2002, http://www.iht.com/articles/75686.html.

Rabies vaccine: Christopher Bodeen, "Deadly Fakes," *The Star* (Penang, Malaysia), June 24, 2004, http://thestar.com.my/lifestyle/story.asp?file=/2004/6/24/features/8119101&sec=features.

Yamaha: "China Bogged Down in IPR Dilemma," *China Daily,* September 7, 2002, http://www.china.org.cn/english/BAT/42162.htm.

Toyota: Tian Ying (Bloomberg News), "Toyota Loses Trademark Suit Against China Carmaker," *International Herald Tribune,* November 24, 2003, http://www.iht.com/articles/118787.html.

DVD machines: "Anti-Counterfeiting Headlines," *QBPC Newsletter,* Quality Brands Protection Committee, May 2004, http://www.qbpc.org.cn/en/about/newsletters/maynewsletter/file.

Bird flu vaccine: Xinhua, "China Fights Fake Bird Flu Vaccines," *ChinaDaily.com,* February 17, 2004, http://www.chinadaily.com.cn/english/doc/2004-02/17/content_306873.htm.

Microsoft: Bloomberg, "China Acts on Pirated Products," *International Herald Tribune,* September 6, 2004, http://www.iht.com/articles/537478.htm.

2. "U.S. Seeking Industry Feed on China Piracy," *Straits Times* (Singapore), September 19, 2004.

3. Robert Marquand, "China's Pirate Industry Thriving," *Christian Science Monitor,* January 9, 2002.

4. Dean Takehashi, "The Billion Dollar Problem," *Electronics Supply and Manufacturing,* May 1, 2004.

5. Phil Tinari, "Why Beijing Vendors Who Built Silk Alley Feel Hung Out to Dry: As Outdoor Market Prospers, City Is Moving It Inside; Piracy and Conflicts Swirl," *Wall Street Journal,* September 21, 2004, 1. Tinari's article is also an excellent tale of how Beijing's rush to development can be disastrous for small businesses.

6. Business Software Alliance, "First Annual BSA and IDC Global Software Piracy Study" (Washington, D.C., July 2004), 3, http://www.bsa.org/globalstudy/loader.cfm?url=/commonspot/security/getfile.cfm&pageid=16947&hitboxdone=yes.

7. Zhu Boru (*China Business Weekly*), "China's Laptop PC Market Remains Attractive," *ChinaDaily.com,* March 3, 2004, http://www.chinadaily.com.cn/english/doc/ 2004-03/08/content_312858.htm.

8. Aloysius Choong, "HP Stands Firm in China Price War," CNET Asia, September 10, 2004, http://asia.cnet.com/news/systems/0,39037054,39193185,00.htm.

9. Sarah Schafer, "Microsoft's Cultural Revolution," *Newsweek,* June 21, 2004.

10. Ibid.

11. Eric Auchard (Reuters), "China Grabs Software Research Deals Despite Risks," *USA Today,* September 21, 2004.

CHAPTER TEN:
THE CHINESE-AMERICAN ECONOMY

1. Press release, "President Signs Jobs and Growth Plan, Remarks by the President at Signing of Jobs and Growth Tax Relief Reconciliation Act of 2003," White House, President George W. Bush, May 28, 2003, http://www.whitehouse.gov/news/releases/2003/05/20030528-9.html.

2. Richard Alm and W. Michael Cox, "A Better Way, Productivity and Reorganization in the American Economy," 2004 Annual Report, Federal Reserve Bank of Dallas. Full report available at http://www.dallasfed.org/fed/annual/2003/ar03.pdf. Statistics on price savings from the China trade, found in a supplemental publication of the same title, can be found at http://www.dallasfed.org/news/research/2004/04it_cox.pdf.

3. Calculated using the Inflation Calculator tool at the Web site of the U.S. Department of Labor, Bureau of Labor Statistics, http://www.bls.gov/.

4. Andrew B. Bernard, J. Bradford Jensen, and Peter K. Schott, "Facing the Dragon: Prospects for U.S. Manufacturers in the Coming Decade," working paper, May 2004, http://mba.tuck.dartmouth.edu/pages/faculty/andrew.bernard/dragon.pdf. The figures cited on the growth of imports are in constant dollars from the year 2000.

5. Yumi Kuramitsu, "Yuan Forwards Drop; China Avoids Setting Deadlines on Currency," Bloomberg, October 4, 2004, http://quote.bloomberg.com/apps/news?pid=10000087&sid=a9F.T_C.IsJg&refer=top_world_news.

6. C. Fred Bergsten, "Is the Chinese Currency, the Renminbi, Dangerously Under-

valued and a Threat to the Global Economy? Over Thirty Important Experts Offer Their Views; a Symposium of Views," *International Economy Magazine* (Washington, DC), March 22, 2003.

7. "A Fair Exchange? China Has Helped to Finance America's Vast Current-Account Deficit," *Economist,* October 2–10, 2004.

8. Dennis Cauchon and John Waggoner, "One Nation Under Debt," *USA Today,* October 4, 2004, 1.

9. "A Fair Exchange?"

CHAPTER ELEVEN:
THE CHINESE CENTURY

1. Kate Bronfenbrenner and Stephanie Luce, "The Changing Nature of Corporate Global Restructuring: The Impact of Production Shifts on Jobs in the U.S., China and Around the Globe" (submitted to the U.S.-China Economic and Security Review Commission, October 14, 2004), http://www.uscc.gov/research reports/2004/cornell_u_mass_report.pdf.

2. Tom Hartley, "As Delphi Eyes China, Mexican Venture Uncertain," *Business First* (Buffalo, New York), August 11, 2003.

3. "U.S.-China Trade and Investment: Impact on Key Manufacturing and Industrial Sectors: Field Hearing in Akron, Ohio, September 23, 2004, U.S.-China Economic and Security Review Commission," http://www.uscc.gov/hearings/2004hearings/transcripts/04_09_23.pdf.

4. ACT, Inc., "Crisis at the Core, Preparing All Students for College and Work" (Iowa City, IA), 2004.

5. Lu Jianhui, Central News Agency, "Propaganda Ministry Reportedly Demands Positive Media Reporting," *The Epoch Times,* September 22, 2004 (*The Epoch Times* picked up and translated the story), http://english.epochtimes.com/news/4-9-22/23366.html.

6. Katrin Bennhold, "France-China Deals Awaken Europeans," *International Herald Tribune,* October 11, 2004, http://www.iht.com/articles/542938.html.

7. Katrin Bennhold, "French Go for Big Stakes in China Talks," *International Herald Tribune,* October 5, 2004, http://www.iht.com/articles/541914.html.

8. David Shambaugh, "China and Europe: The Emerging Axis," *Current History,* September 2004, 243–49.

9. "Sino-EY Trade Volume Witnessing Rapid Growth," *China Daily,* October 6, 2004, http://www.chinadaily.com.cn/english/doc/2004-10/06/content_379983.htm.

10. Jim Garamone, "China, U.S. Making Progress on Military Relations," American Forces Press Service, http://www.defenselink.mil/news/Jan2004/n01152004_200401152.htmlJanuary 15, 2004.

11. Roger Cohen, David E. Sanger, and Steven Weisman, "The Bush Record, Challenging Rest of the World with a New Order," *The New York Times,* October 12, 2004.

12. John J. Mearsheimer, *The Tragedy of Great Power Politics* (New York: W. W. Norton, 2001).

13. "China: Peaceful Rise," *The Economist,* June 24, 2004, www.economist.com/world/asia/displayStory.cfm?story_id=2792533.

NOTES

14. Jane Perlez, "Across Asia, Beijing's Star Is in Ascendance," *The New York Times,* August 28, 2004.
15. Michael Vatikiotis, "Military Alliances: A Diplomatic Offensive," *Far Eastern Review,* August 5, 2004.
16. "Why we cannot negotiate with a pathological liar," *China Daily,* October 10, 2004, http://www.chinadaily.com.cn/english/doc/2004-10/10/content_380961.htm.
17. FY04 Report to Congress on PRC Military Power, U.S. Department of Defense, May 2004, 46, http://www.dod.gov/pubs/d20040528PRC.pdf.
18. "Cash-Rich, Commodity-Starved Mainland Shopping Spree," *China Daily,* September 28, 2004, http://www.chinadaily.com.cn/english/doc/2004-09/28/content_378297.htm.

CHAPTER TWELVE:
ONE LAST STORY

1. Shershow recounted his exploration of the Dongtai eBay sellers in an article in the English-language supplement to the Shanghai newspaper *Orient Express,* "The eBay Revolution Hits China," April 23, 2004.

SELECTED BIBLIOGRAPHY

Abramowitz, Morton I., Funabashi Yoichi, and Wang Jisi. *China-Japan-U.S. Relations: Meeting New Challenges.* Tokyo: Japan Center for International Exchange, 2002.

Alford, William P. *To Steal a Book Is an Elegant Offense: Intellectual Property Law in Chinese Civilization.* Stanford: Stanford University Press, 1995.

Allinson, Robert E., ed. *Understanding the Chinese Mind: The Philosophical Roots.* Hong Kong: Oxford University Press, 1991.

Backman, Michael, and Charlotte Butler. *Big in Asia: 25 Strategies for Business Success.* Houndmills, UK: Palgrave Macmillan, 2003.

Benewick, Robert, and Stephanie Donald. *The State of China Atlas.* London: Penguin Reference, 1999.

Brahm, Laurence J. *Zhu Rongji and the Transformation of Modern China.* Singapore: John Wiley & Sons (Asia), 2002.

Brandt, Nat. *Massacre in Shansi.* San Jose: iUniverse, 1999.

Brown, Melissa J. *Is Taiwan Chinese? The Impact of Culture, Power, and Migration on Changing Identities.* Berkeley: University of California Press, 2004.

Buchholz, Todd G. *Bringing the Jobs Home: How the Left Created the Outsourcing Crisis—and How We Can Fix It.* New York: Sentinel, 2004.

Chang, Gordon G. *The Coming Collapse of China.* New York: Random House, 2001.

Chang, Maria Hsia. *Falun Gong: The End of Days.* New Haven: Yale University Press, 2004.

Chinese Academy of Engineering, National Academy of Engineering, National Research Council. *Personal Cars and China.* Washington, D.C.: National Academies Press, 2001.

Chow, Gregory C. *China's Economic Transformation.* Oxford: Blackwell Publishers Ltd., 2002.

———. *Knowing China.* Singapore: World Scientific Publishing Co., 2004.

Darmon, Reed. *Made in China.* San Francisco: Chronicle Books, 2004.

Davis, Deborah S., ed. *The Consumer Revolution in Urban China.* Berkeley: University of California Press, 2000.

Davis, Deborah S., Richard Kraus, Barry Naughton, and Elizabeth J. Perry, eds. *Urban Spaces in Contemporary China: The Potential for Autonomy and Community in Post-Mao China.* Cambridge: Woodrow Wilson Center Press and Cambridge University Press, 1995.

Dickson, Bruce J. *Red Capitalists in China: The Party, Private Entrepreneurs, and Prospects for Political Change.* Cambridge: Cambridge University Press, 2003.

Dikötter, Frank, Lars Laamann, and Zhou Xun. *Narcotic Culture: A History of Drugs in China*. Chicago: University of Chicago Press, 2004.

Duara, Prasenjit. *Rescuing History from the Nation: Questioning Narratives of Modern China*. Chicago: University of Chicago Press, 1995.

———. *Sovereignty and Authenticity: Manchukuo and the East Asian Modern*. Lanham, MD: Rowman & Littlefield Publishers, Inc., 2003.

Economy, Elizabeth C. *The River Runs Black: The Environmental Challenge to China's Future*. Ithaca, NY: Cornell University Press, 2004.

Farquhar, Judith. *Appetites: Food and Sex in Post-Socialist China*. Durham, NC: Duke University Press, 2002.

Farrer, James. *Opening Up: Youth Sex Culture and Market Reform in Shanghai*. Chicago: University of Chicago Press, 2002.

Feigenbaum, Evan A. *China's Techno-Warriors: National Security and Strategic Competition from the Nuclear to the Information Age*. Stanford: Stanford University Press, 2003.

Gao, Anhua. *To the Edge of the Sky*. Woodstock, NY: Overlook Press, 2003.

Gertz, Bill. *The China Threat: How the People's Republic Targets America*. Washington, D.C.: Regnery Publishing Inc., 2000.

Gladney, Dru C. *Dislocating China: Muslims, Minorities, and Other Subaltern Subjects*. Chicago: University of Chicago Press, 2004.

Gray, Jack. *Rebellions and Revolutions: China from the 1800s to 2000*. 2nd edition. Ed. J. M. Roberts, Short Oxford History of the Modern World. Oxford: Oxford University Press, 2002.

Gries, Peter Hays. *China's New Nationalism: Pride, Politics and Diplomacy*. Berkeley: University of California Press, 2004.

Guthrie, Doug. *Dragon in a Three-Piece Suit: The Emergence of Capitalism in China*. Princeton, NJ: Princeton University Press, 1999.

Gutmann, Ethan. *Losing the New China: A Story of American Commerce, Desire and Betrayal*. San Francisco: Encounter Books, 2004.

Hessler, Peter. *River Town: Two Years on the Yangtze*. New York: Perennial, 2001.

Huang, Yasheng. *Selling China: Foreign Direct Investment During the Reform Era*. Cambridge: Cambridge University Press, 2003.

Hudson, Valerie M., and Andrea M. den Boer. *Bare Branches: The Security Implications of Asia's Surplus Male Population*. Cambridge, MA: MIT Press, 2004.

Hui, Wang. *China's New Order: Society, Politics, and Economy in Transition*. Cambridge, MA: Harvard University Press, 2003.

Johnson, Ian. *Wild Grass: Three Stories of Change in Modern China*. New York: Pantheon Books, 2004.

Kalathil, Shanthi, and Taylor C. Boas. *Open Networks, Closed Regimes: The Impact of the Internet on Authoritarian Rule*. Washington, D.C.: Carnegie Endowment for International Peace, 2003.

Kletzer, Lori G. *Job Loss from Imports: Measuring the Costs*. Washington, D.C.: Institute for International Economics, September 2001.

Lardy, Nicholas R. *China's Unfinished Economic Revolution*. Washington, D.C.: Brookings Institution Press, 1998.

Lee, James Z., and Wang Feng. *One Quarter of Humanity: Malthusian Mythology and Chinese Realities, 1700–2000*. Cambridge, MA: Harvard University Press, 1999.

Lew, Alan A., Lawrence Yu, John Ap, and Zhang Guangrui. *Tourism in China*. New York: Haworth Hospitality Press, 2003.

Leys, Simon. *Chinese Shadows*. New York: Penguin Books, 1978.

Magariños, Carlos A., Long Yongtu, and Francisco C. Sercovich, eds. United Nations Industrial Development Organization. *China in the WTO: The Birth of a New Catching-Up Strategy*. Houndmills, UK: Palgrave Macmillan, 2002.

Murphy, Rachel. *How Migrant Labor Is Changing Rural China*. Cambridge: Cambridge University Press, 2002.

Nathan, Andrew J., and Bruce Gilley. *China's New Rulers: The Secret Files*. New York: New York Review Books, 2002.

Nieukirk, Donald L. *Pekin and Tremont Illinois in Vintage Postcards*. Chicago: Arcadia Publishing, 2000.

Nisbett, Richard E. *The Geography of Thought: How Asians and Westerners Think Differently . . . and Why*. New York: Free Press, 2003.

Ogilvy, James, and Peter Schwartz with Joe Flower. *China's Futures: Scenarios from the Fastest Growing Economy, Ecology and Society*. San Francisco: Jossey-Bass Publishers, 2000.

Panitchpakdi, Supachai, and Mark L. Clifford. *China and the WTO: Changing China, Changing World Trade*. Singapore: John Wiley & Sons (Asia), 2002.

Pomeranz, Kenneth. *The Great Divergence: China, Europe, and the Making of the Modern World Economy*. Princeton, NJ: Princeton University Press, 2000.

Preston, Diana. *A Brief History of the Boxer Rebellion: China's War on Foreigners, 1900*. London: Constable & Robinson Ltd., 1999.

Rosen, Daniel H. *Behind the Door: Foreign Enterprises in the Chinese Marketplace*. Washington, D.C.: Institute for International Economics, December 1998.

Santoro, Michael A. *Profits and Principles: Global Capitalism and Human Rights in China*. Ithaca, NY. Cornell University Press, 2000.

Schrift, Melissa. *Biography of a Chairman Mao Badge: The Creation and Mass Consumption of a Personality Cult*. New Brunswick, NJ. Rutgers University Press, 2001.

Schweke, William. *Smart Money: Education and Economic Development*. Washington, D.C.: Economic Policy Institute, 2004.

Segal, Adam. *Digital Dragon: High-Technology Enterprises in China*. Ithaca, NY: Cornell University Press, 2003.

Seligman, Scott D. *Chinese Business Etiquette: A Guide to Protocol, Manners, and Culture in the People's Republic of China*. New York: Warner Books, 1999.

Shapiro, Judith. *Mao's War Against Nature: Politics and Environment in Revolutionary China*. Cambridge: Cambridge University Press, 2001.

Spence, Jonathan D. *The Chan's Great Continent: China in Western Minds*. New York: W. W. Norton & Company, 1998.

———. *The Search for Modern China*. New York: W. W. Norton & Company, 1990.

Steiner, Stan. *Fusang: The Chinese Who Built America*. New York: Harper & Row, 1979.

Story, Jonathan. *China: The Race to the Market: What China's Transformation Means for Business, Markets, and the New World Order*. London: Financial Times, Prentice Hall, 2003.

Studwell, Joe. *The China Dream: The Quest for the Last Great Untapped Market on Earth*. New York: Grove Press, 2003.

SELECTED BIBLIOGRAPHY

Sun, Yan. *Corruption and Market in Contemporary China*. Ithaca, NY: Cornell University Press, 2004.

Terrill, Ross. *The New Chinese Empire: And What It Means for the United States*. New York: Basic Books, 2003.

Tsai, Kellee S. *Back-Alley Banking: Private Entrepreneurs in China*. Ithaca, NY: Cornell University Press, 2002.

Walsh, Kathleen. *Foreign High-Tech R & D in China: Risks, Rewards, and Implications for U.S.-China Relations*. Washington, D.C.: The Henry L. Stimson Center, 2003.

Walter, Carl E., and Fraser J. T. Howie. *Privatizing China: The Stock Markets and Their Role in Corporate Reform*. Singapore: John Wiley & Sons (Asia), 2003.

Woetzel, Jonathan R. *Capitalist China: Strategies for a Revolutionized Economy*. Singapore: John Wiley & Sons (Asia), 2003.

Wright, Daniel B. *The Promise of the Revolution: Stories of Fulfillment and Struggle in China's Hinterland*. Lanham, MD: Rowman & Littlefield Publishers, Inc., 2003.

Yang, Benjamin. *Deng: A Political Biography*. Armonk, NY: M. E. Sharpe, Inc., 1998.

Yeh, Wen-Hsin, ed. *Becoming Chinese: Passages to Modernity and Beyond*. Berkeley: University of California Press, 2000.

Zha, Jianying. *China Pop: How Soap Operas, Tabloids, and Bestsellers Are Transforming a Culture*. New York: The New York Press, 1995.

Zhang, Li. *Strangers in the City: Reconfigurations of Space, Power, and Social Networks within China's Floating Population*. Stanford: Stanford University Press, 2001.

ACKNOWLEDGMENTS

When I began to tell people I was writing a book on how contemporary China changes the world, I often heard a warning. "Write the book quickly," said many who had spent the better part of their own lives immersed in the country or its culture. "The longer you take the less you'll know." The urgency of the topic pushed the book's deadlines, but true to the warning, I wrote the last page fully aware that China would take ten thousand lifetimes to master. Happily, *China, Inc.* has benefited from the wisdom, generosity, and patience of a long list of people who guided me throughout. First I must thank my editor at Scribner, Colin Harrison. He saw a book on China as a natural extension of our ten-year collaboration and friendship that began at *Harper's* magazine. Colin saw the need for the book and for its accelerated schedule, and made an extraordinary effort to help shepherd it through, bringing his own considerable intelligence and humor to it every day. Before I committed to the book he offered one reservation: that the demand of the schedule might strain our friendship. As far as I can tell, that reservation was his only error throughout the entire process. I am also indebted to Colin's colleagues at Scribner, especially Susan Moldow, Nan Graham, Sarah Knight, Erich Hobbing, Suzanne Balaban, Lucy Kenyon, Kate Bittman, Paul O'Halloran, Mia Crowley-Hald, Elisa Rivlin, and John Fulbrook III, whose enthusiasm for the book was a great inspiration and source of cheer. I must also thank Colin's family, Kathryn, Sarah, Walker, and Julia for letting me monopolize Colin's evenings and weekends over half a year.

Dean Robinson and Gerry Marzorati at *The New York Times Magazine* offered an early vote of confidence with a dream assignment on China. Dean edited my first words on the subject and helped immeasurably when it came to organizing my thoughts and prose on the most vast of topics; I was most lucky to have him as a critical collaborator from the beginning. My advocate, counselor, and friend Sloan Harris at ICM gracefully minded the business end of the book and mental state of its author. Sloan's colleague Katherine Cluverius offered help and perspective along the way. I must also extend my deep gratitude to Lewis Lapham, editor of *Harper's* magazine, for letting me engage on the issues of global capitalism in the pages of *Harper's* and over many long and wonderful conversations. Without the long-term support of *Harper's* magazine, I would have slipped back into the world I left long ago.

I must also thank Jim Rank who helped with research and introduced me to his brother, Dave, who helped launch me into the heart of the subject, and then kept me on track as I progressed. Henry A. Levine at the U.S. Department of Commerce took time out from his incredibly busy schedule to steer me through knotty issues. Brett and Yiyu Sheehan came to my rescue intellectually when I first set out and offered me shelter in Shanghai. Peter Wang helped me out in Shanghai whenever I got in a jam. Francis Bassolino, of Alaris China in Shanghai, generously lent his time and expertise, and showed me in his city where to get off the usual ex-pat roads—physical and conceptual alike. My views of how American and European industries can best respond to and take advantage of China's manufacturing have benefited greatly from the wisdom that Gary Herrigel shared during our talks in Hyde Park. Wu Hung, professor of Chinese Art History at the University of Chicago, provided insight and guidance on China's contemporary art scene and essential introductions. Kris Ercums, Wu Hung's remarkable student, looked over the manuscript at a crucial phase. Saul Thomas, also at the University of Chicago, reviewed the manuscript for historical accuracy and creative spelling. Elise Logemann kept my mind and office ordered and found useful factoids wherever she looked.

Among the first calls I made about China was one to an old friend and China hand, Scott Seligman, in Washington, D.C., who helped provide a road map for my research. With no introduction, I also called Motorola where I found an exceptional team willing to help and trust me. These included Jennifer Weyrauch, Eric Schuster, Karen Pautsch, Richard Brecher, and Mary Lamb. Bo-ning Yang at Motorola in Beijing devoted many days and much effort to help me, and was also a great traveling companion through China's industrial and rural corridors. This book would have been woefully incomplete without Bo-ning's Herculean efforts. Shelagh Lester-Smith, now at CERN in Switzerland, was also an immeasurable help. She became a great friend to my family and introduced my wife and children to the joys of China's great restaurants and bazaars. Among other great favors, Shelagh introduced me to Mr. Sun, my able guide in Beijing. Liu Bing, my first translator in Shanghai proved more than an able assistant; he was also a friend and conscience. I must also thank the Shanghai Academy of Social Sciences for allowing me access to a stellar collection of Chinese scholars. Li Yihai, the director of International Programs at the Shanghai Academy deserves special thanks. Daniel Rosen and the Institute for International Economics thoughtfully and thoroughly challenged my notions of Chinese industry. Richard Miller at the Northwestern University Institute for Neuroscience kindly introduced to me his exceptional group of colleagues and students. Keir Jorgensen and Adam Nelson at the Solidarity Center in Washington gave me a crash course in labor issues. John J. Foarde III at the Congressional-Executive Committee on China generously helped me navigate officialdom. David J. Ohrenstein of the U.S.–China Economic and Security Review Commission opened up the resources of the Commission for my review and kept me current on its investigations.

This book would not have been possible without having Anton Piëch as an associate in Beijing to report, translate, and learn from. George Yueyao Zhao at Baker and McKenzie in Beijing offered friendship and wisdom to a confused traveler. Stephen Terry at Azure International in Beijing did the same. Michael Gagnon and Ashley Liu, of eHero and Mindwalk in Beijing, were also great friends and guides. Ben Ye of V2 Technology Inc. offered a window into the world of young, brilliant entrepreneurs in China. Harry Hong, president of Beijing Smarteye Technology Ltd., did likewise. Tracey Yen at Sterling Communications and C. P. Lim at Netgear went to extraordinary lengths to introduce me to China's place in high-tech manufacturing. Jim Seder made a special effort to ensure that I learned the truth about basic manufacturing in China, and made certain I did not prejudge the Chinese workplace. Norbert Chang, founder of Enorbus, helped me see China's promise in the creative economy. Bradley and Kenneth Davis at Nordson in Hong Kong and Shanghai helped me see how smart American companies adapt and thrive in China.

ACKNOWLEDGMENTS

There are many others who helped with the reporting of this book but whom I have chosen not to mention out of respect for their privacy and confidential advice.

I am also grateful to a circle of friends who were willing to let me tax them with long talks about the book's themes. Ingrid Creppell and Robert Mudge offered me the comforts of home in Washington, D.C., and the benefit of their worldly understanding and amazing circle of friends. One of their friends, Anthony Garrett, offered the formidable resources of Internews. Thanks to Greg Critser and Kurt Elling, who heard me out over many long walks and let me benefit from their own keen observations. Mark Shapiro, who always lends wisdom and humanity to my work, kept a sharp eye out for news on China on my behalf. The brilliant Amy Dissanayake inspired with Bach and Bolcom on the piano and spicy lentils and green beans from the stove. Alan and Julia Thomas weighed in with wisdom on nearly every puzzle. Talks with Alex Benes poured energy right into the book's pages. Dick Babcock and Gioia Diliberto helped hold up my whole family. Brenda Fowler provided a road map for the task before me and encouragement along the way. I offer a special thanks to Chris and Emily Chiu and Gay-Young Cho for being such wonderful fellow travelers, supporters, and extra eyes and ears. The Chiu-Cho family brought an added measure of joy to the whole enterprise. Alexa Knorr, who joined our family in China, bought her own fresh perspective and wonder to all we saw. Regular dim sum lunches with sociologist Xiangming Chen of the University of Illinois at Chicago were enlightening and encouraging.

Last, my deepest thanks go to my family. Most of all to Sara, Elly, and Adam for putting up with both my absences and my presence, tending to my care and feeding and offering love and support every step of the way. The enthusiasm of my loving parents Guy and Elaine Fishman was a constant source of joy, and nothing makes me happier than the sight of them both with the book in their hands. I am blessed to be surrounded by a family who hears me out on any topic, reads my writing untiringly, and fills in when I am distracted. To Zack, Nancy, Jeanne, Rebecca, Emily, Joey, Martin, Phoebe, Jessica, Hilary, Jennifer, Ted, Todd, Ernie, Marty, Cary, Doug, and Gary, I offer my love and thanks.

INDEX